Branching Out

THE PUBLIC HISTORY OF TREES

EDITED BY

LEAH S. GLASER

&

PHILIP LEVY

University of Massachusetts Press
Amherst and Boston

Printed in the United States of America

ISBN 978-1-62534-832-6 (paper); 833-3 (hardcover)

Designed by Scribe Inc.
Set in Adobe Garamond
Printed and bound by Books International, Inc.

Cover design by adam b. bohannon
Cover photo by G. Nagel, *The Angel Oak Tree at Angel Oak Park, Johns Island, Charleston, South Carolina. Estimated to be at least 400 years old*, © 2014. Adobestock.com, #113611810.

Library of Congress Cataloging-in-Publication Data
A catalog record for this book is available from the Library of Congress.

British Library Cataloguing-in-Publication Data
A catalog record for this book is available from the British Library.

Branching Out

A Volume in the Series

PUBLIC HISTORY IN HISTORICAL PERSPECTIVE

Edited by

Marla R. Miller

In memory of the Quadricentennial Bur Oak,
the Sycamore Gap Tree, the Lincoln Park
Oak, the Belfair Douglas Fir, and all the other
historic trees recently lost to age, development,
vandalism, disease, and climate change

Contents

Illustrations

Foreword

TREE TIME

Sonja Dümpelmann, Rachel Carson Center for Environment and Society, Ludwig Maximilian University of Munich, Germany

Trees ground us in place and time. They do so as objects that are alive and that often outlive us humans. Trees change throughout their seasonal and life cycles. And although they, too, must eventually die, they often elicit a sense of permanence and perseverance. Human cultures have developed under and alongside trees. People have worshipped them and used them as materials, markers, memorials, and metaphors. We refer to special trees as witness trees: plants that, due to their longevity, have witnessed history that we have missed and that can tell history if we are able to read them.

Branching Out reveals the role that trees can play in reading, interpreting, and telling the past. Almost no leaf is left unturned, as the contributors to this volume highlight trees in public history, discussing a variety of case studies that show how saving trees also means saving human history. We learn how art can help mobilize for the preservation of notable historic trees, including their surrounding urban space and structures, as in the case of Black athlete Cornelius Johnson's 1936 Olympic Oak in Los Angeles, and how associating select trees with the lynching of Black Americans provides tour guides in Savannah with the opportunity to tell more contextual, evenhanded, and pluralist histories. The chapters also show how turning attention to past and present tree policies and practices in Connecticut can facilitate the state's more sustainable future development and how cultural memory is promoting the backcross breeding program of the American chestnut. Essays range from addressing trees' role in digital storytelling in St. Louis,

Missouri, to their role in fostering place attachment in Cleveland, Mississippi, and from trees' importance for creating the cultural landscape of South Mountain, Pennsylvania, to mulberry trees' relevance in Mormon women's emancipation. Using the examples of George Washington's cherry tree on Ferry Farm and of the Mother-in-Law Tree in Jamestown, Virginia, authors in this volume also reveal the transitive value of trees in storytelling. Many essays show how trees, whether as truthful or fictitious historic markers and makers of place or as symbols and memorials, have been central to cultural memory. Thus, the Fox Oaks in Flushing, New York, appear as the upholders of colonial ideas of religious freedom, whereas the planted pine trees at the site of the Shingwauk Indian Residential School in Sault Ste. Marie, Canada, recall both Chief Shingwaukonse's nineteenth-century vision for cross-cultural education and settler-colonists' practices to forcefully acculturate Indigenous schoolchildren.

Incidentally, while I was reading the chapters that follow, I came across a "double oak" (Doppeleiche) in a small town in northern Germany. The tree was standing next to an enlarged sidewalk bay. Evidently, a new marker had recently been installed: "Planted by citizens on March 24, 1898, on occasion of the fiftieth recurrence of the day of Schleswig-Holstein's upheaval." Memory had been recalled, and the information had been copied from a less intrusive original marker, an engraved plate fastened to a small granite boulder hidden beneath the undergrowth.

The double oaks' characteristic feature is two stems that have grown together, often seemingly forming one tree. They first came to symbolize the close connection between the duchies Schleswig and Holstein in the 1840s, gaining recognition as patriotic and nationalist symbols after Prussia had annexed the duchies in 1867, leading the German states' unification efforts. In 1898, on the occasion of the fiftieth anniversary of the two duchies' initial upheaval for freedom and independence from Denmark, around one hundred double oaks were planted throughout what, by now, had become the German Empire's region of Schleswig-Holstein. Arboriculturalists in the region saw a new business opportunity in the cultivation of double oaks, whereas rural villages welcomed them as inexpensive memorials.[1] Many double oaks related to this phase of "arbornationalism" are still standing,[2] and their memory also lives on in the name of restaurants across the region. Several character traits were decisive in the choice of oak trees. As a native slow-growing gnarly hardwood, oaks in the German states and later empire (as in several other countries and cultures) were considered to embody strength, pride, endurance, perseverance, and sustenance, as well as virtue, liberty, and independence.

Given their longevity, oak trees also featured prominently in a book by former Holstein forestry official Eduard Mielck, published in 1863, just one year before the German-Danish War, considered the first war of German unification. Trees were Mielck's passion. Witnessing increasing encroachments upon the world's arboreal heritage, he warned of the ensuing loss of natural and cultural heritage and of the sense of history. Inspired by the scarcity of information on tree age, he collected data on large and old trees around the world. The culmination of his research is an extraordinary chart measuring the tallest plants against architectural monuments. Entitled *Die Riesen der Pflanzenwelt und die Riesengebilde der Baukunst* (The giants of the plant world and the giant structures of the art of building), Mielck juxtaposes a giant sequoia with the Cheops pyramid and the famous Tenerife dragon tree described by Alexander von Humboldt with the obelisk standing on Rome's Piazza di San Giovanni in Laterano. Among the foregrounded plants in this drawing are "an ancient German oak tree," a eucalyptus tree, a hoop pine, a Douglas and a common fir, a wax palm, the famous Sydney fig tree (known as Port Jackson fig), and the still-existing chestnut tree growing near Mount Etna known as Castagno dei cento Cavalli. The trees are set against a backdrop created by the outlines of the largest contemporary architectural monuments. These include the cupolas of St. Peter's in Rome and St. Paul's in London, the steeples of Europe's major cathedrals, the Torre degli Asinelli in Bologna, the Luxor Obelisk in Paris, and to draw a local relationship, Hamburg's water tower. To add human and animal proportions, Mielck complements his chart with a human figure, an elephant, and a whale in a tank. However, as important as the comparison of horizontal, circumferential, and especially vertical dimensions is Mielck's collection of tree lifespans—that is, the fourth dimension. It ranges from what at the time was thought to be 300 years for north German pine trees to 5,150 years for Senegalese baobabs. These had been ranked already in the previous century as among the oldest living plants known on earth at the time.[3]

Today, more than 150 years after the publication of Mielck's chart, climate change has added another acute threat to trees' lives—old and young—and, with this, to our natural and cultural heritage. Knowing what can be lost is the first step in saving this heritage. The chapters in *Branching Out* therefore make legible the elaborate connections between natural and cultural history. As such, this book stands as one of the first critical assessments of the role of trees in North American public history. May it encourage further tree stories raising awareness of trees' cultural and natural entanglements.

Acknowledgments

In 2016, when Phil was taking over the chairmanship of the Environmental Sustainability Committee of the National Council on Public History (NCPH), one of us raised the topic of trees. Leah commented that she dreamed one day of a book on the cultural value of trees, and Phil exclaimed, "That's a great idea!" We followed with another session at NCPH in 2019, this time in Hartford, and from there began to recruit participants. Special thanks to Carolyn Barske Crawford (contributor) for suggesting the perfect book title.

We owe a debt to those who served on the NCPH's Stephanie Rowe and all of the past and present members of the NCPH's Environmental Sustainability Committee. Thank you for your dedication to making environmental issues integral to public history practice and to the NCPH itself. These members include Chuck Arning, Maren Bzedek, Priya Chhaya, Sasha Coles (contributor), Rebecca Conard, Carolyn Barske Crawford (contributor), Nancy Germano, David Glassberg (contributor), Jackie Gonzales, Donna Graves, Chelsey Harris, Al Hester, Will Ippen, Melinda Marie Jetté, Andy Kirk, Rachel Leibowitz, Carolyn Macica, Tiya Miles, Maggie Ordon, Aislinn Penetcost-Farren, Alena Pirok (contributor), Angela Sirna, Wendy Soltz, and Cathy Stanton for so many conversations about the intersections between public history and natural resources over the last several years.

We are so appreciative of the work done by Matt Becker, Marla Miller, the editorial board of the University of Massachusetts Press's Public History in Historical Context series, and all the press staff who helped this book come together. Essay volumes are unique creatures, and they move at a different pace than monographs. We are very grateful for the editors' and staffs' help and patience. Thanks also to our outside reviewers whose insights made this a stronger work. We are also grateful to the NCPH staff, especially Stephanie

Rowe and Meghan Hillman for their support for integrating environmental issues into the field.

Thank you to grassroots organizations like Hamden for Trees for the inspiration of your activism and passion to push back against tree removal and tree trimming and to Julie Hulten, dedicated champion of Sleeping Giant Park Association. Lastly, of course, we extend appreciation to our patient families.

Branching Out

Introduction

FINDING THE FOREST THROUGH THE TREES

Leah S. Glaser, Central Connecticut State University

Philip Levy, University of South Florida

A beech tree stood on a Providence, Rhode Island, street corner for over one hundred years. In summer, the beech's three stories of leaves and branches matched the colors of the elegant wooden-framed home that sat under its boughs. In autumn, the tree's flame-orange foliage delightfully framed the house's ornate metal roof. Year after year, it went through all the growth cycles peculiar to its genus while shading passersby, storing carbon, slowing erosion, housing birds and squirrels, and serving as a landmark in the neighborhood. House and tree complemented each other as they symbiotically served the needs of generations of Providence residents. In the end, though, the house had human champions that the tree did not.[1]

In 2022, the Providence Preservation Society awarded Brown University its highest honor for the school's work to relocate and restore one of the beech tree's neighbors. This was the 1873 Second Empire–style home of prominent business leader and machinist Lucian Sharpe.[2] The wooden-framed house, with its classic mansard-style roof, had been quietly aging while serving the university as a classroom and office space for some time. But by 2020, redevelopment plans in the neighborhood put the old home in the crosshairs. Rather than tear the building down, Brown chose instead to move it a few blocks over to a new location and, once there, conduct an extensive and well-informed restoration. The project involved students, faculty, and contracted experts. By most accounts, it was a stunning success.

It took a while, though, before a flaw in the plan became clear. Preservationists had focused so much attention on saving the historic Sharpe House that no one had considered that the redevelopment and moving plan called for the killing of the century-old beech tree, which suddenly found itself in an inconvenient location. As one neighbor, who had opposed the university's original plan to demolish the house, watched the removal of the beech tree, he realized the celebrated solution missed something. "Everybody got convinced that this house was more important than the tree," he observed. He summed up the issue, saying, "The tree got lost when people decided the house was more important. Historic houses have more champions than old-growth trees."[3]

Like historical homes, mature trees are limited, irreplicable, and dwindling cultural, as well as environmental, resources. But unlike historical structures, trees' lives are part of the matrix of all life on the planet, and like other American cities, Providence is always stuck between considering the needs and wants of an urban human population and maintaining a thriving treescape. One 2014 count of the city's urban forest showed that its approximately 415,000 trees collectively cleaned up ninety-one tons of various pollutants and kept somewhere close to 4,030 tons of carbon out of the atmosphere.[4] Providence's trees were doing more than shading homes and sidewalks; they were part of a living environment that helped clean up the messes that made life unlivable.[5] Cutting down even one mature tree risks upsetting the balance—and as trees age, they become larger and more effective air filters. Trees like the beech also bring a hard-to-define but deeply powerful charm and historical feel to Providence's streets. This beech was only slightly younger than the Sharpe House, which so many people had worked to save from the wrecking ball. But when Brown's planners worked out the details of preservation, their gaze landed only on the home and not the tree that had stood by it all this time. One of the pair was historical, valuable, and preservable, while the other was expendable.

While work crews set in to move and restore the Sharpe House, strong winds and rain swept over the Gettysburg National Military Park of the National Park Service (NPS) in southern Pennsylvania. Formidable storms are becoming ever more common occurrences thanks to global climate change, and places less accustomed to regular severe weather are finding that Holocene-era development is not always faring well within Anthropocene realities.[6] Fallen trees are second only to floods in the list of climate change–related events disrupting human lifeways.

The storms that rattled Gettysburg in January of 2020 pulled and pushed the park's trees—many of which are relatively young and only poorly rooted in the soil—in dangerous ways. In one case, a pair of pines fell forward and landed on the large stone monument honoring the men of the 143rd Pennsylvania Volunteer Infantry who fought on that site on July 1, 1863.[7] The pines themselves stood out on a landscape otherwise largely free of trees. During the Civil War, these were farm fields, and the NPS has largely maintained that open landscape to retain both the feel and views of the wartime years. These two pines, though, were not local varieties and, in fact, had been planted by the NPS specifically to shade the gray stone monument and those who stopped to visit it.[8] Being conifers, they were full and verdant during the winter months, and in January of 2020, that meant that their coverage offered plenty of surface area to catch strong winds and gather and hold rainwater. Combine that with a conifer's typical shallow root system, and you have a recipe for a tree fall. But at Gettysburg, the problem was made worse by the fact that the monument and both trees sat upon a raised mound of earth—a landscape feature that elevated the memorial's profile while placing its new arboreal cover in unique jeopardy. The furious January winds made a perfect storm of sorts, and instead of sheltering the 143rd's memorial, the trees toppled over onto it.

The pinewood and bark were no match for the monument's hard stone, so in this case, the monument sustained no lasting damage. But it is easy to imagine a scenario in which the tall stone was toppled and damaged in the fall. Likewise, falling trees can easily harm historic buildings and other landscape features. As climate change drives up the intensity and frequency of storms, the danger trees present to historical sites is becoming an increasing concern for preservationists and site managers. The 143rd Pennsylvania monument might have been spared damage, but so many sites are in the crosshairs.

The Sharpe House's beech tree and the Gettysburg pines touch on different ways that trees are complicated parts of the historical landscape. These stories behind such trees highlight the curious ways that historicity lands on some things but not on others and how trees can simultaneously be both visible and invisible on historic sites. Trees can be fragile and vulnerable conveyors of historical memory and serve as aesthetic parts of historic landscapes, meaningful pieces of personal and communal memories, characters in lore, and objects of reverence. From giant sequoias to cherry tree groves to a new trend for funerary trees, the nation is dotted with innumerable charter trees, liberty trees, sour apple trees, strange fruit trees, yellow ribbon–bedecked old oak trees, and commemorative trees all serving as icons of national identity, struggle, and purpose or carrying deep personal significance.[9] While not all the stories attached to trees can be documented and verified, they take on as much meaning in people's and communities' lives, imaginations, memories, and attachment to place as the built environment.

Trees can be isolated on the land, or they can be members of entire forests serving multiple historic, entertainment, or commercial roles—often all at the same time. They exist at the intersection of the human and the nonhuman: independent living entities that are also deeply entwined with human lifeways and meaning. At Gettysburg, rangers have identified about a dozen "witness trees," standing as remarkable survivors of the battle. Throughout the Civil War, Union and Confederate troops decimated forests in battle and felled whole forests for encampments and easier movement.[10] But as the incident around the Gettysburg trees' fall shows, the relationship between people, trees, and landscape is not always happy. Trees are a unique species of *vivifact*, which, unlike other objects of preservation, are vulnerable to diseases and changes in their immediate surroundings and larger environments, making them difficult challenges for those interested in their maintenance and interpretation.[11] In some cases, they are simply a nuisance or an obstacle, like the sixty-three trees on Gettysburg's Little Round Top that the NPS chose to cut down to clear a better viewshed and protect visitors.[12] On the minds of NPS arborists, no doubt, was an incident a few years earlier when an Appalachian Trail hiker near Harpers Ferry, West Virginia, was killed by a falling tree.[13]

As the effects of climate change manifest themselves more and more each year, tree falls like that one are becoming more common and ever-greater risks. At the same time, hard-to-control forest fires present an increasing challenge to cities, homeowners, and historical sites. Particularly in the American West, people have chosen to live in lovely, forested acres only to discover that the changing climate imperils their homes and bodies. The 2018 Camp Fire in Northern California destroyed more than eighteen thousand buildings and caused eighty-five deaths, making it the worst disaster of its kind in the state's history.[14] Among the losses was the Honey Run Covered Bridge—a wooden 1886 structure that was on the National Register of Historic Places.[15] On the other end of the spectrum are massive snowstorms, whose cute nicknames like snowmageddon or snowpocalypse belie the severe damage they can do as they bring down dozens or hundreds of trees and topple power lines, crush cars, and shatter roofs. Increased storm intensity is a global threat, but trees are both the victims of this new weather and its unwitting allies in destruction. A bad blizzard can be a multilayered disaster for inhabited landscapes as communities' desire to preserve older trees directly conflicts with desires for safety. The irony can be quite acute. One singularly strong 2017 storm brought it all together when it toppled Yosemite National Park's much-photographed drive-through sequoia tree.[16] The sequoia had survived a century of cars driving through its huge opening only to be felled in a climate event intensified by a century of cars driving.

Humans have imbued trees with meaning for time immemorial.[17] Americans specifically have long relied on trees to relay their past. The notion of European colonization hewing a civilization out of an untamed wilderness is so deeply ingrained in our mythology that it has survived countless debunkings. The forest and the wilderness have long been sources of both fear and endless possibility in the American imagination. Likewise, logging and forestry are both active economies that some communities commemorate as a way to recall their pasts. Virtually all historical sites, museums, and parks have trees as part of their charge and curated settings—even if they do little more than shade a pathway or parking lot. In all cases, though, trees are a distinctive part of the fabric of American historical sites.

Despite trees' ubiquity, public historians have engaged in little discussion about how trees function in and what they bring to historic sites, and even how they preserve a sense of place. There has been even less conversation, scholarly or otherwise, to address how to handle them as climate change increases deforestation and exacerbates the other problems trees present to historic buildings, landscapes, and archaeological resources. Trees have surrounded, sheltered, and sometimes imperiled the work of public historians, but they have been doing so largely without any substantive analysis. A tree can be an aesthetic part of a historic landscape; it can be a meaningful piece of personal and communal memories; it can be a character in lore, a common landmark for directions, or a marker of boundaries or play; and it can be an object of reverence or significant to cultural beliefs or practices. Viewed this way, trees are often essential participants in the way humans connect to places and recall their pasts.

In his classic 1864 work, *Man and Nature*, George Perkins Marsh argues that the downfall of ancient civilizations had begun with the felling of trees.[18] So if trees can be cultural, personal, and historical resources, as well as natural ones, perhaps we need to start treating and preserving them accordingly. The impact of climate change is demanding a serious and immediate discussion on the intimate, inseparable relationship between trees and people. Historical perspectives might not provide immediate solutions to the climate crisis and all its related calamities, but they can help prevent us from forgetting how knee-jerk responses (forgive us) "fail to see the forest for the trees."

This volume represents the first effort to understand the role of trees in public historical contexts. The following essays begin to fill that gap by looking at a range of trees and forested places in historical and public history settings across the nation to explain how trees have functioned as conveyors of historical meaning, what the climate crisis means for the future they share with their sites, and how trees have been silent actors in public history. The essays grew out of a set of sessions at various annual meetings of the National Council on Public History and the work of its Committee on Environmental Sustainability. The essayists represent a mix of public history practitioners and academicians drawn as widely as possible from anglophone North America. Each essay focuses on an individual tree, a set of trees, or defined forests to explore how trees have been creators and locations of meaning, specific challenges for sites and communities, and objects of curation.

Trees in a Public History Framework

This volume also contributes to a growing literature about the history and origins of public history. In *Museums, Monuments, and National Parks: Towards a New Genealogy of Public History*, Denise Meringolo convincingly reestablishes the "genealogy" of public history as one founded within the realm of natural resource management and the NPS. Beyond Meringolo's study, there is little scholarship that addresses how the perceptions about land conservation translated into historic preservation and resource management. While historical natural resource management practices and policies have moved ideas about culture and nature apart, a distinct separation has proved problematic.[19] Cultural beliefs and behaviors emerge from traditional practices, most often tied to seasonal changes, climate, and topography. Science has dictated some of the public policy toward trees, but management decisions often seem more cultural in practice. National forests and forestry practices have been central to the conservation and development of many regions of the United States, but views toward urban forests have reflected tensions among ecological, economic, and cultural values.

Although (and perhaps because) the National Historic Preservation Act coincided with the passage of the National Environmental Policy Act in the late 1960s, the execution of these laws severed trees from the human landscape. Recent histories have documented the urban forest, but not in the context of the historic preservation movement. Public historians are positioned to think about how trees define our landscapes as well as hold clues about our history, a point few think about until they are gone. How do they fit into efforts to preserve historical places while working toward mitigating the effects of climate change and environmental degradation? What challenges and opportunities do trees present for preservationists, and can we apply standards of evaluation and historical significance to these resources? And finally, can historians utilize trees, forests, and their history to highlight issues of climate change?

Many of these concerns emerge from decades of work by environmental historians, and unsurprisingly, the essays in this volume all owe debts to that scholarship. Environmental history can trace its roots back to conservationist Aldo Leopold's call for an "environmental interpretation of history."[20] Its current iteration, though, really crystallized as the scholarly outgrowth of 1960s social movements. Inspired by choking pollution and Rachel Carson's apocalyptic 1962 book *Silent Spring*, activists began to focus on the residual consequences of over two centuries of industrialization. The 1964 passage of the Wilderness Preservation Act and the first Earth Day in 1970 were both markers that Americans had come to understand that social and governmental actions were needed to restore some balance between the world humans inhabited and what they had made of it.[21] As Donald Worster writes, environmental history rejects the idea that "people are a separate and uniquely special species" and that the "ecological consequences of our past deeds cannot be ignored."[22] Humans therefore are not outside what is commonly called nature. They use, manipulate, and inhabit ecosystems but always imagine themselves as being in charge yet somehow separate—and always acting with divinely mandated domination. Humans have cast themselves as the agents acting upon nature. But this human exceptionalism is ultimately not only wrong but also simple hubris. As Alfred W. Crosby Jr. writes, "Man is a biological entity before he is a Roman Catholic or a capitalist, or anything else."[23] Instead, generations of environmental historians have worked to make the nonhuman an active force in human history. They have challenged the long-standing nature-culture dichotomy in Western thought and brought a host of hard science knowledge into historical inquiry.[24] This work has become all the more urgent in light of human-driven climate change. Nothing better demonstrates the reality that humans and nature are one and the same more dramatically than our disruptions of the biosphere that sustains us.

That point has been most clearly made by scientists Paul J. Crutzen and Eugene F. Stoermer, who in 2000 forwarded a new epochal name, the Anthropocene, to highlight the climatological fact that the planet is no longer in the Holocene era but, rather, has entered a new phase of existence: an era defined by the actions of humans.[25] In this model, climate, something imagined to have been in the realm of nature, merges with time, a concept imagined to have been in the realm of culture. As Dipesh Chakrabarty puts it, "The human being has become something much larger than the simple biological agent that he or she always has been. Humans now wield a geological force."[26]

The twenty-first century brought more studies specifically about the cultural context of trees, including those by Eric Rutkow, Sonja Dümpelmann for city street trees, Jill Jonnes and Ellen Stroud for the urban forests, Jared Farmer for California trees and most recently for ancient trees, Thomas J. Campanella for New England's American elm, and Steven J. Pyne for comparative forestry practices.[27] These histories set up contexts and calls for action in saving, preserving, and managing trees beyond the ecological and public health arguments, but most do not explicitly frame those narratives in ways that might translate to action and policy for tree preservation. As developers and utilities remove trees from the landscape, grassroots environmental groups have primarily taken up this cause, but they are missing a completing piece of their arguments to save trees.

Public history arrives at these concerns on a different path and sees distinct uses in the work of environmental historians. On the applied history side, historic preservationists continue to adhere to traditional guidelines about how and which buildings to preserve, repair, restore, and rebuild, when trees are every bit as critical to maintaining a sense of place as the built environment. In spite of the recent and noteworthy scholarship in environmental history, public historians and historic preservationists still rarely grant trees the type of attention that they give to buildings and structures. There are notable exceptions. The NPS has tried for the last quarter century to blend the work of its cultural and natural resource managers by commissioning cultural landscape inventories and reports to inform management decisions, but the cultural landscape model has not had a significant impact on resource management, interpretation, or practice beyond national park borders.[28]

So how does understanding trees as cultural resources, memorials, and artifacts change how we manage them? If we consider that the natural environment is culturally constructed, should natural and historical parks be managed any differently? Concerns over the limits of natural resources are returning, and planning for an environmentally sustainable future is again on the upswing. Meanwhile, the practice of historic preservation has evolved from saving sacred patriotic spaces and rehabilitating older buildings for economic development to maintaining historic resources as environmentally sustainable. We can begin to adapt our resource management policies by exploring more explicit ways to discuss the intersection of environment and culture through specific resources. Public historians can help tell these stories, making trees culturally as well as environmentally relevant.

Forests and Trees: Macro and Micro Histories

This collection of original essays covers a breadth of perspectives about enlisting trees as rich cultural artifacts, just as material culturalist Thomas J. Schlereth advocated forty years ago.[29] The essays divide into two thematic sections: "Trees, Place, and Communities" and "Trees as Symbols and Interpreted Objects." In the first section, Andrew Hurley's essay, "Arboreal Memories: Recovering Historical Meaning in Neighborhood Trees," surveys popular perceptions of trees in historic sections of St. Louis, Missouri, to show how they can be part of revitalizing urban communities in a sustainable fashion. Carolyn Barske Crawford explores the memory and recovery of chestnut trees, victims of a devastating blight during the first half of the twentieth century, in "'The Most Useful Tree': American Chestnut Stories and Species Restoration." Brian Dempsey's "An Island of Trees Called *Old Hickory*: History and Place in the Mississippi Delta" recounts in personal style the way the memory of a specific grove of trees was central to an understanding of a place. In "When a Tree Falls: Listening to and Managing Connecticut's Historic Landscape," Leah S. Glaser chronicles that state's long-term struggle to manage its treescape in the face of population growth, developmental and industrial pressures, and the devastating impacts of climate change. Liz Sargent offers a long-view landscape history of how one section of Pennsylvania forests has changed meaning over time while serving as a symbol, resource, and recreational area in "The Trees of the South Mountain Cultural Landscape." Finally, Sasha Coles's essay, "Mormon Women, Mulberry Trees, and Environmental Transformation in the American West," explores how one religious community centered its own shared memory on its sentimental and commercial relationship with mulberry trees.

The second section, "Trees as Symbols and Interpreted Objects," begins with Philip Levy's essay, "George Washington's Cherry Tree: Ferry Farm's *Prunus serotina* and Historical Placemaking," describing how a string of actual cherry trees became surrogates for the famous fictional one and were central to making local history. In "Sam Robinson's Sycamore," Mariaelena DiBenigno explores how race, tourism, ghost tales, and one special tree intersect on Virginia's Jamestown Island. In "The Fox Oaks of Flushing, New York: Quaker Pulpit and Bowne Family Shrine," Evan Haefeli recounts how one commemorated tree's story sat at the intersection of centuries of family and community memory and religious sentiment. Krista McCracken's essay, "Pine Trees and the Legacy of the Shingwauk Site," reveals how a set of white pines on the grounds of a Canadian former residential school retain Indigenous meanings within a changing academic setting. In "Oaks of Ill Repute: Dark Tourism, Dissonant Heritage, and Savannah's Hanging Trees," Alena Pirok looks at three of the forest city's trees to show how lore and storytelling situated these trees within ongoing tensions over race. Lastly, in "Living Memory in Los Angeles: Cornelius Johnson's 1936 Olympic Oak in Art, History, and Preservation," Alaina Scapicchio interviews artist Christian Kosmas Mayer about the latter's work to replicate, commemorate, and preserve a unique tree in California, laden with complex legacies of race.

Public historians have experience communicating a sense of place, memory, and the power of objects to the public and might approach these stories from a different perspective. Public historians can partner with environmental historians (if we are not already ones ourselves) and enlist shared authority practices with grassroots conservationists to begin to apply narratives to policy. As editors of this volume, we have tried to achieve a regional balance and actively sought diverse stories across race, culture, class, and practice.

While we did not ultimately receive all the perspectives we solicited, we hope that these essays will advance understanding of the cultural value of trees and how such stories might influence public history practices. In doing so, public historians might enhance our role in environmentally sustainable planning by enlisting trees as compelling tools in advocating for tree preservation and fighting climate change.

PART ONE

Trees, Place, and Communities

FIGURE 1. Mary's Tree. Photograph by Dave Boger, October 2015, St. Louis, Missouri.

Chapter One

Arboreal Memories

RECOVERING HISTORICAL MEANING IN NEIGHBORHOOD TREES

Andrew Hurley, University of Missouri–St. Louis

On a mild October afternoon, Dave trained his iPad on a majestic pin oak sprouting from a residential sidewalk planting strip. Speaking into the device's microphone, he explained the significance of Mary's Tree:

> This amazing tree is at 3665 Russell. Mary Schumacher still lives there. She and her brother planted this tree well over 60 years ago, and it still remains as the biggest tree on the block, and just a locator for the whole surrounding neighborhood. Her original intention with her brother was that they would each pick up half the leaves, the leaves that fell on their side of the tree, and their father would get mad at them when they would argue over whose leaves were which ones, and wouldn't be picking them all up. But Mary has lived at 3665 essentially all her life, and has seen the entire neighborhood come and go, and she's an incredible resource, just for the history of what has happened here.[1]

Mary's Tree, in Dave's telling, was an invaluable neighborhood asset that exuded stability and permanence. Its imposing physical presence, its witness to past events, and its connection to Mary, a guardian of community memory, elevated the pin oak to the status of an unofficial landmark worthy of recognition.

Dave's photo narration, recorded as part of the Missouri Place Stories project, suggests how natural landscape features not typically associated with authorized heritage discourses evoke the past and anchor people in place. Dozens of community conversations and stories elicited in St. Louis between 2015 and 2018 confirmed the extraordinary capacity of trees to enhance the historic character of neighborhoods and provide a sense of continuity amid jarring urban dislocations. The historical meanings associated with trees, however, were far from uniform across geographies of race and class. Whereas the assignment of heritage value to old trees fit comfortably within a trajectory of urban progress among the inhabitants of predominantly white, middle-income neighborhoods, trees were embedded more ambiguously within narratives of urban declension in areas with poorer, homogeneously African American populations.

Appreciating the historical resonances of urban nature matters greatly if we hope to expand the stock of cultural capital that can be activated on behalf of socially equitable urban sustainability. In recent years, greening advocates have made tremendous headway in promoting the conservation and expansion of natural spaces within cities. Yet their efforts have generally proceeded apart from, and sometimes in conflict with, the goals of heritage-based placemaking.[2] Historicizing nature offers an opportunity to align urban greening with historic preservation agendas. Imbuing trees with cultural significance seems an especially worthy endeavor as cities seek to mitigate the many impacts of climate change that threaten poorer communities of color disproportionately.[3] Not only do trees perform the critical function of carbon sequestration, but they also boast cooling properties that reduce health risks associated with excessive heat. Recognizing trees as historical *and* ecological assets while acknowledging the disparate historical conditions that ground people's environmental experiences may well translate into stronger public support for protecting and extending urban tree canopies.

Public historians are well poised to nudge trees into the popular historical imagination. Although old, venerable trees have appeared in fictional works—for example, J. R. R. Tolkien's *Lord of the Rings* and, more recently, Richard Powers's *The Overstory*—they do not figure prominently in representations of historical events or places. The proliferation of heritage tree programs implemented in scattered cities since the 1990s, however, signals a shift toward greater historical recognition. Typically, these programs solicit nominations for trees associated with significant events or famous people. In some cities, official designation affords a modicum of legal protection against indiscriminate felling. Sponsored and administered primarily by arborists, these attempts to recognize and preserve individual specimens have done little to interpret trees as manifestations of urban development.[4] A more innovative approach can be found in the activities of the Heritage Tree Public History Lab at Portland State University. Aiming to raise awareness about how "trees contribute to our urban communities," the lab has collected dozens of "canopy stories" from Portlanders and used them to produce interactive maps and interpretive podcasts.[5] The work described in this chapter reaffirms the benefits of storytelling methodology but also advocates a more activist approach by linking historical revelation to localized sustainability planning and suggests avenues for further constructive interventions in the politics of urban placemaking.

The Place Stories of St. Louis

The Missouri Place Stories project was launched in 2016 to collect historically informed, citizen-produced photo narrations about local landscapes and employ them in local planning exercises. Over five hundred place stories were recorded across seven St. Louis neighborhoods in partnerships that joined faculty and students at the University of Missouri–St. Louis (UMSL) with civic associations, churches, environmental groups, and government agencies. Community partners publicized the project in target neighborhoods, solicited participants, and sponsored forums for collaborative analysis and planning. Project funding was provided by the National Science Foundation under the auspices of the Missouri Transect: Plants, Climate and Community, a statewide initiative to prepare Missourians for the impacts of climate change through enhanced research capacity across multiple universities, scientific institutions, and stakeholders.[6] Initial conversations with community partners revealed that for planning purposes, the theme of climate change was too confining. Hence we adapted our research design to accommodate a more expansive framework of urban sustainability that would include, but not become dominated by, the issue of climate change.

As an experiment in public history, we hoped to elicit historical perspectives on the natural environment through archival research, the extraction of local knowledge, and the activation of personal memory. To this end, UMSL faculty and students prepared informational packets containing brief landscape histories of each target neighborhood.[7] These historical overviews emphasized the role of topography, vegetation, hydrology, and climate in shaping an urban landscape usually conceptualized in terms of streets, homes, churches, shops, and schools. Each packet began with a section about the St. Louis prairie landscape and its role in supporting human habitation prior to the arrival of European colonists. Subsequent sections covered agricultural practices among early French settlers and more dramatic environmental transformations associated with urban development in the nineteenth and twentieth centuries.

Trees played a strong supporting role in this narrative. As developers platted subdivisions and allotted space for recreational parks, they planted trees to enhance the appeal and value of urban real estate. In the twentieth century, the responsibility for planting and maintaining street trees increasingly fell to the municipal government's Forestry Division. Shifting city priorities and budgetary capacities, however, resulted in uneven planting practices across space and time. Ornamental trees were integral to the realization of grand boulevards and an upgraded park system inspired by the City Beautiful movement at the start of the twentieth century.[8] In 1919, the St. Louis Parks Department began working toward its goal of one tree for every home by distributing five hundred specimens annually to residents who paid the requisite $4 fee.[9] Thousands of saplings took root in parks and along sidewalks in the 1930s as money for civic improvements flowed through the New Deal's Works Progress Administration.[10] Another wave of planting occurred in the late 1980s when the city embarked on a $4 million beautification campaign to boost local tourism.[11] Sporadic bursts of urban greening, however, were offset by the otherwise steady depletion of inventory on account of infestations, storms, poor soils, and air pollution. The interplay among these contending forces produced dramatic disparities in canopy coverage not only across neighborhoods but also often from one street to the next. Likewise, some public parks enjoyed elevated status and received more attention than those with less powerful constituencies. Compiling meaningful information thus entailed microlevel analysis of newspaper articles, government reports, and aerial imagery.

Project volunteers from our target neighborhoods reviewed the neighborhood-specific informational packets prior to recording photo narrations using the

Pixstori app for Android mobile devices. Recruits spent roughly twenty minutes perusing the assembled images, charts, and brief textual passages, sometimes pausing to engage in more detailed conversations with project chaperones. Primed with a perspective on landscape that emphasized the relationship between the built and natural environments, community contributors were asked to photograph and provide commentary on five significant places in their neighborhoods. To facilitate the selection and narration process, the packets presented a list of categories that might be employed to describe sites of local importance.[12] Participants who relied on the list were encouraged to apply multiple classifications, where appropriate. Alternatively, they were free to devise their own descriptive categories. Over a period of three years, 116 individuals contributed 506 place stories about parks, churches, businesses, schools, streets, infrastructure, and other landscape elements. Trees and wooded spaces constituted about 13 percent of the total collection. Following electronic submission, the place stories were uploaded to a website and displayed on an interactive map for public viewing. In four neighborhoods, the photo narrations were used to spark discussion at community meetings and planning workshops.

The Trees of Shaw and Botanical Heights

The adjoining neighborhoods of Shaw and Botanical Heights promised exceptionally fertile ground for embedding trees more firmly in popular historical consciousness. Separated by an interstate highway in the 1960s, these distinct neighborhoods had previously been joined in a ribbon of contiguously attached subdivisions that stretched from the 277-acre Tower Grove Park on the south to the Pacific Railroad manufacturing corridor on the north. The presence of Tower Grove Park along with the world-renowned Missouri Botanical Garden made this section of St. Louis unique in its historical and naturalistic associations.

Both Tower Grove Park and the Missouri Botanical Garden owed their origins to amateur botanist and philanthropist Henry Shaw. Born in Sheffield, England, Shaw migrated to the United States in 1819 and shortly thereafter settled in St. Louis, where he maintained a brisk business selling cutlery and ironware to westward travelers. Retiring from commerce at the age of thirty-nine with a small fortune, he devoted the remainder of his life to botany and real estate development. In 1842, he purchased a large tract of open prairie just beyond the city's western boundary. Here, he carved out a country estate with an Italianate villa surrounded by an expanding collection of exotic and native botanical specimens. In 1859, he opened his greenhouses, arboretum, and experimental fruit orchards to the general public. Eight years later, he gifted a large portion of his landholdings to the City of St. Louis for the development of a companion recreational amenity, Tower Grove Park.[13]

Shaw anticipated the outward growth of urban development, which he abetted by opening residential subdivisions on land wedged between the Missouri Botanical Garden and Tower Grove Park. To ensure the district's genteel character, Shaw and adjacent property holder Mary Tyler inscribed restrictions on manufacturing and other nuisances into property deeds. They also planted trees. Along either side of Flora Place, Shaw Avenue, and Tower Grove Avenue, the first streets laid across their subdivisions, they planted a continuous line of mature maples to provide future residents with a protective canopy and a picturesque, country aesthetic. In addition, they bisected Flora Place and Shaw Place with island parks that accommodated shrubbery, flower gardens, grass lawns, and shade trees.[14] As transportation connections with downtown St. Louis improved in the last quarter of the nineteenth century, more developers followed suit, marketing the sale of residential lots with references to nearby parks and the abundance of freshly planted shade trees.[15] Incrementally, a grassy prairie was remade as a sprawling residential district for middle-income households and carefully selected flora.

The influence of Tower Grove Park and the Missouri Botanical Garden on urban development waned in the twentieth century, but these amenities remained relevant. Like many St. Louis neighborhoods, Shaw and Botanical Heights suffered a loss of population and investment in the decades after World War II.[16] In the 1980s, both districts latched onto historic preservation strategies as a means of reversing urban decline. Housing preservation and rehabilitation was more successful in the Shaw neighborhood due, in part, to its proximity to Tower Grove Park and the internationally renowned Missouri Botanical Garden. The certification of a national historic district north of the interstate highway did not achieve similar results, and by the 1990s, the Botanical Heights neighborhood, then known as McRee Town, had acquired a reputation for drug trafficking, violent crime, and poverty. The racial characteristics of the two neighborhoods diverged as well. Once homogeneously white, both neighborhoods witnessed demographic transitions that placed African Americans in the majority by 1990. Thereafter, whites regained their majority status in Shaw, while African Americans approached 80 percent of McRee Town's population by 2010. Subsequently, the Missouri Botanical Garden spearheaded a slum clearance and urban renewal project in McRee Town that replaced two hundred parcels of vacant and condemned properties with new-urbanist single-family homes and rebranded the district as Botanical Heights. Strong ties to the Missouri Botanical Garden in both neighborhoods coincided with grassroots greening activities that resulted in food gardens, bioswales, and native prairie restorations.[17] As historic districts where urban greening was tied to notions of community progress, residents were well disposed toward ratcheting up the heritage value of trees. It was this predisposition that motivated UMSL to select these neighborhoods for piloting the Missouri Place Stories project in the summer of 2016.

Commentary about trees in Shaw and Botanical Heights was overwhelmingly positive. Of the 130 place stories collected, 12 specifically referenced trees, while an additional 22 documented parks, gardens, and vegetative spaces where trees were either prominent or abundant. Robert appreciated trees, first and foremost, for their visual splendor. Pausing in front of a median planting strip on Flora Place, he remarked on the magnificence of foliage displayed by trees when they changed their colors in the fall.[18] Some participants emphasized the cooling properties of leafy vegetation. For Jametta, a playground near the center of Botanical Heights mattered because it was one of the few places where she could sit under shade trees on a hot day.[19] Patrick, one of Jametta's neighbors, drew attention to another ecological benefit when he took note of the fruit provided by the apple and peach trees in the Botanical Heights Community Garden.[20]

Place stories from these neighborhoods also revealed trees as reservoirs of collective memory and welcome components of a historical aesthetic. The place story about Mary's Tree, recounted at the beginning of this chapter, was the most poignant example of a tree that sustained a link to the past by virtue of the people and stories associated with it. More commonly, trees, either singularly or in assemblage, reinforced the authenticity of historical places by manifesting age and elapsed time. Brittany had recently relocated to Botanical Heights from another city, and the neighborhood's historic character was a major selling point. A series of place stories about a freshly restored, hand-painted sign for the Star Saloon and Café; a derelict factory building imagined as refurbished apartments; and an art deco electric utility substation undergoing rehabilitation as a showroom for antique cars constituted a ringing endorsement of historic preservation as a catalyst for urban revitalization. Like many of her neighbors, Brittany privileged old buildings as landscape elements worthy of historical veneration. But before turning away from the rehabbed utility substation, she stopped to take a photo of a towering pin oak that soared upward from the property's front lawn. Aerial photographs show that the tree had been planted about half a century earlier. Although it is unlikely that Brittany would have known its precise age, she was able to surmise that it had been around awhile. Drawing an analogy to the building behind it, she noted that the "beautiful, old tree" had stood the test of time while so many others had been cut down. "Most old trees do not make it this far," she continued, "but I think they are beautiful."[21] For Brittany, a historic preservation ethic extended beyond buildings to include trees.

Unlike Mary's Tree and the utility substation pin oak, the Missouri Botanical Garden and Tower Grove Park were wooded locations that received both popular and official recognition for their historical attributes. Yet place stories about these two premier civic amenities diverged from authorized discourses in their highly localized orientation. The Missouri Botanical Garden earned a listing on the National Register of Historic Places as a National Historic Landmark in 1976 on the basis of its long-standing contributions to plant science and the prominent landscape architects who designed its grounds and structural features.[22] While some residents celebrated the garden for its impressive array of botanical specimens and its conservation work, they more often emphasized its local impact. Of the five participants who recorded place stories about the Missouri Botanical Garden, four viewed it as a reflection of local heritage largely due to its association with the neighborhood's founder, Henry Shaw. Tami and her husband had recently purchased a home in the Shaw neighborhood, and she was eager to explain the garden's importance:

> The Botanical Garden is a place that reflects the neighborhood's heritage. There's a lot of history there because of Henry Shaw and we knew a lot of information about Henry Shaw, the Botanical Garden, Flora Place, and the homes that were built there to reflect his neighborhood home. . . . I think that it offers a lot to the community. A lot of people from all over come here to visit the Botanical Garden. There's been a lot of changes in the community as of late. A lot of new faces, new neighbors.

> And I think that one of the reasons we love this neighborhood is that the Botanical Gardens attracted people from all over so you are able to see new faces and know that the community was building.[23]

For Tami, the Missouri Botanical Garden allowed newcomers like her and her husband to achieve a sense of belonging through attachment to the neighborhood's origins. Equally important, its presence attracted the kind of cosmopolitan population that made the Shaw neighborhood a desirable place to live.

Similarly, Tower Grove Park acquired historical resonance less as an example of nineteenth-century park design than as a treasury of personal memories and an embodiment of long-standing communal values. Peering through an iPad viewfinder, Rob considered several perspectives before settling on a vista that satisfied him. In the foreground, scraggly linden branches cast shadows upon a linear pedestrian pathway. In the near distance, a forking walkway enclosed a stand of silver maples. He spoke into the device's microphone:

> This is Tower Grove Park just a few blocks from my house. This is, of course, where we come just because it's a beautiful place with these wonderful old trees. I love it because it connects it to this late nineteenth century idea that a park was going to make everything perfect. It was this sort of utopian ideal of the park but now that it has been lived in for a hundred plus years and even though it's a natural space, it has this real human history to it and I find it just gorgeous for its own sake but as a place of connection to this old idea of how a neighborhood and its environment were supposed to co-exist.[24]

In Rob's place story, the "wonderful old trees" were notable for their beauty, but in juxtaposition with one of the park's original walking paths, they also evoked and perpetuated a precious civic ideal that harmoniously blended people, nature, and cultural artifacts.

Trees gave definition to vernacular settings as well and were identified as supportive adornments in places where expressions of local heritage dovetailed with friendly social interaction. Sean, who had lived in Shaw for more than twenty years, enjoyed the wide range of architectural styles exhibited in the neighborhood's mansions, bungalows, flats, and apartment buildings. Many of those architectural treasures were located along Flora Place, which he characterized as a pleasant place to stroll, meet companion dog walkers, and admire "beautiful old homes." Further enhancing the setting was what Sean described as a "tree canopy that extends from the park across the street to the homes."[25] Magnolia Avenue, bordering the northern edge of Tower Grove Park, presented Sean with another historic streetscape that merited a place story. As Sean explained, Tower Grove Park, with its "collection of trees," provided a beautiful setting for socializing and athletic activities. The row of craftsman bungalows and early twentieth-century low-rise apartment buildings lining the opposite side of Magnolia Avenue epitomized the range of housing types found in the neighborhood. Completing the narration, Sean again remarked on the value added by "mature, beautiful old trees that hang over the street."[26]

A sylvan lot adjoining the Compton Heights Christian Church extended the roster of places where trees sustained communitarian traditions. To set the scene for her place story, Jacque photographed three wrought iron benches that were arranged tastefully beneath high-canopied oak trees. Although the lot had never received any sort of official heritage designation, Jacque explained what made it worthy of preservation:

> This is the lot attached to Compton Heights Christian Church, at Flora and Grand. This lot is always green space and will always be green space, because of the agreement when Compton Heights [Christian Church] built at this place. I think this is a significant space for the community, as over the years it has become a place where people gather when they come to receive food and assistance at the food pantry here. It's a place where people gather and sometimes find shade under the trees on the benches in the heat of summer, when they are waiting at the bus stop down by the sidewalk. It's a place where the congregation and others in the community have held picnics and ice cream socials and game times, where Isaiah 58 Ministries gathers with those who have family fun days for children in the community. So this is a significant space that will always be open and green space, and I believe it's valuable as that.[27]

In the place stories recounted previously, residents of Shaw and Botanical Heights advocated for hybrid spaces, comprising natural and human-constructed elements, that perpetuated acts of social benevolence and community cohesion.[28] In these places, performative reenactments of time-honored behaviors and practices rooted people to their community. Trees contributed to this placemaking process by evoking stories, marking the passage of time, and completing visual signatures. Their capacity to connect current residents to a remote past also made trees well suited to projecting communal values forward into the future—not only through concerted tree conservation practices but also by placing them into service as memorials.

The use of trees to commemorate beloved people and events has a long-standing tradition in the United States, and in carrying forth this tradition, Shaw residents extended the cultural content of natural landscapes. Ecological objectives, beautification, and memory making converged at the Shaw Memorial Grove, which was established in 2013 by a grassroots environmental organization, Sustainable in St. Louis. The founders, Monte Abbott and Jeanette McDermott, conceived the organization as a way to mobilize citizens around ecologically responsible planting and educational programs. Abbott and McDermott were also eager to revise popular constructions of local heritage to foreground the area's natural history. Among its most ambitious projects was a prairie restoration along the interstate highway berm separating the Shaw and Botanical Heights neighborhoods. The project resuscitated the landscape that Henry Shaw encountered as a young man in the 1840s.

The Shaw Memorial Grove, on the other hand, employed afforestation to facilitate collective grieving among those who had lost loved ones to violence. The issue was heavily freighted in the wake of the fatal shooting of VonDerrit Myers, a Black youth, by a white off-duty security guard in 2014. The death divided the community as social justice advocates squared off, sometimes violently, against law-and-order factions.[29] The grove was conceived as a vehicle to promote community healing by finding common ground and common environmental benefit. In the first year, thirty to forty people gathered to plant trees along another part of the interstate highway berm and affix them with tags indicating their loss. In his place story on the grove, Monte explained, "This planted area has only been in existence for about three years, but it continues to grow as more of our neighbors come and plant a tree to memorialize someone they love, either living or deceased. As we gather and plant our trees, we meet one another and exchange stories of the people we love, and we come back from time to time to tend the trees and to clean the area and renew these new bonds that we're creating across our community."[30]

With minimal prodding, residents of Shaw and Botanical Heights recognized trees as vessels of collective memory that enhanced the historic character of their neighborhoods. Appreciation for the many ways that trees improved neighborhood life animated a community conversation about local tree conservation. In May 2016, a handful of community representatives from a neighborhood association, a local community development corporation, and a grassroots environmental organization met with coordinators of the Missouri Place Stories project to review the collected place stories and brainstorm action items. Of particular concern to the group was the imminent scourge of the emerald ash borer, an Asian beetle species making a slow and steady march across the country infecting and killing ash trees. The conversation focused on possible interventions to save endangered trees and quickly replace trees that had to be removed. Participants noted that different strategies would be necessary to address street trees, where the St. Louis Forestry Department had responsibility, and those on private lawns. An agreement was reached on the wisdom of a preliminary inventory of imperiled trees on both private and public property. One participant also proposed a tree tour to complement the historic house tour sponsored annually by the Shaw Neighborhood Improvement Association to raise awareness.[31] Unfortunately, our project plan did not include a mechanism for following through on these suggestions, and other priorities distracted the various organizations from implementing them on their own. In subsequent partnerships, including the ones described in the next section, this shortcoming was addressed by integrating our work with ongoing planning efforts backed by strong organizational or institutional support.

The Trees of Wells Goodfellow and Walnut Park

A gentleman from Plover Avenue was agitated when he stood to address the gathering at the New Northside Missionary Baptist Church Conference Center on the evening of October 30, 2017. Along with about thirty neighbors, he had come to voice an opinion on a proposed green space that would replace abandoned homes in a struggling section of northwest St. Louis. The workshop attendees had been listening to recently archived place stories, including one from a narrator who claimed that residents of Plover Avenue appreciated the abundance of trees on their block. The speaker disagreed. "Who said they liked the trees on Plover?" he asked incredulously. "We've been trying to get rid of those trees!" The speaker's daughter, also in attendance, injected another dose of skepticism into the discussion by citing the city's poor track record of maintaining grassy lots in the area.[32]

It was within this discordant milieu that UMSL faculty and students employed public history methodologies in the Wells Goodfellow and Walnut Park neighborhoods to integrate historical perspectives into urban planting initiatives. Neither heritage nor greening had figured prominently in revitalization strategies in this northwestern quadrant of St. Louis, where homogeneously African American citizens struggled to overcome decades of population loss, high poverty rates, and systematic disinvestment. Officially designated historic landmarks were few and far between in this area, and the historical narratives that shaped popular understanding of place worked against, as much as in favor of, leveraging the heritage value of trees.

The use of public history methodologies in the Walnut Park and Wells Goodfellow neighborhoods tested the possibilities of extracting historical meaning from trees in the context of a metropolitan initiative to convert abandoned properties into sustainable green spaces. Disappointed in the lack of concerted community action in Shaw and Botanical Heights, UMSL faculty looked for opportunities to embed their public history exercises within ongoing neighborhood-based planning initiatives with greater levels of organizational support. In spring 2016, UMSL entered into a partnership with the Green City Coalition to engage residents in a series of workshops to identify local preferences for the creation of new green spaces. The Metropolitan St. Louis Sewer District (MSD) had recently signed a consent decree mandating the expenditure of $4.7 billion to reduce stormwater discharges into regional creeks and rivers, especially during heavy rainfalls. Some of the reduction would be achieved by capturing surface runoff before it entered the subterranean sewer infrastructure. In depopulated sections of north St. Louis, MSD promised to expand the acreage of permeable ground by demolishing hundreds of abandoned homes.[33] The Green City Coalition joined MSD with the City of St. Louis and the Missouri Department of Conservation to coordinate community-based planning for the green spaces that would replace demolished buildings. Coalition leadership was intrigued with the idea of employing the Missouri Place Stories project to feed community perspectives into its planning process. Between 2016 and 2018, 216 place stories were collected from fifty-five volunteers in Wells Goodfellow and Walnut Park, two neighborhoods slated for land conversion.

Trees took on a supporting, if unheralded, role in the urban development of St. Louis's northwestern reaches. As St. Louis grew from a commercial entrepôt to an industrial city in the years surrounding the Civil War, wealthy families carved small farms and country estates from the abandoned prairie lands.

Both the Wells and Goodfellow families owned large tracts of land in the areas that would bear their names as city neighborhoods. Rolla Wells, who served as the mayor of St. Louis from 1901 until 1909, recalled the family estate as "the source of much pleasure and recreation," adding that his father "enjoyed the products of the orchard, the vineyard, the melon patch and the garden." He also remembered Sunday afternoon gatherings of friends and family who conversed and joked under shady trees.[34] Alongside the plank roadway that led from St. Louis to the outlying village of Florissant, entrepreneurial families established truck and dairy farms to supply growing urban populations with foodstuffs. This area was also known for the walnut groves that eventually gave the neighborhood of Walnut Park its name.[35]

Urban development came late to this remote district due to poor drainage and periodic flooding from meandering streams. Sewer construction, streetcar service, and the establishment of manufacturing plants eventually initiated the subdivision of large properties into residential parcels around the turn of the twentieth century. Horticultural remnants from previous land uses survived as inducements to prospective homebuyers. A 1912 newspaper posting for a nine-room brick home on Goodfellow Avenue advertised the presence of "shade and fruit trees," along with fixtures, screens, steam heat, and hardwood floors.[36] Another nearby lot boasted a "grape arbor and several fruit trees."[37] Until 1906, property owners relied on their own initiative to adorn their streets, resulting in haphazard canopy distribution. Thereafter, the office of the city forester rationalized planting practices with the goal of decorating every residential street with trees.[38] Discrepancies persisted, however. Street trees suffered short lives, and although the city forester, and later the Forestry Division, sought to replenish inventory, budgetary constraints impeded comprehensive replanting. By the time these neighborhoods underwent a demographic transition in the late 1950s and early 1960s, with African American households replacing the predominantly white working-class populations, the streets of Wells Goodfellow and Walnut Park exhibited considerable variation in the extent of canopy coverage. Over the next decades, canopy maintenance was further impeded by the spread of Dutch elm disease, which eliminated a staggering 50 percent of the city's street trees in the decades after 1950.[39]

Primed with information about the natural history of their neighborhoods, participants of the Missouri Place Stories project had plenty to say about trees and other green spaces, although they were hard-pressed to categorize such landscapes as historic. Unlike the yearning for connection to neighborhood origins that we observed in Shaw and Botanical Heights, historical consciousness in Walnut Park and Wells Goodfellow was more tightly entwined with personal memory and African American identity. This divergence may be partly explained by contrasting demographic profiles. Many residents of Wells Goodfellow and Walnut Park traced their local lineage to the racial transitions of the early 1960s, when African American purchasers became the sole inheritors of a housing inventory rapidly abandoned by whites. Due to the slack demand for real estate in subsequent years, homes purchased in the 1950s and 1960s found few buyers and were passed on to children and grandchildren. For many residents, history began when their families sunk roots and accrued meaning through associations with personal memory and the struggle to sustain a viable African American community. Typical sites designated as historic by participants included schools, churches, and African American–owned businesses.

On the other hand, only two tree-adorned spaces were explicitly recognized by place story narrators as embodiments of local heritage. Bellefontaine Cemetery is one of only two Level II ArbNet arboreta in St. Louis, along with Tower Grove Park. Established in 1849 as a private graveyard for elite St. Louisans, the cemetery contains five thousand arboreal specimens, including two State Champion trees, a 109-foot shingle oak, and a red mulberry with a 57-foot canopy spread. The site is also listed on the National Register of Historic Places.[40] Unlike Tower Grove Park, a widely accessible and highly venerated community resource, Bellefontaine Cemetery is gated off from surrounding residential areas and functions less effectively as a focal point for local identity and collective memory. Despite its proximity to the Walnut Park neighborhood, it only merited one place story. Barrett Brothers Park, a large recreational space in Wells Goodfellow, elicited more testimonials, but neither trees nor other forms of greenery figured prominently in these place story narrations. Appended to the neighborhood's urbanized fabric in 1947, Barrett Brothers Park was not part of Wells Goodfellow's origin story. Although its original design distributed shade trees alongside one peripheral and two interior walking paths, the greater part of its acreage was given over to softball diamonds, a football field, a playground, and a pavilion.[41] Place stories about the park's contribution to local history mostly recalled the athletic events and organized youth activities that took place there during the first generation of African American settlement.

If arboreal landscapes were rarely categorized as "historic" by Walnut Park and Wells Goodfellow residents, they were nonetheless implicated in notions of neighborhood identity and ingrained in personal memories. Trees contributed to a sense of place, and for some narrators, they enhanced neighborhood appeal. The place story that elicited consternation at the Walnut Park Workshop meeting was one example. "The best thing I love about my street," recounted John, "is to keep cool in the summertime, we have a lot of trees on the block. Thank God for them." Although John was unable to point to a surviving walnut tree on his block, he implicitly acknowledged them as part of the neighborhood's heritage and a reminder of his childhood: "This is what the neighborhood is, was named from walnut, Walnut Park. . . . We do have walnut trees in my neighborhood because we used to take the walnuts that was in the hull and throw them at each other for fun."[42]

Several blocks away, Reggie expressed his long-standing admiration for a tree that occupied the corner of a vacant lot across the street from his home. At one point, he had considered purchasing the property. "I liked that tree," he said in a place story that he titled "Lot with Tree." "I wasn't going to cut it down. I was going to build a treehouse in it once I got the lot. It looks like somebody holding their hand like that."[43]

What was most striking about the trees featured in this set of place stories was how many of them had vanished from the landscape. Seven project participants elaborated on places where a tree or multiple trees once stood. Their stories were remarkable in their specificity, and with one exception, the trees were remembered fondly. Sylvester grew up in Wells Goodfellow and continued to live in the home that was purchased by his parents in 1965. Recalling the neighborhood of his youth, he reminisced, "This was a beautiful neighborhood in 1965. There was a lot of fruit trees and flowers. There were a lot of neighbors who were proud of their homes."[44]

For Sylvester, ghost trees made a lasting impression due to their association with a period of time when the neighborhood was vibrant and intact. He was not alone in connecting trees to a declension narrative. As Ernest toured the Walnut Park neighborhood, he constructed a series of place stories around a history of subtraction—streets where houses had been demolished, homes that had fallen into disrepair, abandoned stores, and sidewalks deprived of trees. On several intersections, Ernest was quite precise in his retrospective identification of vanished trees, such as the "beautiful apple tree on Thrush and Harney" and the apple and peach trees near the intersection of Genevieve and Harney.[45]

For some, these landscape erasures were simultaneously sad and perplexing. Reggie pondered, "We had a whole bunch of trees in the hood: walnuts, cherries, peaches, apples, all kinds of trees. Now we don't hardly have anything. I don't know why because they should still be here if they were growing. But you don't see them."[46] His query was echoed by Joyce in Wells Goodfellow, who asked, "So why don't we have them in our community? They should be on every block, every major street."[47]

Whereas Joyce and Reggie were baffled by the absence of trees, other residents were keen on explaining their disappearance. Tyanna recalled how elms on her block succumbed to disease and how storms felled trees that once lined West Florissant Avenue.[48] Her emphasis on natural causes, however, was counterbalanced by explanations that linked a narrative of urban decline to governmental neglect. William captured this sentiment as he described Walnut Park in 1967, the year he moved into his home: "Then, the neighborhood was real viable and it had a lot of trees. On my street at noon, it was so shady and cool there. And all of the streets were tree-lined and the homes were manicured. The alley was taken care of. They were clean. And the city was helping then. They were there. In fact, we had inspectors riding the area. . . . But as the years went by, we see less and less of the City help."[49]

Valerie, who grew up in Wells Goodfellow during the 1960s, gave a similar account: "We used to have more trees than we have now. Every year they come and cut trees down and do not replace trees. What do they say on the commercial that replaces trees? They haven't replaced one tree since they cut them down."[50]

Strong convictions about systematic governmental negligence in low-income African American neighborhoods also provided an explanatory context for negative views about woody spaces that proliferated in the present. In particular, narrators directed their ire at the St. Louis Forestry Division for its failure to clear wild vegetation from vacant properties and its practice of mowing the center portions of abandoned lots while allowing trees and bushes to propagate at their edges. Residents cited these overgrown patches as breeding grounds for wildlife nuisances and criminal activity. Viewed as artifacts of urban decay and manifestations of governmental malfeasance, trees became objects of contempt and candidates for elimination wherever they appeared—on vacant lots, lawns, and sidewalks.

Some residents, however, adopted a more nuanced stance. Eltereon photographed a cluster of trees that straddled a fence dividing two residential properties in Walnut Park. He began his narration by recognizing their contribution to local heritage, noting that his neighborhood was named for the walnut trees that were once abundant. Turning his attention to the trees in his viewfinder, he continued: "We have a bunch of trees . . . what everybody knows as volunteer trees. Trees that nobody planted grew, trees that nobody wanted. They represent neglect, and areas people don't care about anymore. It promotes crime, it promotes violent acts, people use them to hide behind. . . . Planting trees is nice but those are the ones that you are going to take care of and the ones that are planted in certain spots."[51]

To reconcile the contradictory impacts and meanings of trees, Eltereon contrasted those that were deliberately planted and assiduously maintained with those that grew wild. It was this kind of information gleaned from place stories that ultimately proved invaluable for orchestrating combative, yet productive, sessions at a series of community workshops on local green space creation. At each of these public meetings sponsored by the Green City Coalition, UMSL faculty and students presented historical research along with a sample of place stories to help frame issues for discussion. In both neighborhoods, skeptical residents reasserted negative associations between trees and public health, safety, and quality of life. Yet fond recollections of trees, especially fruit trees, also resonated with workshop participants. Eltereon's distinction between unkempt happenstance vegetation and carefully cultivated greenery helped focus discussion on the matter of maintenance. Whereas a history of poor service provision from public and quasi-public authorities made residents wary of any officially sponsored greening program, they were less hostile to arrangements that assigned responsibility for upkeep to a coalition of environmental organizations, governmental agencies, and local citizens. Likewise, the idea of creating a community land trust in cooperation with a local university generated more favorable feedback.[52]

Drawing on fond remembrances of fruit trees and reassured by promises of adequately funded and democratically governed maintenance regimes, citizens in Wells Goodfellow and Walnut Park endorsed the inclusion of community orchards within newly proposed green spaces. In Wells Goodfellow, a community development corporation, the Hamilton Heights Neighborhood Organization, assumed sponsorship for a fruit orchard on the southern edge of a planned seven-acre green space. A nearby shop owner and passionate advocate for increasing access to fresh and nutritious foods volunteered to coordinate the distribution of produce in her capacity as orchard steward. At a ward meeting in September 2019, residents were invited to sample a variety of fruits and berries that could be grown safely in compromised urban environments. The session concluded with a survey of planting preferences. Two months later, a group of about twenty local volunteers gathered on a chilly morning at the orchard plot to position apple, peach, pear, persimmon, plum, cherry, and pawpaw saplings firmly in clean soil. By noon, twenty-four trees had been planted. The first crop was harvested in fall 2022. In Walnut Park, green space designs included a quarter-acre strip of fruiting trees for open foraging.

Storytelling, History, and Nature

In the book *Black Faces, White Spaces: Reimagining the Relationship of African Americans to the Great Outdoors*, Carolyn Finney argues that African American environmental perspectives are heavily mediated by personal and collective memories. For this reason, Finney stresses the necessity for recovering personal stories and including them in public decision-making processes that have tended to marginalize African American environmental experiences. Only by acknowledging the distinct and often tragic relationship between African American people and nature can white environmentalists expect to forge alliances across racial divides.[53] Finney's observations and insights were borne out by our work in St. Louis, especially in the African American neighborhoods of Walnut Park and Wells Goodfellow, where story sharing and frank conversations ultimately led to community endorsement of green infrastructure installation.

Facilitated by the proliferation of electronic media, digital storytelling has become a powerful instrument in the public historian's tool kit. More so than its close cousin, oral history, it gives contributors wide latitude over content and interpretation through creative mixing, such as audio narration and imagery.[54] While it has been used successfully in a variety of public-facing projects that seek to confer interpretive authority over our collective past, the work we performed in St. Louis illuminates its specific utility for bringing nature into the realm of history. Stories like "Mary's Tree" and "Lot with Tree" give trees that otherwise might be seen as mere botanical specimens an added historical dimension through their associations with people.

The imperative of forging a sustainable urbanism demands a sensitive navigation of social differences and divisions. Stories that personalize the past, couch individual experiences within broader currents of urban development, and give voice to both the pain and joy derived from interactions with nature can clarify and validate distinct environmental histories. Sharing those stories can cultivate empathy across wide audiences, shatter stereotypes, and ultimately ensure equitable and democratic responses to urgent challenges, environmental and otherwise. As historians look for opportunities to contribute to policy discussions and planning initiatives, projects such as Missouri Place Stories suggest a promising agenda for constructive engagement.

FIGURE 2. George Hepting stands with an American chestnut tree in North Carolina. Hepting spent most of his long career with the US Forest Service's Division of Forest Disease Research at the Southeastern Forest Experiment Station protecting American forests against disease. He wrote extensively about the failure to control the American chestnut blight, which led to the collapse of the species in the first half of the twentieth century. Photograph by George Snowden, n.d. Forest History Society, Durham, NC.

Chapter Two

"The Most Useful Tree"

AMERICAN CHESTNUT STORIES AND SPECIES RESTORATION

Carolyn Barske Crawford, University of North Alabama

> We really didn't talk about the chestnut very much. The chestnut was always there, and we never thought it would not be a part of our lives. . . . I can recall picking up chestnuts with my father on the Black Moshannon State Park in Pennsylvania during the 1930s. Collecting nuts was a typical Sunday outing and we would literally collect gallons of chestnuts. We would roast and eat the nuts, they were a real treat.
>
> —Bryan Burhans, "Who Will Remember the Chestnut"

At one time, more than four billion American chestnut trees spread from southern Canada all the way to Mississippi and Alabama. While it was rarely the dominant tree in the forests, this giant of the eastern woodlands was hard to miss.[1] It could stand over one hundred feet tall, the trunks straight and truc. To those who lived in the eastern United States, especially Appalachia, the tree was invaluable. It provided food for both people and animals and wood for cabins and fence posts. In cash-poor regions, the tree could even put some money in people's pockets when they sold nuts to brokers to take to the cities of the Northeast. Some joked that the tree could take you from the cradle to the grave, as the wood was used to make both furniture for babies and caskets.[2] It was certainly "the most useful tree."[3] In the early twentieth century, however, the chestnut came under serious threat. A fungus, first identified in New York in 1904, began killing chestnut trees. It quickly spread south across Appalachia, resulting in the almost complete loss of the species by the mid-twentieth century. This loss had enormous ecological impacts on the forests of the eastern United States and contributed to a decline in the population of many species of wildlife, including turkeys, bears, and squirrels.[4] Today, while millions of American chestnut sprouts remain in the forests of the East, almost all the large trees, as well as most of the people who remember the trees' dominant place in the forest ecosystem, are gone.[5]

Since 1983, the American Chestnut Foundation (TACF) has taken the lead in restoring the American chestnut. While scientists coordinate the project, volunteers play an important part in planting and caring for trees in TACF test orchards. One of the tools TACF uses to connect with volunteers are chestnut stories, like the one that prefaces this chapter. In TACF's publication, originally published as the *Journal of the American Chestnut Foundation* and known since 2015 as *Chestnut: The New Journal of the American Chestnut Foundation*, chestnut stories can take many forms—oral histories, essays, poems—but they all document the relationship between humankind and the American chestnut tree. Chestnut stories serve an important purpose: reminding people of the value of the species and the many ways people used the tree before its decline. In documenting the story of the American chestnut through the journal, in sharing and interpreting this story, and in using it to mobilize volunteers and resources, TACF has demonstrated the value that practices rooted in the field of public history and the study of memory can bring to the realm of environmental science. Public historians are well aware of the power that narrative has in prompting action and encouraging people to rethink the status quo. The chestnut stories documented by TACF help create a historical narrative and also serve as a justification for the reintroduction of the species into the modern landscape. This chapter explores the story of the American chestnut and how TACF has shared and used chestnut stories to fulfill its mission. As we deal with the long-term consequences of climate change, the emergence of new diseases, and the loss of habitat, the work of TACF can, perhaps, provide a road map for other organizations to employ science, technology, public history practices, and memories to mobilize people to solve environmental challenges.

The story of the American chestnut has been told in many ways and on many pages over the years. The chestnut appears in Native American myths and legends, and its medicinal use by Indigenous peoples has been documented.[6] Scientific articles chronicled the spread of the fungus and the demise of the tree in the first half of the twentieth century—and today report ongoing renewal efforts. Poets write of its spreading branches, straight trunks, and lofty heights, as well as the blight that brought it low.[7] Henry David Thoreau writes of the chestnut in *The Dispersion of Seeds* (1862). Journalists have told the story from many angles—including Susan Freinkel, whose *American Chestnut: The Life, Death, and Rebirth of a Perfect Tree* (2007) helps contemporary readers understand the tree and its place in American society long after the tree itself has all but disappeared. Environmental advocates and historians, including Donald Davis and Ralph Lutts, and many amateur historians, including Dr. William Lord, also document the history of the tree.[8] Combined, these resources give us a good understanding of how people lived with the American chestnut, how they used it in their daily lives, and how important the tree was to the forest ecosystem. Those pieces written after the decline of the American chestnut also help us understand the void that the loss of the species left in people's lives and in the forests of Appalachia. While the historical explorations of the American chestnut do include chestnut stories, their use as a motivating factor in the restoration effort by TACF has not yet been explored.

While it is difficult to pinpoint the exact moment when the fungus that devastated the American chestnut arrived in North America, it is possible to date when and where someone first noticed its effects. In 1904, in the Bronx Zoological Park in New York City, employee H. W. Merkel noticed that large sections of the park's chestnut trees' bark were dying, and the overall health of the trees appeared to be deteriorating.[9] Dr. A. A. Murrill, who worked for the New York Botanical Gardens, was called in to study the affected trees. He identified the cause: a new fungus, which he called *Diaporthe parasitica* (the name was changed in 1978 to *Cryphonectria parasitica*).[10] It is highly unlikely that the trees in the Bronx Zoo were the first to be infected by the fungus, which had come into the port of New York from Asia, but rather it was the first place that someone paid enough attention to notice it.[11]

The "chestnut blight," as it was commonly called, spread quickly, infecting trees in other locations in New York, as well as in New Jersey and Connecticut. Scientists studying the blight, such as Dr. Haven Metcalf and Dr. J. F. Collins, published bulletins about the disease, which contained recommendations for how to slow the spread. These recommendations included checking nurseries for blighted trees and quarantining those suffering from the blight, creating blight-free zones where chestnuts were removed in the hopes that the blight's progress would be stopped if there were no chestnut trees, and performing surgery to remove cankers from infected trees. Unfortunately, the advice they gave did not stop the blight, and it began pushing farther south. In Pennsylvania, the Chestnut Blight Commission had permission to enter private property and remove trees infected with or threatened by the blight. In all, the commission spent over $500,000 to fight the blight. But, again, their efforts did not halt the spread. The blight reached West Virginia by 1911, pushing into the heart of Appalachia, where the tree had an important place in the lives of mountain communities.[12] Combined with ink disease, which had been attacking chestnut trees in the southern end of the tree's range since the nineteenth century, the blight caused widespread devastation.[13] By 1950, 80 percent of the American chestnut trees were gone.[14] In all, the upper portion of over 3.5 billion trees died, the equivalent of approximately nine million acres of forest.[15] The root structure of many trees, however, did not die, and stump sprouts continue to emerge from root systems today, well over a century later. Unfortunately, before they are able to grow very large, these stump sprouts become infected by the blight and die back. So today, while millions of stump sprouts do exist, few mature trees are left.[16]

The blight was able to spread so rapidly for a couple of reasons. First, the fungus issues both spring and winter spores. The spring spores come in the form of a sticky mass, which sticks to birds and insects that then carry it to other trees. In the winter, the wind carries dry spore clouds from infected trees to other trees nearby. If the fungus finds a crack in the bark—quite common in the American chestnut—it can invade the tree, leading to the formation of cankers that eventually girdle the tree, killing it.[17] Other species of trees, including the pin oak, scarlet oak, white oak, post oak, southern live oak, sumac, and more, also carry the blight, though they are not negatively impacted by it.[18] This means that even where there are large gaps between chestnut tree stands, the blight can still travel across them.

Work on developing blight-resistant American chestnuts began shortly after the fungus's arrival. By 1913, the fungus had been identified by a US government plant explorer in China, where it had no negative impact on chestnut trees.[19] In the 1920s, the government sent another plant explorer to gather nuts from Asian chestnuts, especially from those that were straight and tall, important characteristics of the American chestnut. Government employees planted some of these nuts at a government research station in Maryland and distributed seedlings. The problem, however, was that these imported Asian trees needed fertile soil with good tilth (i.e., allowing for good air and water infiltration) to grow well, meaning that using them in place of the American chestnut in unmanaged forest settings was not practical.[20] Work on developing hybrid chestnuts began in Connecticut in 1931, when A. H. Graves, who worked at the Brooklyn Botanical Garden, began crossing American chestnuts with Chinese and Japanese trees on property he owned in Hamden. In 1947, the Connecticut Agricultural Experiment Station (CAES) took over the management of Graves's property.[21] The site continues to serve as a CAES research orchard today.

While these efforts and others demonstrated a real desire to solve the problem of the American chestnut, a solution seemed out of reach. Progress often halted when researchers passed away or lost interest in the issue.[22] In 1981, things changed. To tackle the chestnut blight problem, Dr. Charles Burham, professor emeritus of the Department of Agronomy and Plant Genetics at the University of Minnesota, applied the methodology he had used to develop hybrid strains of corn to the American chestnut, developing the backcross breeding program subsequently used by TACF. While the American chestnut was very susceptible to blight, the Chinese chestnut was not. However, most Chinese chestnuts lacked many of the characteristics that made the American chestnut such an integral part of life in the eastern United States, including the height and straight trunk.[23] Working with both Chinese chestnuts and American chestnuts that showed some signs of blight resistance (e.g., the famous Clapper tree, which originated as part of the United States Department of Agriculture [USDA] chestnut breeding program and survived for twenty-three years after being infected with the blight), Burham advised backcross breeding, selecting for the desired characteristics of the American tree and the blight resistance of the Chinese tree.[24] While he knew the breeding program would take a long time to bring about the desired results, as trees grow much more slowly than corn, others recognized in the idea the potential for a true solution to the loss of the American chestnut. Early supporters, including Philip Rutter and Dr. Harold Pellet from the University of Minnesota, began implementing Burham's program. They also formed TACF, recognizing that gaining long-term financial support would be fundamentally important to the success of the breeding program.[25] Founded in 1983, TACF took the lead in chestnut restoration efforts. The establishment of Meadowview Research Farms in 1989 and other research orchards in subsequent years allowed TACF to develop a sustained breeding program.[26] With the restoration of the chestnut inscribed as the organization's core mission, TACF provided the continuity and resources necessary to find a real solution: the organization could continue the restoration efforts even when contributing scientists retired or changed focus.

Other partners and allies have joined the effort to restore the chestnut, including colleges and universities.[27] SUNY's College of Environmental Science and Forestry's American Chestnut Research and Restoration Center in Syracuse, New York, successfully developed a blight-resistant transgenic chestnut tree.[28] Other organizations have also worked on the tree's restoration, including the American Chestnut Cooperator's Foundation (associated with Virginia Tech and Concord College), which focused on developing blight resistance in all-American chestnut trees rather than in hybrid trees.[29]

TACF began formally documenting its progress in 1985 with the publication of the *Journal of the American Chestnut Foundation*, published as *Chestnut: The New Journal of the American Chestnut Foundation* since 2015. In the first edition, the then editor Donald Willeke lays out the mission of the journal: "We hope that it will be both a scientific journal and a means of communicating news and developments about the American Chestnut to dedicated non-scientists (such as the lawyer who is writing this Introduction) who care about trees in general, and the American Chestnut in particular. and wish to see it resume its place as the crowning glory of the American deciduous woodlands."[30] Over the years, the journal has moved from a volunteer publication released once or twice a year (depending on the year and on capacity) to a glossy, professional magazine released three times a year.

In the journal, the progress of the backcross breeding program is broken down into terms nonscientists can understand. The journal, however, is not only about the science behind the restoration effort. One of the most significant sections of the journal in its early years was the "Memories" section, which documented "chestnut stories." From its inception, TACF recognized the importance of the chestnut story. In the early years, "Memories" often appeared in the middle of the journal, the symbolic heart between reports from TACF's Meadowview Research Farms and articles discussing a broad range of scientific topics connected to the chestnut tree. With a few exceptions, the "Memories" section remained a fixture in the journal until 2010, when the journal's format changed. Between 2010 and 2015, memories, recollections, and recipes handed down over generations were woven throughout the journal (now referred to as a magazine). In 2015, when the magazine changed format again, chestnut stories became a semi-regular series called "Reflections."

"History & Culture," which first appeared in 2019, also highlights the impact the chestnut had on the lives of people in the eastern woodlands. While many of the memories included in the journal came to TACF unsolicited, TACF also recognized the importance of documenting people's chestnut stories in a more organized fashion. In 2003, the then membership director Elizabeth Daniels wrote about the American Chestnut Oral History project, which aimed to preserve chestnut stories for future generations.[31] In the spring of 2006, the then editor Jeanne Coleman let readers know she was interested in gathering chestnut stories. Stories came pouring in, and as Coleman says in the fall 2006 issue, "These stories are heartwarming [and] often funny."[32] Today, in essence, the journal itself acts as the archive of TACF's chestnut stories, preserving and sharing them simultaneously.[33]

Just as science takes place outside of Meadowview Research Farms and the other TACF orchards, so too does the gathering of chestnut stories. University of Tennessee at Chattanooga (UTC) student Bethany Baxter gathered oral histories for her master's thesis "An Oral History of the American Chestnut in Southern Appalachia." The interviews are available online through the UTC Library's website. Chestnut stories also appear in folklore collections, such as *Foxfire 6* (1980), as well as in the folklore and memories gathered by Charlotte Ross of Appalachian State University.[34] Today, the chestnut community also has a strong online presence. In Facebook groups such as "The American Chestnut Research and Restoration Project," people share their chestnut stories and pictures of the trees they have planted or found, as well as ask for help identifying trees and for advice about caring for chestnuts. In 2007, TACF also published *Mighty Giants: An American Chestnut Anthology*. The anthology includes reprints from the journal, excerpts from the *Foxfire 6* interviews, photographs and drawings of the trees, and chestnut stories gathered by TACF.

In reviewing all seventy-nine issues of TACF's journal that are available online (as of January 2022), as well as other sources, the significance of the chestnut stories becomes quite clear. The work of the scientists engaged in backcross breeding and genetic modification is essential to the restoration of the chestnut. But the success of TACF also has come from thousands of members and volunteers who have supported the work of the scientists. From the beginning, TACF understood the importance of engaging with people outside traditional scientific research circles to accomplish restoration. Backcross breeding at the scale necessary to breed a blight-resistant chestnut takes a lot of time, a lot of land, and a lot of help. The journal's contents reveal the variety of people who have become involved with the project over the years. These have included students, hikers, medical doctors, landowners, journalists, and retired veterinarians—even former US president Jimmy Carter lent his support to the organization, serving as an honorary director. Unifying such a diverse group requires educating them about why the tree matters. What better way to do so than to use the voices of people who remember the forest giant or of those who may never have seen the tall, straight trunk themselves but can share memories passed down from their parents or grandparents?

It is not just memories of the American chestnut tree's beauty and its role in the forest ecosystem of the eastern woodlands that the journal documents. Many chestnut stories demonstrate the value of the trees and nuts to communities, especially in Appalachia, where the tree made up approximately 20 percent of the forest.[35] Work on the topic by environmental historians has helped substantiate the stories and provides important historic context to these memories. For example, Ralph Lutts points out the nut trade's economic significance in Virginia, though he also notes that the monetary value of the nut varied dramatically across the region, with transportation networks and economic circumstances having an impact.[36] In *Where There Are Mountains: An Environmental History of the Southern Appalachians* (2000), Donald Davis highlights the important role the chestnut played in the diet of man and wildlife alike. The loss of this important resource contributed to Appalachia's shift away from "a semi-agrarian and intimately forest-dependent way of life" and toward a more industrialized culture focused in larger population centers, a story that played out in both Black and white communities.[37] For example, the African American community of Coe Ridge in Kentucky faded away as lumbering and farming became less profitable and the chestnut trees disappeared. Residents made their way to cities in Ohio, Virginia, Pennsylvania, and Illinois seeking work.[38] Chestnut stories also document the important role the chestnut tree played in the logging industry as well as in the production of tannins, which brought the leather tanning industry to the mountains of Appalachia.[39]

Memories of the tree's usefulness and its place in American culture are also built into the landscape. Furniture and carvings made from chestnut help keep the memory of the tree alive as much as the words recorded in an oral history interview about the tree.[40] Combined with chestnut stories documenting the experience of working with the wood to make furniture, whether in shop class as a child or as an adult woodworker, these physical reminders document the place the chestnut tree occupied in material culture.[41] Other examples of memories embedded in the landscape include stumps, fallen trunks, and deadwood still standing, though, like the people who remember the tree in the wild, these physical reminders in the landscape are fading as well.[42] While most chestnut stories connect to the senses of sight, touch, and taste, one contributor to the journal recalls the "heart rendering [*sic*] 'thud'" that the dead chestnuts made as they fell to the ground in the mountains of North Carolina.[43]

Despite the clear economic and cultural value of the tree, it would be easy to dismiss the chestnut stories as nostalgic reminiscences. The stories do take the reader back to a time that feels less complicated. The trees seem taller, the forests more alive, and the pace of people's days much slower. Even Jeanne Coleman, the journal's editor who put the call out for chestnut stories in 2006, notes the stories people sent in were "always nostalgic."[44] In *The Past Is a Foreign Country*, David Lowenthal opens with an examination of nostalgia, a romantic remembering of a past that relies less on research and more on "collecting its relics and celebrat[ing] its virtues."[45] A nostalgic past is one that "does not need to be taken seriously."[46] It is "memory with the pain removed."[47] Philip Rutter, the first president of TACF, recognized this pitfall of nostalgia. As he says in the second issue of the journal, "Several scientists with long-standing familiarity with chestnut biology have expressed the sentiment to me that some of the stories regarding chestnut trees and forests must be exaggerated. 'It probably wasn't *that* great. You know how stories tend to grow with each telling.' I certainly do. Human nature is familiar to us all. It is very easy to look back on our childhood with rose-colored glasses."[48]

Digging deeper into the chestnut stories complicates matters. The past people describe does include pain. People recount their feelings when the trees began to die. The sense of loss they felt is palpable. They describe the loss of income, the loss of wildlife, and the loss of an essential food source. The word *tragedy* or *tragic* appears repeatedly—for example, in Jack Stillman's recollections in "A Chestnut Treasure" and Ellsworth Barnard's *In a Wild Place: A Natural History of High Ledges* (an excerpt of which appears in the journal).[49] Lowenthal also describes how "mistrust of the future" creates nostalgia.[50] However, more recent work on nostalgia and environmental sustainability suggests that there are important applications for nostalgia in creating a better world for tomorrow. For example, in "Sustainable Nostalgia," Jeremy Davies argues that being nostalgic for a future when we occupy a more sustainable world helps motivate environmentally conscious action today.[51]

In the case of TACF, people who mourned the past also supported work to bring about a future where the chestnut once again plays an important role in the ecosystems of the eastern woodlands. TACF members have been "trying to do something about the problem rather than just lament the loss," which certainly challenges the argument that nostalgia can reduce the ability to act in the present.[52] Rutter, after writing the previous lines, determines "that our unicorn [the American chestnut] had a real basis in fact."[53] While maybe not quite as tall or as wide as remembered in chestnut stories, the American chestnut tree occupied a significant place in the forest and in the lives of those who lived under its spreading branches—and it is certainly worthy of the work to restore it.

Chestnut stories document this significant place chestnuts held in the forest ecosystem, and the sharing of the stories reminds people of the value the tree brought to Americans before the blight destroyed it. In an interview with Charles A. Miller, William Good remembers how farmers fattened their hogs off chestnuts: "In the fall, because people didn't raise corn to feed their hogs, farmers would let them run in the mountain where they fattened up on chestnuts. The hogs would have to eat through the big burs on the outside to get the nut out. . . . The hogs must have liked the nuts so much they would chew through them until their mouths were bleeding."[54]

In an interview that appears in *Foxfire 6* and is reprinted in TACF's journal, Noel Moore recollects that people in the Appalachians did not build fences to keep their stock in; they instead fenced around their homes and fields to keep out the free-range stock wandering the woods. Each fall, farmers would round up and butcher their hogs that had grown fat on acorns and chestnuts.[55] Chestnuts also served as an important food source for wild animals, including turkeys, black bears, white-tailed deer, gray fox squirrels, and the now extinct chestnut moth.[56] These animals, in turn, fed those who hunted them.

Chestnuts also were an important food source for people. Myra McAllister, who grew up in Virginia, recalls that she liked chestnuts "raw, boiled, and roasted by an open fire."[57] Cecil Clink, who grew up in North Bridgewater, Pennsylvania, remembers filling old flour sacks with the nuts, which his mother would store in the family's "butry," or buttery, "with the smoked hams. . . . [They ate] the nuts boiled, or put them on the cook stove and roast them."[58] Other people made stuffing and traditional Cherokee bread out of the nuts, though they could not grind the nuts into flour because they were too soft; the nuts had to be pounded by hand into flour instead.[59] And it was not just the nuts themselves that people loved. Noel Moore remembers the taste of the honey that bees made from the chestnut blossoms.[60] The leaves also had medicinal uses: the Mohegans made tea to treat rheumatism and colds, and the Cherokee made cough syrup.[61]

Some stories recall the act of selling chestnuts, which gave many families cash that they might otherwise not have had—likely making it a memorable moment. In *Where There Are Mountains*, Donald Davis shares the chestnut story of John McCaulley, who as a young man had gathered chestnuts for sale. The nuts he gathered sold for four dollars a bushel in Knoxville, Tennessee—and McCaulley could gather up to seven bushels a day.[62] Jake Waldroop remembers seeing wagons loaded with chestnuts in his northeast Georgia mountain community. The wagons headed to "Tocca, Lavonia, Athens, all the way to Atlanta, Georgia."[63] Noel Moore recalls seeing families coming from the mountains and heading to the store in the fall, laden with bags of chestnuts. They traded the bags for "coffee and sugar and flour and things that they had to buy to live on through the winter."[64] Exchanging chestnuts for supplies or cash was "much less risky than moonshining."[65] To the north in Vittoria, Ontario, Donald McCall, whose father owned a store in the village, recollects that "farmers counted on the money from their chestnuts to pay taxes on the farm."[66] The trees themselves also had value. William B. Wood recalls that his father tried to save the family farm during the Great Depression by felling and selling the wood of a huge chestnut tree dead from the blight that Wood calls the "Chestnut Ghost." Unfortunately, the plan did not work, and the family lost their farm.[67]

Other stories connect to the "usefulness" of the tree. Because chestnut wood is "even grained and durable . . . light in weight and easily worked," the tree was used for a wide variety of purposes.[68] Georgia Miller, who was 101 when she wrote "Chestnuts before the Blight," recalls the split rail fences that lined the edges of pastures. The chestnut wood split easily and lasted longer than that of other species, making it a good material for what some called "snake fences."[69] Daniel Hallett, born in New Jersey in 1911, says his family used chestnut to trim doors and windows and also for chair rails in the houses they built.[70] Dr. Edwin Flinn's story (told by Dr. William Lord in 2014), which focuses on the extraction of tannins from dead chestnut trees, shows that the tree remained valuable even after the blight struck.[71]

Chestnut stories recount more than memories of the tree's usefulness or the role it played in Indigenous and rural economies. Many stories have documented how an encounter with the tree mobilized someone toward engagement with the restoration effort, demonstrating that chestnut stories can provide a pathway to a wider recognition of the natural world. Patrick Chamberlin describes such an experience in "A Practical Way for the Layman to Participate in Breeding Resistance into the American Chestnut."

Chamberlin tells readers how his grandmother used to reminisce about the tree when he was a young boy and then how he came across a burr from an American chestnut while in high school. He started looking for trees as he explored the woods on his parents' farm. Eventually, while wandering near the old homestead site where his grandmother grew up, he came across two flowering chestnut trees. Returning later in the season, he found nuts from the trees. Through this experience, Chamberlin became involved in the backcross breeding program—and, at the end of his essay, encourages others to do the same. A chestnut story from the distant reaches of his youth started him on his journey, and science helped him continue his work into the present.[72] Fred Hebard, who directed TACF's Meadowview Research Farms for twenty-six years, saw his first American chestnut sprout while helping round up an escaped cow with a farmer he worked for. When the farmer told him the story of the American chestnut, Hebard ended up changing his college major, earned a PhD in plant pathology, and began researching the chestnut. It became his life's work.[73]

Sometimes the work of chestnut advocates crosses generations. Ernest Souther shares a story about coming across a tree while deer hunting with his father in the Maine woods. After his father, Leroy, identified the tree, Ernest climbed it to knock a clump of burrs loose. His father collected the nuts. Over the years, Leroy went on to plant chestnuts on his property and care for them. Two trees survived long beyond the others (at least thirty-five years). These experiences in the winter woods of Maine turned Ernest and Leroy into chestnut advocates.[74] In "One Man's Dream—the Return of the American Chestnut," Jill Willson writes of her father's relationship with the chestnut tree. When her father, Charles Tracey Matthews, was a boy in Virginia in the 1930s, loggers still harvested chestnut trees, though their numbers were dwindling. According to his daughter, Matthews became interested in the tree's restoration for several reasons. He saw value in the wood, the nuts he loved to eat, and the significant role the tree played in the forests of Virginia. He identified two important chestnut trees that survived long after other chestnuts around them had died—the Amherst and the Mawyer trees.[75] While the Mawyer tree has since succumbed to the blight, the Amherst tree remains, though its health is in decline.[76] Matthews also grew chestnuts, participating in the massive effort to restore the tree. After years of listening to her father's stories and watching him work, Willson too became an advocate for the tree. She, like her father, identifies herself as a "chestnut watcher," keeping her eye on several large trees to see how they handle the blight.[77] In the November 2010 issue, Jim Casada retells the stories his grandfather told him, then shares how he in turn tells those stories to children in his granddaughter's class in school, thus using oral tradition to preserve chestnut stories.[78]

In 2011, TACF began highlighting the work of volunteers in the journal. The volunteers often share how they became interested in the restoration of the American chestnut—in effect, telling their own chestnut stories. For example, Vermont / New Hampshire chapter board member Terry Gulick recounts that as a young boy he discovered an American chestnut tree in the woods around Springfield, Vermont. The tree, being unfamiliar to him, led him to research the species, which in turn connected him to the story of the American chestnut. This led to a lifelong interest in the tree and his eventual involvement with TACF.[79] Others, including Curt Laffin, James Curtis, Tracey Coulter, and Ellery "Woods" Sinclair, found their way to TACF after seeing trees in the wild, because of a family member's passion for the tree, or because of the chestnut stories older generations had shared with them.[80]

Chestnut stories will continue to help move the work of TACF forward in the coming years. Educating the next generation will be fundamentally important to the long-term success of TACF. The full restoration of the American chestnut cannot be accomplished in ten years—or even in fifty. To keep the restoration effort alive years into the future, TACF has increasingly emphasized the passing of knowledge about the tree to younger generations. As TACF board president Glen Rea noted in 2011, "Most of us don't remember the American chestnut as it once was. And we continually lose people who have first-hand knowledge and memories of the chestnut. We must educate our youth about the history and importance of the American chestnut. TACF has a 75-year or more mission; we must educate our youth today."[81] Gathering chestnut stories from those who remember the tree thus serves a purpose that goes well beyond just documenting people's memories of the tree. These memories, combined with hands-on learning activities (such as planting chestnut trees that children can watch over and care for), can help create a new generation of stewards for the American chestnut.[82]

The restoration effort, despite its cadre of dedicated volunteers, does face challenges. The forests of the eastern woodlands have changed since the chestnut succumbed to the blight. Other trees, especially oaks, have filled the spaces chestnuts once occupied, a problem identified early in the restoration effort.[83] Chestnuts will have a difficult time competing for light in a mature forest setting. There are landscapes that provide opportunities, including strip-mined areas, where American chestnuts will not face the same pressure from other tree species.[84] The transgenic chestnut developed at SUNY has also raised concerns about the introduction of a genetically modified tree into the forest landscape. Despite a rigorous review process underway by the USDA, Food and Drug Administration, and Environmental Protection Agency, some groups are worried that introducing the transgenic chestnut will open the door for other transgenic trees and will cause degradation to forest ecosystems.[85] Overcoming these challenges requires perseverance, and one way to persevere is to build a narrative that keeps people mobilized and motivated. TACF's perseverance does appear poised to pay off, as we are "now on the cusp of perhaps the largest reintroduction effort to date for a plant species."[86]

There are examples of organizations that have embraced scientific elements of TACF's program while working on the restoration of other tree species, for as Ralph Lutts points out in "Like Manna from God: The American Chestnut Trade in Southwestern Virginia," the chestnut is just one species of tree that has been impacted by disease or insect infestations.[87] For example, the Forest Restoration Alliance uses TACF's backcross breeding program as a model to develop hemlocks and Fraser firs resistant to insects called woolly adelgids, an invasive species from Japan that has devastated both tree species in eastern woodlands.[88] The effort to restore the American elm, which began to disappear from the urban and rural landscapes in the 1930s when the Dutch elm fungus arrived in America, is also underway. The restoration work does not use the backcross breeding method, instead focusing on propagating clones from "survivor" trees, with the US Forest Service, the Nature Conservancy, and universities playing important roles in the process.[89] While the solution to the elm problem may be different than that of the chestnut, those working on the restoration of the elm have looked at the work of TACF to learn about "management strategies . . . to improve reintroduction success."[90]

As Dr. Kim Steiner and Bryan Burhans point out in "Why Bring Back the American Chestnut?," while the scientific work of TACF can help save other tree species threatened by diseases and insects, the model of narrative storytelling can provide a *why* for these trees too, just as it has for the American chestnut.[91] The Ozark Chinquapin Foundation (OCF) has modeled its work closely on that of TACF, which makes sense in this case as the tree is closely related to the American chestnut and was affected by the same blight beginning in the 1960s. Like TACF, the OCF recognizes the importance of stories to motivate action. Because the species was impacted by the blight later than the American chestnut, there are more people alive today who remember them, which also helps motivate restoration.[92] For other species, creating supporters for a restoration effort may be a bit more challenging. The very reason why so many people have "chestnut stories" or "chinquapin stories" is that the trees played an important role in the lives of hundreds of thousands—if not millions—of people. What of a plant or a tree that does not provide the same type of resources, or what if only a small group of people understand the importance of the species? Perhaps then the narrative becomes even more important, but developing it and sharing it may be difficult.

TACF shows how having a compelling narrative can drive action, something public historians are well aware of. The science behind the restoration is, of course, essential, but it is the story that mobilizes a wide range of people. TACF cofounder and the first editor of the journal, Donald Willeke, noted this in his address at the thirtieth anniversary celebration of TACF. He warns against apathy as one of the biggest threats to restoration. Willeke argues the best way to fight apathy is to "make a strong effort to tell others of both the past and the future of the American chestnut so its history and potential are not lost."[93] It is the mobilization of people that makes the project successful. Restoring the tree is truly a grassroots effort.[94] While those gathering and publishing chestnut stories may not have realized it, they were engaging in public historical practice, documenting and sharing the past with the public. Public history is rooted in activism, in challenging narratives, and in creating an engaged citizenry, principles TACF has embedded in its own work.

TACF is an organization that blends science with history and art. Poetry, drawings, and photographs grace the pages of its journals. Recollections of bygone days when the chestnut provided sustenance for Indigenous people, mountain families, and their animals appear on pages following complicated (to a nonscientist's eye) charts showing the specifics of the chestnut breeding program. It is because of this blending—because the organization has figured out how to appeal to both sides of the human brain and the diversity of human interests and experiences—that TACF has found so much success in its efforts. People who participate in the breeding program are not only part of a scientific project; they are also involved in an act steeped in history, a history TACF has consciously worked to preserve through the gathering and sharing of chestnut stories. Memories included in the journal may recall a simpler time and be nostalgic in tone, but they also help shape a path forward to a future where the American chestnut once again spreads through the eastern woodlands of the United States.

FIGURE 3. Internal view of Old Hickory, 2022.
Photograph courtesy of Will Jacks.

Chapter Three

An Island of Trees Called *Old Hickory*

HISTORY AND PLACE IN THE MISSISSIPPI DELTA

Brian Dempsey, University of North Alabama

"You are forbidden to go to Old Hickory." This was a strong statement from my mother, given the wide range I typically enjoyed as a seven-year-old adventurer living in the Mississippi Delta. As a kid growing up in the early 1980s, I was free to roam my neighborhood and even travel considerable distances on my bicycle. This freedom equated to a daily reconnaissance of every dirt path, ditch, secret hideout, and backyard in a two-square-mile radius. So it was quite a surprise to hear my mother's directive against going to a familiar place the older kids talked and bragged about.

I could see it in the middle of the field across the street from my neighborhood: a stand of woods at the end of one of those ditches, lurking unto itself in a treeless expanse. At this edge of town, cotton and rice spread across the land, revealing a horizon line that met the sky twenty miles away. Any remaining trees, lone buildings, water, or man-made piles created a striking contrast, drawing one's eye and interest. Old Hickory was such a place, and it looked like an island of trees. I remember being persuaded by its winking mystery—sitting there both within and apart from the flat, ocean-like fields abutting its three sides. For a young kid, an exotic and possibly dangerous clump of woods just within reach was simply too much to resist.

By the time I was nine years old, a bit older and more courageous, I was walking or riding my bike the half-mile distance to Old Hickory fairly often. Approaching the woods from the open field pulled up a sense of fear and vulnerability. As I walked closer, details came into focus, and the whole triangular complex seemed to grow with each step. I remember marveling at how big the trees were when I finally entered the border space between the woods and the farm field.

Before I actually walked into the woods, I could hear them. There seemed to be more birds there, and I could only imagine the other animals that might take cover under the thick canopy. I was sure snakes were around, given the proximity to the water-lined ditch on two sides. I could also see and hear flashes of kid activity through the dense undergrowth that acted as a closed barrier between the outside world and the secret goings-on inside. The whole place was alive and aware of my presence. I was transfixed, but I was scared and feeling my youth.

When I stepped inside, the thick edge of the woods opened into another world with tightly packed and defined dirt trails running around huge trees and swampy plants. There were wide, dug-out depressions punctuating the slightly rolling and cleared floor, indicating years of use and the hard work of kids bent on a serious ride. I could see standing water in other carved depressions as I looked across the space, and I remember feeling the pure exhilaration of arrival as I peddled around this place. Soon, older kids were passing me on their dirt bikes with precision and speed, turning the water holes into black pits of roiling mud.

Since my mother grew up in our house, she was well acquainted with the wild tales emanating from the site. She said it wasn't a place for me, as teenagers went out there and did things they weren't supposed to do. A few years later, after moving away to Virginia, I found myself thinking about Old Hickory and whether similar places existed in my new hilly home. We had woods, a creek that actually ran, and plenty of backyards to explore, but I never found a place that made me feel like that clump of trees in the middle of the Delta. I didn't know why, but I always tried to find a new Old Hickory.

The name, *Old Hickory*, is not written on regional maps, nor is it the subject of any previous official history. This patch of woods is an everyday place known to people living within a two-square-mile radius on the outskirts of Cleveland, Mississippi. It is the kind of place that remains unnoticed by casual passersby. It measures 140 yards (north/south) by 100 yards (east/west) and sits at the corner of two drainage ditches that service the surrounding agricultural fields. The distance from the primary road to Old Hickory is 730 yards.[1] While there are various tree representatives at the site, overcup oak is the dominant species in this stand, and they thrive in "poorly drained, alluvial, clayey soils mainly on southern river flood plains." They can grow up to ninety feet and live as long as four hundred years, and their acorn fruit, identified by a distinctive cupped crown, mature in about one year. The lower trunk is generally free of short branches, and the canopy is full and rounded. While the wood is "hard, heavy, and strong," overcup oaks are not historically valued for refined uses. Therefore, they tend to predominate at cutover sites.[2] From above, the trees at Old Hickory form a triangle, but this stand resembled a circular island in an otherwise cleared and open landscape before a bordering neighborhood expanded Cleveland's residential footprint in the early 1970s.

Old Hickory is largely taken for granted by locals. However, the site possesses deep cultural meaning dating to the early days of Mississippi post-frontier development. When prompted to think about it, many locals connect their memories of being a child growing up in the Delta with their visceral experiences at Old Hickory. The memories are often expressed through emotional language, and their affective content relates to wider themes regarding a sense of place, identity formation, and ecological change. Evidence indicates that successive generations of children created and added multiple layers of meaning to this site, transforming a collection of trees into a named, valued, and protected space. While these alterations mimicked some of the changes wrought by industrial agricultural values and practices in the region, this cultural activity, combined with the physical configuration of the landscape, worked to safeguard the trees as farming and development expanded in the area.

For some adults recalling their childhood experiences at Old Hickory, the woods are part of an assumed wilder, older, more authentic landscape, now only visible in scattered pockets across the vast flatland. These memories and associations are embedded within a region shaped by historical, cultural, environmental, and ecological forces. In this sense, Old Hickory exists within a *bioregion*, or a visually discernible area defined by a particular and complex "linkage between ecological locale and human culture."[3]

As a remnant of a pre-cleared old-growth forest, Old Hickory was and continues to be a place in which many cultural traits that animate the Delta play out. Historically, the site was a close, confined area for local children to interact with nature on their own terms. It allowed for the formation of friendship bonds, and it served as a space for rebellion against dominant parental and societal conventions. Because open agricultural fields surrounded this patch of woods prior to the 1970s, a juxtaposition made possible by human development and the Delta's unique topography occurred—setting the woods apart and creating a destination and generational refuge. This tiny vestige possesses an intrinsic value separate from economic or political considerations alone, and the affective memories associated with these trees shed light on how people interact with and embody nearby landscapes.

Additionally, since identity is understood to accrue through "the transactions between people and their everyday socio-physical environments,"[4] trees and local wooded areas should be considered active agents in this process. By situating Old Hickory within a bioregional and historical context, this project seeks to uncover why a tiny patch of trees survived the removal of surrounding forests to make way for cotton; to understand how people engage, think about, and remember everyday natural places; and finally, to embrace my own subjectivity and familiarity with the site to evaluate its utility as a repository of local memory and gauge its capacity as an agent acting upon sense of place, historical thinking, and environmental awareness.

The Mississippi Delta: Bioregion

Historian James Cobb called the Mississippi Delta "the most southern place on earth" in his influential book about the region published in 1992. He was interested in the historical development of a place defined by competing realities: severe poverty, racial violence, and oppressive heat intertwined with lavish wealth, artistic genius, extreme beauty, and a lingering impression that geography and dirt connected all. Cobb recognized the Mississippi Delta's uniqueness as he tied the region to wider currents shaping American history.[5]

Other historians, journalists, and artists echo similar themes, just as Cobb picked up on earlier work about the region. In his best-selling 2015 memoir, *Dispatches from Pluto: Lost and Found in the Mississippi Delta*, Richard Grant refers to the Delta as "the most American place on earth" as he describes his experiences with the people, land, and sounds of his new alien home.[6] Mississippi native Ralph Eubanks surveys the impact Mississippi's geographies have had on homegrown literary talent, from Faulkner to Eudora Welty. Interweaving memoir with literary analysis, Eubanks writes, "Suffering and injustice permeate visions of the Delta landscape as much as the wail of the blues . . . but whatever it is, for a brief part of the day beauty soothes the echo of the ghostlike weary blues that seem to howl and scream across this wide and often empty berth of land."[7]

The Mississippi Delta was a swampy frontier before humans introduced levee systems to wrestle control of the Mississippi River. It is part of a large alluvial complex stretching from Illinois to the southern extreme of Louisiana. As the river moves southward, thousands of acres of streams, creeks, and lesser rivers funnel into the main channel, conveying water and sediment that once spread outward during routine flooding periods prior to the twentieth century. This "entire watershed drains all or parts of thirty-one states, two Canadian provinces, and over 1,000,000 square miles before it finally reaches the gulf [of Mexico]."[8] The area in northwest Mississippi that locals call "the Delta" is part of the Yazoo-Mississippi River Delta, carving a two-hundred-mile half oval from Memphis to Vicksburg. The region's shape is clearly discernible from Google Earth, and the abrupt change in topography from bluff to flatland is similar to riding down a steep hillside onto a parking lot. Writer, photographer, and Mississippi native Eudora Welty recalled in 1972, "The Delta is very rich and visually striking, but completely flat. I would find it maddening after days with nothing but the horizon."[9]

Thick forests and varied tree populations have existed in the Delta for thousands of years, sheltering immense varieties of flora and fauna. Hernando DeSoto encountered junglelike conditions as he traversed the Delta in the 1500s, while subsequent pass-through expeditions revealed fleeting glimpses of deep soils hinting at future agricultural potential. The trees were part of the broad southern bottomland hardwood forest that blanketed much of the region until the nineteenth century, and they included "red maple, water hickory, sugarberry, persimmon, green ash, sweetgum, swamp chestnut oak, water oak, American elm, and bald cypress." Native American groups lived on and worked these bottomland zones prior to European settlement, altering their surroundings by controlled burning. This process "created a southern landscape of prairies, fields, savannas, woodlands, and dense forests." European settlers continued burning practices, but subsequent steam and mechanized technologies accelerated intensive logging that carved open spaces out of the thick southern bottomland regions.[10]

In the seventeenth century, forests covered an estimated 90 percent of the entire acreage area of modern-day Mississippi. By the early 1800s, as land values in the Delta were rising parallel to the idea of taming this wilderness for cultivation, James Audubon wrote vivid descriptions of immense old-growth forests covering the Delta, offering protection for a huge variety of animal species. Oxbow lakes created from the millennial swings of the Mississippi River also dotted the region, held in place by cypress trees recalling ancient flora. Eastern planters with access to enslaved labor soon relocated their considerable resources to the Delta to begin the long, complicated process of establishing working farm operations. Cobb notes that by 1830, "Washington County's population stood at 1,976—of whom 1,184 were slaves." Enslaved people represented 87 percent of the total population in Bolivar County by 1860, reflecting the hard history of draining and clearing the landscape to establish a cotton empire.[11]

After the Civil War, the Delta continued to attract wealthy white farmers, railroad companies, and northern speculators interested in cotton and timber, as well as hunters pulled by the allure of exotic game. The land itself was imposing and unforgiving: a "'wild country' . . . covered with 'heavy timber and thick cane . . . fifteen to twenty feet high.'"[12] The postbellum regional economy was unstable, however, and many of these initial would-be developers sold or leased deeper backcountry lands to ease debt burdens imposed by Reconstruction governments. Newly freed African Americans and poor whites leveraged this opportunity by purchasing or renting land to set up farming operations of their own.[13] While this moment of expanded opportunity was fleeting, it highlighted the close and complicated relationship between land and people in the Delta, as the wrenching process of cutting open, dry spaces for planting also created economic, emotional, and cultural ties to the region.

As the twentieth century dawned, global demand pushed cotton prices upward. Boosters understood the economic potential of clearing wider swaths of the Delta landscape for cotton, and advertisements soon blanketed local and foreign markets touting profits and a return to antebellum ease. In 1911, for example, British investors sensed the windfall and purchased "thirty to forty thousand acres" of what would become the Delta and Pine Land Company. Others with capital and command of labor joined the fray, implementing precision management and industrial-scale production. In the process, the Delta's social and political systems coalesced around a new plantation ethos using sharecropping and tenant farming to drive cotton production and white supremacy. While this system afforded real benefits for the owner and worker if the crop was healthy and debts were manageable, whites largely controlled Black labor and social mobility. Thus, this system reversed postbellum gains for African Americans. By 1910, "92 percent of the area's farms were operated by tenants," and "approximately 95 percent of the Delta's tenants were black."[14]

The wilderness also endured significant change, as "timber companies clear-cut the swampy forest of its hardwoods, making land available for sale, and railroads laid tracks that connected Delta planters to outside cotton markets." Land clearing in the Delta reflected wider historical processes across the country. American forests drew people from around the world in the early days of colonization and pushed settlers farther into Native American territories after the Revolution. Wood was a critical engine for growth, serving as raw material for new infrastructure and as a framework for economic expansion. Lumbering operations cut large forest stands across the East, as agricultural production continued apace; both pushed industrial development. As the Southwest (Alabama, Mississippi, Arkansas, Louisiana, and Texas) opened to white settlement after the Indian Removal Act of 1830, these processes moved into the extremely dense and fertile frontier region. By the end of World War I, "[lumbering and clearing] of southern timber stands had reduced the primeval forest by approximately 40 percent." Albert E. Cowdrey writes of the South generally that "every part of this primordial landscape—woods, soil, and waterways, and the animals that used them—was altered by the demands of a society with many wants of its own, and foreign markets to serve, as well."[15]

In 1911, W. W. Boone (chief engineer of the Bolivar County Drainage Commission) reflected prevailing attitudes about land control and regional development, writing, "The time was ripe and conditions demanded that the thousands of acres of rich swamp and timbered lands lying useless and a burden for the lack of drainage be reclaimed and turned into channels of usefulness." Walter Sillers Sr. (Delta native, cotton planter, and politician) wrote about Bolivar County in 1924, conveying an excited boosterism that connected progress with human mastery over a subdued landscape. Bolivar County was, according to Sillers, "a vast, open stretch of the most fertile land in all America! There [were] no hills, only a few scattering Indian Mounds." Because of this, "every foot of land [was] capable of cultivation, there [were] no waste lands or obstacles in the way of tillage."[16]

Boone and Sillers utilized a contemporary value system in the United States and within forestry management circles "that emphasized the exploitation, use, and development of resources, dominance of economic over noneconomic values, and human control over nature." Sillers also connected progress with white rule, reflecting attitudes held by significant portions of Delta leadership during this era. By the 1930s, approximately three-fifths of the Delta had been cleared for agricultural pursuits, with cotton serving as the dominant crop. Across the South, cotton spread over forty-two million acres.[17]

Today, agriculture still dominates the Mississippi Delta landscape, while forests cover only between 5 and 25 percent of the region. What remains is an open, flat land utterly transformed by the human hand, bearing "little resemblance to the Delta inhabited by Native Americans or even mid-nineteenth-century American settlers." This striking cutover landscape was largely in place by World War II, and the remaining forests and collections of trees stood in stark contrast to the meticulously sculpted and increasingly weedless agricultural fields stretching for miles. The economic advantages of clearing the Delta were widely understood, as mechanization in the middle of the twentieth century reflected new technological approaches to controlling the land, spurring waves of Black and white labor out-migration. Farmers also recognized the economic opportunities crop diversification would bring, ushering in a new era in Delta planting in the latter part of the twentieth century. Catfish, rice, soybean, and corn spread across the Delta landscape and quickly positioned the region as a significant contributor to total commodity production in the United States.[18]

With so many acres of land in cultivation, the spatial organization of the Delta assumed unique characteristics compared with other parts of the country. While the upper South and eastern regions certainly engaged in heavy agricultural production, those landscapes tend to be hilly and mountainous, thereby reducing large-scale contiguous farm fields. Since the Delta is a giant floodplain, once the forests were cut over and the swamplands drained, the landscape opened. Private farming operations could therefore butt against other landowners engaged in agricultural production, and the Delta assumed its vast, garden-like appearance. The remaining trees and understory demarcated field ownership, often rendered in thin, straight lines. Trees left in the middle of these boundaries were anomalous, surrounded by managed farm fields. The affective impact of this spatial arrangement is palpable and often overwhelming, as an unfettered horizon line seems to melt into the sky. At night, dense networks of stars pierce through the blackness, as rows of lights appear from towns in the far distance.

Such a visual reality can quickly turn into romantic flights of fancy, and countless native-born and foreign artists and writers have all added to the Delta's mystique. Ralph Eubanks argues that "imagination is stamped into the cultural fabric of the Delta, making it central to Mississippi's literary landscape."[19] Indeed, literature and music are inextricably linked to the region's identity. Faulkner was fascinated with the Delta, while blues artists like Robert Johnson, Son House, Charley Patton, and hundreds more musicians introduced the world to *Delta* blues.

The Mississippi Delta is therefore a place of contradictions, echoing discordant themes in American history. Delta landscapes physically harbor this ambivalence, and it is tempting to overlook the social, cultural, and ecological consequences of human-induced development while watching thunderhead clouds billow up and out as they cast anthropomorphic shadows on a perfectly flat Delta stage. The current distribution of Delta towns, agricultural fields, and developed areas reflects patterns centuries in the making, and these alterations to the land directly impact the way humans and animals organize their daily routines and understand their immediate world.

Before drainage and clearing transformed the land for massive-scale agriculture, the Delta was also home to a wide variety of animal species. The ivory-billed woodpecker is a famous example of a now extinct native bird, but wolves, cougars, and the Carolina parakeet, among others, also called the forests of the Delta home. As contiguous forest habitats disappeared and tree stands grew distant from each other, animals felt increased pressure to locate other sources of cover and sustenance, causing other changes down the chain. Extinction rates increased as this process intensified. Mikko Saikku connects large faunal extinctions in the Delta with established biological theory, suggesting, "Newly formed fragments of forest that previously composed larger islands tend to be supersaturated with species that cannot be sustained for long."[20]

In "The Delta and Yoknapatawpha: The Layering of Geography and Myth in the Works of William Faulkner," Phillip Gordon discusses the many ways Faulkner intuited these human and biological processes as the Mississippi author incorporated the Delta in his work. In "The Bear," Faulkner captures the impact of land clearing and cotton expansion, in which a disappearing wilderness is being overtaken by the saw, while ancient characters negotiate the new reality. Gordon parses Faulkner's words:

> But the wilderness is only "apparently impenetrable." Boon will kill Old Ben. The old Chickasaw hunting guide, Sam Fathers, dies at virtually the same time. Within two years of killing Old Ben, Major de Spain has sold the old hunting camp to a logging company. When Ike travels to the old camp two years later, he finds in its stead a lumber mill and newly laid railroad. He finds Boon hunting squirrel in the one remaining tree in a vast clearing, the tree teaming with squirrels because it is the last place they have for refuge. Boon warns Ike clear with the hoarse exclamation, "Get out of here! Don't touch them! . . . They're mine!" Indeed, he should feel proprietary. This is all that is left of that old wilderness, one tree full of trapped squirrels.[21]

Gordon's analysis illustrates Faulkner's understanding of changes to the human and nonhuman Delta world. In this reading, the lone tree stands as a signifier of change, inhabiting a charged space in which people and animals must now find new ways of relating to the land. The squirrels are crowded as they retreat to the last few natural spaces of cover, while the hunter desperately fights to maintain ownership and control over a world slipping away. The tree is an anchor to the past and an active agent within these ongoing dramas, and the lives of all are intertwined in this historical and ecological matrix. James Cobb also understood the wider implications of Faulkner's perspective about a changing Delta, South, and America, arguing that he "used the Delta to explore transcendent questions of greed, cruelty, and the ravages of man and modernity against nature."[22]

Faulkner's fictionalized account speaks to the complex processes by which humans derive meaning from their surrounding landscapes to develop their sense of identity and place. Increasingly, various academic disciplines describe an interplay among everyday landscapes, sense of place, and identity.[23] In the environmental humanities, place is understood as "co-produced by ecological and cultural processes," and much emphasis is given to "the implications of thinking of humanity as dependent upon environment, and of the environment as a domain which is as much cultural as ecological."[24]

In "Mining Memories in a Rural Community: Landscape, Temporality, and Place Identity," Rebecca Wheeler conducts fieldwork interviews in a rural English village in Cumbria, whose residents remember its mining history through "residues embedded in the landscape." Rather than inert pieces of material lacking agency, Wheeler discovers that remnants of mining infrastructure, along with subtle "phantom environment" alterations extant on the previous industrial site, all contribute to a process by which "the past is thus presenced through remembering *with* the landscape." Wheeler finds that children use these remnant and "un-heritageised" landscapes as "unofficial playground[s]," "allow[ing] space for ambiguous local tales or myths, that might otherwise have been erased through being labelled 'incorrect,' to live on." This physical and creative interaction with the everyday or "unmanaged" landscape pulls "memories of past people and places into the present," contributing to an important historical perspective and sense of place knowledge for local inhabitants.[25]

Wheeler's findings suggest that identity is bound up in routine interactions with everyday places, and this work has clear implications for land management, conservation, interpretation, and preservation practices in a variety of contexts. It also speaks to the agency of landscapes and their capacity to engage the full range of human perception and sensory experience. In *Topophilia: A Study of Environmental Perception, Attitudes, and Values*, Yi-Fu Tuan surveys the myriad emotional connections that exist between humans and their environments. Different types of landscapes, their features, and their spatial characteristics generate affective environments within which humans interact, form emotional associations, and derive meaning. Tuan writes, "Open space signifies freedom, the promise of adventure, light, the public realm, formal and unchanging beauty; enclosed space signifies the cozy security of the womb, privacy, darkness, biologic life."[26]

Similarly, Jennifer Ladino considers National Park Service sites in the American West as affective environments and argues that their spatial and built configurations on the landscape prompt emotional responses that shape historical thinking. At each memorial site, she "track[ed] several affective registers: the *textual*, as represented emotion; the *corporeal*, as affect and/or emotion felt in [her] own body; and the *environmental*, as affect emanating from landscapes." By engaging and evaluating her felt presence along with other fieldwork methods and archival research, Ladino finds that the physical configuration, other features including nonhuman elements, and interpretive narratives at each site all act to condition affective registers in the visitor, expressed as "shame, regret, grief, pride, fear, anger, guilt, and others." These serve as pathways to build empathy, generate historical thinking, and work toward social and environmental justice. This perspective also applies to non-memorialized natural spaces.[27]

Old Hickory: An Island of Trees

Old Hickory is a non-memorialized site located on the southern edge of Cleveland, Mississippi. Incorporated in 1886, Cleveland developed as a railroad town and as one of two county seats for Bolivar County. Between 1900 and 1933, the town's population and residential housing stock expanded dramatically, while local timber operations cleared surrounding fields for cotton production. Delta State Teachers College opened its doors in 1925, offering postsecondary training for whites and ushering in new development to accommodate the "influx of students and teachers who would need temporary housing."[28] By 1940, residential housing had expanded to within half a mile of the Old Hickory site.[29]

Cleveland, like most Delta towns, is still essentially segregated, a product of the long, often violent history of enforced separation in Mississippi. Old Hickory is located in a predominately white section of town. Therefore, this study represents an incomplete evaluation of how the many cultures living in the Delta understand and interact with local wooded areas and remaining natural spaces in the region. Subsequent work must explore the experiences of the many communities living in the Delta to form a more complete understanding of cultural exchanges with similar places.

I was born in Cleveland and lived there as a child. My family moved away to Virginia in the mid-1980s, but we maintained a close connection to the Delta. As a public history graduate student many years later, I studied blues music tourism and spent countless hours doing fieldwork in the region. When back in Cleveland, I found myself going to the Old Hickory site to see if the trees were still standing. Indeed, they were. I was curious about similar experiences or recollections about this place, so I asked family members and old friends about it. Their stories and memories were very similar to my own, and it was apparent that the site's cultural history would be worthy of more study.

I visited Old Hickory again in 2019. Walking across the fallow field in late spring felt comfortable and familiar: an affective reminder from thirty years ago. A path leading into the woods bordered a drainage ditch separating the adjacent neighborhood and the site. Once inside, I saw the tamped trail systems again, with pools of standing water punctuated by low, swampy vegetation and mature trees. A teenager named "Edgar" was riding an all-terrain vehicle at a distance just beyond the trees. Through serendipity, I was able to field-test early questions and compare my own childhood recollections with Edgar's contemporary experience.

Edgar was a great informant. He confirmed that the site is still called "Old Hickory" and that he and his friends have been going there since they were little kids to "mud ride and swim in the holes." He remembered initially learning about the site through "friends and their parents and family," indicating knowledge passed down and around local friend and kin networks. This place "has been important for everybody around here," he said. "After school . . . any time [I] need time for myself, I just come out here and ride."[30]

Edgar was covered in thick, clay-infused mud—residue from riding around the site that afternoon. He pulled at the globules and worked them in his hands as he thought about and responded sincerely to my questions. Had I never moved away from the Delta, this image would not have registered in any meaningful way. But with time and distance, I could see that Edgar was completely at ease in the trees and dirt he'd played in and ingested all his life. As a place to get away, ride, and meet with friends, Old Hickory was clearly important to Edgar, and our interaction reinforced the idea that the site was important.

In addition to speaking with local officials, landowners, and forestry experts and conducting archival and secondary research, I posted a general query about Old Hickory in a private Delta Facebook group hoping to clarify early questions.[31] This group contains members from all walks of life. Most are adults who live in the region, while many moved away and maintain close connections to the Delta. The group is dedicated to sharing Mississippi Delta memories, culture, history, anecdotes, and family relations, and it came up in conversation many times as I spoke with people in the early phases of research. The query established my ties to the area and that I was conducting research about the site for an upcoming publication. It also made clear that in addition to other forms of research, gaining local perspective was critical to the project.[32]

There are significant challenges associated with using social media for research purposes, including data bias due to "social desirability influences and other censoring by a given participant," as well as the inherent ease and rampant practice of posting misleading or false information. Employing social media as research text should therefore be a cautious endeavor and preferably in conjunction with primary and secondary research methods that offer context and checks on the data. Facebook is used by approximately 69 percent of Americans and by 2.8 billion people worldwide. While most Americans (59 percent) "said they distrust the platform as a place to get [political and election] news," Daschel argues that if done carefully, these "platforms provide an information-rich opportunity to reach diverse populations that would otherwise be difficult to identify."[33]

In July 2019, my query received 432 interactions—a surprising and reassuring figure, given the lack of any previous formal study of the site.[34] The responses varied between short statements of support, lengthy descriptions, and detailed remembrances. The posts were nostalgic, and many connected their experiences at the site with a bygone era. Quite a few were surprised and excited that the woods were even being discussed:

> Boy [those] were the good ole days, it's bringing a tear just thinking about those woods. I was there everyday, boy I miss em.[35]

> Oh wow! Old Hickory! I spent many days, many hours playing in those woods growing up in the 1960s. We made a lifetime of memories for sure.[36]

> Man we had bicycles, four wheelers, dirt bikes, and even a few of the really crazy ones took dads lawn mowers! mud holes that would swallow you whole! then when rice was planted in [the] field behind it, we would cool off in the pump water.[37]

A significant number of replies served as prompts for discussion within the group, as members recalled experiences that were echoed and developed by others. This dialogue revealed patterns of use, themes, shared emotions, and consistent descriptions that breathe life into an otherwise hidden history.

There were posts about BB gun fights, secret meetups, smoking "grapevine," stocking up on candy at the local store and then heading out to the site all day, and elaborate fort- and trail-building projects. One poster mentioned that his family moved to the adjacent neighborhood in 1977, adding, "The inside of these woods will forever be etched in my mind. I remember every hill, trail, and mud hole in there."[38] Another wrote, "We built bridges across the ditch to get to [Old Hickory]. Sometimes we would take a cooler and float in that ditch. Our parents knew exactly where to find us or some of them were loud enough to yell or whistle and we knew which parent was calling for which kid. It was our little world. . . . We made forever family and friends in those woods."[39]

Some described an insider/outsider scenario in which kids in the know claimed ownership over the site. They also described efforts to keep the space clean, as if the site belonged to their little group. This proprietary sense evolved over time due to spatial changes after the construction of the adjacent neighborhood in the early 1970s. These stories appeared in stand-alone posts and throughout intragroup discussions, and members supported and playfully chided one another in their shared memories. This was the first time most group members reflected upon and discussed the site in detail, and the volume of responses indicated a collective desire to remember and share in this place once again.

I reached out to several respondents who participated in group discussions requesting a more comprehensive interview based on their dialogue. "John" quickly agreed to a telephone conversation. His posts were quite detailed, and he was clearly surprised that so many people were talking about Old Hickory. In his first post, he wrote, "During the mid-fifties, we had a group that hung out there. At the SE corner of the woods we dug the center out of the spoil bank beside the ditch and built 2 underground rooms, each about 8 feet long and connected. They were buried with hidden trap doors in the roof. We spent many entire weekends there and enjoyed cooking frog legs that we gigged in the ditches. Many of our friends visited our underground hut. We had a lot of fun days and nights at hickory woods."[40] Another poster independently offered a memory of a "mound with collapsed caves/tunnels dug by earlier explorers."[41] John excitedly responded, "Wow . . . I wonder if the mounds that caved in for you were the old tunnels that I referred to earlier. Our older group dug into two spoil banks and built two underground rooms about 4′ × 4′ × 8′, connected them and buried them with trap doors from the top."[42]

John's family moved to Cleveland in 1942, and they lived in a house that stood one mile from Old Hickory. John was eleven years old when he first heard about "hickory woods" from his neighbor friends. Our conversation revealed timelines and details that surfaced in other interviews. He remembers playing at the site primarily from 1951 to 1956, but he also visited as a teenager in later years. He described riding his bike with friends to the local store at the southern edge of town and then taking a dirt path across the open farm field to the site. At this time, Old Hickory was the only stand of woods he could recall in the area, confirming the island effect. He mentioned that there were "not many other places to go" and that it was their "non-adult world away from home."[43]

As we talked about his elaborate cave and tunnel systems, John mentioned a sense of ownership of the site. He recalled "running off . . . fighting . . . and kicking [another kid] out," laughingly saying that they "ran that Yankee off"[44]—a direct expression of territorial defense and an allusion to lingering post–Civil War animosities. John was not sure how this boy found his way to the woods, and he remembered acting out a protective posture. John moved away from Cleveland many years ago, but when back in town, he "salutes Old Hickory . . . trying to see if the woods are still there."[45]

Other respondents posted separately about an insider/outsider memory. Once the neighborhood adjacent to Old Hickory was completed in the early 1970s, the proprietary boundary from John's earlier years contracted. The new neighborhood offered resident children immediate access to the site, generating a new sense of ownership. For example, one respondent commented, "Heard my older brothers talking about [Old Hickory] when I was just a little kid in the mid-70's. Buddy of mine in ninth grade lived on one of the offshoot roads [in the adjacent neighborhood]. That's when I started hanging out there. Neighborhood kids were very protective of Old Hickory."[46] Another recalled, "As a kid I had a dirt bike, in the late 70's early 80's. We rode on many turn roads, but I became a little fearful to venture into Old Hickory. . . . There were many, many kids that lived [in the adjacent neighborhood]. You see, these kids seemed to have territorial rights to 'Old Hickory.' I wish I could claim great memories there, as it was a special place, but not living in the immediate closest area, I never had the chance to enjoy it as did 'the protective locals.'"[47] Once completed, the neighborhood expanded the residential footprint in Cleveland. It also altered the spatial and visual orientation of the site, filling in some of the open context that previously set the woods apart on all sides. Kathy Rhodes, a writer and Cleveland native who now resides in the Nashville area, posted that she remembered the "Big Woods" from her childhood in the 1950s/60s and that she had written a short story about it years later. Apart from one- or two-line mentions about Old Hickory on a few social media posts prior to this study, Kathy's short story is the only fully rendered account of the site I have been able to locate. Her elegant prose and our subsequent interview captured the affective impact of the site prior to the 1970s. She wrote in "The Big Woods,"

> The dusty trail narrowing as it got further away and the defined leaves of early cotton blurring into walls of green. The flat, open field stretched out as far as the eye could see—except for one thing. A patch of woods a mile or two down the road. One circular structure of trees rising up out of the cotton. We called it The Big Woods. It was mysterious. It was out of place. It was far away. Yet, it beckoned, its wailing sweetness sliding across waves of heat, wrapping around us, pulling us like it knew us well and we knew it. . . . As we stepped into the forest, we entered a whole new world. It was the difference between summer and winter, light and dark. Sunlight couldn't penetrate the thick vegetation, making it damp and cool. It was like Tarzan and Jane's jungle we'd seen on TV. Virgin forest. . . . We marveled at nature's playhouse—this place that seemed to belong to us alone.[48]

The physicality of the site—a lone stand of trees on the outskirts of town in the middle of an open Delta field—generated intense childhood feelings of mystery, intrigue, and alluring adventure for Kathy, and these memories remained for her as an adult. In our interview, she reflected, "It was more than a little forest; it was a feeling—a feeling that I belonged to this place, and this place belonged in that cotton field, and my heart knew that we were all part of something bigger. Maybe all Delta-born children are connected to the spirit of 'place' with a sense of belonging and a longing to be there."[49] This recollection speaks to Tuan's description of the many cultural associations with islands across the world. He writes, the island's "importance lies in the imaginative realm . . . symboliz[ing] a state of prelapsarian innocence and bliss" and thus "identifying enchantment with insularity."[50]

During the course of my research, I learned that the City of Cleveland had recently acquired the land on which Old Hickory sits, and they were actively planning to build a soccer complex at the site. I wrote a letter to the mayor of Cleveland informing him of this project and discussing the site as a cultural landscape that was clearly important to local residents over a long period of time. He responded immediately and generously offered to help. Mayor Billy Nowell is a lifelong Cleveland resident, and his father's construction company built the neighborhood adjacent to Old Hickory. He played in the woods as a child in the 1960s, so his recollections and our conversations about the site proved invaluable.

FIGURE 4. Aerial view of Old Hickory, 1964.
Photograph courtesy of Historic Aerials.

Mayor Nowell felt the trees remained standing because the site must be low and prone to retaining water and thus not worth the effort and expense to clear years earlier. He also mentioned that if this were not the case, his father certainly would have attempted to develop that part of the field when he began construction on the adjacent neighborhood development.[51] Dr. Brady Self, associate extension professor of silviculture at Mississippi State University, corroborated this line of reasoning. Dr. Self agreed to join me for fieldwork at Old Hickory, and he identified concentrations of overcup oak trees at the site. These trees thrive in low, wet areas with clay soils—exactly the content found at Old Hickory. Self also connected elevated pH values in similar ecological zones with overcup oak stands and lower crop yields.[52] Therefore, it is likely this tiny section of ground simply would not support consistent agricultural practices.

Dr. Self's analysis of the site also supports Mikko Saikku's environmental history of the Delta, which establishes that early "logging operations had customarily concentrated on timber stands of highest economic value. Consequently, half of the remaining old-growth forest was dominated by Overcup Oak and Water Hickory, two species that in 1932 were 'in limited demand.'"[53] Historic topographic maps and aerial images from the 1930s and 1940s indicate a stream and parallel thin strip of woods next to the Old Hickory site. Most of the wooded area, along with the stream, disappeared during the midcentury drainage and clearing. Modern aerial images show a clear subsurface trace of what appears to be the stream footprint running to the south of the remaining patch of woods called Old Hickory. These early maps and images therefore indicate a feature that likely contributed to prolonged periods of standing water in the slightly lower elevation at the site.[54] A soil survey of Bolivar County published in 1958 indicated that "most of the county has been cleared, and all the forest has been cut over," and "small areas of timber are distributed throughout the county, mostly on poorly drained heavy soils."[55]

This suggests that Old Hickory is part of an old-growth forest that was culled and cut over in the early twentieth century and that the economic value of the trees on this damp, low ground was deemed insufficient to the concerns of planters and developers in that era. As the forest around the site receded, the remnant stand was a physical anomaly within a cleared and ordered agricultural context that took on new meaning for locals seeking a secluded place to gather and play. Because this stand included overcup oak, whose trunks grow few small branches before larger branches appear toward the crown, there was some room to move around the interior within an enclosed space. As multiple generations of children visited, carved trails, and left their own traces, their accumulated experiences added new layers of meaning to the site. In many ways, these alterations mirrored wider agricultural practices and values that sought to subdue and control the land, yet this activity also helped safeguard the patch of woods. The trees and ground left alone due to their lack of economic viability in earlier post-frontier clearing stages were later valued because of their scarcity in the cutover Delta, and a small, distinctive cultural landscape emerged.

Old Hickory attracted Dr. Alan Feduccia as a child in the 1950s. It was part of a larger eighty-acre tract owned by the Feduccia family, with cotton and soybeans farmed primarily by tenant farmers until 2019. Dr. Feduccia is the S. K. Heninger Distinguished Professor Emeritus of Biology at the

University of North Carolina at Chapel Hill. He is a leading scholar in the evolutionary origins of birds, and his work complicates theories that posit a direct line between dinosaurs and modern bird species. While he hasn't lived in the Delta for decades, he maintains a deep connection to the region and Delta State University.

After I informed him of the initial findings, Dr. Feduccia wrote, "It is absolutely amazing to me how many people saw that little piece of property as something of value; and for me it was an integral part of my childhood."[56] While he is uncertain exactly when the woods acquired the name, he feels that many trees in the current stand are approximately one hundred years old. He also offered that "it was well established as Old Hickory," and he "recall[ed] [his] grandmother referring to it by that name" when he frequented the site in the mid-1950s,[57] suggesting that the name has existed for at least seventy-five years.

In addition to overcup oak, water hickory trees thrive across the Delta's rich, loamy soil. President Andrew Jackson established direct ties to the Delta in 1838 when his adopted son, Andrew Jackson Jr., purchased the Halcyon Plantation in Coahoma County. Prior to that, white Mississippians celebrated Jackson, famously known as "Old Hickory," as the primary negotiator of the Treaty of Doak's Stand (1820), a land cession that opened the Mississippi Delta to frontier development. While highly speculative, it is possible that Jackson's nickname remained in area lore, and the presence of water hickory trees at or near the original Old Hickory site could explain early naming.[58]

Dr. Feduccia lived within walking and riding distance of the woods as a young teenager. Describing his solitary explorations fueled by a keen interest in the natural world, he wrote, "I was likely in my early teens (12–13 plus or minus), when my natural history wanderings began. After school I would walk along Jones Bayou and often go all the way to Old Hickory, sometimes by bike halfway and then follow the drainage ditch over to the woods." He credits Old Hickory as a catalyst for his early interest in biology and later career, adding, "I suppose some five or more of my [Eagle Scout] natural history merit badges owed a large debt to Old Hickory."[59]

Discussing the decision to sell the land to the City of Cleveland, Dr. Feduccia indicated that he was seeking a way to "give back to the city,"[60] and he described the process by which his family partners "joined in deciding" to sell "their share for half the projected value as a partial gift." Feduccia maintains "a long-term sentimental attachment to the [Old Hickory] parcel of family land," and he was "opposed to turning it into a development." After negotiations with the city, Feduccia and the family's charitable trust[61] agreed to terms that would "convey the land to the City of Cleveland for a park" in 2019 for about one-fourth of the total value.[62] Feduccia was happy to hear that the city had received a grant to build a soccer complex on a portion of the land after the sale, but he "urged, if possible, that old Hickory be preserved as a remnant of the original Delta."[63] Like Kathy Rhodes, Dr. Feduccia feels that Old Hickory "shows what the [Delta] landscape was like prior to clearing."[64]

As he repeated his desire to see Old Hickory preserved, Feduccia stressed that "keeping the small woodland as it is could be an asset and of teaching value for conservation, etc., as well as for scouting."[65] Many social media respondents also exhibited a strong sense of place value, projecting emotional ties between the physical site and their childhood.[66] This relates to southern attitudes about the environment, suggesting "an emerging noneconomic orientation to forests" over the past few decades.[67] In recent years, Dr. Suzanne Simard's work revealed communication networks across plant communities that suggest "sentience in forests," requiring a potential reordering of how we think about the traditional binary relationship between human and nonhuman worlds.[68]

From an economic perspective, initiatives like the Natural Capital Project are quantifying the value of forests and natural landscapes, measuring returns on investment if municipalities consider trees and natural areas within their developmental strategies.[69] They offer frameworks to argue for data-driven preservation and conservation of natural areas by converting seemingly intangible assets into economic value. For example, the project found that "street trees in California provide $1 billion per year in ecosystem services, through atmospheric regulation and flood prevention, and Mexico's mangrove forests provide an annual $70 billion to the economy through storm protection, fisheries support, and ecotourism."[70] These findings reinforce the need for interdisciplinary research to fully measure impacts upon and threats to ecosystems and human and nonhuman communities. Sites like Old Hickory reveal personal attachments to everyday natural areas, and they open pathways to understanding bioregional histories. Their small-scale and affective resonance therefore introduces contexts for enhanced dialogue regarding environmental change and the climate crisis.

It appears that Old Hickory will remain standing even as its surrounding context witnesses another significant change. Mayor Nowell expressed a desire to mark or interpret the site in some way, acknowledging his personal experiences with the woods, their connection to the community, and the preservation interests conveyed by Dr. Feduccia in the land sale. As this next phase of development continues, Old Hickory will no longer resemble a partial island, and its position between the neighborhood and soccer complex will create a new visual and spatial dynamic. The transition from commercial agriculture to organized recreation will have immediate impacts on land use and public perception, as new infrastructure and access routes will alter the way locals approach and think about the woods.

The dialogue from the land sale and this project have also introduced questions about historical and cultural relevance, and this information may play a role in shifting perceptions about Old Hickory that contribute to some type of heritage recognition at the site—a change that is both beneficial and not without complication or negative consequence. The soccer complex will provide a needed space for organized play, while decreased usage of agricultural pesticides in the immediate area should contribute to a healthier ecosystem. Old Hickory might live on for another hundred years, offering opportunities to experience a unique Delta landscape, but official recognition and visitation may also bring unwanted attention to a space previously understood as a hidden local privilege and unofficial oasis.

These issues are inherent in public history work and within any type of local development. While the ramifications of interpreting spaces like Old Hickory must be fully considered, including how and whether to recommend preservation strategies, the potential for useful knowledge regarding how these sites function within communities is clear. Local residents should participate in this information exchange, and future efforts to interpret or preserve these landscapes will benefit from sustained community research and input.

This study offers a brief glimpse into a long and complicated story. Social media feedback, interviews, and fieldwork all suggest that children played a direct role in creating and maintaining a distinctive cultural landscape in Cleveland since at least the mid-twentieth century. Knowledge transfer through generations and physical interactions with the woods over time contributed layers of meaning that anchor the site within the local community and sustain memories about living in the Mississippi Delta. For Kathy Rhodes and Alan Feduccia, Old Hickory elicits reflections about what the Delta must have looked like before the land was transformed by the human hand, and it prompts historical thinking about their formative years and their later lives.

Future research may shift Old Hickory's timeline back a few decades to reveal the genesis of the site's name, along with earlier associations. It could uncover troubled histories and stories consciously forgotten, recalling Delta themes related to race and a post-slavery society. More investigation might establish the presence of other similar cultural landscapes scattered across the Delta, prized for their obscurity and sustained by local children. If more of these sites exist, it is a safe bet their visitors maintain emotional connections that span generations and bolster their sense of place. For now, Old Hickory retains much of its mystery as it stands like Faulkner's lone tree: a survivor pulling the past into an ever-changing present.

FIGURE 5. The former pine grove picnic area in Sleeping Giant State Park, Hamden, Connecticut, before the tornado on May 15, 2018. Photograph by Julie Hulten, September 25, 2017.

Chapter Four

When a Tree Falls

LISTENING TO AND MANAGING CONNECTICUT'S HISTORIC LANDSCAPE

Leah S. Glaser, Central Connecticut State University

Just before 5 p.m. on May 15, 2018, a microburst touched down in suburban Hamden, Connecticut (the town's first since 1989), taking out hundreds of trees, trapping schoolchildren in after-school programs and people in their homes, and knocking out electrical power for weeks. A hiker documented the twister from the top of a stone WPA (Works Progress Administration) tower in Sleeping Giant State Park. The first tornado to hit the town in over thirty years leveled swaths of the park's forest cover in about thirty seconds, including dense pine grove picnic and parking areas at the main public entrance.

The damage precipitated community-wide mourning. Hamden's town seal identifies it as "The Land of the Sleeping Giant," and local tribes have identified it as a significant sacred site. In addition to the damage to homes, transportation routes, and power lines, the town lost its defining landscape. A 739-foot forested mountain of incredible tree variety—pine, hickory, chestnut oak, white and red oak, birch, beech, red cedar, hemlock, sugar maple, and Connecticut's state flower on the mountain laurel shrub—hosts dozens of hiking trails. The park serves as one of the town's most valuable recreational assets. It took over a year to reopen the park to an eager public, and it remains difficult to reconcile the absence of so many trees with one's place memory. Open grass fields replace the former pine forest, but there are plans to at least partially reforest the area.[1]

This saga of Sleeping Giant State Park, founded in 1924 to preserve the landscape for recreational purposes, reflects the environmental, cultural, and economic importance of trees to a local sense of place and memory amid a changing climate and unpredictable weather events. Over the three decades, climate change–induced weather events have amplified the significant roles that hurricanes, storms, flooding, fires, drought, industry, agriculture, technology, disease, insects, and urban development have historically played in altering our cultural landscape, destroying trees, and for all of us who call Hamden home, shaking our sense of place.

In a 2015 article for the *New York Times Magazine*, writer Helen McDonald asks, "We measure our own lives against the trees we grew up with. What does it mean for us when they disappear?" She offers Australian environmental

FIGURE 6. The former pine grove picnic area in Sleeping Giant State Park, Hamden, Connecticut, after the tornado on May 15, 2018, illustrates the impact of weather events on places defined by trees. Photograph by Julie Hulten, May 18, 2018.

philosopher Glenn Albrecht's word *solastalgia* to describe "people's emotional distress when their home landscapes become unrecognizable through environmental change."[2] Trees grow in forests but also within and near our suburban and urban communities, our built environment. It is among these cultural or hybrid landscapes that we feel loss most acutely. Our man-made infrastructure—including roads, utility lines, and now even solar and wind farms—frequently competes with natural resources, most often trees, for space on our streetscapes, in our open spaces, and in our viewsheds.

While we often hear these trees fall, whether from natural disaster or urban development, are we listening? Are we paying attention to the impact of these losses, environmentally, culturally, or psychologically? How will we respond to climate change in ways that do not sacrifice one of our most powerful ecological, economic, cultural, and physiological assets? The field of historic preservation has developed various frameworks and tools for identifying and preserving significant cultural resources from our past that define our sense of place. We can extend these tools to natural resources, particularly those that we have culturally managed. Natural disaster responses range from tree hugging (preservation) or tree planting (replacement) to tree trimming (rehabilitation) or clearing (demolition).

By absorbing and storing carbon from the air in their roots and trunks, trees remain one of our greatest environmental assets for slowing climate change. They are also integral to our cultural infrastructure, literally and metaphorically framing, connecting, and rooting individuals and communities. It is therefore critical, culturally and environmentally, that we as humans maintain trees in the places we live. Dendrochronology can not only date building materials but also reveal environmental events, ecological and climatic. In the last few years, scientists have even relied on trees to broaden data about hurricanes in the Caribbean back to the fifteenth century by comparing the tree studies against historical shipwreck data.[3] Urban development historically and continuously threatened trees (and their environmental, sociological, and psychological benefits) even before we acknowledged the effects of storms and fires on trees. Roads, utility lines, subdivisions, retail, and other commercial endeavors are essential to modern life. Urban renewal projects caused a devastating landscape disruption in the 1950s and '60s, launching the national historic preservation movement and formalizing historic preservation practices. For better or worse (and often for worse, environmentally speaking), economic interests and sociocultural values can be more influential than ecological science in how we respond to the destruction of our natural resources.[4] Enlisting policies and strategies consistent with the historic preservation of other cultural resources can help maintain place and encourage resilience.

Recent years have produced many scholarly studies about trees, and such works are critical for providing the context necessary to understand the cultural significance of trees on the landscape and the streetscape. Here I offer additional context for how people and policy responded to landscape-altering storms in Connecticut's past, arguably the birthplace of forestry in the country, with the hope that this history and its cultural significance might provide guidance for maintaining this character-defining and critical carbon-absorbing resource as we move into an uncertain future.

> At 6 a.m. on August 15, 1635, fifteen years after the settlement of the Plymouth Plantation, a 130-mile-per-hour windstorm tore through eastern Connecticut and the Long Island Sound on its way up the Massachusetts Bay Colony. Puritan settlers reported that a fourteen-foot storm surge killed several Narragansett as they scrambled to find higher ground by climbing trees along the coast. Few reported what happened in the southern part of the colony, now known as Connecticut, which the English had just begun to colonize with a few forts and trading posts. However, Plymouth leader William Bradford described the storm as "strang & fearfull to behould." The winds uprooted "an inconceivable number of trees," twisting many like ropes and shattering others. It destroyed much of the recently planted harvest, and the landscape bore the scars for years afterward. With a diversified diet and migratory tradition, the local Native people often found trees a rich source of food: nuts, berries, and syrups. In competition with foreign English settlers, the food scarcity following the storm helped precipitate conditions leading to the Pequot War just a few months later.[5]

Connecticut's close and complex relationship to trees extends back centuries to the lifeways of precolonial woodland tribes. This seventeenth-century storm is one of the earliest recorded in colonial New England about a major weather event in the heavily forested region. Settlements in Hartford, Wethersfield, and Windsor merged into the Connecticut Colony the following year, but the place-defining landscape dates back to the Native peoples, whom anthropologists identify as the Eastern Woodland tribes. Native people across New England enlisted controlled burns to facilitate the endurance of certain tree species through regrowth, creating forests at various stages of ecological succession. Mature forests supplied them with tools, shelter, and food as they kept seasonally mobile between inland forests and the shoreline. Older, larger trees on the landscape also served as landmarks, offered directional and spiritual guidance, and often functioned as vessels to preserve memories and stories.

Part of the Mashantucket Pequot tribe's seal includes a lone tree to represent "much wooded land." Four "trees of life" point out from between the four sacred directions on the Mohegan tribal seal. Trees mark and recall Mohegan tribal stories—for example, the site of the annual Green Corn / Wigwam Festival is located within a grove of red cedar trees at the rock marking the Algonquian spiritual figure Moshup's footprint. Mohegan women designated the sacred site of an annual gathering of Mohegans, Niantics, and Pequots with a church, crushed shells, and the red cedar grove that serves as an important place for communal remembrance and marks the site of Sachem Uncas's village. The red cedar tree remains sacred to tribal members. Located inland, one already long-standing Native "peace tree" that survived the 1635 hurricane remains the central artifact of Connecticut's own treasured creation story. The local Native people (likely the Sicaogs or possibly the Tunxis or Wangunks) reportedly held councils beneath this massive oak tree (*Quercus alba*) in what is now the city of Hartford.[6]

Upon their arrival, Europeans marveled at Connecticut's "infinite thick woods" and vast forests of hardwoods as practically biblical gardens of Eden but soon cleared the lands for agriculture. Colonists planted invasive species strictly for use as lumber and fuel but saved certain individual trees around settlements that reminded them of the English landscape.[7] Far from Native ideas about the reciprocal nature of communal land stewardship, New England colony surveyors also used trees to mark property boundaries, symbolizing the idea of individual property ownership.[8] As part of the colonization process, the English and their descendants appropriated this Native "peace tree" both literally and culturally into their own origin story, claiming the land and its resources for themselves. When in 1662, England's King Charles II granted the Connecticut Colony a royal charter that stipulated self-rule, a delegation of Native people pleaded to the English settler who claimed the land as property not remove the tree to clear for farming. Not only did the tree possess spiritual significance, but its springtime leaf development helped indicate when to plant maize. Another popular colonial-era story explains that in 1686, King James II threatened to revoke the colonial charters under his new Dominion of New England. While he was able to seize Massachusetts's charter, Connecticut refused to give up its colony's charter, and with it, its autonomy. When newly appointed governor Edmund Andros came in person to seize the charter, settlers used the tree to assert their own claim to the region. They literally hid the physical charter in the eight-hundred-year-old hollow oak on South Meadow. The Glorious Revolution deposed James soon afterward, but Connecticut was able to retain its charter, and the Charter Oak became a colonial origin story and symbol of colonial resistance and independence for the growing colony. The Charter Oak legend serves as Connecticut's original story, reflecting the central role trees will play in Connecticut's political and economic development over the next three centuries.

> When in September of 1815, a "Great Gale" hit Connecticut's shoreline towns and seaports—sweeping through the coast with six-foot waves, killing thirty-eight people, and taking down sturdy oaks, maples, and walnuts—the Charter Oak remained standing near the center of the state, safe in Hartford. But forty-one years later, lightning fatally struck the estimated one-thousand-year-old monument, by then twenty-one feet in circumference. The community mourned, draping two national flags over the fallen tree and memorializing it with a ceremony and speeches. Church bells rang. A band from the Colt Armory played dirges. The city hosted a parade. Connecticut residents made precious mementos from the oak's trunk, the most prominent being a chair in the state senate chamber.[9]

Connecticut dodged the worst of New England's storms through most of the nineteenth century.[10] The long respite may be at least partially responsible for the evolution of the state's commitment to a forested landscape. Farms, mills, and factories created "culturally modified landscapes" that even today define the character of the New England region. In his regional environmental history *Second Nature*, historian Richard Judd argues that in New England, "nature and culture dissolved into an organic whole . . . a confluence of land use, collective memory, and natural processes that is widely accepted as distinctive to the region."[11] Colonists favored exotic trees transplanted from elsewhere, and by the early republic, antebellum New Englanders began to appreciate and desire native shade trees.[12] Towns became beneficiaries of tree philanthropy, whereby the wealthy donated saplings to plant in public spaces and along byways, in keeping with Europe's urban landscape traditions. However, New Englanders largely valued *rural* trees as economic resources. Almost every early industry (tanneries, shipping, mills) used wood for construction or energy (making charcoal to heat homes and blast iron furnaces), effectively eliminating virgin forests. By 1860, Connecticut had less than 30 percent tree cover.[13]

After the Civil War, northeastern manufacturing fueled the settlement and development of western lands, but those same activities conversely helped redefine local tree management. Certain local industries such as carriage making, furniture making, and shipbuilding required lumber, especially hickory, elm, and white ash.[14] Regenerated forests could not always produce large enough logs for quality lumber products, but the second-growth wood served as material for railroad tracks and eventually electrical poles erected throughout cities and suburbs.[15]

When historian Ellen Stroud describes this era in her book *Nature Next Door: Cities and Trees in the American Northeast*, she excludes Connecticut from the study, although it naturally shares the entwined history between forestation and urbanization. "The urban Northeast and the northeastern woods grew up together; they can become impoverished together," she explains, "and can nourish each other." Stroud argues that reforestation in the Northeast resulted from deliberate decisions of politicians and businessmen motivated by urban concerns, such as a dependable supply of drinking water.[16] The Connecticut landscape reflects decades of deliberate decisions by administrators and activists in response to deforestation from the early twentieth-century industrial economy. The larger leaf shade trees—especially the sycamore (*Platanus occidentalis*), oak (*Quercus*), chestnut (*Castanea*), and elm (*Ulmus americana*)—historically and culturally define its major cities, and these hardwoods make up the majority of managed forests. Trees are intertwined with the early twentieth-century conservation movement and later recreational economy.[17] Connecticut's vast network of state and municipal parks and forests makes it one of the most forested states in the country, over 60 percent for the last half century, with much of that urban tree cover. Connecticut became the first state to establish policy on forestry, the first to hire a state forester, and the first to purchase forestlands to protect watersheds and timber supplies. At the same time, state law often lacked clarity over the purpose of trees. This ambiguity included the management of the forests but also the trees we live among in the urban canopy.

Puritan tradition permeates the Connecticut River Valley, but as historian Mark Stoll explains, the early Connecticut Congregationalists' ethic of the common good and their agrarian values regarding land use as a tool for economic and social equality heavily influenced Progressive Era conservationists like Gifford Pinchot, Henry Graves, Stephen Mather, and Conrad Wirth, all from Connecticut.[18] Pinchot, born in Simsbury, Connecticut, embraced a philosophy that advocated the development of natural resources, and in particular forests.[19] In his role as the first chief of the US Forest Service, Pinchot asserted, "The first principle of conservation is development, the use of natural resources now existing on this continent for the benefit of the people who live here now."[20] Pinchot, often associated with the conservation movement in the American West and Pennsylvania, where he later served as governor, cofounded the US Forest Service and the Society of Forestry. He also continued to influence practice in Connecticut and helped begin the Yale School of Forestry in New Haven to train the nation's first professional foresters.

In 1895, Reverend Horace Winslow of Simsbury called the first meeting of the Connecticut Forest Association (CFA) to advocate the preservation, restoration, expansion, and scientific maintenance of forests. The group lobbied the Connecticut General Assembly to develop a forest policy, appoint a state forester and town tree wardens, and use state funds to purchase land to establish state forests. Meanwhile, after the chestnut blight, several uncontrolled fires, and sawmilling, Connecticut became the first state to assign a state forester with research and advocacy duties.[21] The state's earliest foresters closely associated their practices with agriculture, but forestry eventually became a wholly separate profession.

According to longtime Connecticut state forester Austin Hawes, the thirty-year period of Connecticut's forest and park development between 1913 and 1943 followed "the coming of the Professionals," specifically those from the Yale School of Forestry in New Haven. By the Great Depression, activists and bureaucrats disagreed upon what it meant to be a "conservationist." The mission of "public enjoyment" held by the National Park Service (NPS) aligned far more with John Muir's view of landscape preservation than with the foresters who initially wielded more influence in Connecticut. After gaining practical experience in Europe and the American West, they "scattered" their views of natural resources like seeds. Hawes credited Pinchot with advocating for coordinated programs in private and public forestry that encouraged resilience: "Fires have been greatly reduced, acreage in Woodlands increased, and the economic returns from scientific forestry are being felt by farmer and industrialist."[22] Henry Graves would become the dean of the Yale School of Forestry and president of the private but influential CFA. Yale continued to provide office space for the CFA between 1906 and 1927, even after Graves took over from Pinchot as chief forester of the US Forest Service. Many of Connecticut's conservation efforts launched from New Haven, where advocates promoted forest legislation. However, the fact that most land in the state was privately owned challenged the overzealous philosophy that Connecticut's conservationists promoted. Pinchot solicited support for extending the land reserve power of the federal government to eastern states, which unlike much of the West, largely required purchasing private land for public use.[23]

The Northeast's version of conservation evolved from agrarian-influenced notions about forest management to "newer Romantic, urban-based visions of the forest" that resembled ideas about natural public parks.[24] Legislation required appointing tree wardens to every municipality to meet the growing urban forests, largely in parks. Municipal parks, designed for recreational use, had proliferated throughout the Northeast since the 1860s with Hartford native Frederick Law Olmsted and his work creating New York City's Central Park. In the 1870s, Jacob Weidenmann introduced several tree species into Hartford's urban park system, and Olmsted designed parks in industrial New Britain and New Haven, Connecticut. Olmsted advocated the city park as a naturalistic landscape, where urban residents could escape the harsh realities of industrial work without losing the comforts of the city. Industrial cities set aside areas for grass, ponds, and trees for the enjoyment of urban workers and to soften the hard industrial streetscape. These designed landscapes echoed the aesthetic of the Hudson River Valley (HRV) School of painters, founded by Hartford's Frederic Church, one of the earliest advocates for public parks.[25] HRV artists joined poets and writers in persuading Americans that nature served as America's cathedrals. This notion shaped public perceptions of state parks and forests as essential to public health—not only physically but also spiritually.[26]

Urban parks remained popular, but Connecticut also followed national trends in creating public parks outside of the city. The state legislature appointed the State Park Commission (SPC) led by seven commissioners, including New Haven agricultural station forester and Yale alumni Walter Filley in 1913 to manage both parks and forests.[27] This administrative model, which fused cultural use and scientific conservation into the rigid Progressive Era administrative models (known as Taylorism), influenced how the state and its 169 towns stewarded their trees. Foresters worried about the competition between managing trees for economics or for recreation.

Yale alumni and field secretary Albert Turner candidly complained about the lack of definition between parks and forests in his annual reports to the SPC, and the lack of clarity haunted him for at least two decades. Unlike many of his peers, Turner's ideas about public land use aligned with the Yale-trained foresters, and he wrote prolifically about those ideas in letters, reports, and speeches. He believed that state parks had a specific purpose quite different from "museum-like" city parks, which were more art than science. State parks could serve as more natural alternatives to the cities' Olmstedian parks. "Let the formal museum stay in the city where it is now, and have field study in the field," wrote Turner. He liked Hartford's second park superintendent, the aptly named George Parker, because Parker drew a clear distinction between a state and city park.[28] That distinction persisted even as the State Park Commission became the State Park *and Forest* Commission (SPFC), and the Connecticut Forest *Association* added "and Park" to their name (CF&PA), thus absorbing recreation into their mission of scientific forest management and balancing the two goals.

In the meantime, the *Hartford Courant* published a full-page article in 1919 sounding the alarm that unless Connecticut paid attention to its forests and maintenance of hardwoods, its hills would be bare of trees and "as timberless as China," and it would have to build houses out of concrete.[29] It was then that the state hired forester Austin Hawes, who practiced scientific forestry for economic development. This meant discouraging clear-cutting and producing quality lumber for industrial purposes rather than for purposes of aesthetic and recreational enjoyment. Hawes had served as a "student assistant" under Gifford Pinchot's national forestry program in New York's Adirondacks in 1900; later in Washington, DC; and even out west in Arizona. He returned with the belief that no one without the proper training could manage public forests in this way.[30] He subscribed to the European notion of forest management for public and *multiple* uses, including recreation: "So long as a distinction is retained between parks and forests, parks must stand for recreation and forests for multiple use."[31] However, he saw the East as more challenging, since it had "no reserves of large timber" but was "more nearly like the European countries where forestry [had] played such an important part in the economic life of the people."[32]

Forestry was agriculture "to be harvested, reseeded, improved, and reaped again," but as emphasis on recreational needs rose, Hawes acknowledged, "Besides the necessities of modern life which the forest furnish, they have great indirect value for their effect on climate and upon water flow, for their healthful qualities, and lastly for their beauty and attractiveness as places of amusement and rest for thousands of people tired of city life."[33] Hawes understood the demand and economic appeal of attracting tourists seeking to escape the hardscape of the industrial cities to the softer landscape and "romantic scenery" of the state forests.[34] He also further undermined a strictly scientific forest management approach, noting that roadside shade trees served a distinctly aesthetic and cultural purpose integral to the state's heritage and identity. He observed that trees resembled colonial settlement patterns and values, and trees could attract tourism:

> There are sections of the Connecticut Valley in general appearance not unlike the rolling country of the middle west, and the tobacco fields of the region would doubtless be of interest to any agriculturalist. But of course, Connecticut is primarily an industrial state. The great brass industry of the Naugatuck Valley; the silver industry of Meriden; the great munitions plants of New Haven and Bridgeport have created great wealth, but it is not these that the summer tourist wished to see . . . where splendid colonial houses nestle attractively among rows of great shade trees. These rows of maple and elm are monuments to the robust characters who planted them long ago, and every house is a memorial to the virgin forest of Connecticut from which the oak timbers were hewn and the pine paneling was sawn. Every village has its "green" and many of the trees are of historic interest. . . . Tourists passing through Connecticut remark on the general prosperous appearance of the countryside. No factor has added more to this reputation than the splendid shade trees and well-kept lawns.[35]

Throughout the 1920s, the citizen-directed CF&PA launched an educational blitz on the care of shade trees in the city and along the streets and roadways. Suburbanization expanded the urban forest along transportation routes where shade trees blended rural and urban settings. The CF&PA and private civic organizations promoted the beautification of roadways with shade trees and helped establish the Bureau of Roadside Development in the State Highway Commission. Such work culminated in a distinctive roadway designed and built in the 1930s primarily for recreation, the Merritt Parkway.[36] The expanding transportation network thus connected rural and urban landscapes not just with roads but with trees and power lines.[37]

Street tree planting as part of urban street design dated back to the colonial era and continued through the industrialization periods.[38] Henry Ward Beecher promoted planting a different kind of tree to identify each street fifty feet apart in 1859.[39] By the late nineteenth century, Progressive Era environmentalists and policymakers advocated planting shade trees along roadways in and outside the city, at the same time that they erected power lines and other technological infrastructure. Topography and existing rights-of-way often dictated the location of utility lines and who had access to those services. The telegraph poles and wires ran alongside railroad lines to connect the coasts. Telephone and electric power lines soon joined them. Economic expediency piled them all on the same poles and towers. Connecticut often maintained its landscape by literally and metaphorically hiding the power lines among the trees. In 1912, the City of New Haven appointed a superintendent of trees and teamed up with Walter O. Filley, then the assistant state forester, to provide guidance on how to best preserve and maintain mature street trees as municipal responsibility in cooperation with citizens. The guidance included what and where to plant, as well as how and how much to prune, address diseases, and manage utilities like gas and electrical lines around them. One suggestion stipulated zigzagging trees across the street or running lines beneath the canopies.[40]

Between 1919 and 1926, the general assembly passed at least six acts placing the planting of roadside trees under the regulatory eye of the SPFC, the highway commissioner, and/or the Public Utilities Commission, but the laws remained uncoordinated and overly complicated. Claiming modern times required more systematic care than in the past, the advocacy groups urged the general assembly to pass the Arborist Law, requiring licensing for anyone responsible for planting public trees or selling services related to tree care and management. The CF&PA began issuing detailed care guidelines in the 1920s in several pamphlets that repeatedly stressed the need to coordinate planting around utility wires, providing photographs, diagrams, and instructions for establishing what the group called "roadside plantations" either in rows or in clusters, in preference to individual plantings.

The organization partnered with the state to publish another pamphlet advising local tree wardens, who at the time maintained fairly broad powers in the state for local regulation and best practices for planting and maintaining shade trees. The pamphlet's advice urged that trees never be planted beneath wire, and it included precise techniques for regular pruning to form the crown, especially around wires, with precise examples and lists of different points of conflict between safe wire installation, use of sidearms on utility poles, and healthy trees. One tip was to remove lower limbs to secure clearance for wires and vehicles, but it also advised the careful siting of utility lines by workers knowledgeable about both trees and wires. When unable to avoid interference, pruning should develop the tree's crown to avoid utility wires. Such wires should ideally run above, below, or to the side of trees. It stipulated planting, spacing, and pruning schedules. One photo illustrated the ideal: one in which nature obscured but did not interfere with modern living. The guidance acknowledged that not much could hide larger long-distance transmission towers, but it urged architects and engineers to improve their appearance. Other ideas offered that roadside trees should be planted in rows or groups but in their own "lane," separate from power lines. On narrow roads, trees should flank the wires so workmen can reach them and the tree canopy curves over private property, but on wide roads, trees could hide wiring or other objectionable structures. Tree plantings should avoid water and gas mains beneath or block viewsheds, stressing that if utilities could consolidate electric and phone wires, the entire street does not need to be tree-lined.[41] Several local chambers of commerce also designed street tree plans that regularly placed trees on the opposite side of the street from power lines or on private property six to ten feet from the sidewalk to avoid even underground utilities.[42] Yet in 1927, even "Elm City" (also known as New Haven) felled a still-healthy sycamore—first planted by colonists on the city's historic green and reportedly still bearing the bullets from British rifles from the American Revolution—ironically to widen Elm Street.[43]

American elms, *Ulmus americana*, can be deciduous and semi-deciduous, with about five-inch long pointed oval, double-serrated leaves. They can grow from thirty to one hundred feet tall. The SPFC had urged towns and cities like New Haven to plant smaller trees but also to stipulate type to provide uniformity. This aesthetic decision of planting the same tree type to identify place, known as monoculture, placed trees at risk for disease. Epidemics targeting certain species could destroy the tree-lined greens and urban streetscapes of the state and region. For example, Dutch elm disease, which had already decimated European trees, arrived in America via a shipment of logs from abroad. Despite efforts from the state's Agricultural Experiment Station to stop it from entering the "gateway to New England," the disease arrived in Connecticut in 1933, initially spreading slowly. By the decade's end, however, New Haven could no longer accurately claim the moniker of "Elm City." The impact "struck deeply in the heart of all New Englanders" and undermined decades of policy, cultivation, and advocacy.[44] Then, following the ecological pandemic, the region's worst hurricane in the historical memory of anyone living in New England at the time further devastated Connecticut's carefully cultivated tree canopy in and outside the cities.

On September 21, 1938, the 186-mile-per-hour winds of the Great New England Hurricane arrived without warning. Trees fell, blocking trolley lines and roads and flattening homes. Connecticut's transportation and utility infrastructure was crippled. The next day, the front page of the newspaper summarized, "Raging Storm Hits New England Causing Death and Destruction." Many residents still remember the storm as the most devastating weather event in the history of the northeastern region. They would measure all future storms against it. As the first state hit by the hurricane winds, Connecticut experienced several devastating floods and lost most of its hardwood trees over sixty years old (about 10 percent). Unlike states like New Hampshire and Massachusetts, the forests were relatively young, having rebounded in the 1910s as coke replaced charcoal as a fuel to fire forges and blast furnaces.[45]

Even as roadside trees blocked transportation routes, the vast majority of the newspaper articles, volunteer groups, clubs, and editorials all called for replanting bigger, stronger trees, citing the environmental and health benefits.[46] The state had committed to an economic future around recreational activity, and that depended upon forest resilience.

In 1935, the State Planning Board pursued recreation as the primary function of not only state parks but also state forests. In a report exploring the use of natural and historic resources, the authors observed that visitors seeking recreational opportunities rarely distinguished between parks and forests; thus "the best forestry practice becomes immediately available for the benefit of wooded parks, while the best park management becomes available for forests supporting extensive recreational use."[47] New Deal agencies and programs emphasized recreational development through the WPA and the Civilian Conservation Corps (CCC) in order to (1) bring in revenue-generating tourists and (2) relieve and solve social problems generated by the cities.[48] Speculating that modern urban life caused anything from malaise to crime, one report predicted that, in the depths of the Great Depression, increasing access to recreation would decrease the state's mental health costs.[49]

Connecticut was a leader in the New Deal's "tree army," a response to Roosevelt's executive order that invested $10 million in tree planting across the country. Under Hawes, CCC workers across twenty-one camps cleared hundreds of miles of hiking trails, access roads, sawmills, dams, picnic areas, swimming ponds, and fire towers throughout the forests. They also enlisted the latest scientific reforestation techniques and revived a commercial forest products business by building wood treatment plants, charcoal kilns, and a state sawmill. Hawes proudly boasted the achievements on a lunch date with his mentor, Gifford Pinchot, at the October 1940 meeting for the Association of State Foresters in Washington, DC: "I had the best visit with him I had ever had. He inquired about Connecticut and I told him of our 80,000 acres of state forests, and he expressed pleasure that his 'native state' was making such good progress."[50]

The growing popularity of the automobile meant that travelers in and through the state would encounter its woodlands in both journey and destination. The Highway Department's Bureau of Roadside Development cared for 5,500 miles of trees, but the state (like with forests and parks) tried to maintain separate highways for separate purposes, commercial and recreational. The Merritt Parkway became one of the first roads built primarily for the latter purpose. It lured drivers away from the commercial stress of the Boston Post Road and closer to nature with a winding scenic drive through an open, naturalistic landscape of fields and perfect picnic sites under shade trees.[51]

By the 1930s, many trees had achieved cultural significance. Trees sometimes served as historical destinations for day travelers. Several communities attached significance to mature trees that had survived generations, fueling political and cultural claims to local places, as the economic distress and competition for work exacerbated nativist sentiment. In 1934, Katherine Matthies of the Connecticut Daughters of the American Revolution, like similar chapters across the country, recognized over one hundred individual trees for their size and beauty. *Trees of Note in Connecticut* included commemorative apple trees in Litchfield and scions of the Charter Oak, but others achieved inclusion due to their historic association. Until 1815, Litchfield residents used the elm near their county jail as a whipping post. A sycamore tree survived as one of thirteen planted by Governor Oliver Wolcott, a signer of the Declaration of Independence. An oak in Watertown had "witnessed" the first unfurling of the American flag in 1812.[52]

> Just months before VE and VJ Day, the Great Atlantic Hurricane swept the Eastern Seaboard at category 3 on September 4, 1944.[53] While fallen trees caused blackouts, adequate pruning and preparation since the 1938 hurricane limited the damages. The GI Bill welcomed former soldiers into new jobs and newly designed suburban neighborhoods, but those with tree cover reflected the discriminatory housing policies of the Cold War era.

During World War II, the Arbor Day Foundation promoted tree planting as an act of patriotism because manufacturers, prior to plastic products, commonly used cork as a seal.[54] The second half of the twentieth century subsequently committed to maintaining the rural and urban forest, but statewide policies gradually grew less rigorous in their conservation, care, and management as suburbanization blurred urban and rural boundaries. Postwar housing and commercial building reflected the proliferation of the automobile, and using Levittown, New York, as a model, developers stipulated evergreens and flowering shrubs, as well as "at least four fruit trees," on each mass-produced, uniform property.[55] The influential *Community Builders*

Handbook encouraged developers to choose sites with minimal tree clearing to save costs but emphasized that trees could screen out unwanted views and noise.[56] The CF&PA doubled down on roadside trees, insisting that streets served as the "front yards of the nation" and emphasizing the need for ongoing community maintenance. The newspapers printed regular articles on proper tips for tree plantings. Sometimes the utilities worked with the local tree warden to plant.[57] Over the years, though, cities and towns rarely replaced destroyed and damaged shade trees, particularly if they were near utility lines.

During this postwar period, several of the state's most stalwart trees finally succumbed to previous storm injuries and disease. The Wethersfield Elm was almost as old as the town itself (dating from the 1750s). It was one of the largest and oldest in the nation in the 1930s. Over the years, several storms had broken off branches, but the resilient tree continued to grow, outlasting several property owners and their homes, even continuing after losing two of its main six branches from the 1938 hurricane. The old tree had then survived the 1944 Great Atlantic Hurricane, but Dutch elm disease finally reached it a year later. At the time, it was the largest recorded elm in the country at thirty feet in circumference and almost one hundred feet tall. The town desperately tried to save it through pruning until only its stump remained in 1953. Schoolchildren lined the street as a truck carried the massive remains away.[58]

In the meantime, those who had moved away from urban areas sought locally accessible leisure opportunities adjacent to their new suburban homes. A group of businessmen, inspired by trips to the national parks out west, became interested in further developing Connecticut's forests and parks for recreational use. They successfully challenged the foresters and conservationists who had controlled state policies, acquisitions, state institutions, and private associations regarding forestry for three decades. Despite years of efforts to prove forests could serve multiple uses, Austin Hawes and his Yale-trained forester colleagues no longer managed the state's forests.

Claiming budgetary efficiency, the State Park and Forest Commission hired a former NPS administrator, Donald Alexander, to oversee the state forester in 1943. Hawes and the remaining foresters on the commission, Walter Filley and Yale faculty H. H. Chapman, insisted Alexander knew nothing of scientific forestry. Outnumbered on the commission 5–2, the foresters maintained that "state forests should be administered by a technically-trained state forester responsible directly to the Commission," not a middleman. The new commission chairman, Bridgeport newspaper editor George Waldo, dismissed their concerns, claiming that forestry was not something that only the "experts can understand." Quoting a British dramatic critic, he spouted, "No I cannot lay an egg either but I am a better judge of omelets than any hen in England."[59] Hawes retired early to protest the continued management of the forests and parks with the single, primary purpose of "public enjoyment." When Chapman tried to regain control of the commission, even appealing to the governor, he instead lost his senior position, but he continued to fight for forestry through the private State Forest and Park Association. When Alexander left to join the Veterans Administration in Virginia three years later, the foresters tried to exert influence on the new commissioners through the CF&PA but, according to one historian, with little impact during postwar development.[60]

Despite these efforts, the postwar development of rural Connecticut proceeded more or less without the foresters' direct guidance for new-growth trees. In 1949, the Department of Natural Resources hardly made any administrative distinction between forests and parks.[61] Meanwhile, the mature street and park trees that cities planted in the 1920s blocked views, often becoming hazards in highly trafficked areas. They suffered from air pollution, road salts, multiplying utility lines, and vulnerability to storms. The role of the municipal tree warden evolved into someone much more concerned with safety and removal than conservation, even amid the rise of the modern environmental movement. And by the late twentieth century, fewer tree wardens had training or possessed even basic knowledge about trees.[62]

Meanwhile, the Federal Housing Administration's racially discriminatory lending practices, now known as "redlining," ensured that such shaded housing complexes built outside the city targeted white middle-class ownership. Urban renewal projects caused similar landscape disruption in the 1950s and '60s. These schemes focused on access for the car and not the pedestrian or resident. Large-footprint, modern Bauhaus inspired affordable housing complexes made of artificial materials like glass and concrete.[63] This trend stripped city residences of natural features to build, pushing the public stewardship of natural resources out of urban neighborhoods, places people of color now primarily lived. A lack of trees created heat islands and continues to diminish property values. These development initiatives redefined streetscapes, eliminated urban cores in favor of highways, and precipitated Congress's passing of the National Historic Preservation Act in 1966, which formalized historic preservation practices, even before the National Environmental Policy Act.

> Following Hurricane Gloria in 1985, utilities began contracting with tree companies to trim around power lines, only with owner permission, and credited that activity for fewer outages in subsequent storms. The public still pushed back on what some called a "search and destroy mission."[64] Then in 2011, both Hurricane Irene and an October snowstorm felled still-leafy trees and knocked out electrical power across Connecticut for days. The *Hartford Courant* headlined, "Connecticut's Love of Trees Threatens Electrical Service," and the general public, living without electricity for over a week, hated the power company and the trees. Governor Dannel Malloy complained, "We [have] too many trees alongside of roads that also have wires adjacent to them. . . . We're going to have to do something about that. . . . When we start to do that . . . there are going to be people wrapping themselves around trees."[65]

Along with thousands of trees, the frequency of extreme storms of the early twenty-first century seemed to blow away collective memory about the local attachment and history of trees, the state's conservation heritage, and long-standing debates about tree management policies in forests and parks. Science has historically dictated some of the public tree policy, but management decisions often reflected vacillating tensions among ecological, economic, and cultural values. Those cultural beliefs and behaviors emerge from traditional practices, most often tied to seasonal changes, climate, and topography.

As strong storms become more frequent in Connecticut and the Northeast, the tree canopy becomes the most obvious and frequent disruptor of electrical, transportation, and communications networks. And when they fall, trees can literally destroy, if not severely disrupt, lives. The mass power outages following the storms of Irene and Sandy convinced many of the state's policymakers that modern life could no longer coexist with the urban forest.

If we recognize, however, that the physical, aesthetic, and historical relationship between trees and urbanization is intertwined, we can balance our love of trees with our need for electrical power and other infrastructure. The manufactured poles that carry electric wire compete with trees for roadside space and are ironically milled from trees. Cellular towers are now often not so well camouflaged with synthetic conifer branches and leaves to blend with actual live shade trees.[66] Preservation might mean allowing "sustainable forest management," but for mature street trees with large canopies, it might also mean considering utility lines as part of a larger "eco-cultural" system on the urban streetscape.

As the Connecticut SPFC marked its centennial in 2013, the local utility company initiated a vegetation plan to trim or remove *all* roadside trees within an eight-foot zone on either side of power lines and utility poles.[67] This response marks a shift in how we have historically thought about trees and their value as integral to individual and communal well-being. We have increasingly associated trees only with the natural world, not the human one, and we no longer "hear" them when they fall. They have become neither economically nor culturally valuable at precisely the time they are most environmentally critical.[68]

> In 2009, a resident of Tolland, Connecticut, filed a lawsuit to stop the utility company from removing trees on the town's green because they were interfering with power lines.[69] In Collinsville, the Historic District Commission planned to replace its older trees by carefully considering tree type and, as critically, plans for care and maintenance.[70] A five-hundred-year-old white oak in Granby required cabling, and the nearly three-hundred-year-old Pinchot Sycamore in Simsbury—Connecticut's largest tree at twenty-eight feet circumference and almost one hundred feet tall—lost 35 percent of its 120-foot canopy in 2011.[71]

Citizens exhibited concern over the fate of mature and historic trees on their landscapes even in the years between Gloria and Irene. Newspapers regularly reported how new construction had damaged "historic" trees across the state. The *Hartford Courant* printed several stories that lamented the loss of older trees, particularly those in historic districts. The articles focused on preserving the historical, economic, and also environmental benefits of the tree canopy. These well-organized grassroots environmental groups have vehemently protested, mainly on environmental and scientific grounds: trees pull carbon from the air. Trees provide shade and mental health benefits to urban residents. Yet these arguments still have trouble being heard and gaining the kind of political traction that could override the threats trees pose to the power grid.[72] Tree advocates lack the vocabulary and knowledge to address tree preservation policy from an additional perspective—a historical one focused on how these resources became part of our landscape and how they environmentally, economically, and culturally hold communal memory and define the places we live.

In a time of climate crisis, we need to preserve both the cultural and the natural. Trees are natural resources, certainly, but as history attests, they are also as culturally important as power lines. With thoughtful planning, research, and interdisciplinary management, communities do not have to decide between mature trees and modern life. In partnership with environmental historians, public historians effectively communicate a sense of place, memory, and the power of objects to the public and might approach these stories from a different perspective.[73] Ways to assess environmental resources in a cultural context exist. Many states keep databases of notable trees (albeit absent of historical context). Connecticut began building one the same year as Hurricane Gloria, and the database—maintained by Connecticut College, which has preserved an arboretum adjacent to its campus—lists over forty-five thousand individual trees across the state. Some towns have tree ordinances for "heritage trees."[74] Existing nominations and contexts include some models. Identification is one protective measure for culturally significant trees, but preservation and management present other challenges. Some trees achieve significance because they are old, but such significance clearly has a limited time frame (which seemingly contradicts the objectives of preservation). Trees grow, change, deteriorate, and unlike buildings, eventually and inevitably die naturally. As Superintendent Ross Diamont wrote of the Marsh-Billings-Rockefeller National Park, "Trees are moving along their own unique trajectories influenced by the dynamics of competition and disease, and the availability of light, soil, water, and nutrients. The pull of forest succession never rests." Preserving historic trees must therefore be less about exact replication and more about maintaining their character and ecological health. In keeping with the fifty-year mark for historic significance, a tree would already be well matured and of a substantial size. When they are not alone, preservation might mean allowing "sustainable forest management," but for mature street trees with large canopies, it might mean considering utility lines as part of a larger "eco-cultural" system on the urban streetscape.[75]

Like other objects of material culture, trees are artifacts through which to explore both natural and cultural history, not to mention explore ideas about recreation, aesthetics, public memory, and public health. Thomas Schlereth, a longtime advocate for material culture, observed that tree plantings can mark historic migration or travel routes, document patterns of landownership, mark settlements and property lines, influence housing types, and drive local industry.[76] The NPS pushed the cultural landscape model that emerged in the 1990s as a method for describing "cultural properties [that] represent the combined works of nature and of man." The NPS has provided fairly specific guidelines for tree "restoration" within a cultural landscape from the treatment of the stump to replanting. There are several options consistent with preservation practices to consider. These include stabilization, maintenance, repair through field conservation, repair through pruning, and in-kind replacement to maintain integrity. Trained preservation arborists can assess and maintain the health and management of older trees.[77]

The commemorative role of trees and tree groves may qualify for the National Register of Historic Places, under Criteria Consideration F as a commemorative property. Native Americans often cite "witness trees" that recall communal stories, but like the Charter Oak, such stories are not specific only to Indigenous belief and practice. The distribution and replanting of commemorative tree saplings has become a time-honored, often communal ritual involving "germplasm conservation" to preserve species. In-kind or environmentally sustainable "replacement" captures the function and spirit of restoration.[78] Just months after the storm that hit Sleeping Giant State Park, the Hamden Tree Commission designated a Colorado blue spruce as a "notable tree," as one of the only survivors of the former picnic grove, "as a memorial to all the trees that were lost."[79]

History, like that in Connecticut, provides the context through which to approach tree preservation policies through cultural as well as natural resource management strategies. Examining the state's historical relationship with and response to trees and forests may allow us to craft more sustainable policies for the economy and the environment that could mitigate future damage from ever more frequent storms to our urban infrastructure and our cultural landscape. We have traditionally enlisted historic preservation documentation and practice only for the built environment, but the field can offer tools and models for protecting the urban canopies that define the places we live, combat *solastalgia*, and help preserve our memories as well as our planet.[80]

FIGURE 7. Rock outcroppings and mountain laurel near the summit of South Mountain in Michaux State Forest. Photograph by Liz Sargent, May 2015.

Chapter Five

The Trees of the South Mountain Cultural Landscape

Liz Sargent, Liz Sargent HLA, Charlottesville, Virginia

South Mountain—the northernmost outpost of the Blue Ridge Mountains—rises as a broad, hulking mass above the farmland of Pennsylvania's Great Valley to the northwest and the rolling terrain of the Fruit Belt to the southeast. The forests that cloak the area have been the focus of cultural use and activity for hundreds of years. Hidden beneath the tree canopy and emerging more definitively within clearings is an assemblage of features that reflects the deep intertwining of nature and culture connected to the region's forest heritage. As such, South Mountain represents a cultural landscape, a unique place formed when humans interact with the physical environment. One of the ways that a cultural landscape can be viewed is as a *palimpsest* of layers of history visible at the same time on the same ground. The palimpsest of South Mountain reveals a landscape history of resource extraction, industrial technology, ecology, and conservation, all related to trees and forests. During the nineteenth century, logging and industry denuded South Mountain, leaving spindly trees, stumps, burning slash, and eroded soils. Today, the same forests have been transformed into accessible open space, an abundance of recreational elements, and a preserve of natural diversity. As the cultural landscape of South Mountain was better understood and the forest regenerated, a similar transformation of people's attitudes about nature and stewardship of public resources arose.

You may already have seen South Mountain while traveling Interstate 81 between Greencastle and Carlisle, Pennsylvania, or walking along the Appalachian Trail. Although a part of the Blue Ridge Mountain range, it rises high above the surrounding terrain, separated visually from the rest of the Blue Ridge by a miles-long gap near the Maryland-Pennsylvania border where softer geological formations have worn away over time. Today, much of South Mountain is protected from development as part of Pennsylvania's Michaux State Forest, an eighty-five-thousand-acre public reservation established in 1901. This conservation gesture, rare for its time, could not have been accomplished without the work of one man—Joseph Trimble Rothrock.

It was Rothrock's lantern slideshows that first illustrated how logging and other natural resource extraction, coupled with resulting wildfires, had devastated woodland health and were contributing to soil erosion that was damaging farms and diminishing drinking water quality for all Commonwealth citizens. Rothrock made South Mountain, which had become denuded of trees by charcoal production in support of iron companies, the poster child for his lectures and later the object of his advocacy for large-scale conservation and protection of Pennsylvania's forests.

Rothrock also inspired the establishment of one of the nation's first forestry schools at South Mountain, as well as the first state tree nursery. Both contributed to the nation's heritage of land conservation by introducing innovative approaches to forest management that were adopted elsewhere within the state and elsewhere within the United States. The suite of forestry initiatives introduced at South Mountain established its reputation as a cradle of American forestry and Rothrock's stature as the father of Pennsylvania forestry.[1]

For more than 120 years, Pennsylvania has managed Michaux State Forest for sustainably harvested timber, native plant community health and diversity, soil and water conservation, and public recreation. The Commonwealth's approach to forest management has evolved with the science of ecology. Today, the Commonwealth also works to balance cultural landscape heritage values while promoting resilience in the face of climate change. These efforts have contributed to the successful reestablishment of forests over much of South Mountain. No longer denuded of trees, South Mountain has taken on a much different appearance than that of 1901. Hidden beneath the present-day mantle of the forest overstory, however, is the surviving evidence of South Mountain's industrial past. The trees help tell the story through stand age and woodland composition.

South Mountain as Cultural Landscape

With its trees as the touchstone, South Mountain embodies many important themes in conservation, recreation, education, and stewardship, providing lessons from the past that can inform future management. As such, the area represents a *cultural landscape*. But what is a cultural landscape, and why is this important? Cultural landscapes are special places that reveal aspects of a specific region's origins and development—as well as our relationship to the natural world—through their form, their features, and the ways in which they have been used. Often associated with a historic event, activity, or person, they represent the combined works of nature and of people. Examples vary in complexity and include historic homes, military sites, national parks, farms, urban plazas, parks, and gardens. Cultural landscapes provide people with a sense of place and identity; they map our relationship with the land over time. They are part of our national heritage and narrative.[2]

South Mountain fits neatly into this framework as a cultural landscape in three distinct, yet intertwined, ways:

for the way that the dramatic landform shapes the farm communities around its perimeter and becomes an object of orientation and identity
for the evidence of an extensive historic complex of iron forge companies, logging, mining, and other industrial activities
for the Michaux State Forest and other early forestry efforts involving conservation

The South Mountain cultural landscape offers a mosaic of historic associations, each of which builds one upon the others to reveal important aspects of our evolving relationship with the natural world. The trees that bear witness to South Mountain's heritage also provide an interesting way to read the cultural landscape palimpsest. Looking at the South Mountain cultural landscape as a many-layered palimpsest allows us to compare cultural survival strategies, community structures, and attitudes about stewardship of—and responsibility to—the environment. Today's forest management practices represent only the newest layer in a series of cultural strata. By reading the palimpsest, we learn how American culture has evolved over time.

South Mountain Geography and Geology

The South Mountain landform has served as a cultural marker for centuries. The landform is sandwiched between two valleys, traversed by Interstate 81 to the west to US Route 15 to the east, in south-central Pennsylvania. It spans portions of four counties—Franklin, Cumberland, York, and Adams—and measures nearly seventy miles from end to end. Although the majority sits within Pennsylvania, a small portion crosses into western Maryland. The northern terminus occurs near Dillsburg, Pennsylvania, where the broad form of the mountain breaks into a series of small rocky hills. North of the hills is a sizable gap that is among the largest breaks in the Appalachian barrier. The gap ends at the Reading Prong, part of the New England Uplands province of the Appalachian Highlands. The gap played a critical role in westward migration during the eighteenth century. After passing through the gap, travelers could reach the Great Valley of Pennsylvania. Continuing on in a southwesterly direction, settlers found fertile lands in Maryland and Virginia without crossing the mountains. European American settlers who followed this route were in fact echoing the footsteps of Native Americans before them, as well as migrating wildlife.

The Great Valley is part of a continental-scale trench that continues nearly uninterrupted for two thousand miles between Quebec and Alabama. Near South Mountain, the Great Valley is known as the Cumberland Valley; to the north, it is referred to as the Lebanon Valley and the Lehigh Valley. In Maryland, it is known as the Hagerstown Valley. Within Virginia, it is referred to as the Shenandoah Valley. Regardless of the names, the Great Valley is characterized by fertile limestone soils. The Great Valley formed the backbone of colonial agrarian settlement and remains an important agricultural region today.

To the east of South Mountain lies the Triassic Lowlands, an area of undulating terrain that eventually morphs into the Piedmont region of southeastern Pennsylvania. Composed of red shale, sandstone, and conglomerate, the Triassic Lowlands offer some reasonably workable soils suited for agriculture, as well as intrusions of volcanic diabase, a geologic formation that is highly resistant to weathering and poor for farming. Today, the intrusions appear as wooded ridges and knobs dotting the lower slopes of southeastern South Mountain, set between cultivated fields. Inventive local farmers eventually determined that the intrusions could support fruit tree cultivation. After years of pome fruit production, the crescent-shaped region has been christened the Historic South Mountain Fruit Belt, recognized as a unique and important growing area.

In between these agricultural powerhouses is the steeply sloped and elevated core of South Mountain, composed of sandstone and quartzite geology. It is highly resistant to weathering. Ridges oriented north to south form the spine of the mountain's topography. The east-facing slope of South Mountain is also underpinned by metarhyolite, a low-grade felsic metavolcanic rock that Native Americans used to carve projectile points.[3] Over millennia, the sandstone and quartzite have undergone a relatively slow weathering process. Gravity has carried mineralized soil down the mountain's slopes, resulting in thick wedge-shaped deposits of colluvium—a combination of rock, sediment, and soil—that can measure up to two and one-half miles in width and one hundred feet in depth above the resistant bedrock. Due to the nature of the local geology and complex chemical weathering processes, iron ore deposits formed beneath the colluvium in numerous locations at the base of South Mountain over millennia.

South Mountain's Forests

Prior to the destructive logging practices of European Americans engaged in iron mongering, South Mountain was blanketed by dense forests containing a patchwork of community types suited to slope, orientation, available moisture, and elevation. The majority of the forests were mixed oak and northern hardwood forest types. Mixed oak forests include such species as northern red oak, chestnut oak, shagbark hickory, red maple, and tulip poplar. Northern hardwood forests, occurring in the higher elevations, typically include sugar maple, black cherry, aspen, birch, hemlock, and ash. Historically, the American chestnut was a dominant component of these forests, but it was wiped out by a fungal disease introduced to North America from Japan during the early to mid-twentieth century. American elm trees have also been impacted by Dutch elm disease since the mid-twentieth century, and today, hemlocks have been decimated by the invasive, aphid-like woolly adelgid. Ash trees are currently succumbing to the emerald ash borer.

Regeneration of the South Mountain forests that began after the establishment of Michaux State Forest in 1901 and the Mont Alto Forestry Academy in 1903 has been extremely successful in returning tree cover to the steep slopes and stream valleys. Forest management today balances resource protection with the Commonwealth's policies of ensuring that the state forest remains a working landscape and provides value to Pennsylvania citizens in the form of pure water, recreation, scenic beauty, plant and animal habitat, sustainable timber, and natural gas, among others.[4]

South Mountain's Cultural Heritage

When we discuss the cultural heritage of a place, we focus on the ways people interact with it. The landscape of South Mountain and the surrounding valleys has remained a unique part of Pennsylvania's historical and cultural development. The landforms of South Mountain and the surrounding valleys—including the geology, soils, and waters—influenced settlement patterns, land use, and community development over centuries.

Throughout Pennsylvania's history, from the predominantly Native American era when the region was home to the Conestoga-Susquehannock (an Iroquoian people of the Susquehanna River Valley), as well as to a lesser degree the Lenape (or Delaware; an Algonquian people), to the present, South Mountain itself served as a significant source of natural resources—from timber to iron ore, limestone, gravel, and plants and animals useful to support cultural lifeways—while the adjacent lower-lying areas yielded agricultural bounty. Diverse, yet interconnected, the intensive cultivation and extraction of these available resources by people has shaped the south-central Pennsylvania landscape we see today. European settlement within the region was a devastating affair for the Conestoga-Susquehannock peoples, involving armed conflict and the eventual dispossession of the tribe from their ancestral homeland as settlers increasingly sought control of the region's desirable resources.[5] The fur trade for beaver pelts during the seventeenth century diminished an important resource and fueled conflict between nations as well as with colonizers. Coupled with the introduction of disease, warfare, and colonial raids, the Conestoga-Susquehannock suffered a massive population decline by 1700 and political disruption. Tribal members increasingly left their ancestral homeland, many joining the Ohio Mingo people. The Mingo today are federally recognized as the Seneca-Cayuga Tribe of Oklahoma, one of several tribes with historical kinship with the Conestoga-Susquehannock. Descendants today continue to work to protect and preserve the cultural legacy of the Conestoga-Susquehannock within the Susquehanna River region and their ancestral homelands.[6]

Aspects of the present-day personality of the Pennsylvania landscape, especially the South Mountain region, began to emerge during the eighteenth century as various groups of European immigrants began to form small settlements and a patchwork of farmsteads. William Penn's policy of tolerance welcomed a wide variety of European groups, particularly English, Welsh, Scots-Irish, and several varieties of ethnic Germans. Immigrants came as families, extended families, and community groups, many to escape religious persecution.

To the west of Philadelphia, settlers found an abundance of available good farmland. Southeastern Pennsylvania offered a vast area of rolling topography with excellent soils that were easily converted to prosperous farms. The region's temperate climate favors grain-based agriculture. During the late eighteenth and nineteenth centuries, settlers began a great migration through the Great Valley to lands to the south and west. The cultural traditions of southeastern Pennsylvania moved with them. Today, the region is often referred to as the Pennsylvania Cultural Area or Pennsylvania Cultural Hearth.[7]

South Mountain sits at the western edge of the Pennsylvania Cultural Hearth, known for its settlement by "yeoman farmers" who created a relatively homogeneous, yet diverse, agricultural landscape of small independent farms tied to small market towns. The agricultural market system that evolved in Pennsylvania spread down Virginia's Shenandoah Valley and eventually across the Appalachian Mountains into Kentucky and Tennessee after the discovery of a passageway west through the Cumberland Gap. Lifeways representative of the Pennsylvania Cultural Hearth became a bedrock feature of the nation's heartland because of this migratory pattern, while the plantation system that originated in Tidewater Virginia was adopted more consistently in the coastal regions of the Southeast. Although not at the scale found in Virginia's Tidewater, these farmers did rely on the labor of enslaved people even though Pennsylvania passed "An Act for the Gradual Abolition of Slavery" in 1780.[8]

Transportation was critically important to this regional settlement experience. Trails established by migrating animals and Native American tribes involved in trade, such as the Conestoga-Susquehannock and Lenape to the east and the Shawnee to the west, allowed passage through the Great Valley. Many were eventually transformed into wagon roads, turnpikes, railroads, automotive roads, and interstates, all of which followed a similar alignment through the Great Valley. South Mountain, with its steep and arduous terrain, was an impediment to this movement. Settlers, however, found two routes of passage through the seventy-mile-long landform, one being a gap that occurs near its center at a geologic fault line that is now marked by US Route 30 (also known as the Lincoln Highway) and the other a relatively level corridor near its southern end used today to carry State Route 16.

Today, agricultural practices similar to those introduced during the mid-eighteenth century remain the predominant land use around South Mountain. Supporting market towns and crossroad villages established then, such as Mt. Holly Springs, Shippensburg, and Cashtown, remain at the heart of community life today. Although suburbanization has occurred around some of these areas, settlement patterns established by the early nineteenth century continue to characterize the cultural landscape.

The roads, communities, and network of well-tended, fenced farms that occupy the pastoral landscape of the Great Valley encircle a wilder landscape, that of South Mountain, an undeveloped island of green, a tangled mass of trees and regenerated forest.

Within the forest, a landscape of surviving cultural evidence coexists with the public recreational use mission of Michaux State Forest. Trails, swimming areas, and other amenities take advantage of infrastructure established in support of iron production. Limestone extraction sites now form swimming areas. Rail lines that used to carry ore to market are hiking trails. Charcoal hearth and logging roads have been repurposed as bicycle paths. South Mountain also serves the local economy today as a center of heritage tourism. Sites located nearby, such as Gettysburg National Military Park, have become international destinations for tourism, while historic valley towns like Carlisle, Shippensburg, Chambersburg, Greencastle, and Waynesboro are popular for visitors seeking bed-and-breakfast inns, festivals, and local craft foods.

The Iron Industry

Mineral resources have long played a key role in Pennsylvania's economy since colonial times and continue to do so today. The state's diverse geology has been extracted for economic uses and, as such, is part of the national story of economic growth and expansion; in some regards, the state has led the way in mineral exploitation. At South Mountain, the principal mineral resource exploited was iron ore.

Iron ore extraction and iron production began in southeastern Pennsylvania in locales like Valley Forge. Between 1784 and 1830, iron production rapidly expanded westward with the settlers, as new sources of iron ore were discovered. During the late eighteenth and nineteenth centuries, South Mountain was extensively exploited for the mining and processing of iron ore, industrial activities that were to dramatically impact its landscape. Although coal fueled Pennsylvania's dominance in steel and manufacturing in the late nineteenth century, it was wood from trees that fueled iron production for a century prior. Iron production required several components to be successful—iron ore, limestone, waterpower, wagon roads, and enormous quantities of wood to make charcoal. South Mountain had all these resources in abundance. Of these, the iron ore deposits were the most difficult to locate, as they were buried beneath many feet of colluvium. Iron ore was also a relatively heavy resource to transport, and so processing needed to occur near the source. Besides location and weight, other variables influenced iron ore mining. Because it forms chemically through the interaction of elements and compounds in the soil, the amount available for extraction can vary tremendously. It is only when concentrations of iron ore form in high-enough densities that the labor required for its extraction becomes economically viable.

At South Mountain, the iron ore deposits associated with the Tomstown dolomite formation and other dolomite bedrock were the most well suited to extraction. The earliest deposits to be extracted were where the residuum and associated iron ore were located close enough to the surface to reach with relatively little work. Initially, it was local farmers with land along the base of the mountain who excavated the ore as a way to supplement their income. Later, iron companies began to buy up land or the mineral rights associated with the land and extract iron ore on a much larger scale. Over time, as the shallower deposits were depleted, the iron companies began to extract deeper deposits using equipment and technical innovation. To avoid the expense of transporting the ore to production facilities, they built iron furnaces on-site in order to remove the iron from the ore, as well as forges where the iron was further refined. The iron companies powered their furnaces and forges using charcoal, a concentrated form of fuel derived from slowly burnt wood.

Another important raw ingredient needed to make iron was limestone. This element was used as a fluxing agent to help separate contaminants from the ore. When both iron ore and limestone were placed in a heated furnace to melt, impurities in the ore would float to the top of the resulting liquid. A combination of liquefied limestone and nonmetallic impurities formed a slag that could be raked from the surface, resulting in purified iron ore. Today, slag, clearly discernible as a glassy rock in a variety of colors often containing small holes formed by gas bubbles, can be found scattered around furnace sites at South Mountain. The locations of former iron furnaces often indicate sites where limestone was extracted, since the heavy rock posed a transportation challenge for industrialists due to the generally poor condition of roads at the time.

A third key ingredient for iron production was waterpower. The movement of water across a wheel was harnessed to provide furnace blast used to power the forges and associated machinery. Furnace blast forced air inside the furnace, helping to superheat the limestone and ore to a temperature where it would melt. To create furnace blast, a waterwheel was located near the furnace, and water from a nearby stream or river was channeled to the wheel. The wheel powered a bellows that forced compressed air steadily through a duct in the walls at the base of the furnace. The forced air fed oxygen to a wood fire, increasing the heat and hastening the separation of iron from the ore. The need for waterpower also meant that iron furnaces had to be located along streams that could provide a reliable flow of water year-round via a headrace. Today, visitors often find dams and ponds located near defunct iron furnaces. After the water powered the wheel, it was directed through a tailrace back to the natural stream. Constructing the dam, pond, headrace, and tailrace, as well as the furnace, required a specific arrangement of topographic relief allowing for adequate fall for the water channel and level space for the construction of the furnace structures—and not a little wood. The cultural landscape of iron production thus tells a highly specialized industrial story that is deeply connected to environmental conditions.

In addition to the key components discussed previously that were needed in close proximity to one another, iron production also required a fuel source. At South Mountain, as elsewhere during the eighteenth and nineteenth centuries, the fuel source used most frequently was charcoal, which was needed to reach and sustain a temperature of 2,700 degrees Fahrenheit, sufficient to melt iron ore and limestone. Maintaining such hot temperatures required great quantities of charcoal. At full capacity, an average furnace burned 800 bushels of charcoal every twenty-four hours.

Charcoal itself also had to be produced. The process of charcoal production involved felling trees, cutting them into cordwood, and charring the wood in large circular leveled areas known as charcoal pits or hearths. Before setting fire to the wood in a process known as coaling, it was stacked ideally into a pile measuring ten to fourteen feet in height and thirty to forty feet in diameter. A mound this large required thirty to fifty cords of wood. The wood was then burned slowly into a concentrated form of fuel under the watchful eye of a collier. Upon completion, the hearth yielded between 800 and 1,200 bushels of charcoal, enough to power a furnace for a day to a day and one half.

Each burned charcoal mound represented the equivalent of about 1 acre of forest with twenty to twenty-five years of tree growth. Over the course of a year, powering one furnace required 240 or more acres of forest trees. Assuming the need for twenty to twenty-five years of forest regrowth, iron companies would need to own enough land that they could rotate their clearing of trees over twenty-five plots. Calculating the output, this suggests that they needed to own at least 6,000 acres to power their furnaces continually.

During the heyday of the iron industry in the region during the nineteenth century, three iron companies operated at South Mountain. Although written records have not revealed the number of hearths established on South Mountain, the emerging remote sensing technology known as Light Detection and Ranging (LiDAR) has been used to locate more than three thousand charcoal hearths at the northern end of South Mountain alone.[9] The hearths appear through LiDAR technology because of the way in which they were built, whereby the ground was graded and carefully leveled to establish a circular hearth that would ensure even burning of the charcoal. Constructing a wide, level, circular area on the side of the mountain required cutting into the slope on the uphill side and using the borrow material to fill on the downhill side. LiDAR clearly depicts this aberration in the natural topography. Other evidence of charcoal production atop South Mountain includes hut foundations and traces of trails and roads used to access the hearths.

Those involved in charcoal production were known as colliers. One or two skilled wood colliers and one or more helpers carefully stacked the mounds, lighted them, and monitored them continuously, night and day, for several weeks as they slowly burned. As many as twelve colliers were needed to produce the charcoal needed to keep one furnace going. While working at the hearths, the colliers lived in crude huts. Teams of two to four colliers would take turns sleeping in one of the huts or tending to as many as nine nearby charcoal hearths simultaneously.

The three iron companies in operation on South Mountain during the eighteenth and nineteenth centuries were Pine Grove Iron Works (later South Mountain Iron Company; ca. 1764–1895), Caledonia Iron Furnace (1837–70), and Mont Alto Charcoal Iron Furnace (1807–35). Each operated within its own sphere on the mountain. The Pine Grove Iron Works was located in the north portion of South Mountain, with approximately twenty thousand acres of land under their ownership (see figure 8). Caledonia Iron Works was located at the western end of the gap in South Mountain through which US Route 30 passes today. Mont Alto Charcoal Iron Furnace was located in the narrow gap of the West Branch of Antietam Creek, as it descends from the west side of South Mountain near the southern end of the formation.

Even as South Mountain supported three iron companies during the nineteenth century, it was recognized that the iron ore deposits were not of the highest quality. During the latter part of the century, higher-quality iron ore deposits were identified in Minnesota and elsewhere within the Midwest. By

FIGURE 8. Pine Grove Furnace at Pine Grove Furnace State Park. Photograph by Liz Sargent, May 2015.

the 1870s and 1880s, iron companies had begun to target the higher-quality ore of the Mesabi Range in Minnesota. In this, their transport needs were supported by a growing network of railroads. Through this period, the poorer-quality ores at South Mountain became increasingly less viable economically. Also contributing to the decline in iron production was the rise of the steel industry, which began in Pennsylvania in 1867. Through the late nineteenth century, steel production and manufacturing increased in importance, reducing the markets for iron. At South Mountain, the iron companies attempted to adapt by extracting the various resources available to them on their land, including limestone, gravel, and any remaining timber, but ultimately could no longer remain profitable. By the 1890s, iron production on South Mountain had run its course.

Forestry and Conservation

Like many places in Pennsylvania, logging for timber and iron production left behind vast wastelands that became known as the Pennsylvania Deserts.[10] In his Michaux lantern lecture series that began in 1877, Joseph Rothrock noted that when William Penn first experienced the Commonwealth's "woods" in 1862, forest covered approximately 99 percent of the twenty-nine million acres comprising Pennsylvania. By the 1870s, Rothrock observed that less than half of the state's land remained in forest.[11] In *A Century of Forest Resources Education at Penn State*, historian S. W. Fletcher is quoted as saying, "There is no more shocking example of greed and utter disregard for public welfare than the ruthless devastation of the forests of Pennsylvania by the lumber companies between 1840 and 1900."[12] Rothrock's observations were instrumental in calling attention to the problem. In his book *Forestry Education in Pennsylvania*, Henry Clepper notes, "The growth of forestry in the commonwealth was essentially an Indigenous development, principal credit for which belongs to Dr. Rothrock, who gave half his life to it."[13]

Forestry

As mentioned earlier, by the early twentieth century, the Commonwealth had taken the unprecedented step of establishing Michaux State Forest as

Pennsylvania's first public reservation atop the foundation of defunct iron ore extraction and processing sites. The legislation had two goals—management of forest resources for commerce, recreation, and other public values and conservation of soil, water, and biotic resources. The reservation is notable for predating the establishment of the US Forest Service in 1905 and the national forest system that followed the passage of the Weeks Act in 1911 (36 Stat. 961).[14]

With Michaux State Forest, Rothrock was also successful in appealing to the Pennsylvania legislature to concurrently establish the Pennsylvania State Forest Academy, also known as the Mont Alto Forestry Academy. The school was instrumental in laying the foundation for early forestry practices within the state reservation and effectively served as a model for national practices as well while also allowing Americans to be trained at home. Prior to 1898, the emerging field of forestry was based in Germany and France, where the Industrial Revolution first took most forest stands. The European profession of forestry was imported to the United States by such notables as Gifford Pinchot, who helped implement a scientific forestry plan at Biltmore for George Vanderbilt near Asheville and his successor, Dr. Carl A. Schenck. Pinchot had been trained in Europe, while Schenck was a German immigrant. Schenck later founded the Biltmore Forest School in the late 1890s as the first school of forestry in the United States, while Pinchot would later serve as the first chief of the US Forest Service and as governor of the Commonwealth of Pennsylvania.

The profession of forestry slowly emerged in America through schools like Mont Alto, which applied management practices to both conservation and extraction purposes. Established on the former Mont Alto Charcoal Iron Furnace property, the school utilized the ravaged hillsides of South Mountain as an incubator of forest management concepts and experiments related to planting, thinning, harvesting, and treating pest infestations.[15] Students at Mont Alto Forestry Academy repaired the damage caused by logging and charcoaling on South Mountain. Past tree removal had led to soil erosion, the movement of silt- and debris-laden stormwater into streams and rivers, and other problems. At the same time, the loss of topsoil and the associated seed bank had severely limited the ability of the forest to regenerate. Early American foresters realized the need to adapt European principles to the specific needs of forests at home. They focused on stabilizing land that had been badly treated, working to cease and ameliorate practices that had led to topsoil loss, stream degradation, and wildfires. Then came rejuvenation and developing sustainable methods of timber harvest. Unlike conservation, the goal of good forestry practices was a form not of preservation but of managed resource extraction.

Pennsylvania State Forestry Commission

In his crusade to steward Pennsylvania's forests, Joseph Rothrock did not rest after seeing the Michaux State Forest and Mont Alto Forestry Academy established during the early years of the twentieth century. He continued to point out the problems he observed with logging and tree clearing throughout the state. In his view, forest management practices on a large scale should help regenerate forests, improve water and air quality, control flooding, and enhance hunting and fishing and other community amenities as a way to improve the physical health and well-being of its citizens.

Based on Rothrock's lantern lectures, a group of women formed the Association for the Promotion of Scientific Forestry, with a mission to advocate for the protection of state forests. The association routinely joined forces with other Philadelphia-based groups, such as the Historical Society of Pennsylvania, to expand their sphere of influence and garner support for the cause. Later, the association sought to influence the state legislature to act. By the early 1890s, legislators had begun to debate the role of government in forestry policy. By May 1893, they had passed Public Law 115, which allowed for the establishment of a state forestry commission to tackle the issues related to the fact that Pennsylvania was practically devoid of trees.[16] The law charged the governor with appointing two persons, one a competent engineer and the other a botanist, to examine forest conditions within the state and suggest appropriate actions by March 1895. The botanist hired was none other than Joseph Rothrock.

The two-man team produced an exhaustive study that said the Commonwealth should establish a state forestry program geared toward protecting public drinking water supplies through active forest management. In the study, Rothrock touted the economic value of forests, as well as their aesthetic value. He also recommended the creation of a full-time forestry commission office to deal with state forestry issues, acquire land suitable for growing forests to protect the headwaters of streams, and demonstrate the benefits of forestry to the public.

Based on the commission's report, the legislature formed the Division of Forestry within the Department of Agriculture in 1895. Rothrock was named the first commissioner of forestry and head of the State Forestry Reservation Commission, a position he held until 1904.[17] During his tenure, Rothrock set in motion the purchase of lands for state forestry reservations, the training of foresters for state service, the establishment of state forest tree nurseries to support reforestation, and the formation of a system to detect and extinguish forest fires. Under Rothrock's guidance, the Commonwealth of Pennsylvania acquired 924,798 acres for forest reservations or reserves between 1901 and 1910. The chestnut blight caused by an Asian fungus that struck Pennsylvania in 1910 was an early blow to the program and was followed closely by an outbreak of white-pine blister rust. Believed to arise on currant and gooseberry plants, the rust outbreak led foresters to destroy all evidence of the two shrubs near white pine trees. In support of the need to replant where vegetation was removed, Rothrock established a tree nursery at Mont Alto in the spring of 1902. The nursery was the first of its kind, born through the sowing of six pounds of pine seed. Many other state parks would eventually include tree nurseries based on the success of Mont Alto.[18]

Recreation

Rothrock envisioned promoting and accommodating recreation within the new forest reserves. By 1902, the Commonwealth had acquired land near Michaux State Forest that had been associated with the so-called Mont Alto resort, dedicating it to public recreation as part of the public land reservation on South Mountain. Hunting, fishing, camping, and hiking were permitted as uses compatible with forestry reservations. As noted, recreational opportunities have become an important part of the South Mountain cultural landscape, with former industrial features being converted to other uses, such as extraction sites serving as swimming holes.

One of the premier recreational features of Michaux State Forest today is the Appalachian National Scenic Trail, a publicly accessible footpath that extends for more than 2,200 miles between Mount Katahdin, Maine, and Springer Mountain, Georgia.[19] Completed in 1937, the Appalachian Trail continues for 30 miles through Michaux State Forest and 60 miles through South Mountain between the Potomac River and Boiling Springs, Pennsylvania. In

1968, President Lyndon B. Johnson designated the Appalachian Trail the first National Scenic Trail.[20]

The Appalachian Trail is affectionately known as the "Green Tunnel" for the canopy of trees that covers the trail for much of its route. The Pine Grove Iron Works company headquarters occurs at the midpoint of the trail. One of the company buildings now serves as the Appalachian Trail Museum. Hikers stop at Pine Grove and purchase a half gallon of ice cream at the company store. Eating, or attempting to eat, the entire half gallon of ice cream is a traditional way that through hikers mark the milestone.[21]

Conservation, Forestry, and the Great Depression

In addition to the state forestry school and management program, Michaux State Forest later benefited from New Deal-era programs introduced by President Franklin Delano Roosevelt during the 1930s to address unemployment during the Great Depression. One of the programs targeting conservation needs resulting from poor farming practices, exhausted and depleted soils, and poorly managed forests was the Agricultural Adjustment Administration, which led to the expansion of national forest reserves and public parks. Another was the Civilian Conservation Corps (CCC). CCC enrollees built roads, cleared land, fought fires, and also undertook conservation of the nation's natural resources—timber, soils, and water—on public lands. Between 1933 and 1942, more than three million young men participated in the massive conservation effort. CCC camps were built around the nation in close proximity to the areas of proposed projects.

The CCC had a profound impact on the Commonwealth of Pennsylvania, helping to improve the health and viability of the forests and natural areas while also enhancing state parks. Pennsylvania had the second-highest number of CCC camps and enrollees in the country. The state also benefited from the foresight of Governor Gifford Pinchot, who extended the conservation arm of Roosevelt's New Deal. During their tenure in Pennsylvania, the CCC enrollees built roads, bridges, and dams; reforested areas that had been cleared by industrial activity; and helped establish and improve many recreational areas within public lands. Five CCC camps were established within Michaux State Forest during the 1930s. One occupied land formerly owned by the Pine Grove Iron Works. In concert with Mont Alto, the CCC continued to enhance the forests that had been impacted by the iron industry by planting trees. The CCC enrollees also engaged in developing the Appalachian Trail through Michaux State Forest, including the construction of several bridges and shelters for hikers.

World War II

Although the CCC program was dismantled following America's entry into World War II, some of the camps were left in place. The US War Department secretly appropriated the CCC camp at Pine Grove in 1943 to serve as Camp Michaux, a prisoner-of-war interrogation facility hidden from public view by the now wooded landscape of South Mountain.[22] More than 1,500 prisoners, including officers and noncommissioned officers of the German navy and Rommel's Afrika Korps, as well as Japanese military personnel, were brought to Pine Grove and housed in former CCC barracks. The US Army constructed additional buildings on the site, including a hospital and several guard towers, as well as perimeter security fencing, to protect against prisoner escape. Evidence of the prisoner-of-war camp survives in the form of names etched into concrete structures built on-site and artwork prepared by some of the prisoners that illustrate camp life. Visitors to Michaux State Park can follow an interpretive trail through the campsite and learn about both the CCC and Camp Michaux.

Contemporary Forest Management

Over time, the Commonwealth of Pennsylvania has updated its forest management protocols and strategies based on emerging science. In 1995, the Bureau of Forestry completed a strategic plan titled "Penn's Woods Sustaining Our Forests" that identified the critical issues to be addressed by the Bureau of Forestry in the future. With a goal of ensuring "the long-term viability, health and productivity of our forests while providing benefits to all Pennsylvanians," the plan heralded a fundamental shift in forestry management toward taking an ecosystem approach over the extractive approach that had driven the commission since the early 1900s.[23]

Today, the Commonwealth recognizes the importance of preserving evidence of cultural land use history and heritage while continuing to manage for natural resource values. Management strategies are anticipated to continue to evolve based on science, particularly as the Bureau of Forestry struggles to meet the challenges posed by climate change and ensure the resiliency of the recovering forests at Michaux.

The forests that occupy the ridgelines of South Mountain today are 120-year-old stands of successional woodland dominated by a variety of oak and hickory species slowly reasserting their importance following the devastation wrought by charcoal production. Although the forest is slowly returning, it will never return to the condition known to Native Americans and early settlers. Human activity, from logging to the introduction of the parasitic fungus that caused the chestnut blight and of non-native invasive plant species, has influenced the composition of the contemporary forest. Also influencing present-day forest composition are contemporary state forest management practices and a cultural dependence on fire suppression. While fire, both naturally occurring and of anthropogenic origins, was traditionally a key component in forest ecology, fire suppression introduced in the nineteenth century has had a profound impact on forest composition. Before Europeans settled the region, Native Americans regularly set ground fires to clear the understory for hunting. Later, however, European settlers feared the destructive power of fire to their homes, crop fields, and wooded lots and sought to suppress fire rather than employ it to manage the landscape. The iron companies that operated on South Mountain, with their charcoal production and timbering practices that left dry piles of slash across the landscape, were often responsible for starting dangerous forest fires that led to the development of fire control strategies during the late nineteenth century. With the establishment of Michaux State Forest in 1901, the Commonwealth of Pennsylvania introduced fire suppression programs that promoted fire-sensitive species at the expense of fire-tolerant or fire-dependent species. The fire control practices implemented at South Mountain were similar to what was implemented at the federal level with the passage of the Weeks Act in 1911, which initiated the practice of cooperation among federal, state, and private landowners that is the foundation of fire control and protection today.[24] It was not until much later, as the importance of fire in plant community ecology became better understood, that the Commonwealth of Pennsylvania began to incorporate fire as a management tool into its forestry programs.

Although science plays a key role in forest management at South Mountain, the woodlands that cloak the mountain remain important as both a natural and a cultural resource. The South Mountain cultural landscape stands as evidence of several interrelated heritage values, multilayered features that can be read by the visitor and history detective to witness the evolution of an American worldview toward trees and the natural world. Although tempered by a mission to provide resources such as timber, the forests of South Mountain are also recognized for the habitat they provide to plants, animals, and insects and their ability to combat climate change through their capacity to remove carbon from the atmosphere and to serve as a buffer against the impacts of storms and floods while feeding our rivers. Tasked with working toward a future with healthy and sustainably managed forests, the Commonwealth of Pennsylvania can draw from a unique cultural heritage in devising forest management strategies that consider South Mountain's value as a cultural landscape. With many competing interests tugging at land managers today, digging (literally!) into a site's history, heritage resources, and connection to larger trends and modes of belief helps us solve a host of environmental, social, and political problems. Cultural landscape investigations involve explorations of place—past as well as present—to generate ideas of how physical change may be managed in the future. South Mountain offers a microcosm for understanding these principles and a fascinating history waiting to be discovered through the lens of trees.

Visiting South Mountain

At South Mountain, it is the trees that bear witness to our evolving relationship to the land. The evolution of South Mountain's forests since the nineteenth century has been nothing short of astonishing. From the devastation wrought by iron industry charcoal production to the establishment of the state's first forest reservation and forestry school, with the implementation of reforestation and conservation-minded forest management plans, the landscape has changed dramatically. Michaux State Forest is a vital part of the regional landscape, providing recreational opportunities to the residents of surrounding communities and managing and preserving important natural resources. The maturing woodlands of Michaux State Forest shelter but do not obscure the many-faceted history of the South Mountain cultural landscape that depicts a deep connection between environmental conditions and the eighteenth- and nineteenth-century iron industry in Pennsylvania. As a cultural landscape, South Mountain must be managed in such a way as to balance natural and cultural resource values so that the significant stories of cultural heritage, deeply connected to the land and its unique environmental conditions, survive and can be understood. For visitors, there are many ways to enjoy South Mountain and the intersection of the natural and the cultural. Beneath the leafy overstory of the young woodland of today's Michaux State Forest, the palimpsest of land use history remains evident, while rich stories of the past are revealed, with trees helping to tell the story.

FIGURE 9. The Daughters of Utah Pioneers Silk Industry Monument, Yalecrest neighborhood, Salt Lake City, Utah. Designed by Avard Tennyson Fairbanks. Photograph by Sasha Coles, June 21, 2022.

Chapter Six

Mormon Women, Mulberry Trees, and Environmental Transformation in the American West

Sasha Coles, Penn State University

In November 1941, a group of women assembled in the Yalecrest neighborhood of Salt Lake City to nail a copper plaque to a seventy-four-year-old mulberry tree. The Daughters of Utah Pioneers (DUP)—a group dedicated to preserving and commemorating the history of the people who passed through or established settlements in Utah from 1847 to 1869—had planned the meeting. At the time of the ceremony, the mulberry tree grew on D. Eugene Livingston's property at 1784 Herbert Avenue. Decades before, it had been part of a five-acre grove planted to sustain a nineteenth-century silk industry (mulberry tree foliage is the ideal food source for silkworms).[1] A brief description of the DUP event appeared in the pages of the *Improvement Era*, an official magazine of the Church of Jesus Christ of Latter-day Saints, more commonly known as the Mormon Church. The article explained how local silk production "flourished in pioneer times" and earned prizes at the Chicago World's Fair of 1893.[2] But things had changed. By the 1940s, very few Utahans still raised silkworms. Also, not many mulberry trees remained from the nineteenth century.[3] From the five-acre grove that Yalecrest used to host, Livingston's tree seems to have been one of only a few still standing. But the DUP's 1941 celebration was not a stand-alone event. It was part of a longer tradition of women leveraging mulberry trees to spin a story about domestic labor and environmental transformation.

The mulberry tree's history in the western region of North America begins in the middle decades of the nineteenth century, when Latter-day Saints, or Mormons, migrated to the Great Basin region—what was at that point Mexican territory—in pursuit of land and religious freedom. Once they arrived, these colonizers used negotiations, bribes, and violence to compete with Ute, Paiute, and Shoshone people for dominance over resources and territory.[4] They also threw their weight behind an economic independence program designed to provide employment, income, and commodities to their growing settlements. Church leaders called on Latter-day Saints to make food, clothing, and other necessities at home.[5] Silk production quickly became a part of this self-sufficiency initiative.

Right away, the introduction of the mulberry tree was a top priority. Industry boosters imbued the tree with the ability to grow easily, provide shade, and convert the free time of women and children into profit. While Mormon men helped advance local silk, women delivered the largest share of industry labor and organizing. They plucked leaves from trees and raised worms in homes and cocooneries. They also earned wages, won awards, and published pamphlets.[6] Their efforts kept the industry going for several decades. But financial limitations, time constraints, and environmental conditions made tree planting and worm raising difficult. Ultimately, these producers could not overpower cheaper, better-quality imports from Europe and Asia. By the early 1900s, many had stopped seeing the benefits of still-living mulberry trees, and very few people continued to cultivate silkworms in Utah.[7]

The silk industry lived on, however, in the realm of memory. Even before hopes for a viable independent industry had been completely extinguished, women Latter-day Saints became preservers, articulators, and celebrators of local silk's history. They created exhibits of cocoons, thread, and cloth for the Chicago World's Fair of 1893. Subsequent commemorations featured mulberry trees more prominently. A parade float for Utah's 1897 Pioneer Jubilee presented the audience with horse-sized representations of mulberry tree leaves. In subsequent years, Utah's mulberry trees saw a severe decline in popularity, but they never fully disappeared. In the 1940s, for example, tree planting was a centerpiece of centennial anniversary celebrations for the Relief Society, a Mormon women's organization invested in charity, education, and spiritual uplift. Relief Society members in the southern Utah town of St. George saw fit to mark the occasion with brand-new mulberry trees. In Salt Lake City's Yalecrest neighborhood, DUP members nailed a plaque to D. Eugene Livingston's tree. They also commissioned a concrete monument to the silk industry. With these mulberry tree mementos, Mormon women argued for the economic value and environmental impact of an industry that failed to replace imported goods or turn a regular profit. In this respect, they reworked an unsuccessful experiment into a source of pride.

These commemorations represent just one piece of a much larger pioneer memory landscape that operates as a "civic religion" for Latter-day Saints.[8] Scholars have long been interested in how individuals and institutions mobilize versions of the past to suit the present. Museums, historic sites, nation-states, corporations, and communities are constantly engaging in acts of remembering (and forgetting) to align with present-day mentalities and agendas.[9] This dynamic is evident among Latter-day Saints, who have a long and strong tradition of recalling and celebrating the nineteenth-century settler experience.[10] Each July 24, for example, Mormons around the world celebrate the anniversary of the day in 1847 when a contingent of Latter-day Saints entered the Salt Lake Valley.[11] It is also common for young Mormons to participate in annual "treks," during which they don pioneer clothing, assemble into "families," and pull handcarts.[12]

Several scholars have pointed out that these rituals perform an important identity-forming function. For one, they bring Latter-day Saints closer together. Mormons get a chance to live out the actions of the ancient Israelites, inculcate new converts in an agreed-upon set of values, and create a shared history for an increasingly diverse and international institution.[13] Pioneer commemorations build bridges between Latter-day Saints and the outside world, primarily by erasing controversial elements of the church's past.[14] In other words, Mormons use commemorative activities to perform a balancing act. These expressions permit Latter-day Saints to generate in-group solidarity while also aligning with mainstream American myths, values, and institutions.

This scholarship has not fully considered how trees behave as witnesses to the past, repositories of value systems, and agents in the community. By taking trees seriously, this essay offers new insights into the agents and agendas of Mormon pioneer memory. Since at least the 1890s, Mormon women have mobilized real and imagined mulberry trees to challenge their subordination in a patriarchal religious institution. In fair exhibits, parades, publications, ceremonies, and monuments, mulberry trees and their cultivators received credit for establishing an enlightened way of life in the Salt Lake Valley and converting a barren wasteland into a well-irrigated paradise. Much like other commemorations of nineteenth-century Mormon settlers, these representations squeezed out many historical realities. Gone were the Native people whose communities flourished in the Great Basin region for centuries.[15] Also gone were challenges with mulberry tree cultivation and the tree's unpopularity with community members. By layering together arguments about the long-term significance of women's work to economic success and environmental change, mulberry tree mementos provided a powerful counternarrative to the declining authority of women Latter-day Saints in their church-affiliated organizations and an increasingly conservative gender mentality in their religious community.

"It Was Too Hot for Them": *M. alba* and Women's Silk Production in Utah Territory, 1850s–1890s

There are three main species of mulberry tree: white (*Morus alba*), red (*Morus rubra*), and black (*Morus nigra*). The "mulberry" in the name refers to the blackberry-like fruit produced by pollinated flowers. Contrary to popular belief, fruit color is not a reliable indicator of species. A white mulberry's fruit, for example, can appear white, pink, black, purple, or some shade in between. The trees can be better distinguished using flower bud color, trunk curvature, and leaf shape and texture.[16] While the three main species boast unique characteristics, in general, mulberry trees are "hardy evolutionary athletes," writes historian Ben Marsh.[17] This organism originated in eastern Asia, more specifically central and northern China. Now, mulberry trees can be found all over the world. They live in low-lying river bottoms, woods, and orchards and along fences, streams, and city streets. They can thrive in temperate, dry, and tropical climates. They can also survive droughts, flooding, harsh winds, and salty soils.[18]

The tree's impressive territorial expansion is a product of its hardiness combined with the widespread allure of silk fabric and profitability of silk production. Of the roughly twenty recognized species in the *Morus* genus of the Moraceae family, *M. alba* has assumed the mantle of the superior food source for silkworms. Chinese people made this discovery roughly 4,700 years ago after witnessing wild worms consume *M. alba* leaves and then form fibrous protective shells. Observers drew on this information to create the human-directed, mulberry-fueled cocoon-raising process known as sericulture. It took time for knowledge of these hard-won and, according to some accounts, carefully guarded techniques to spread via trade networks, diplomatic interactions, and even romantic interludes. Once they did, enthusiasts in the Mediterranean, the Middle East, and other parts of the world turned to a local, readily accessible food source—the black mulberry tree, or *M. nigra*—to sustain their silkworms. They eventually realized, however, that white mulberry trees could supply multiple crops of leaves per year while also delivering more raw silk of a higher quality. Monarchs, politicians, and businessmen actively invested in the tree's importation and cultivation. Some retained black mulberry trees for their pleasant shade and tart-tasting fruit. Meanwhile, *M. alba* began to take up more and more space in gardens, orchards, informational pamphlets, and state economic agendas. By the early 1500s, writes mulberry tree expert Peter Coles, it was "the tree of choice for Western sericulture, as it had been in China for millennia."[19]

People in colonial North America and the antebellum United States arrived at the same conclusion. The North American continent has its own native species of mulberry. *M. rubra*, the red mulberry tree, has long grown on land spanning from today's Canada to southern Florida and across much of the US Midwest. For generations, the Cherokee, Comanche, Creek, Iroquois, Seminole, and other Native American groups relied on *M. rubra*'s fruit, leaves, bark, and wood for food, medical treatment, textile production, and bow manufacturing.[20] To European settlers, these trees looked amenable to local silk production. Experience soon proved, however, that *M. rubra* did not perform as well as the tried-and-true *M. alba*, which could provide better-quality silkworm food much more quickly.

Colonists responded enthusiastically to these findings. In their minds, homegrown silk offered to resolve many problems at once. They predicted that the American colonies could generate raw materials for manufacturers in Europe and then purchase finished products. In addition, industry boosters believed that silk would transform individuals they categorized as economic "liabilities"—women, children, the elderly, sick people, and enslaved people—into assets. Workers supposedly too young, too old, too weak, or not skilled enough for other tasks could generate capital by collecting leaves, raising silkworms, and reeling thread. These arguments provided the foundation for robust mulberry tree programs. Officials imported *M. alba* and installed taxes, bounties, and other economic incentives to encourage its cultivation in New Spain in the sixteenth century, New France and Virginia in the seventeenth century, and Pennsylvania, Georgia, and the Carolinas in the eighteenth century.[21]

Silk's popularity declined during the American Revolution but rebounded quickly. The fabric's association with old-world luxury did not sit well with revolutionary republican ideals. But concerns about industrialization and economic uncertainty in the early 1800s catalyzed a short-lived silk resurgence, primarily in the Northeast and along the Atlantic coast.[22] This revival coincided with the arrival of an even more promising white mulberry tree variety, *Morus alba multicaulis*, which could deliver abundant leaf harvests two, even three times a year. Enthusiasm for this specific tree rose to the level of a speculative "craze" followed, not surprisingly, by a severe market collapse.[23]

Still, the introduced *M. alba* persisted and even found new adherents. Nineteenth-century Mormon settlement pushed the white mulberry tree farther into the North American interior. Beginning in the late 1840s, a series of migrations brought thousands of Latter-day Saints to the Great Basin, a region claimed by the Mexican state that had long sustained a diverse group of Native peoples. Over the next decade, Mormons from the US and abroad established almost one hundred settlements in the American West. Right away, these colonizers transformed their natural surroundings. Individual- and community-wide attempts to cordon off land, plant crops, install irrigation systems, raise livestock, collect timber, and build homes, businesses, and places of worship had a profound impact on the environment. To protect their imported cattle, pigs, and sheep, for example, farmers and ranchers battled with bears, coyotes, wolves, and mountain lions. Growing populations of domesticated animals feasted on native grasses, which created an opening for non-native vegetation to move in and take over.[24]

Various "home industries" left their mark as well. Church leaders agreed that Mormonism's survival depended on economic independence. They argued that Latter-day Saints had much to gain from the production of metals, textiles, and other commodities at home. These industries, they proclaimed, would reduce reliance on imported goods, keep valuable hard currency within the community, generate employment opportunities, and encourage investment into secular and spiritual initiatives. Factories, foundries, ranches, plantations, orchards, and other infrastructure went up to support an economy by and for Mormons.[25] Silk production constituted one important pillar of this home industry movement.

Utah Territory needed lots of trees for a self-sufficient silk industry. This makes sense. Consider the modern estimate that the foliage of thirty mature mulberry trees roughly translates to just one yard of silk fabric.[26] Worms cannot spin their valuable cocoons without a generous supply of leaves. In the 1860s, Louis A. Bertrand, a French Mormon convert with exposure to European sericulture, stated that a single worm could consume twenty pounds of mulberry leaves during its short lifetime.[27] Bertrand and other industry boosters recognized that local silk would stall without a reliable food source. The first step necessary to support the "infant" industry, according to an article Bertrand published in December 1868, was to "plant mulberry trees everywhere."[28] Bertrand predicted that these "magnificent mulberry plantations" would bring the land into the light of "humanity."[29] Other pro-tree propaganda from Latter-day Saints wove together confident reports about soil and temperature with proclamations about the tree's positive qualities. In the late summer of 1865, Brigham Young—the church's second president and prophet—told an assembly of Latter-day Saints, "The mulberry tree, which produces the natural food of the silk worm, will flourish on all our bench lands, and our climate is exactly adapted to the healthy condition of the silk worm. I would recommend the planting and propagating of the mulberry tree. . . . Let our cities and gardens be adorned with trees that are both ornamental and useful."[30] A few years later, George D. Watt, Young's private clerk, expressed similar ideas with even more optimistic rhetoric: "The soil of our extensive benches skirting the mountain ranges, is most admirably adapted to the cultivation of the Mulberry tree. . . . I know of no tree so full of usefulness, profit and blessing to the human family."[31]

Like other contributors to this edited volume have recognized, discussions about trees can provide clarity about the values that humans attach to the natural world. To nineteenth-century Mormons, the fusion of religious, economic, and environmental affairs in mulberry-related rhetoric was quite familiar. Scripture, sermons, and prophetic revelations explained that the kingdom of God on earth would be built not just by prayer, church meeting attendance, and other religious ceremonies but also by planting gardens, caring for livestock and children, and constructing roads, homes, fences, and irrigation ditches. These temporal labors supported a sacred mission, and church leaders intervened directly in organizing economic life.[32]

Religion played an instrumental role in the Latter-day Saints' relationship to the environment as well. The church's founder and first president, Joseph Smith, instructed the Latter-day Saints in what historian Thomas G. Alexander describes as "the spiritual unity of humans, the earth, and its nonhuman inhabitants under the fatherhood of God." This "salutary environmental theology," as defined by Alexander, taught that animals and plants possessed eternal spirits. It also attributed the ownership of the earth to the Lord and defined humans as temporary caretakers of natural resources.[33] Brigham Young made similar pronouncements about stewardship. In his mind, Latter-day Saints had a "divine covenant" with nature, argues historian Sarah Dant.[34]

Scholars disagree about the extent to which these ideals shaped on-the-ground interactions with the natural world. When compared to other white settlers of western areas, Mormons tended to adopt a communal, centrally planned system of land, water, and timber distribution that helped them succeed in their arid surroundings. There is also evidence that Latter-day Saints exploited resources to secure individual profit and compete in the capitalist marketplace, especially after the completion of the transcontinental railroad in 1869.[35] Historian Jeff Nichols's study of livestock, for example, suggests that communitarian ideals coexisted in tension with market competitiveness, which made Mormon environmental stewardship "selective and anthropocentric."[36] The silk experiment confirms that multiple incentives shaped Mormon economic activities.[37] For example, Latter-day Saints instructed one another to smother cocoons—with gas, in ovens, or in the hot sun—to kill the chrysalis inside and ensure an unbroken silk thread.[38]

Before they could get to that stage of silk production, however, Latter-day Saints needed mulberry trees. Brigham Young raised some at one of his Salt Lake City properties, an experimental agricultural station known as Forest Farm. After seeds arrived from France, Hamilton G. Park, Young's business manager, planted them on one Forest Farm acre.[39] In July 1865, the *Deseret News*—an outlet owned by the Mormon Church—reported "100,000 young mulberry trees" growing there.[40] By 1868, according to another newspaper report, Young had 600,000 trees available.[41] Paul A. Schettler, a Latter-day Saint convert from Prussia, cultivated another critical mass of trees—hundreds, according to one account—on his farm in what would eventually become Salt Lake City's Yalecrest neighborhood.[42]

This was not Schettler's first or last silk-promoting activity.[43] In the 1870s, for example, he traveled with three other Latter-day Saints to Europe and the Middle East. Schettler took this opportunity to connect with sericulturists and silk manufacturers and ask them their opinion of cocoons raised in Utah Territory. These agents, reported Schettler, "pronounced the sample of cocoons which I had brought along from home of very excellent quality, and expressed the opinion that this branch of industry would prove to our people an almost inexhaustible gold mine."[44] Later that decade, Schettler assumed a leadership role in the Deseret Silk Association, established in 1877. During an organization meeting held in March of that year, he offered to distribute mulberry trees to interested parties once the plants reached the appropriate age for relocation.[45]

While men made key contributions as cultivators, promoters, investors, and landowners, Utah Territory's church-sanctioned silk experiment depended primarily on women. Much like industry enthusiasts who came before, Latter-day Saints assumed that women made ideal silk laborers. The longtime categorization of spinning, reeling, and weaving as women's work, combined with assumptions about women's biological predisposition to delicate nurturing, made the relationship between women, worms, and silk manufacturing seem quite natural, even preordained.[46] Silk also offered to resolve anxieties about an industrializing economy. In the early nineteenth century, a large share of textile production moved out of the home and into factories. Waves of young women left family farms to accept those wage-paying positions. These developments prompted concerns about the extra time that women had, since they no longer produced the family's clothing. Commentators also worried about the threat that urban environments posed to women workers free from the supervision of their parents.[47] Mulberry tree cultivation and silkworm raising offered the perfect solution to perceptions of women's declining household productivity and eroding parental authority.[48] These assumptions motivated Latter-day Saints to invest in silk production. So did the desire to create an independent Mormon-oriented economy.

From the 1850s to the late 1890s, Mormon women powered local silk. They handled the tasks required to make silk of a high-enough quality to use and sell. Some raised a few worms in a cupboard. Others dedicated entire rooms or outbuildings to the enterprise. Many elements of the industry took place within the home, often with the assistance of children. But silk's success also necessitated action far beyond the domestic sphere. Women staffed cocooneries, presided over silk-centered organizations, lobbied politicians, presented their goods at local and national fairs, and planted mulberry trees up and down the Wasatch Front.[49] They staffed a local factory in Salt Lake City. In the 1880s, for example, Scottish-born Margaret Cullen arrived in Utah Territory and used her skills with a power loom to produce a "cut," or sixty yards, of silk fabric.[50]

Mormon women also spread the tree-growing gospel. At one church organization meeting in 1875, for example, Zina D. H. Young—a recognized leader of women Latter-day Saints—commented, "If some of the Sisters would go into the silk culture and get mulberry slips and plant them, around your houses, they grow rapidly and would make excellent shade trees as well as being food for silk worms."[51] In silk, Mormon women discovered the many challenges involved with cultivating worms and trees. They also found opportunities to foster far-flung commercial networks, earn respect for their skills, and turn an occasional profit. Many of these activities depended on ward-level Relief Society organizations, which provided financial support and a source of leadership. Zina D. H. Young, for example, served as president of the Deseret Silk Association and the Relief Society at the same time.[52]

Latter-day Saints believed they had hardy trees, welcoming land, and a ready and willing labor force, but on-the-ground experiences with *M. alba* left much to be desired. While mulberry trees are flexible, they are not invincible. Young plants cannot survive shocks to their system nearly as well as mature plants can.[53] Droughts, frosts, and floods stood between Latter-day Saints and a consistent silkworm food supply. Lydia McLellan's experience is illustrative. She tried her hand at mulberry tree cultivation in St. George, a settlement located on the southern edge of Utah Territory. In February 1878, McLellan reported that her plants "looked well for a season and then looked yellow as tho it was too hot for them or the soil not right."[54] Clearly, mulberry trees have vulnerabilities. McLellan's fledgling trees probably needed more water than they got. Latter-day Saints also discovered the skill and delicacy involved in the synchronization of egg hatching with tree maturation.[55] Silkworms went hungry, even at the well-sponsored Forest Farm.[56] Men, women, and children found themselves traveling great distances at all hours to locate available trees.[57] Some experimented with alternative food sources, like lettuce and the leaves of the Osage orange tree (*Maclura pomifera*), but these could not challenge the white mulberry's supremacy.[58] Repeated requests from prominent Latter-day Saints to invest in the enterprise suggest that not everyone wanted to dedicate their land, money, or time.[59] In at least one instance, Mormon women sold off their tree orchard and applied that money to grain cultivation instead.[60]

Ultimately, these silk producers found themselves in the same position as the American sericulturists who preceded them. When reflecting on the state of Utah Territory's industry in 1893, one commentator explained that the Latter-day Saints had "no market for cocoons and no machinery suitable for working the native silk."[61] That same year, another observer lamented that "very few new mulberry orchards are planted now a-days."[62] Some abandoned silk for more reliable, more profitable pursuits instead. As the industry fell by the wayside, so did the mulberry tree.

Interested parties did their best to keep the industry afloat. In 1892, for example, Zina D. H. Young asked fellow Latter-day Saints "not to destroy the mulberry trees."[63] She also supported tree cultivation as chairwoman of the Utah Silk Commission (USC), established and funded by the Utah legislature in 1896 to shore up the local silk production. USC sponsored a cocoon bounty, hosted reeling classes, and distributed mulberry tree seeds and cuttings. It also tried to revive *M. alba*'s reputation. USC's 1897 pamphlet on sericulture described the mulberry tree as "endowed with many properties which render its cultivation, whether on the farm or as an ornament around our dwellings, an object happily combining utility, convenience and pleasure." These positive qualities, wrote the board members, "*should at once put a stop to its destruction in all parts of the State*."[64]

USC's initiatives did give local silk additional energy, but only for a short time. Utah legislators voted to dissolve the commission and cancel the cocoon bounty in 1906.[65] For some producers, this was the last straw. That year, one church leader recommended the dissolution of a silk association in Provo, Utah. His rationale? "Silk could be purchased from China and Japan."[66]

"An Oasis in the Great American Desert": Pioneer Memory and Mormon Women's Authority, 1890s–1940s

As the potential for homemade silk faded into the background, mulberry trees and other silk industry ephemera appeared in public commemorations designed to celebrate the so-called pioneer era of the nineteenth century. When Utah observed Arbor Day for the first time in April 1919, for example, one commentator celebrated the long-term impacts of tree cultivation in a Salt

Lake City paper. When the Latter-day Saints began to colonize the Salt Lake Valley, said this account, they found "several hundred thousand acres of dry land covered with sagebrush to be rooted up." Brigham Young and his followers imported and planted fruit and shade trees, including the mulberry. "By the time [Brigham Young] died," wrote this local resident, "his love for trees and gardening had become the ardent desire of the community."[67] This description linked the mulberry tree to popular plotlines about white settlers, westward expansion, and environmental conversion. Tree-centered commemorations helped audiences register Latter-day Saints as an assimilated component of the American body politic. They also created an opening for Mormon women to assert their authority.

Latter-day Saints have long used public venues to reconcile their religious principles with the expectations of American citizenship. Over the course of the nineteenth and early twentieth centuries, tensions over polygamy, the political dominance of church leaders, and other practices flowered into internal schisms, violent confrontations, and federal government intervention. They also prompted more of the church's attention to public relations. At the turn of the twentieth century, Latter-day Saints embarked on an ambitious campaign to improve their reputation and ease conflicts with outsiders. Members put on performances for tourists, forged strategic alliances with politicians, and bribed newspaper editors and railroad tycoons.[68] Church leaders also began relinquishing control of local economic institutions and instructed Latter-day Saints to abandon or downplay some of their most controversial activities, including, most famously, polygamy.[69]

This evolution did not always bode well for women Latter-day Saints. As their church's male leaders and bureaucracy began to align more with the American mainstream, the marital and familial ties of plural wives lost legitimacy. Mormon women's organizations also lost some of their autonomy.[70] Even so, Mormon women continued to act independently and build community.[71] They participated in the suffrage movement and ensured that Utah's state constitution included women's access to the ballot.[72] They used Progressive Era traditions of improvement, reform, efficiency, and modernization to enter paying professions and determine legislative agendas.[73] Memory politics also helped them shape their surroundings. Historian Jennifer Reeder's study of hair wreaths, quilts, and other material culture, for example, shows how Mormon women created a usable past that imbued them with the qualities of middle-class respectability.[74]

Even before the cancellation of Utah's cocoon bounty in the early 1900s, women created space in Mormon pioneer memory to assert the transformative impact of a (largely failed) silk industry. Thread, curtains, and other goods appeared at the 1893 Chicago World's Fair, for example.[75] The elites responsible for the fair intended to pay homage to a white, Protestant, industrializing United States by papering over class conflict, economic depression, and racial antagonisms.[76] This event also offered "a secular back door by which the LDS Church entered upon the stage of national legitimacy," writes historian Konden Smith Hansen.[77] Exhibits of male-dominated agricultural and mineral industries defined Utah Territory as open to capitalist development and Latter-day Saints as central to westward expansion. Mormon women made arguments of their own at the fair. They fostered alliances with major figures in the suffrage movement and aligned themselves with progressive causes, according to historian Andrea Radke-Moss.[78] They also placed homemade silk goods alongside the material and human remains of Native people. To event attendees, these objects confirmed Mormon women's sophistication and Utah Territory's market integration.[79]

Symbols of the mulberry tree performed a similar function at the 1897 Pioneer Jubilee, put on to celebrate Utah's transition to statehood and mark the fiftieth anniversary of the Mormon migration to the Great Basin region. Parades in Salt Lake City credited Latter-day Saint settlers with bringing productive enterprises to Utah and enveloping western territories into the United States. Individual counties submitted floats communicating their material contributions to the state's prosperity. One float from Tooele County included mining tramways carrying ore. Another from Box Elder County presented a literal cornucopia overflowing with fruits and vegetables.[80] Silk appeared in this tableau of local economic development as well. Atop one parade float sat a small group of sun-bonneted women. Larger-than-life figures of silkworms and mulberry tree leaves composed the rest of the display (see figure 10).

These high-profile presentations brought visibility to women's work with local silk. But they were not enough to keep the state-sponsored cocoon bounty going.

At around the same time, still-lingering mulberry trees began to attract negative attention. Much like some of the other trees discussed in this volume, the mulberry came to be seen as outdated, inconvenient, and expendable. In a 1914 newspaper article, a resident of St. George wrote, "The mulberry trees

FIGURE 10. Silkworm float, Pioneer Day Parade, 1897, Salt Lake City, Utah. Charles R. Savage photographs, circa 1866–1906, PH 500, box 1, folder 21, Church History Library.

are a nuisance. The fruit falls on the sidewalks attracting swarms of flies and are disagreeable to walk upon."[81] Nineteenth-century trees also caused commotion in Ogden, located roughly forty miles north of Salt Lake City. "Up to a few years ago nearly every street in Ogden had one or more mulberry trees," but the "fly-attracting smear" caused by dropping fruit drove people to cut them down, reported one newspaper in 1915.[82] As early as the 1930s, city councils and commissions started regulating and proactively removing mulberry trees in the name of "beautification."[83] Individual property owners and community leaders also uprooted them to make way for construction projects.[84] This push to remove mulberry trees might explain why, by the 1940s, the tree on D. Eugene Livingston's property was one of the few remaining in Salt Lake City's Yalecrest neighborhood.

Decaying, sidewalk-smearing fruit aside, some local mulberry trees survived. Newspaper reports from the first half of the twentieth century clarified how these trees could provide shade, screen homes from curious neighbors, or be used as windbreaks on the farm.[85] Commentators also suggested using harvested fruit to feed farm animals or make pies, soups, preserves, and wine.[86] By making room for the mulberry tree, these residents joined a long tradition of flexibility among tree cultivators. *M. alba* could feed silkworms, but it could also be used to make paper, textiles, furniture, medicine, and food items. Long after learning about the white mulberry tree's superiority for silkworm feeding, for example, communities continued to nurture *M. nigra*. *M. alba*'s fruit is good enough for livestock and for jams, pies, and other popular desserts, but *M. nigra* delivers a fruit that is much more succulent.[87] In a similar vein, some Utahans continued to acknowledge the mulberry tree's usefulness.

The organism also attracted attention as a symbol and catalyst of Utah's economic, environmental, and religious maturation. In a 1930 letter to the editor of the *Salt Lake Telegram*, an unnamed Salt Lake City homeowner explained how "in some parts of the city the Mulberry predominates, due to the fact that years ago mulberry trees were planted to aid the silk industry of the state." These and other "beautiful trees" of Salt Lake City deserved protection because they "attract the attention of visitors."[88] Other commentary incorporated the tree more explicitly into Mormon pioneer memory. In a 1934 article, George M. Cannon—a direct descendant of the Latter-day Saints who colonized southern Utah Territory in the nineteenth century—described how "the attitude of the Pioneers of Utah toward tree planting was one of deep interest from the beginning." Walnut, ash, elm, and mulberry trees came up on farms, in nurseries, along streets, and around church buildings. Cannon saturated the resulting "abundance" of trees with religious significance. His article reproduced the ancient prophet Isaiah's statement that "the Lord shall comfort Zion; he will comfort all her waste places, and he will make her wilderness like Eden, and her desert like the garden of the Lord . . . (Isa. 51:3)." Cannon believed that this forecast had come to pass. He wrote that "from the very beginning Utah became noted as an oasis in the great American Desert."[89]

This narrative proved useful to Mormon women as well. In 1944, local politician, art enthusiast, and longtime Relief Society leader Alice Merrill Horne described how Mormon pioneers—"history's most intrepid adventurers," in her words—made an "inaccessible, remote, dormant" desert "habitable." While interested in men's contributions, Horne also credited pioneer women with animating a supposedly lifeless place. "Silk worms were fed mulberry leaves," and "silk cocoons presently emerged into silk evening dresses," she wrote. These activities created the foundation for "the redeemed desert."[90]

Here, narratives about the mulberry tree and the silk industry intersected with a long-standing tradition of celebrating the dramatic environmental conversion of colonized landscapes and the success of an envisioned "civilization" over so-called savagery. Latter-day Saints have their own version of this nostalgic trope. Since the middle decades of the nineteenth century, Latter-day Saints and their observers have advanced a line of argumentation that historian Jared Farmer calls "the desertification of Zion." According to this thesis, nineteenth-century Mormon settlers confronted a water-starved, game-depleted, pest-ridden natural world in the Salt Lake Valley and miraculously rendered it productive.[91] Church leader and historian Orson F. Whitney's *Popular History of Utah* (1916) provides one illustration of the longevity and popularity of the desertification thesis. Whitney describes nineteenth-century Mormons as "the vanguard of progress, the builders of empire in the barren heart of the West." According to Whitney, the Latter-day Saints "planted civilization in the midst of savagery, and to them, more than to any other people . . . is due the redemption of 'Arid America.' Their industry and that of their successors made the desert Basin habitable."[92]

The desertification thesis does not stand up to available historical evidence or scholarly literature. Generations of Native people have made their homes in the Great Basin region. Also, some of the first Latter-day Saints who established settlements there expressed satisfaction with available natural resources and did not always go to great lengths to exploit them.[93] In addition, when it comes to the silk industry specifically, many factors—weather, available land, lack of capital, and outright eradication—severely constrained the mulberry tree supply. These realities contradicted a simple story about an empty and difficult but conquered environment. Even so, for Alice Merrill Horne and George M. Cannon, the desertification thesis had utility. By establishing Latter-day Saints (and their trees) as essential agents of progress, this myth excised the rich history of Native societies and defined westward expansion as a benevolent process.

In the 1930s and 1940s, women Latter-day Saints placed a spin on the desertification thesis that highlighted women's activities during the pioneer era. Relief Society leaders kicked off a membership drive in 1938 in preparation for the organization's centennial anniversary four years later. The popular slogan "members old and members new, one hundred thousand by '42" captured the drive's ambitious goal.[94] By the time the centennial arrived, the eruption of World War II had significantly disrupted the implementation of large-scale celebrations. Still, individual Mormon communities in the US and abroad managed to host special events, including pageants, concerts, and tree-planting ceremonies.[95] In August 1941, a bulletin disseminated by Relief Society leaders encouraged members to plant trees to mark the one-hundred-year anniversary. In addition to improving the aesthetics of church property, the trees had symbolic value. "A majestic tree slowly but surely growing with its roots firmly planted in the earth and its branches ever reaching heavenward is typical of our great organization and its century of service," the bulletin stated.[96] According to one estimate, Relief Societies in the United States and Canada planted 874 trees in 1942.[97] While the inspiration for tree planting might have come from a top-down directive, local flavor infused the choice of tree. Women Latter-day Saints planted maple trees in New York, eucalyptus trees in California, and magnolia trees in the southern states.[98]

Mormon women in Utah used tree-planting ceremonies to acknowledge women's past contributions and communicate the Relief Society's vitality. On March 17, 1942, for example, Relief Society board members gathered at Temple Square, a church-owned complex in the heart of Salt Lake City, to plant an English elm.[99] That day, Relief Society president Amy Brown Lyman delivered an address, broadcast over radio, about the organization. "Even though the shadows of war hang heavy over many lands, this hundredth birthday is not forgotten," Lyman said. Relief Society members had spent the last year preparing for the anniversary by combing through historical records. In her speech, Lyman revealed their findings. "We have learned of [Mormon women's] work as pioneers in the West where side by side with men they helped to blaze trails and lay the foundation of an empire," she said.[100] The English elm they planted recalled these contributions. Lyman predicted the trees would be "loved and cherished by future generations of Relief Society women—symbolic of the strength and steady growth of the organization."[101]

Relief Society members in St. George, Utah, marked the centennial with a similar ceremony in March 1942. Instead of the English elm, however, they opted to plant non-fruit-bearing mulberry trees.[102] It is worth noting that a mulberry tree only produces fruit when a male flower's pollen fertilizes a female flower. A monoecious tree can self-pollinate because it grows both male and female flowers. A dioecious tree, on the other hand, grows only one or the other, which explains why male and female dioecious plants need each other to produce fruit. The decision of Relief Society members to plant dioecious trees in the 1940s makes sense, considering the resentment some residents felt toward the pest-attracting mulberry mess on the sidewalk.[103] By opting for that variety, Relief Society members provided a living illustration of the community's defunct silk industry as well as the worldwide presence of their organization.[104]

The Great Depression and World War II fundamentally shaped the dynamics of these commemorative activities. As the Great Depression got underway, church leaders asked Latter-day Saints to eschew government support and utilize the church's own charity program—what became known as the Church Welfare Plan—for food, clothing, and job assignments instead. Not all Mormons divorced themselves from government funding. For some, the economic crisis cut too deep to say no to government aid. Others saw no contradiction in accepting help from the state as well as the Church Welfare Plan. Whatever avenue individual church members chose, the church's nineteenth-century pursuit of economic self-sufficiency took on heightened significance. As Latter-day Saints weathered the storm of economic downturn, they valorized hard work, thrift, self-reliance, and other qualities associated with the pioneer generation.[105] Latter-day Saints continued to foster this connection during World War II. The scarcity and loss caused by the global conflict generated yet another reason to recollect the presumed fortitude and independence of nineteenth-century settlers.[106]

When analyzed alongside other Relief Society programs from this era, the organization's 1942 tree-planting celebrations reflected this church-wide attention to the pioneer generation but from a gendered perspective. Relief Society members engaged in many activities designed to amplify the value of women's work, past and present. In 1937, for example, members opened a consignment store in Salt Lake City stocked with quilts, wreaths, infant clothes, gloves, and other handmade items. In addition to providing women with a source of income, this outlet communicated the instrumental place of women in community support and financial security.[107] In a similar vein, the organization began incorporating images of wheat into its official insignia, membership pins, parade floats, and commemorative activities in the 1940s. The wheat symbol recalled the Relief Society's wheat storage program, which began in the 1870s to shore up against poverty and famine. The program lasted until World War I, when male church leaders decided to sell the stored wheat to the US government. At the time, this sale signaled a prodigious loss of autonomy and control for the organization.[108] But the crises of the mid-twentieth century prompted the Relief Society to revive wheat as a symbol communicating the membership's immediate and historic investments in the community.[109]

The Relief Society's utilization of mulberry tree mementos may have also been a response to changing church programs and shifting gender expectations. In the 1930s, the Church Welfare Plan took over the collection and distribution of resources to Latter-day Saints experiencing poverty. This responsibility had long been the purview of the Relief Society. Since the organization's founding in Nauvoo, Illinois, in the 1840s, members had collected and distributed clothing, food, and other donations to vulnerable populations. These activities took on a more modern shape during the Progressive Era. The Relief Society created its own Social Services Department, which utilized professional casework methods and relationships with private charitable institutions and government agencies. Much of the momentum for this approach came from Amy Brown Lyman. Lyman held various Relief Society leadership positions from 1909 to 1945, including the presidency. She used her platform to encourage women's involvement in public life as politicians, administrators, doctors, and educators. This explains why, for Lyman and other like-minded Mormon women, the Church Welfare Plan's co-optation of a Relief Society centerpiece was a source of frustration. While the organization's members continued to support poor relief, high-level decision-making came under the purview of male church leaders. A growing emphasis on a traditional domestic ideal accompanied the Relief Society's declining influence. In the 1930s and 1940s, church leaders celebrated the divine qualities of modesty, motherhood, and housekeeping for women. Wage work, policymaking, and political activism, on the other hand, belonged to men. Historians have found that while some Mormon women worked within these expectations, others found ways to reject or subvert them.[110] In this context, recollections of women pioneers who blazed trails, transformed the wilderness, and established an empire may have been one way for Latter-day Saint women to critique their marginalization.

A similar approach can be found in commemorative activities sponsored by the DUP, an organization composed primarily but not exclusively of women Latter-day Saints. When Anne T. Hyde formed the DUP in April 1901, her stated goal was to "[cement] together in the bonds of friendship and love the descendants of those who were instrumental in redeeming the desert and making it blossom as a rose."[111] DUP camps—the term used to designate neighborhood-based groups—have pursued this mandate for over one hundred years. Much like that of the Daughters of the American Revolution, the DUP operates on a lineage-based membership system. A woman does not have to be a Latter-day Saint join, but she must be able to trace her ancestry to a person who traveled to or through Utah Territory (or its predecessor, the proposed State of Deseret) after July 1847 but before the completion of the transcontinental railroad in May 1869. She must also be at least eighteen and "of good character." According to the organization's website, more than twenty thousand women belong to roughly one thousand DUP camps. Members are currently engaged in a wide range of projects—everything from genealogical research and archival collecting to museum education, pamphlet and book publication, and a scholarship program.[112] DUP camps also fund landmarks. According to a recent estimate, the DUP has installed 591 historical markers in twelve different countries.[113]

One of them honors Utah's homegrown silk industry. In the 1930s, DUP members put a plan into motion to install a monument in Yalecrest, the previously mentioned Salt Lake City neighborhood where DUP members nailed a copper plaque to a mulberry tree.[114] In September 1935, Gertrude S. Romney, president of DUP's Yale camp, sent a letter to Ida M. Kirkham, president of DUP's Yale Crest camp. The establishment of two DUP camps in the Yalecrest neighborhood had occurred only very recently. The addition of new subdivisions made it necessary to divide the community's single DUP camp in two. Romney wrote Kirkham to ask permission to mark several "places of historical interest" on land that "was originally Yale Camp" but, due to Yalecrest's recent expansion, was now under Kirkham's jurisdiction. "One of these places . . . is where the silk industry was first fostered in this western country," Romney wrote. Margaret Cullen Geddes Eccles, the silk weaver mentioned earlier, "figured prominently in the manufacture of the first silk made," Romney told Kirkham. As it happens, Eccles was also a charter member of DUP's Yale camp.[115]

In addition to securing permission from Ida M. Kirkham, Gertrude S. Romney sought support from Leona Holbrook, the president of the entire DUP organization. Romney told Holbrook that the Yale camp wanted to place a "suitable marker" where "the pioneers planted many acres of mulberry trees for the purpose of helping along the silk industry." She took care to clarify silk's significance when she said, "Since the venture was successful and beautiful silk was made here in the early days, it seems that a marker on this location should be much desired by us all."[116]

In the end, the Yale and Yale Crest camps came together to sponsor a monument designed by prominent Latter-day Saint sculptor Avard Tennyson Fairbanks. To the DUP project, Fairbanks brought a passion for Mormon subject matter and years of art education. Fairbanks grew up in Utah. As a teenager (and with the support of his artistic father), he left for New York City to study with famous American sculptors at the Art Students' League. Fairbanks earned a BFA from Yale University in 1925 and studied art in Europe on a Guggenheim Fellowship. After that, he became a faculty member at the University of Michigan's Institute of Fine Arts. During his decades-long career spanning most of the twentieth century, Fairbanks created several high-profile sculptures in a conservative realist style. He aspired to do justice to human proportions and features, a goal advanced by his doctoral degree in anatomical science. He also approached his art as an instrument of, in his words, "large-scale education and community uplift and pride."[117] During his career, Fairbanks represented famous figures from American history, including George Washington, Abraham Lincoln, and Pony Express riders, as well as iconic people and moments from Latter-day Saint culture, like the Angel Moroni, Brigham Young, and Joseph Smith's first vision.[118]

Fairbanks also played an instrumental part in the twentieth-century revival of the nineteenth-century Mormon pioneer period. Historian Cynthia Culver Prescott has argued that Fairbanks's sculptures from the 1930s and 1940s emphasized the centrality of family units to Latter-day Saint migration and settlement roughly one hundred years earlier. In his renderings, a sturdy patriarch tends to lead his gentle wife and their children into unknown western lands, protect them from hostilities, and provide "material support and spiritual guidance."[119]

This vision shaped the bronze plaques he completed in 1942 for the Relief Society's centennial memorial in Salt Lake City's Temple Square. The structure's centerpiece is a freestanding bronze bell tower designed by architect Lorenzo S. Young. The bell inside originally resided in the Mormon temple in Nauvoo, Illinois. Fairbanks's plaques encircle the base of the tower.[120] One introduces the memorial by narrating origin stories for the Relief Society and the bell from Nauvoo. A second is called *Benevolence*. A third is titled *Education*. The fourth, *Pioneering*, deserves a lengthier description. It depicts a Latter-day Saint family crossing an icy Mississippi River after being expelled from Nauvoo by mob violence. The father cradles an infant in one of his arms and embraces his wife with the other. The couple's older child, a son, stands on the other side of his mother. She has a shawl draped over her head and one of her hands placed on her son's shoulder. The Nauvoo temple sits on top of a hill in the distant background, while leafless trees and a bare winter landscape surround the family.

Several tools of labor—an axe, spinning wheel, and shovel—appear in the scene.[121] Much to the disappointment of the Relief Society's central leadership, World War II significantly delayed the centennial memorial's construction. It took until the late 1960s to erect it.[122] But Fairbanks managed to complete his contribution in time for the anniversary. The plaques include the artist's signature and a date: 1942.

Pioneering and other art of this genre reflected the internal dynamics of Latter-day Saint communities as well as the circumstances shaping American culture in the 1930s and 1940s. These commemorations tethered Latter-day Saints to cherished myths about manifest destiny and white racial superiority while promoting key components of Mormon theology, including the eternal nature of family relationships. In this respect, representations of pioneers balanced Latter-day Saint exceptionalism with American assimilation.[123] They also attended to the conditions of depression and war, when Latter-day Saints found solace in the tenacity and survival of nineteenth-century settlers. In addition, they communicated a conservative mentality regarding dominant patriarchs and child-focused, domestically oriented women. The tools, environmental conditions, and characters represented in *Pioneering* confirmed that Latter-day Saint family units headed by male household heads prepared themselves to work the land, generate self-sufficient communities, and install civilization. A short phrase running along the bottom edge of the *Pioneering* plaque—"No Toil Nor Labor Fear"—underscores this message. While this and other Fairbanks pieces spoke to Latter-day Saint audiences, they also had a calculable impact on US society more generally. During his "remarkably long and productive career," Cynthia Culver Prescott explains, he catapulted "idealized images of [nineteenth-century] white settler families . . . into a national American family ideal."[124]

The piece Fairbanks created to memorialize Utah's mulberry trees, silkworms, and women workers for the DUP, on the other hand, drew different boundaries around gender. The rectangular cement sculpture (see figure 9) is located next to an in-use Latter-day Saint meetinghouse constructed in the 1930s. It is across the street from 1784 Herbert Avenue, what used to be D. Eugene Livingston's property. Fairbanks's art features local resident, DUP member, and weaver Margaret Cullen Geddes Eccles. She is depicted using a loom to work silk thread into fabric. From the imagery alone, the viewer cannot discern the loom's precise location or the weaver's marital or familial status. She could be at home preparing cloth for her and/or her family. She could be in a factory earning wages. Either way, this rendering departed from how Fairbanks typically cast women of the pioneer generation, likely because of the goals DUP members had for the monument. The depicted weaver is not attached to her children or leaning on a male household head. Instead, she is alone, mobilizing her weaving skills to produce a valuable fabric and reduce her dependence on imported silks.

While the independent weaver is the centerpiece of this Fairbanks monument, the raw materials of silk production also feature prominently. Eight moths with their wings outstretched create a border beneath the worker and her loom. Two lively silkworms—one in each of the structure's bottom corners—bend upward, as if they plan to climb up the marker's edges. Delicate *M. alba* trunks, branches, and leaves frame Eccles's weaving.[125] These elements recall the pioneer values of hardy industriousness and self-sufficiency. They also point to the silk project's environmental impacts. While not many mulberry trees still lived in the Yalecrest community, the ghost trees represented in concrete confirm the statement that Latter-day Saint settlers made this region "blossom as a rose." In this rendering, women's work receives the credit for economic independence and landscape improvement.

Much like other mulberry tree mementos, the Fairbanks piece narrates local silk as a triumphant success story. Some elements of this storytelling recall people's actual experiences in the nineteenth century. By depicting Eccles at a loom but not clarifying her precise location, for example, the image captures the public/private duality of silk production. Latter-day Saint women acted on behalf of homemade silk in their homes but also in factories, community celebrations, and other public spaces. In addition, the monument acknowledges Schettler's relative success with mulberry trees. The inscription on the bronze plaque affixed to the bottom of the monument reads, "In 1867 Paul A. Schettler, an ardent supporter of the silk industry in Utah, acquired this land and planted five acres in mulberry trees, the leaves of which were used to feed silk worms. He built two cocooneries near this location. Elizabeth Von Bergen (Beck), a Swiss weaver, came from France to operate the looms installed by Schettler. Several types of looms were used." Schettler did establish himself as an authority on silkworm raising and a reliable source for mulberry trees in the later decades of the nineteenth century. But the monument also engages in a major historical manipulation. Newspaper coverage from the monument's official unveiling on July 13, 1941, clarified that Margaret Cullen Geddes Eccles "is honored as the predominating figure on the monument."

The article identified her as a DUP member and "the first weaver of brocaded silk in Utah."[126] While Eccles's body is on the monument, her name is not. Elizabeth Von Bergen's is instead.

Polygamy may be to blame. As mentioned earlier in this essay, Margaret Cullen gained employment at the Salt Lake City silk factory in the 1880s. Scholars have described this decade as the low point of the relationship between the Church of Jesus Christ of Latter-day Saints and the US federal government. In this period, Congress embarked on an ambitious campaign to criminalize plural marriage, disenfranchise believing Latter-day Saints, and strike at the economic influence of the church. Federal legislation made it much easier to send polygamous husbands to prison for "cohabitation," or living with more than one woman.[127] But Margaret Cullen decided to become a plural wife to William S. Geddes anyway.[128] William died in 1891, the year after church president and prophet Wilford Woodruff officially withdrew the Mormon Church's support of plural marriage. Even so, Margaret's experience with polygamy continued. She became wealthy industrialist David Eccles's third plural wife in 1898 and gave birth to their son, Albert, the following year. But mother and child used "Geddes" as their last name, and Margaret lied publicly about her marriage to David. When he suddenly passed away from a heart attack in 1912, however, their relationship became public. Margaret asserted her and Albert's claims to their portion of the Eccles estate. They received no sympathy from the "legitimate" family. A well-publicized lawsuit settled the matter. The court awarded Margaret and Albert $150,000.[129] The family may have directed some of this money toward the purchase of a home in Salt Lake City's Yalecrest neighborhood in the 1910s.

Margaret Cullen Geddes Eccles's role in the silk industry earned her respect from the local community as well as a place on the DUP monument. She was also present on the day that her DUP colleagues attached a bronze plaque to D. Eugene Livingston's still-living mulberry tree.[130] But explicitly naming her in the Yalecrest monument's inscription may have been a step too far. The Latter-day Saint history with polygamy had long posed a threat to the church's effort to embody mainstream American ideals and institutions. By the middle decades of the twentieth century, Latter-day Saints had spent decades trying to leave behind that controversial aspect of their past and cast themselves as Christian, monogamous, patriotic American citizens instead. This quest for realignment could explain Eccles's partial erasure.[131] Her well-known participation in plural marriage may have been enough to keep her name off the monument.

In the same spirit as the other scholarship in this volume, this essay makes the case that it is worth paying attention to trees. Real and imagined trees and treescapes have played a central role in history narration, memory construction, identity formation, and preservation. An exploration of Utah-based mulberry trees illustrates that Mormon women have formed deep attachments to the nineteenth-century silk industry and dramatically expanded the historical significance of a relatively unsuccessful experiment.

These trees also offer a story about the shifting gender dynamics of a religious community.[132] As other scholars have explained, the increasingly global membership of the Church of Jesus Christ of Latter-day Saints has long depended on recollections of nineteenth-century settlers to balance external public relations with internal solidarities. Mormon pioneer memory permits members to reassert the authority of church prophets, appreciate the material sacrifices of early church members, and recommit to their spiritual traditions. These activities have simultaneously remodeled Latter-day Saints into a palatable shape for non-Mormon audiences.[133] While symbolic and actual mulberry trees exist within this framework, they also had something unique to offer to women experiencing a decline in their individual autonomy and organizational influence. With their twentieth-century commemorative activities, women Latter-day Saints established a direct link between mulberry trees, silk producers, and the beauty, order, and productivity of the Great Basin region. These narrations offered a politicized reminder about the value of women's work to westward expansion and environmental change.

Mulberry tree mementos needed to obscure certain historical realities to function this way. Exhibits, parade floats, and monuments papered over the role of polygamy in Mormon communities and the longtime presence of Native societies in the Salt Lake Valley. They also left out any challenges Utah-based cultivators had with mulberry trees and local silk's demise by the early twentieth century. But, as we have seen, a tree can have tremendous value without being deeply rooted in actual fact, truth, or authenticity.

PART TWO

Trees as Symbols and Interpreted Objects

FIGURE 11. A man in a driving cap stands before Washington's cherry tree at Ferry Farm in about 1917. Photograph courtesy of the George Washington Foundation, Fredericksburg, Virginia.

Chapter Seven

George Washington's Cherry Tree

FERRY FARM'S *PRUNUS SEROTINA* AND HISTORICAL PLACEMAKING

Philip Levy, University of South Florida

In figure 11, a suited man in a crisp white shirt, a bow tie, and a big floppy driver's cap stands with his hands respectfully folded behind his back. We viewers cannot see it at this angle, but there is a large book stuffed in his jacket's left pocket. Behind the man is the two-and-a-half-story Corson family home, built sometime in the 1870s but moved a few dozen yards in the 1910s from its original site to where it sits in the photo. The windows are all shuttered closed, and simple flat gingerbread trim adorns the roof edges. A lightning rod sits at the peak. To the left in the photo is the board-and-batten siding of the icehouse, which farm owner J. B. Colbert put there in 1903. One of his work sheds also sits right next to that. The wood all looks tidy but unpainted. A lattice fence cuts across the view from the left side of the photograph, separating the man in the cap from the Corson house. That fence forms a T with another rougher one made of wire and sharpened logs stuck in the ground so that their points look rather menacing. This is a workmanlike farmscape—efficient but not elegant.

The fences enclose the man in the driving cap in a small yard that has little in it except a few spindly saplings arranged in a row. The man stares neither at the plain buildings that frame him nor at the saplings; rather, he looks into the distance out over the wire fence and out of the frame to the Rappahannock River and, beyond that, the city of Fredericksburg, Virginia. The man's look is serious, considered, and respectful. The photographer is capturing a significant moment.

The most curious thing, though, is that for all the formality of the man's stand-to-attention posture, he is not at the center of the image—he is not even the subject. Instead, the focus of the image is a tall, tapering tree. At least sixteen heavy branches reach out and up from its trunk before it ends in a split V. It would be graceful, but a large offshoot branch awkwardly reaches back toward J. B.'s icehouse and thwarts the symmetry. It does not seem to fit, and it is almost as if it were the result of some accident—an injury in the tree's past that caused errant growth in an otherwise perfect form. The year is 1917, and the respectful man is an unnamed visitor to Ferry Farm, the childhood home of George Washington. The real sitter in this portrait was the tree itself because, as the man would have told you, this was the cherry tree that young George attacked with a new hatchet just under two centuries earlier, which had survived lo these nearly two hundred years. Or perhaps it was a descendant of the original—either would be fine. What was certain was that somehow Washington, the cherry tree, and Americanism converged at this spot.

This chapter recounts the story of that specific tree, the one that stood from about 1890 to about 1933 on a prominent part of the farm where Washington spent his childhood. What follows centers on the tree to show how its specific genetic traits segued with the needs and desires of storytellers to create a distinct form of historical-site meaning not possible with other categories of entities, living or otherwise. The tree was not what its promoters claimed—that statement will not come as a surprise. But it nevertheless played an important and overlooked role in Ferry Farm's twentieth-century commemorators' attempts to turn the farm into a preserved historical site. In that way, the story of this tree sits right at the juncture of what is usually called the natural and the cultural, and in this case, its innate traits helped drive the historical narratives that encrusted it.[1] Historians have been slow to put trees at the center of their analyses and make them active agents in unfolding pasts. Forests and wildernesses have long been part of historical narratives, but making them participants and not simply concepts has proven difficult until fairly recently. Eric Rutkow and Stephen Pyne have made forests primary agents in their histories. Sonja Dümpelmann's study of street trees, as well as works by Jill Jonnes and Ellen Stroud, explored the relationships between cities and forests to bring trees into what were usually treated as human-only stories and places. Jared Farmer and Thomas J. Campanella have shown how trees have worked to define American regions in writing that rethinks the forest while engaging with the nature of individual trees.[2] The popularity of books like Richard Powers's *The Overstory* and Peter Wohlleben's *The Hidden Life of Trees* offers current commercial proof that the cultural and emotional significance of trees, which scholars have discussed, is alive and well.[3] The special place people give to trees makes them uniquely important in the creation of historical and public history sites.

Making Ferry Farm a preserved historical place, though, was not an easy task.[4] From the time of the man in the driving cap's visit, at a rate of almost one a decade, a succession of failed preservation efforts have centered on a vision of Washington informed heavily by the writings of Mason Locke "Parson" Weems. The cherry tree—the most famous of Weems's inventions—became an imagined living artifact and a rallying point for these failed efforts.[5] But all this enthusiasm came together when Weems and his tales could not have been more out of favor in the eyes of the mainstream historical establishment. That meant that a preservation project organized around Weems's most famous and most derided anecdote was destined to fail from the start. Yet visitors like the man in the driving cap, and others whom we will meet, all understood the tree to have been a unique link to the nation's past. For them, Weems was far from "debunked" or irrelevant; in fact, the tree proved their point for them.[6] All these visitors shared a version of what Jared Farmer calls "arbornationalism," rooted in the conviction that *the* cherry tree, whatever that meant, was vital to Ferry Farm, to the nation, and to themselves—a view that even the tree's death did not end.[7] The cherry tree was hardly unique in being both real and fake. Americans were adept at creating this specific type of arboreal-historical connection.[8] This tree's excellent documentation provides a rare opportunity to see how a single tree contributed to a historical site's complicated preservation story.

The genetic qualities of this tree's specific subgenus of the family *Prunus cerasus* are crucial to the role it played in historical placemaking. The attributes the tree carried in its DNA allowed it to take on projected meanings in ways otherwise unavailable to other trees. It was not an accident that this single tree became *the* cherry tree, and had it been another variant of *cerasus*, it might not have. Other trees came and went on the land, but no other one was so important in creating historical meaning. In this way, this tree's innate physical characteristics worked with its advocates to create a set of meanings that rooted the tree-ness of trees in the stories enthusiasts told.[9]

The man in the driving cap was not the only one to pose before Ferry Farm's cherry tree. In a second photo from two decades after his visit, a matronly middle-aged woman in a springtime dress and white shoes stands before a shrubby blossom-filled cherry tree only slightly taller than she is (see figure 12). Script on the photo's edge tells us that her name was "Miss Mollie" Latham. In the photo, her right hand clasps one of the tree's small limbs. Her hand tells us that seeing was not enough; another form of physical connection was needed to fully experience the tree and its value.[10] Miss Mollie's chin is up, and she has a serious look on her face—there is an unmistakable pride in her air. As it was for the man in the cap, this is a significant moment.

Behind Miss Mollie is, again, the same Corson house, with its plain trim still in place and its shutters still closed. The board-and-batten of J. B.'s icehouse, though, has sprung free of its nails at the bottom, thanks to decades of soaking, drying, curving, and twisting of the unpainted wood. The stones of the icehouse pit show on the ground as well. Some of those stones had been part of the Washington family home that once stood only a few yards away. For all his digging, reusing of stones, and moving of buildings, though, J. B. never really knew where that lost home was, even though he made its memory the most valuable commodity on his farm.

By the time of Miss Mollie's photograph, J. B. himself had been dead for four years. He spent his last years in a herculean attempt to cash in on the fact that he was farming the site of George Washington's childhood home. There were no aboveground remnants of the eighteenth-century homestead. But there were stories. There was an 1870s wooden farm office the Corsons had built, which J. B. would erroneously tell visitors had been standing in Washington's day. For all we know, he believed that lie—plenty of others sure did. And there was the cherry tree, the best Washington childhood story of them all. J. B. worked up a deal to sell his farm, which he had craftily renamed the George Washington Farm, to a party of patriotic preservationists. The price of $130,000 was well over five times what it was worth as 470 acres of farmland.[11] He also secured a lifetime tenancy for himself and his wife. The buyers wanted the farm in time for the 1932 bicentennial of the first president's birth. The crash of 1929 shut down their fundraising but not before Colbert had

FIGURE 12. Miss Mollie stands with one of the newly planted cherry trees in 1937. Behind her are the 1890s Corson house and the bent batons of J. B. Colbert's 1903 icehouse. To her left is the decaying stump of Washington's cherry tree. Photograph courtesy of the George Washington Foundation, Fredericksburg, Virginia.

garnered over $80,000 of the asking price. The Depression, though, eventually scuttled the deal and made a mess of the titles and deeds.[12] J. B.'s 1933 death left the ownership of his farm unclear and regular maintenance deferred. By the time Miss Mollie made her pilgrimage to the site of Washington's childhood, its fake Washington building and its famous tree were a bit shopworn. In the past, J. B. would walk visitors over the land—for a small fee, they could even spend a night on the site. That was why he had moved the old Corson house closer to the cherry tree. It was better for business—more enticing to patriotic visitors. But when Miss Mollie and her friends (someone had to have taken the photo) came, it was J. B.'s daughter, May Belle, who played hostess and recounted the lore of the "George Washington Farm," while her dogs—including one German shepherd named Lady Martha—would run around, excited by the visitors.

To the right of Miss Mollie's photo—significantly, now no longer in the center of the frame—is the darkened trunk of the 1917 cherry tree, its bark peeling and its wood splintering. Even as the tree died, its role as conveyor of Weemsian truth transferred to the vibrant blossom-laden young boughs of the new trees planted in the shadow of the old one. Historical significance had a unique transitive quality when trees were involved. Since the same soil produced the same sort of tree under the same sun, one was as good as another—each was a suitable vehicle to recall the boy with the hatchet and the American values the tale shared. In the photo of Miss Mollie, the tree to her left was dead, but the new sapling in her own aging hand showed the fullness of youth. The circle of life was joined with Miss Mollie standing in the middle of Weems's Washington-infused space (see figure 12).

By the time of Miss Mollie's visit, self-professed serious historians had long ago turned their backs on Weems. The story of the cherry tree, and the story of a young George Washington who tested out a new hatchet on its bark and then confessed his misdeed when his father confronted him, was the best-known and most derided tale the parson had spun. A justifiably unshakable consensus still sees the tree and its story as being the invention of Weems sometime just before 1809 and before the publishing of the fifth edition of his popular *Life of Washington*.[13] For most of the next one hundred years, he was either treated with humor or taken seriously. At the end of the nineteenth century, though, a newly professionalizing historical field vocally rejected Weems and his fables in favor of a new sense of mission, an emerging idea of objectivity, and current science-inspired uses of evidence.[14] Henry Cabot Lodge was one of the most prominent of the new anti-Weemsians when, in 1889, he spoke for his fellows in stating that "until Weems is weighed and disposed of, we cannot even begin an attempt to get at the real Washington."[15] Readers of the early twentieth-century Washington biographies were encouraged to see the old fiddle-playing bookselling parson as a purveyor of "fairy stories" of "dubious dependability" that were a "slush of plagiarism and piety."[16] Iowa painter Grant Wood's 1939 canvas *The Cherry Tree Fable* effectively sums up the bemused way Americans had relegated the tale to the colorful folklore file by featuring a young George man-child hiding his offending hatchet.[17]

But even if it was a "brazen piece of fiction," the cherry tree has remained, arguably, the most famous tree in American history—or at least the subject of the most famous American tree story.[18] Scholars have treated it as a unique gem of American literature and have seen Weems's *Life of Washington*—hate it or love it—as representing an important moment in the development of American biography infused with a message of unity for a new nation with an uncertain future.[19] The bundle of Weems's meanings, though, has landed with the loudest thud on the specific Virginia landscape where this story was imagined to have taken place, and each retelling of the tale was also a recounting of the farm as at least a bit player. Likewise, each rendering in art (there have been many) features some reference to the land and even to the Washington home itself.

Weems's cherry tree was a constant feature of all this cultural production, so its stand-in maintained pride of place as a living icon and embodiment of an entire body of lore and a worldview. Each of the failed efforts centered on Weems's version of Washington's "boyhood" and the values that project backers saw these tales as representing. All this took place against a backdrop of a version of what John Bodnar influentially calls "official memory," which, by the time of the man in the driving cap's visit to Ferry Farm, had turned solidly anti-Weems.[20] This left an older, but nevertheless deeply rooted, popular embrace of the cherry tree subject to highbrow ridicule. That in turn distanced true believers from the sorts of funding streams and powerful allies that each successive group of failed Ferry Farm commemorators discovered, to their cost, were vital to achieving their dream of saving Washington's home. The federal government's George Washington Bicentennial Commission entirely bypassed the farm and its environs in its plans for a national celebration in 1932. This left local residents angered that "the city where George Washington spent his boyhood" and "where originated the legends of the cherry tree" had no seat at the event's planning table.[21] That oversight was no accident. At the same time, the Daughters of the American Revolution largely ignored Ferry Farm's attempted preservation. When their magazine did share news of Fredericksburg's historical trees, the focus was on a horse chestnut Washington was said to have planted near his mother's home.[22] Another anti-Weemsian dismissed the Ferry Farm backers' efforts as resting on little more than "popular belief" or "so-called tradition" and "cherry tree stories."[23]

Cherry tree fans did not go softly, though. Some cast themselves as protectors of tradition and viewed embracing the new anti-Weemsian consensus not as it saw itself—the triumph of fact over folklore—but rather as a matter of choice. A bit of 1909 doggerel by Lydia Chatton spoke for many in saying, "Above iconoclastic views; That little hatchet gleams!; 'I cannot tell a lie,'; I choose The Washington of Weems."[24] Others sought a middle ground that would acknowledge the core anti-Weemsian claims of fabrication while still retaining the legitimacy of their own belief. Progressive Era travel and science fiction writer George Allan England summed up this view when he claimed that while "some critics" might condemn the tree as a fiction, "time and popular belief have crystalized it into solid reality."[25] England accompanied that assertion with his own photo of the tree circa 1928—a view that looks almost identical to the 1917 image but without the man in the driving cap. His caption heralded the tree as being the "scion of George Washington's immortal cherry tree."[26] Still others were simply indignant at the threat to what they saw as a valuable national possession. A *Washington Post* letter writer declared himself "a firm believer" that young George's "chopping the cherry tree" was fact and had not been "debunked." His conviction came from his having "studied" the story "most thoroughly" and finding "no occasion to raise a doubt" about its veracity.[27] Theologian and Abraham Lincoln biographer W. E. Barton claimed that Lodge and his anti-Weemsian ilk were guilty of "bad sportsmanship" and were "lacking in the historical spirit."[28] Barton conceded that "of course" Weems "dressed it up and gave it what he thought a proper literary form," but he wondered, "What is there about the story apart from its verbiage, that suggests a lie?"[29] To cap his point, he turned to verse: "Though they've beaten and flayed you, by the living Lord that made you, you're a better man than they are, Parson Weems."[30]

The passion came from different places. Barton clearly was making a not-so-hidden defense of the Bible and dressing the old parson up as a Christ figure. Others were simply using faith in the old story as an anchor amid the rapid changes of the first few decades of the twentieth century—a concern that itself was a motivator for a host of colonial-revival impulses and preservation efforts, such as Colonial Williamsburg and Henry Ford's Greenfield Village.[31] Personal identity investments were also always running strong just underneath the surface, as people resented having elites, eggheads, and other "debunkers" challenge stories fans had cherished since childhood. The cherry tree as an idea thus was at once a symbol of a chosen worldview and a synecdoche for a bundle of American values. As an actual tree, whether seen as the original or one of its descendants, it made physical a set of values—including ancestry, the power of belief to make things real, and an unironic assertion of an ironic view of truth—and bound it all with a Weems-inflected George Washington imprimatur.

Ferry Farm's actual cherry trees became the vehicles of a special kind of historical meaning—a transmissible essence at once perishable and immortal and denied other landscape components.[32] What was never in doubt, though, was the fact of the story. The leaders of Ferry Farm's first failed attempt at preservation in the 1920s were clear and emphatic about where they stood on the Weems question. Their promotional literature decried "modern historians of a certain iconoclastic school" who "attack the veracity" of the cherry tree story, and it argued, rather remarkably, that "the burden of proof rests on those who would" deny the story "and not on its defenders."[33] Their certainty that Ferry Farm was "the place where occurred the incident of the cherry tree" drove their preservation efforts.[34] Having an actual tree made the stories physical and tangible, and the tree itself aided their project.

Weems described his tree as being a "beautiful young English cherry-tree," a term perhaps referring to origin but not genus.[35] The 1917 tree, though, was of a distinct subgenus of the family *Prunus cerasus*. It was of a type uniquely tall—far taller than the productive fruit trees that commonly grace most orchards or the ornamental ones favored in parks and gardens. The specific tree in figure 11 was about thirty inches in diameter at the base of its trunk and stood a bit taller than the two-and-a-half-story Corson house. It probably reached close to forty feet, although others of the same kind could grow to twice that height. It was an American black cherry (*Prunus serotina*), a deciduous fruit-bearing tree that is native to North America and can be found all over the eastern side of the continent.[36] The tree is not the preferred one for fruit growers but is not without its uses and charms. Its bark is often made into cherry-flavored cough syrup, while its long, gradually tapering trunk is ideal for timber. Much of the cherry wood used for furniture or fine carpentry comes from tall black cherries, which produce long planks with even grain. Its fruit, though, is bitter, containing—as does the bark—a nice dose of cyanide and amygdalin, which can be toxic in quantity.[37] To eat its cherries, one has to cook them for preserves, mull them in wine, or soak them in hard liquor.[38] Spring is when the black cherry shines. Its branches fill with white blooms, each with a little yellow core. Right as other deciduous trees are filling out their green leaves, the black cherry stands out with a coat of shimmering white. In the fall, it steals attention once more, this time by turning, top to bottom, into a stand of fiery red and orange. Who cares if the fruit is vaguely poisonous? The tree is a beauty.

As figure 11 shows, the black cherry held pride of place at Ferry Farm in 1917. It stood alone right at the point where the farm's flat plateau of land began a sharp thirty-foot drop down to the river's floodplain. A cluster of larger hardwoods stood farther back on the plateau and a bit west, where they shaded J. B. Colbert's home. But alone in its little fenced-in yard, the black cherry was clearly singled out as something special.

When Washington described this landscape in 1771, he noted the site's "clear and distinct view of almost every house" in Fredericksburg.[39] Nearly a century and a half later, things had not changed all that much. A railroad bridge blocked the view somewhat, but Ferry Farm and the small city opposite were still on each other's doorsteps. All this made the lone black cherry not just an on-site Washington icon but one that was visible at a distance as well. At its full height, it was like a flagpole or a ship's prow, easily seen and singled out from the other side of the river. Railroad passengers traveling between Washington, DC, and Richmond had a view, too, as they crossed the Rappahannock—at least, those with seats on the east side of the train did. Most importantly, as the black cherry cycled through its dramatic seasonal colors, it would have been an unmistakable beacon, shifting from snowy white (a shade so full of meaning in the Jim Crow South) to its autumnal flaming red and orange. While George Claude's first neon signs were still a Parisian novelty, Ferry Farm's cherry tree was boldly flashing a Weemsian message for all who cared to decode it.

Black cherry trees generally live for between sixty and one hundred years, although some examples have survived over two centuries.[40] It was therefore not beyond possibility for this black cherry to have been alive during Washington's childhood a century and a half earlier. Indeed, in photos, the tree certainly looked aged. But *serotinas* grow very quickly—faster than the other deciduous trees with whom they usually share terrain.[41] A mature specimen can add over two and a half feet each growing season, and by the time the tree has lived ten years, it will already have a dark, scaly, cracked bark.[42] That fast rate of growth is a significant boon for commercial growers, but it also can be quite deceptive. A fairly young tree can have an air of venerability despite its few years, and the rough, dark bark of a mature *serotina* can cause the casual viewer to wildly overestimate its age—especially if that viewer had no real knowledge of the land's history and use. In other words, the perception of an individual *serotina*'s historicity can be simply an effect of its innate traits and not the life story viewers might hang on it. The tree's genetic makeup conspired with Weemsian desire to make this particular specimen an object of interest. For embattled turn-of-the-century Weems fans seeking some sort of confirmation of their beliefs, a tall *serotina*, like the 1917 black cherry, was a gift.

There is no documentation to show exactly when this tree was planted or just who set it in the ground. But a sequence of landscape art and photographs gives us a timeline of changes on the land.[43] Artist John Gadsby Chapman painted Ferry Farm in 1833, just as the last remnants of the Washington home were crumbling away. His painting made clear that no trees of any kind were on the site then—anything anyone saw after 1833 was planted after that date and offered no connection to the Washingtons.

Civil War sketch artist Alfred Waud visited the site in the winter of 1862, when the Rappahannock's north bank was the staging point for the Civil War Battle of Fredericksburg. Waud's drawing of the Union lines also included the only rendering of Ferry Farm in its prewar incarnation—a set of buildings and a cupola-adorned barn, all built after 1833. His drawing also showed the farm lane that led to the buildings, and standing at the end of that path was a lone tree roughly where the 1917 black cherry stood. Waud was not concerned to make clear what kind of tree it might be, but its size and shape are consistent with larger cherry trees. There certainly were cherries on the land, because Northern Civil War soldiers wrote about them in their letters home. In the summer of 1962, soldiers encamped here sent home cherry pits they had collected or made "all sorts of crosses, pipes, rings, etc., that can be sent away by mail," carved from wood from "the original tree of the famous hatchet story."[44] Just what tree that was, though, is lost to time. Abraham Lincoln himself—a self-professed fan of Weems's "small book"—visited the site when he came to Fredericksburg that summer.[45] Even in wartime, the "'ol' plantation' where Gen. Washington spent the early days of his life" had visitor appeal for Americans who knew the place only through Weems's work.[46]

The commanding view Washington had extolled took on new significance after the winter battle that made Fredericksburg a household word all across the land. Commercial photographers produced several views of the vista once the guns were silent. Although the city in the background was the photographers' principal subject, the images also documented Ferry Farm's changes during and after the war. In the winter of 1863, photographer James Gibson made a glass-plate image that was a photographic version of what Waud had drawn the year before.[47] But between the time of the sketch and the photograph, all the farm buildings that Waud showed had been taken down by soldiers making their own shelters from any material on hand. All that was left was a cluster of small fruit trees surrounding cellar holes where the buildings had once stood. There also were larger deciduous trees that Waud had shown. Two flanked the farm lane that led to the farm site, a third stood near where the buildings were, and a fourth stood alone at the end of that path.[48] Gibson's photograph showed the four trees to be essentially identical and all the same height.[49] Their matched heights and placement along the lane tells of an intentional simultaneous planting. All four also could easily have been cherry trees. Their trunks were branchless for about ten or twelve feet and then bifurcated to become an upward-reaching canopy—patterns consistent with larger cherry trees. Any of these many trees could have been the cherry trees that beguiled the soldiers and showed an early link between visitation and Weems's take on Ferry Farm's trees.

In 1864, Timothy O'Sullivan came to Stafford Heights to produce his own view of Fredericksburg. By then, the city was filled with Union wounded, but very few of its prewar inhabitants remained. Though Gibson's 1863 view of the demolished farm was sad, O'Sullivan's was even grimmer. By 1864, the effects of years of war, two battles, and long encampments had denuded the land. Not only were the buildings gone, but even trees had been cut down.[50] Only the stumps of the two lane-flankers were left aboveground. Even the cellar holes had been filled in, and there was almost nothing to show that this had been a crowded and shaded home lot.

By 1880, new folks were coming into the Fredericksburg area, drawn by cheap land and a rebuilt road and rail network. The Corson family moved down from Pennsylvania, bought the ruined farm, and started anew. They built a balloon-framed home on the site, several cattle barns, and the farm office that would later be misidentified as a Washington building. The Corsons had no firsthand experience with what the war had done to the farm and the area. But they knew the site's Washington history and made much of it. An 1885 *Frank Leslie's Popular Monthly* Fredericksburg travelogue revealed that the Corsons had intentionally built their home "immediately on the stone foundations of the Washington homestead" and that they were "quite proud of the memory of the original tenant."[51] The reporter wrote that Washington "pictures adorn the interior of the cottage" and then went on to retell Weems's original version of the cherry tree story.[52] Significantly, though, there was no mention of the tree still standing on the land—something that the Corsons surely would have highlighted. The new residents were then reviving the farm's treescape, but there was as yet nothing that invoked the cherry tree as a living object. The only photograph of the Corson farm circa 1880 shows a line of about a dozen bare trees along the farm lane, but at that time, there was nothing yet visible where the black cherry would stand.

An 1888 panoramic photograph of downtown Fredericksburg, taken from a local church spire, also showed the Corsons' Ferry Farm in the distance.[53] The large white house is unmistakable in the image, but there did not appear to be any trees of noticeable size on the land by then. It had to have been the Corsons who planted the black cherry in its place of prominence, probably as a living addition to their home filled with Washington pictures. All this would mean that our tree had to have been planted—or perhaps may have been a mere sapling—around 1890. That would make it only twenty-seven years old when the man in the driver's cap visited.

J. B. Colbert bought the farm in 1903. Like the Corsons, he was not originally from Fredericksburg but instead was from Warrenton, about forty miles northwest of town. Also like the Corsons, he did not bring to the farm all that much knowledge of the landscape and its trees before his time—he was fertile ground for any possibly fabulous yarns locals cared to spin for him. He was more than capable of making up a few tales of his own as well. He was the one who started telling visitors that the Corson farm office was a Washington family survival. This was a whole-cloth fabrication but one that caught on, and what became known as the "George Washington Surveying Office" spent a few decades as a sort of local attraction and object of Weemsian devotion.[54] The facts were on hand, though, for anyone able to tell nineteenth-century circular-sawed lumber from eighteenth-century pit-sawed wood.

When Historic American Building Survey architects examined the office in 1937, they dismissed the tale as local "tradition" based only on "hearsay."[55] Colbert built his new farmhouse on the site of the old Corson one (after moving it nearer the black cherry). He incorporated the cellar stones that the Corsons had found into his own cellar. He called the little patch of eighteenth-century wall set in newly poured concrete a piece of the Washington home. He was partially right, at least—archaeological study showed these stones to have been part of a Washington-era kitchen.

But it seems a bit much to have imagined that J. B. both planted the black cherry himself *and* passed it off as the original from Weems's story. It was possible (he was pretty wily) but a stretch. Given a growth rate of between twenty-four and thirty-six inches per year, the tree could have been already as high as thirty feet when Colbert bought the farm. Its mature, cracked, dark bark would have made it seem far older than its actual age. The fantasy of its age depended on people not really knowing trees very well. Colbert owned the farm, but most of his life was spent selling dry goods, producing ice, taverning, and buying and selling buildings in town—he was hardly a man of the land. He might have known little or nothing about trees and simply fallen for the allure of the tale (and its financial possibilities). Likewise, the small parade of visitors had to be either ignorant of dendrology or untroubled by anti-Weemsian vision of fact, or both.[56] But that was where the black cherry's special allure resided. It did not need to be factual in the literal sense—it did not need to be *the* tree to be *the* tree in people's hearts. It thrived on plausibility. It *could have* been the tree, or it could have been a descendant, and if neither was true, it at least was growing on the same farm and therefore, in some way, a link to the stories of the little boy with the hatchet.

By 1933, though—the year after the Washington birth bicentennial—the black cherry was dead. A photograph of the Colbert farm from directly opposite on the Fredericksburg side of the river shows it to have been cut down, leaving a trunk of about eight feet in height. This means that the black cherry lived for only about forty years—that is short for most trees but especially so for a genus with examples having lifespans nearly five times that long. There is no way to know for sure why it died young. One 1936 news story claimed that a tree of the same "variety" as the one Weems described had died at Ferry Farm, "having blown down a year ago."[57] The reporter was wrong on most of the details, though storm damage is as likely a killer of the black cherry as is anything else. But there are other possibilities.

The 1930s saw a devastating wave of "little cherry tree disease," which wiped out most of the trees in British Columbia, Canada, but the virus did not make it far east.[58] But even without an epidemic, *serotinas* are susceptible to a host of ailments that could have ended the black cherry's life prematurely. It is also possible that the tree was simply loved to death. Historical tourists were famous for feeling free to take what they wanted from the sites they visited, and trees' seeming ability to heal made them particular targets for patriotic vandalism. The trees at Washington's Mount Vernon, for example, suffered terribly from an early nineteenth-century craze for stealing low-hanging limbs and turning them into souvenir walking sticks.[59] A *serotina*'s cracked bark might have proven just too tempting to pull off, and the unknown number of visitors over the years could have simply, bit by bit, made the tree no longer viable.

Whatever the reason, Colbert had the tree cut back so that it was less a tree than a standing column of wood. Once the black cherry was no longer a living memorial, the process of its own memorialization took off. On Washington's birthday (the recurring date for such events) in 1935, Colbert's widow welcomed a party of midlevel dignitaries, including a former mayor of Fredericksburg, the president of the Virginia Bar Association, and a former US Senate chaplain to offer a benediction for the placing of a granite block and brass marker at the foot of the dead black cherry. Notably, the marker did not face the land—the place from where visitors would approach. Rather, the plaque faced the river so that tiny letters close to the ground could send its message out to the world. The awkward wording of the plaque itself captured the underdog homespun quality of this easily derided movement of Weemsian enshrinement. It proclaimed,

Washington's Cherry Tree

Beside this stone stood the cherry
tree which according to tradition
George Washington when a boy
Cut down the prize cherry tree
Was placed by the
Fredericksburg Chamber of Commerce

February 22, 1935

The text makes an interesting contrast to other plaques that marked storied trees. "Hangman trees" in California were sometimes marked with grimly concise signs declaring their past role.[60] A brass sign of the same era marked the Old Pine at New Hampshire's Dartmouth College—a tree that also came and went and came again. The Old Pine's plaque specifically noted that the tree was "replaced in 1912," making it clear that anything visible after that date made no claim to being the original.[61] The black cherry's plaque's twisted prose, though, confused more than it clarified and thus allowed a nuanced reading. It mentioned the cherry tree three times in thirty-three words, phrasing that inadvertently made a distinction between the *serotina* that stood "beside" the stone—the recently living tree whose remains were right there—and Weems's written one "cut down" by the boy, which was an object of literature and secular veneration. Both of these cherry trees collectively became "Washington's Cherry Tree" announced at the top of the text.[62] The plaque merged several ideas and incarnations of trees, thanks to the English language's odd paucity of synonyms for *tree*. It also expertly threaded the veracity's needle by at once claiming the absolute reality of the tree *and* invoking "tradition" in describing its fate. Many a Weemsian, though, did not hear the word *tradition* as an insult—it was part of their mission. The plaque was the perfect example of how invoking the "cherry tree" allowed for whichever meaning the user wanted. Weems would have been proud.

The second part of memorialization was replacement, a practice that even further blurred the lines between Ferry Farm's physical and rhetorical trees. Photographs make clear that other young *Prunus cerasuses* were being planted next to the black cherry's tall stump as early as 1933. The presence of saplings near the aging stump added weight to the idea that one or all were descendants of Weems's original. By 1933, though, the nation was already two decades into a Japanese cherry tree craze that filled Washington, DC, with lovely annual blooms.[63] But planting *cerasuses* had a special resonance at Ferry Farm. The 1935 ceremony also included a new cherry tree donated by the Traverse City, Michigan, Chamber of Commerce, to be planted "as near as possible to the original spot" where the old one stood.[64] One of these new trees was the one that Miss Mollie Latham posed with a few years later. In 1936, promoters launched a plan to line the road from Fredericksburg to Ferry Farm with "a double row" of cherry trees, two hundred of which were to be "supplied by Ambassador Hirosi Saito of Japan"—a faint echo of the three thousand cherry trees Tokyo's mayor had donated to Washington, DC, in 1912.[65] Half the trees would be Japanese, the other half American. The plan never got too far. Planters only set a few *cerasuses* along the road, and these survived at least until the road was widened a few years later.[66] The trees, though, showed that contemporary elites found the cherry tree as symbol far more acceptable than a single black cherry said to be *the* original. From then on, planting a new cherry tree on the site became an almost annual ritual—usually taking place on February 22, in honor of Washington's birth. Cub Scouts, Boy Scouts, civic groups, and a slew of individual enthusiasts put an unknown number of successor trees on the land. No one ever argued that these trees were anything more than a good-natured tribute to Washington and the Weemsian vision of American boyhood. The proliferation of new trees on the farm celebrated the spirit of the original story, but their sheer number and the publicity surrounding each February's new crop made it impossible for any single one to ever gather the lore of being *the* cherry tree.

Amid an ever-increasing number of new *cerasuses* of many varieties, the old black cherry retained a special place, even in death. In 1940, the farm's confused ownership was resolved when May Belle Colbert won Washington's childhood home at auction. The *Washington Post* ran a picture of May Belle kneeling reverently before the black cherry and its awkwardly worded plaque.[67] Her reverence was quite fitting. That cherry tree had been very kind to the Colbert family, who had netted more than $80,000 from the failed preservation. May Belle paid a mere $25,000 to regain the farm.[68]

Time and weather, though, were not being so kind to the remains of the old black cherry. By 1940, it was suffering the inevitable effects of the environment on untreated wood. It was split and splintered and was slightly leaning away from the plaque that announced its identity. A decade later, it was in even worse condition. By the early 1950s, photographs show that only the addition of tension wires was keeping it from falling over entirely. But all this damage only gave the stump an even more pronounced air of venerability. After all, the sight of the tree in poor condition accorded better with Weems's story of a chopped tree than the living version just a decade earlier.

Oral histories bring the voices of farm residents into the story. One woman who lived at the farm in the 1950s and '60s recalled that visitors most wanted to see "that cherry tree that he [Washington] had cut down" and that they showed less interest in any other part of the site.[69] Visitors also wanted to touch it, she noted, saying, "You had freedom. You could—people could touch the cherry tree." Some, indeed, thought it was the original, but the residents often told visitors that it was a "scion" of the one of Weems's story that somehow "came up from the root of the original tree that Washington hatcheted down as a boy."[70]

Cold War–era freedom to touch the black cherry meant freedom to possess a bit of it as well. Visitors were constantly pulling off little pieces, while the residents—a succession of renter families by then—either gave slivers of the "stump that was there" to friends and family as patriotic keepsakes or, in some cases, sold them as souvenirs. Some of the boys living on the farm turned bits of the tree into extra cash through the sale of splinters, little hatchets, and other trinkets carved from the stump's wood.[71] It was common practice for renters to "hack off fragments" of about "six inches by two inches and sell them for one dollar each."[72] One recipient of one of these wooden lengths was so proud of his icon that he gave it a place of prominence on the mantel in an inn he ran. When the inn later burned down, the fragment of the black cherry was the only thing he ensured was saved as the fire raged.[73]

At some point in the 1950s, the tension wires could no longer keep the shrinking stump in place. Residents took it down and stored it in the work shed that J. B. had built next to his icehouse—the building that was visible in the left foreground of the man in the driving cap's photo. At some point after that, the residents accepted an offer to buy the remains of the black cherry. Just like that, the tree that had been Ferry Farm's focal point, that had flashed a *serotina*'s seasonal glory and had been a moving patriotic link to Washington and the roots of the nation for so many vernacular Weemsian true believers, simply vanished from the land and from the historical record. The cherrywood souvenirs continued to be on sale, though. The enterprising boys simply crossed the road and clandestinely cut down one of the *Prunus cerasuses* that were meant to line the road from Fredericksburg. The resulting log was laid in the shed, and the carvers were back in business. Weems's cherry tree had been English, the black cherry was American, and there is a very good chance that some unsuspecting Ferry Farm tourists ended up with Japanese splinters.

By the 1960s, the black cherry had vanished from the landscape. One 1974 visitor noted, though, that "several new cherry trees" were then "growing there," the result of years of annual planting commemorations.[74] But for the most part, the farm looked to be a forgotten place. Only the plaque remained to mark the spot where the tree stood, and the buildings that had framed the 1917 photograph were gone. People driving by on Route 3 saw only a "thick barrier of evergreens and underbrush" that hid the place from view and a state historical marker that proclaimed the land to be the place of Washington's childhood.[75] That state-sponsored sign did not mention the cherry tree.[76]

Decay was a garment Ferry Farm had frequently worn. When Weems wrote about the farm, he described the home as having a "low and modest front of faded red."[77] When Chapman painted the landscape, he centered on the ruins of the Washington home. Civil War photographers turned their lenses on the gradually disappearing antebellum farmstead. The Corsons boasted about building on the remains of the original Washington home. The cherry tree story itself centered on the death or damage of a living part of that landscape.

The site's actual decay and even the very real threat of commercial development were vital parts of what justified its preservation and motivated decades' worth of citizen groups. But decay also worked to create the air of venerability that undergirded the site's claim to being historical at all. Pride of place in this concern has generally gone to the built environment. The nineteenth-century farm office reimagined as Washington's Surveying Office is only an example of how well-meaning enthusiasts transformed an aging quotidian structure into something special and imbued it with deep historical resonances.[78] Early twentieth-century icehouse foundations followed this same path, as did J. B.'s farmhouse, a 1960s vintage school building, and a set of utility structures built by Stafford County. Buildings, though, stand long enough on the land to enable many eyes to see them and many experts to raise troubling questions about their alleged identity. Even as they rendered the Surveying Office on paper in the 1930s, Historic American Building Survey architects made their disbelief clear.[79] Museum interpreters today make it clear to visitors that nothing they see on the land dates to Washington's time.

But trees are quite different. The expert eye that lands on them is often not that well informed about their many forms and types, and there remains the prevailing tendency to see trees as a thing of nature and thus not subjected to the same analytics and movements as might attend a historic structure. The inherent growth traits of Ferry Farm's black cherry tree allowed it to seem aged enough to be granted a new and imagined past, but its rootedness in the natural world, its relatively short life, and a prevailing skepticism about Weems in general allowed it to escape any serious discussion. It was a symbol for those who wanted one and essentially invisible or irrelevant to those who did not. Weemsian fantasy and the version of patriotism it fostered created a fertile environment for Ferry Farm's *Prunus serotina*, innate traits to enable new tree-based historical meaning.

FIGURE 13. Blair tomb postcard, which includes a man, who is presumably Sam Robinson, looking at the base of the tomb of Mrs. Harrison Blair. The large sycamore now growing atop of it has been the subject of much superstition and storytelling and has been at the intersection of race and interpretation at Jamestown Island in Virginia. The back of the postcard reads, "Blair Tomb, Jamestown Virginia—Showing old Sycamore Tree, which dismembered the tomb of Mrs. Sarah Harrison Blair, wife of Dr. James Blair (Founder of the College of William and Mary)." Published by Walter H. Miller, Williamsburg, Virginia, ca. 1960.

Chapter Eight

Sam Robinson's Sycamore

Mariaelena DiBenigno, William & Mary's Highland

> The mother-in-law didn't get a chance in life to separate her daughter Sarah from Dr. Blair but she did come back and plant the old sycamore to separate her.
>
> —Sam Robinson, "1957 Audio Recording," Archive Williamsburg, YouTube

On a crisp fall day in 1957, England's Queen Elizabeth II and her husband, Prince Philip, visited Jamestown Island, located roughly 160 miles south of Washington, DC, to commemorate the 350th anniversary of the first permanent English colony in North America. In their opening act for the 1957 Jamestown Festival, the royal couple spent a short twenty minutes on the island, attending a short service and receiving gifts. Then, they heard a ghost story popularly known as "The Mother-in-Law Tree." Sam Robinson, a Black man who gave highly detailed tours of Jamestown—then interpreted as the cradle of white civilization in North America—was the storyteller. The ghost story involved a sycamore tree. Under the shade of said tree, Robinson told a tale about gender, agency, and the environment as racial segregation and violence spread across the United States—and white people listened.

Robinson's encounter with the queen shows how stories define historic sites for visitors and why it is important to examine *who* does the storytelling—what sociologist Avery Gordon calls "ghostly matters," or the overlooked components of a story that centers haunting.[1] How and why did Robinson become connected to a spectral sycamore tree in Jamestown's mid-twentieth-century public memory? The immediate answer is that Robinson told a story to and appeared alongside the royal couple in numerous media accounts that introduced both him and the sycamore to international audiences. In the decade following the 1957 visit, before his death in 1965, Robinson and the sycamore appeared together in countless tourist imaginaries. His connection to the tree was primarily visual, preserved via commemorative materials—but how much control did Robinson have over this linkage? Without his explicit reflection on this relationship, it is difficult to recover how Robinson felt about "his" sycamore. However, a more nuanced reading of this connection requires the deployment of historical and literary studies alongside recent scholarship on Black ecologies and ghost tourism. This chapter explores the many histories, institutional and public facing, that haunt one site of US mythmaking. It grows out of the ghost story to explore setting and storyteller before branching out to the broader cultural and historical context. Ultimately, this encounter beneath a tree shows how Samuel Andrew Robinson both reinscribed the commemorative landscape of Jamestown and, paradoxically, unsettled it.[2]

The Story

"The Mother-in-Law Tree" is one of Jamestown Island's most popular ghost stories. In 1957, Jamestown Festival coordinators published the story as a commemorative booklet with Sam Robinson as its author. The booklet opens with a note to Robinson from Queen Elizabeth that thanks him for the "instructive and entertaining account of the 'Mother-in-Law Tree' outside the Jamestown Church."[3] The publication's cover depicts the sycamore tree, with its roots wrapped, viselike, around an aboveground tomb. Other flat tombs rest nearby. The tree is not overtly menacing, with lacy green leaves above uneven green grass, but there is a dark hollow in the tree trunk's center as if it is shouting in outrage. Visitors familiar with the Jamestown landscape might recognize the scene as the graveyard adjacent to the island's small brick church. In regional ghostlore, the imposing sycamore, known as the Mother-in-Law Tree, spectrally separated two lovers after death.[4]

Robinson's narration begins as many ghost stories do: with a broken engagement and an untimely death. Sarah Harrison, of Virginia's Berkeley Plantation, wed the much-older James Blair, "founder and Commissioner of William and Mary College," despite her family's objections.[5] Harrison allegedly ended a previous engagement, and her fiancé died of a broken heart. Her mother, father, and younger sister were also killed in a freak lightning storm en route to prevent the marriage. However, this powerful desire to inhibit Harrison and Blair's marital bliss extended beyond (and into) the grave. As Robinson narrates, after her 1713 death, Harrison was buried outside her family plot on Jamestown Island. Following Blair's 1743 death, husband was reunited with wife in side-by-side tombs.

Robinson's conclusion provides the ghostly denouement: "7 years later that old sycamore there . . . came up between 'em as a little while sapling." It grew up between the couple's side-by-side tombs and pushed Harrison's tomb "up out de groun' above Dr. Blair and push de back of the head end 7 feet from her husban' back over to de right within 6 inches of her [family]." Blair's grave remained solitary and separate from his wife. The tree was referred to as the Mother-in-Law Tree because Harrison's mother "didn' get a chance in life to separate her daughter Sarah from Dr. Blair, but . . . she did come back and plant the old sycamore to separate her." Deep analysis of the story's plotlines is better suited by a follow-up essay. The story requires a close reading, with its hypergendered characterizations and historical referents, but the following examination centralizes the story's narrator and protagonist: Sam Robinson and the sycamore.

For Robinson to be linked to a tree is not without its complexities. For centuries, trees played a violent and traumatic role within African American collective memory. They were the settings of public torture for enslaved persons. They were frequently the sites of extrajudicial lynching. Trees were also harvested for their timber and sap using enslaved labor—an exhausting process.[6] Post-emancipation, white supremacists used tree timbers in cross burnings and other intimidation tactics. This collective memory of trees—often expressed through poetry, literature, song, art, and cinema—represents a deep transgenerational trauma among African Americans that reaches into the present moment.[7] However, as scholars point out, trees were also spaces for gathering, worshipping, resting, and escaping. Treescapes terrorized, but they also provided refuge and sustenance.[8] These oppositional meanings exist simultaneously when examining Robinson's story.[9]

The site of Jamestown, too, is a place of historical trauma. For decades, Jamestown Island's brutal histories of colonization, disease, violence, and abandonment were overlaid with the thick, sanitizing topsoil of the United States' founding mythos. Now, thanks to years of archaeological, architectural, archival, communal, and environmental scholarship, Jamestown's visitors learn about the past, ask questions in the present, and consider destructive futures like the effects of climate change and the James River's ever-present and devastating erosion on the site.[10] Public historians share the island's genealogy of habitation and labor: Indigenous peoples, English settlers, enslaved Africans, indentured servants, imported wives, colonial merchants, agricultural workers, preservationist societies, commemorative committees, trained and untrained archaeologists, tourists, scavengers, caretakers, soldiers, sailors, curators, and tour guides. Despite these interventions, Jamestown remains a fraught space within an imagined American past.[11]

The Jamestown Colony

Briefly, Jamestown as a site of English colonization commences in the early 1600s. Under the protection of the English king James I, the private Virginia Company recruited colonists with the following imperatives: secure permanent settlement, locate material wealth and natural resources, and find safe passage to the Pacific Ocean.[12] The group of men and boys landed at Jamestown Island in May 1607 and moored their ships to strong trees on land.[13] The local Indigenous people, understood by the English as the Powhatan paramount chiefdom, attacked the temporary English camp almost immediately. As a result, the English colonists began the first layer of their built environment using timber from the island. The triangular, palisaded fort—now reconstructed on Jamestown's public history site—protected inhabitants for a time.

Despite efforts to secure the colony and exploit natural and human resources for England's imperial benefit, Jamestown experienced a near-constant cycle of famine, disease, and fighting both with the Indians and with one another. English-Powhatan peace followed Powhatan ambassador Pocahontas/Matoaka/Rebecca's marriage to English farmer John Rolfe, and the colony's prosperity was further solidified by the introduction of the cash crop tobacco.[14] Although the triangular fort disappeared from written documentation about Jamestown by the 1620s, the colonial capital flourished as a port city. As the centuries passed, commerce and dense habitation moved inland. By the nineteenth century, only a few families worked the island on a plantation system. As the land emptied of people and buildings crumbled, the natural landscape consumed the Jamestown city.

Storytelling at Jamestown

Jamestown's slow disappearance into Virginia's vegetation created a tabula rasa for storytelling about the United States. In the nineteenth century, tall grasses, scruffy bushes, and massive trees obscured any ruins from the seventeenth-century built environment.[15] For decades, popular belief stated that the original Jamestown fort eroded into the James River, yet the site was revered by heritage tourists.[16] In the late nineteenth century, preservationists "rescued" Jamestown from total environmental encroachment. The Association for the Preservation of Virginia Antiquities (APVA) received 22½ acres, including the general area where the fort once existed. With its preservation efforts, Jamestown's histories flattened into a monolithic narrative in support of specific political and social needs.

According to historian James Lindgren, the APVA organized in an era of white anxiety. As immigration swelled cities on both coasts of the United States, late nineteenth- and early twentieth-century urban populations increasingly did not resemble white elite Virginians.[17] In response, white southerners took refuge in agrarian romance that imagined an Anglo-Saxon origin story for what became the United States.[18] The APVA's choice of projects reflected a racist and xenophobic perspective with preserved spaces purposefully emptied of Africans, Native Americans, and English women.[19]

To avoid being revised out of the national founding myth and to combat the androcentric historiographical power of New England scholarship and Frederick Jackson Turner's frontier mythology, the APVA increasingly stressed the "strong, virile" leadership of John Smith as ancestral to the "cult of martial vigor" during the era of Theodore Roosevelt.[20] Storytelling was key to this project. Sentimental stories about Pocahontas saving Captain John Smith circulated via tourist materials from this period. Phallic monuments were erected, and while white women worked to preserve the site, white men dominated the narratives found on tours and pedestals.

As the APVA restored Jamestown in the American mythos, it also beautified the island with anachronistic landscaping.[21] Treescapes reinforced the one-dimensional stories as the twentieth century unfolded. In 1938, the US

Department of Agriculture published *Famous Trees*. It states that "trees by their very nature are landmarks and memorials" and highlights trees "identified with human happenings"—specifically, those of famous white enslavers and their progeny. *Famous Trees* aligns the United States with abundant natural resources, industrial might, and legacy building.[22] After a listing of trees affiliated with "notable people," there is an ordering of trees by state. Tucked toward the end, there is a two-sentence mention of Virginia's "Jamestown Churchyard Sycamore" that "has attracted attention for many years because of the havoc it wrought."[23]

The sycamore tree's "havoc" was a Jamestown focal point for almost 150 years.[24] Though the sycamore's story has been told since the early nineteenth century, it is only attributed to one particular tour guide: Sam Robinson. Historical ghostlore affects public understanding of sites, with stories set in a specific era, involving long-dead protagonists, beneath a tree that now only lives on in ghost tourism. Scholars, like historians Celia Naylor and Tiya Miles, implore academic and public audiences to take ghost stories seriously, especially those concerning historically marginalized persons.[25] In Miles's recent study, she argues that "ghosts represent history in a way that feels like magic."[26] However, Miles also cautions ghost tour guides, especially those who operate within museums, to depict African American spirits with "integrity."[27] In her exploration, Miles experienced only one ghost tour, conducted by an African American man, that offered "a usable take on plantation tourism."[28] Miles commends the following elements of this specific tour: the sardonic treatment of romanticized plantation storytelling, an acknowledgment of extant descendant communities, an amplification of diverse knowledge producers, and the decentering of the white perspective.

Sam Robinson's story occurred before the explosion of the ghost tour industry, but the sycamore ghost tale still provided visitors with an affective experience where they could "touch the past in both material and immaterial ways."[29] Though Robinson's story centered a white family, unlike Miles's example, his experience is remarkable given his interpretation at the height of Jim Crow in Virginia. While his storytelling did not challenge racial or social or gender hierarchies, Robinson had lasting power on the commemorative landscape and offers a "usable take" on Jamestown Island's tourism persona. Robinson's delivery treated James and Sarah Blair as star-crossed lovers, but he quickly displaced the couple as the central narrator of the sycamore's story. As a Black man, Robinson shared knowledge about white elite persons in his own voice and did not mimic white speech patterns in what Miles argues, borrowing from Black queer theorist E. Patrick Johnson, is "a subtle symbolic reversal of plantation power dynamics."[30] Listeners, past and present, tend to remember Robinson and the sycamore, not the Blairs and the sycamore.

Samuel Andrew Robinson

Almost all that is currently known about Sam Robinson comes from mid-twentieth-century ephemera connected to the sycamore tree: newspaper articles, tourist programs, and commemorative planning materials. In the twenty-first century, he still receives nostalgic treatment in regional retrospectives.[31] Robinson's ephemeral treatment was spotty, with less-than-rigorous attempts to recover his biographical details. Storytelling about Robinson reached epic proportions around the 1957 Jamestown Festival, but he left few clues about himself. Government documents offer some glimpses into his residences, occupations, and networks. Robinson's World War II draft card and death certificate name South Carolina as his birthplace, but other newspaper sources state Winnipeg, Canada—almost certainly inaccurate.[32] The exact date of his birth varies from April 6 to 15, from 1901 to 1906.[33] According to the 1940 census, Robinson completed school through grade eight.[34] He worked a series of jobs, including as a circus roustabout, before a mid-1930s encounter with Ellen Bagby, the then chairperson of the Jamestown Committee of the APVA.[35] Bagby met Robinson on a Richmond, Virginia, street corner and later hired him as a custodian for Jamestown Island.[36] It was this role that linked Robinson to Bagby and, eventually, the sycamore tree.

During Robinson's tenure at Jamestown, Virginia's historic sites "reshaped and redefined the built and natural environment of the United States . . . [and] influenced the way people defined and identified themselves as Americans."[37] National or heritage tourism served "as a ritual of American citizenship."[38] However, this ritual was not for everyone. Virginia's white population maintained social and racial order through "managed race relations." This system "wholeheartedly supported segregation and disenfranchisement but rejected the rigid racial oppression and violence trumpeted elsewhere in the South." Elite Virginians—lawyers, doctors, politicians, judges, and preservationists—considered themselves paternalistic toward the Black population. They "promised to provide a modicum of basic services and even encouraged a certain amount of black educational and economic uplift. In return, white elites demanded complete deference and expected blacks to seek redress of their grievances only through channels deemed appropriate by whites."[39] Bagby and Robinson certainly fit into this paternalistic relationship, though there is scant evidence from Robinson's perspective.

Much like the turn-of-the-century visitor, Robinson traveled east from Richmond to Jamestown for the tourist season. Each April, William Harrison Smith, superintendent of the grounds for the APVA at Jamestown, would bring Robinson from his home in Richmond to the island, where Robinson lodged for six months.[40] Robinson and Smith appeared to have a collegial relationship; at the very least, the men traded travel advice. Smith wrote, "Sam warned me last summer [about cabs overcharging] before I came up here [New York City] for school."[41] According to Bagby, Robinson "proved apt and interested in history" and began to give tours on the island.[42] By 1954, Robinson had been appointed sexton of Jamestown Church, a small brick building with structural elements dating back to the 1630s. In this capacity, Robinson interpreted the church and its adjacent graveyard using material provided by the APVA and conducting his own research.[43] Robinson's sycamore stood in this graveyard.

Robinson left behind a few clues to his personality. Beyond reading him through correspondence by Smith and Bagby, in newspapers, and by way of his *Mother-in-Law Tree* booklet, there are three extant letters from Robinson.[44] His handwriting is clear and broad and slants to the right. He writes in pen and always includes the date: April 7, April 14, and May 1. In each note, Robinson inquires about transportation from his home at 108 West Hill Street in Richmond to his temporary quarters at Jamestown. Robinson lived in the Gilpin neighborhood, known as Apostle Town in the 1890s, transformed into the Gilpin Court Housing Project in the 1940s, and cut off from downtown Richmond by Interstate 95 in the 1950s.[45] In one letter, he asks after Alice, an African American woman who did domestic labor on Jamestown Island. Two letters directly reference Bagby, who was also Robinson's next of kin on his World War II draft card.[46] He asks after "Benchie and Pup," makes an indecipherable joke about "Pocanatos [*sic*]," and apologizes for his bad handwriting. He closes each letter with "S. A. Robinson." He is comfortable and conversational but refers to his addressee as "Mr. Smith." In an audio recording of his Jamestown tour, Robinson is confident and comfortable with his historical material.[47] His work has value, and he appears to have enjoyed its seasonal arrival. Robinson's self-worth may also be read through census data. In 1940, his job is "janitor," but a decade later, he lists "guide . . . [at] Grounds at Jamestown Virginia" as his occupation and industry. This shift might indicate not only Robinson's promotion but also an elevated sense of self and purpose.

Robinson died in November 1965 and was buried in Richmond's East End Cemetery.[48] His grave is simple, untended, and difficult to find. However, Robinson's seasonal position preserved him within Jamestown's built and natural landscape during the mid-twentieth century. His retelling of "The Mother-in-Law Tree" allowed him to act as an arbiter of knowledge for white audiences. As Sarah Harrison Blair's tomb rose up in Jamestown's ghost-lore, Robinson's biography partly emerges from the 1957 Jamestown Festival records. Within Jamestown's public history, the seventeenth century comingled with Robinson's mid-twentieth-century experience via the sycamore.

A "Strange" Sycamore

As a popular mode of public history, Jamestown's ghost stories both maintain a particular social order and utilize familiar elements from the landscape and literature.[49] One example: Robinson's tree was an American sycamore (*Platanus occidentalis*), a tree species native to North America that thrived along the James River. As seen with the "Mother-in-Law Tree" narrative, sycamores grow abundantly along the Eastern Seaboard of the United States.[50] They are among the largest trees on the continent, often growing as tall as one hundred feet and as wide as ten feet. Their branches shed their bark with the passage of time and the growth of the trees. As the trees grow, the olive-colored bark peels away to reveal smooth white branches that look almost skeletal in the winter months.[51] Their root systems are destructive and capable of uprooting the built and natural environment as they skim along the ground level. They lift stone walkways, small sheds, and tombstones.[52] They are old trees, possibly witnessing the passage of multiple centuries from the same location. As they age, older sycamores can hollow out and create small caves within their still-living trunks—animals, insects, and even humans have been known to inhabit their massive interior spaces.[53]

The sycamore is an ancient tree, with religious symbolism found in ancient Egypt, Christianity, and Judaism.[54] It is a powerful tree that helps hold "river banks in place"—a useful natural tool for sites susceptible to erosion, like

Jamestown Island.[55] In Fiona Stafford's *The Long, Long Life of Trees*, she describes the sycamore tree as "too much" in its dominating physical presence, significant sap output, and acting as an "apian and avian cafeteria."[56] In 1971, sycamore seeds orbited the moon on the Apollo 14 mission. Upon returning to Earth, these seeds were planted around the country and referred to as "Moon Trees."[57] As a strong historical and natural marker, it is significant that a sycamore features prominently within Jamestown's origin stories. They are a visually and symbolically striking species.

In nineteenth-century US newspapers, sycamores were frequently mentioned for their exceptional characteristics. *Frank Leslie's Illustrated Newspaper* described a sycamore located outside Chester, South Carolina, as "curious" and completely unknown to nearby residents despite its advanced age and multiple trunk systems.[58] Fifty years prior to the aforementioned Chester sycamore, a "remarkable" sycamore tree in Ohio caused a sensation when its hollowed trunk provided enough space for thirteen persons on horseback to remain dry in "a falling shower of rain."[59] In 1824, the *Raleigh Register* labeled a South Carolina sycamore "wondrous" for its size, "circumference," and shelter for families during the American Revolution.[60] One year later, the *Register* lauded a "large tree" on the Ohio River that took "76 long paces to go around."[61] These descriptions center the sycamore as otherworldly—as settings for quasi-fairy-tales about people inhabiting tree caverns.

Increasingly, the "strange" Jamestown sycamore, later known as the Mother-in-Law Tree, gained notoriety in regional histories as well as national newspapers.[62] Descriptions animate the sycamore as "embrac[ing] . . . the tomb of Mrs. Blair, one-third of which lies embedded in the body of the tree and is held immoveable."[63] The narratives suggest a Sleeping Beauty–like fairy tale, with a fair maiden imprisoned. According to early twentieth-century historian Lyon Gardiner Tyler, the sycamore "was among the objects which attracted attention" from visitors during the 1807 commemorations. At that time, the sycamore was a young barrier between the Blairs, but a century later, the tree had "shattered both tombstones," and a "fragment" of Sarah Harrison Blair's tombstone was "imbedded partially in its trunk." In 1895, the churchyard was cleaned, and the tombstones were temporarily removed, thus momentarily releasing Sarah Blair from "the embrace of the tree which has since proceeded to close the cavity."[64] The tree eventually grew back between the two tombs. Throughout the 1890s, its description turned ghoulish, with imagery of the tree "wrenching" and "breaking" the tomb of Sarah Blair to the point that one can barely read the "mutilated sentence of [her] epitaph."[65] Commemorative postcards state how the tree "dismembered" Sarah Harrison Blair's tomb—another curious suggestion of the sycamore's nefarious agency.

As the twentieth century began, proto-heritage tourists visited the sycamore before Robinson's tenure at Jamestown. At some point in the 1930s, the sycamore was featured in two popular syndicated cartoon strips: Robert Ripley's *Believe It or Not* and John Hix's *Strange as It Seems*.[66] Using similar layouts, Ripley and Hix illustrated strange stories from all around the world into households across America. They were predicated on travel, even if vicariously, and encouraged tourism, even if voyeuristically. (At least one Jamestown tourist mentioned knowing about Ripley's *Believe It or Not*'s coverage of the Mother-in-Law Tree in 1939.[67]) The cartoons often depicted unusual things from nature, like remarkable trees and rock formations. Ripley served as a source for Robinson's later recitation of the sycamore's story, though Hix's version was most likely also known to Robinson.[68]

Stories about the sycamore were encouraged—perhaps even created—by Jamestown administrators. In mid-1940, APVA "official" Ellen Bagby shared a spooky story about a mysterious fire that almost destroyed the sycamore tree: "Of course it's preposterous . . . but maybe the spirits of Mr. Blair and his wife had something to do with it."[69] Bagby's story feels like a publicity stunt, complete with a longer recitation on the sycamore tree's staying power. The tree has a hollow center that figures in this "mysterious fire." It also houses a group of reptiles. According to Robinson and Bagby, the sycamore was home to five snakes that often cooled themselves on the nearby church floor; Robinson gave them names, though Bagby had him run them off to keep tourists happy.[70]

Beginning in the early 1950s, newspaper headlines began to link the sycamore tree to Robinson: "Caretaker Spins Yarn about Jamestown Sycamore," "Guide and Historian: Sam's Fame," and "'Mother-in-Law' Tree Story Spices Visit to Jamestown." The sycamore roots Robinson to Jamestown, and he is often incorrectly described as the originator of the legend.[71] These mid-twentieth-century accounts depict the tree as less carnivorous and more folkloric. In photographs, Robinson frequently stands close to the now massive sycamore, with one hand resting on the tree's gnarled trunk and his face upturned to the wide branches. In another image, he is standing with his hand on his hip and eyes looking down at Sarah Harrison Blair's tomb. In these images, the Blair grave blurs. It is completely woven into the sycamore's roots. One might interpret the sycamore as feeding off the tomb, perhaps balancing on it, or even reaching toward the sky from its solid stone grave. Robinson and the sycamore tree unite in tourist materials.

Robinson's sycamore is part of a larger ecosystem in Jim Crow Virginia. Every summer, he would travel from his predominantly Black urban Richmond neighborhood to rural white Jamestown Island. His annual journey, from city to country, reverses the typical Great Migration movement and might suggest Robinson's deliberate decision-making process and connection to the island. Recent scholarship about Blackness, whiteness, agency, and place also helps dislodge Robinson's sycamore story from the realm of innocuous storytelling. It is important to interrogate where and when this story took root. Cultural geographers encourage conversations around how free and unfree persons moved through the landscape and how regions racialized over time and space.[72] Environmental historians also remind us that nature must be contextualized and historicized; place does not exist outside of time and space.[73] Black ecologies link historical and environmental approaches to examine "Black insurgent and practical knowledge in the face of environmental degradation, geographic dislocation, and territorial violence."[74] To understand Robinson's presence on the white commemorative landscape, it is important to know how white supremacy employed the natural environment to enforce, overtly and covertly, racial categories. Robinson, as a Black man in Virginia, undoubtedly witnessed or experienced this enforcement. Public historians must also consider how sites interpret their natural landscape.[75] Too often, now pastoral places remain unexamined by the visitor. Though historic sites appear pastoral and restorative now, they often have legacies of physical and psychological trauma.

Trees and Racial Terror

Sycamore trees are particularly prevalent in depictions of lynching and racial violence. In both fiction and nonfiction, the linkage of trees to violence reverberated from the plantation into the post-enslavement experience. In the opening pages of the spectacular and spectral novel *Beloved*, Toni Morrison's main character cannot shake the images of "boys hanging from the most beautiful sycamores in the world."[76] Morrison's use of a sycamore tree is a deliberate artistic choice, and it illuminates the sycamore within "treescape memory"—specifically, how trees commemorate both historic space and "longer-term patterns of signification."[77] However, in the mid-twentieth-century accounts of Robinson's sycamore tree, this racialized connotation is never acknowledged. The sycamore tree's story commemorates the Blairs' separation and signifies "an idyllic past" in the white collective memory of Jamestown.[78] Though it is unknown if the Jamestown churchyard sycamore witnessed racial violence during or post-enslavement, its inclusion within the 350th commemoration and its interpretation by a Black man reveals a network of power dynamics for consideration in the twenty-first century.

In the early years of Robinson's employment with the APVA, "lynching was an infrequent and extraordinary occurrence" that nevertheless deeply and painfully impacted African American communities and other people of color.[79] Virginia was the site of eighty-four reported extrajudicial murders of Black persons from 1880 to 1930.[80] Despite the low number comparative to other states in the Lower South, the "everyday humiliations and hostilities that black southerners endured under Jim Crow" were constant—especially for individuals who worked among white people.[81] As other scholars have pointed out, news of lynching circulated via photography, news media, and souvenirs that "served to normalize and make socially acceptable . . . the utter brutality of lynching."[82] Often, this media included the lynching setting: a scaffold, a bridge, or a tree. For a Black man to be photographed alongside a large tree may imply violences that Robinson and his contemporaries would have recognized.

After World War I, African American communities began to push back against white paternalism and racial inequality. In retaliation for such "betrayal," white Virginians codified white supremacy through Jim Crow laws and restrictions in the 1920s and 1930s.[83] In this increasingly tense environment, "as paternalism eroded, urban whites increasingly turned to the state legislature and city councils to redefine the terms of white supremacy; rural whites, who dominated the state's politics, enthusiastically embraced such measures."[84] As the twentieth century rolled on, African Americans were increasingly restricted by Jim Crow regulations. In March 1924, the Virginia General Assembly passed the Racial Integrity Act, which "defined a white person as an individual with 'no trace whatsoever of any blood other than Caucasian'" and outlawed interracial marriage.[85] Walter Plecker, director of the Bureau of Vital Statistics, led this legislative charge and "waged a campaign of intimidation and threats aimed at classifying all Virginians by race."[86] Other white Virginians aided in Plecker's quest to bureaucratically delineate between the races.[87] This ordering increased in the aftermath of the 1954 *Brown v. Board of Education* Supreme Court decision. In Virginia, the federal mandate to integrate public schools led to Massive Resistance from elected white officials and community leaders. Municipalities first tried to simply ignore the ruling, then chose to close schools forced to integrate by federal judges.[88]

Racial codification also affected access to historic sites, where Black visitation was increasingly limited and/or prohibited. In 1929, undergraduate students from the Hampton Institute, a Black college in Hampton, Virginia, were denied entry to Jamestown Island based on skin color, and the APVA refused entry to a Black man visiting with his white employer.[89] The Black press called out these affronts. The *Norfolk Journal and Guide*, a regional African American newspaper, pointed out the importance of the site within the "history of the Negro in America" and decried their inability to visit.[90] Interestingly, an unnamed writer appealed to the paternal persona of elite Virginians who felt they knew best for Black populations: "For Virginians of all people to deny to Negroes the privilege of making a physical inspection of a place so important in their history is indeed unlike true Virginians."[91] Though the platitude may have been disingenuous, its tone shows how African American communities bristled at the exclusion.

As planning began for the Jamestown Festival of 1957, people were violently threatened by publicly advocating for equal rights, specifically school integration efforts. Often, this threat occurred using tree limbs burned in the shape of a cross. In 1955, attorney Oliver W. Hill's Richmond, Virginia, home was targeted with a cross burning, and in 1957, only a week before Robinson interpreted for Queen Elizabeth II, a cross burned on the lawn of Maryland governor Theodore R. McKeldin.[92] Was Robinson aware of this ongoing violence and intimidation? Currently, there is no evidence of Robinson's feelings on race relations, but he must have been aware of local and national events. In particular, when the Virginia Chamber of Commerce organized a commemorative dinner in May 1957, several prominent Black Virginians declined their invitation in response to public outcry. Journalist Alton Levy editorialized the moment in a column titled "Mr. James Crow Invited to Attend," where he decried the "neglect . . . of the Negro contribution to Virginia and to our nation."[93] One wonders if Robinson kept up with such news stories, especially given his role in the 1957 commemorations.

It was into this racially segregated environment that Robinson guided white audiences across the colonial foundations of the United States. He gave tours to white audiences seeking a great Anglo past at the height of McCarthyism and amid the turmoil of the Cold War. As the Commonwealth of Virginia fought *Brown v. Board of Education* tooth and nail, Robinson educated white visitors about *their* colonial history. Ten years before the 1967 *Loving v. Virginia* Supreme Court decision, he lectured to foreign dignitaries from England and Greece. In available accounts, white reporters described Robinson's behavior as jovial, but the tone is overtly stereotyped: "With gold teeth sparkling, he boomed out the tale in his series of memorized phrases and slurred syllables."[94] Robinson was "an uneducated Negro [with] no knowledge of grammar" who "knew a good story when he heard one."[95] Though he is sometimes labeled a "historian," Robinson's knowledge of the sycamore's story is often attributed to extant sources provided to him by Bagby.

Though there were a few African American interpreters in nearby Colonial Williamsburg, Robinson achieved fame among white audiences as the 350th anniversary of Jamestown's founding approached.[96] Vivian Smith, wife of William Harrison Smith, wrote to Bagby in anticipation of Robinson's annual arrival: "The nice class of people are coming here now . . . the ones that really appreciate Sam."[97] Robinson's recognition peaked in 1950, when he was featured on the back cover of April's *Reader's Digest*. In the watercolor rendering, Robinson stands below the John Smith statue in a red tie and short-sleeved collared shirt. An all-white audience, dressed in springtime attire, surrounds him. Robinson gestures up at the treelike Smith statue in a typical tour guide pose, but Smith's statue faces away from him in striding mid-step toward the river. This image places Robinson on the landscape, but he is decentered, separate and beneath. Though the focal point, he is dwarfed by Smith's memorial and unacknowledged in the image caption. Notably, Robinson disliked the choice of tie color: "I ain't never wore a red tie in my life. I don't like 'em."[98] It is impossible to know if his statement was pushback against the *Reader's Digest* representation, but Robinson was clearly comfortable in white commemorative spaces.

In available travelogues from the 1940s and 1950s, visitors went to Jamestown expecting to hear the sycamore's story from the "legendary" Robinson.[99] Robinson's storyteller role drummed up Jamestown within tourist imaginaries. As literary scholar Sarah Gilbreath Ford argues, white audiences were accustomed to Black storytellers from the literary works of Joel Chandler Harris, William Faulkner, and Eudora Welty—all white authors themselves.[100] Robinson-as-tour-guide may have felt familiar to white audiences with his colloquial storytelling using trees, snakes, and storms. As he engaged with white tourists and worked for white women, his behavior was innocuous within the racially codified expectations of white supremacy.[101] Robinson's few direct quotations unrelated to the sycamore are expressive but not argumentative. For example, he is quoted as unfazed by Queen Elizabeth's visit ("I ain't given it no thought yet"[102]). Despite these hints at a unique personality, Robinson remained within the racially ordered bounds of the mid-twentieth-century United States.

The Jamestown Festival of 1957

In early November 1956, W. E. B. Du Bois pointed out specific dates that "deeply affect the history of the Negroes and of this country" in a letter to the National Association for the Advancement of Colored People (NAACP) board of directors. Du Bois saw 1957 not as a date to commemorate Jamestown but as the centennial of the Dred Scott decision. He also noted, "If we [presumably the NAACP and other Black leaders] neglect to mark this history, it may be distorted or forgotten."[103] Du Bois was undoubtedly noting the erasure of Black history from the Jamestown planning. As pointed out by other scholars, efforts to commemorate African American history faced resistance and zero participation from white people.[104] As the 350th anniversary of Jamestown approached, white Virginians readied for an influx of visitors but purposefully excluded vocal Black participation. How might Robinson's presence push back against this deliberate ghosting of Black histories at Jamestown?

Robinson's presence was not the only example of African American labor for the commemoration. African American labor was required to halt Jamestown's decay in material and memorial ways. Blackness was also commoditized in tourist publications and through national or heritage tourism in what Grace Elizabeth Hale terms "making whiteness American culture."[105] In order to consume the landscape at Jamestown, to soak up its Anglo-Saxon work ethic and American "ancientness," Black labor needed to recover it from the ground. African Americans worked on building a seawall along the James River, dug trenches for National Park Service archaeologists, and worked as custodians and cooks for white APVA employees.

Though there had been celebrations in 1807, 1857, and 1907, the Jamestown Festival of 1957 was the most ambitious commemorative endeavor. It was a two-pronged affair, organized at the state level by the Virginia 350th Anniversary Commission and at the federal level by the Jamestown-Williamsburg-Yorktown National Celebration Commission.[106] The APVA had a limited role and busied itself with the beautification of the island acreage.[107] In early planning documents, festival organizers wanted the celebrations to be "nationwide in scope," though the historic focus would be Virginia. The eight months of "living events" would ideally pay for themselves.[108] In a public letter to the Virginian population, the then governor Thomas B. Stanley discussed the "great heritage" that required Commonwealth citizens "to properly commemorate this anniversary."[109] Virginia would transform into a shrine itself, as the festival would "create a great national historical monument before it is overrun and destroyed by increasing industrialization and urbanization."[110] The history on display, however, was not reflective of the whole population, and it was designed to evoke nostalgia for a white supremacist version of colonial expansion. The planned events focused on Anglo-European arrival and permanent imprint on the landscape, with some anthropological discussion of Virginia Indians. Despite an interest in "learning [Jamestown's] story more completely," the festival activities at Jamestown, Williamsburg, and Yorktown failed to discuss African indenture, enslavement, and material existence on the landscape.[111]

In addition to the history, only white guests were invited to Queen Elizabeth's visit and sit-down dinner in October 1957.[112] The monarch presented a "17th century casket (box) made of tortoise shell and with some reference to American Indians on the exterior" as a gift, but there was no Native American delegation to greet her formally.[113] Virginia's Mattaponi chief, O. T. Custalow, did ask to meet the queen. In September 1957, Custalow wrote to Stanley to remind the governor how Virginia Indians "greeted the first English settlers," and the queen's visit was a "particularly appropriate" opportunity for the Mattaponi chief to present her with "a trinket symbolic of the early gifts of [his] ancestors to those first white settlers."[114] Stanley's response is unavailable, but Lewis A. McMurran, delegate and chairman of Virginia's

350th Anniversary Commission, responded with a firm no: "This commission very much appreciates and understands your interest." McMurran suggested Custalow and his tribe see the queen when she visited the Festival Park at Jamestown. No Virginia Indians were present at the queen's official reception and dinner at the Williamsburg Inn in Colonial Williamsburg.

Though Virginia Indians were excluded, Robinson did interpret for the queen. Guided visitor tours were necessary, "since so much of Jamestown [had] disappeared and [had] to be conjured up for the visitor by means of oral explanation."[115] Though William Harrison and Vivian Smith were still in residence on the island, Robinson personally interpreted for three of the twenty minutes that Queen Elizabeth II was on Jamestown Island.[116] Robinson's reputation had preceded him: he had shared the same tale for Elizabeth's mother, Mary, during a visit in 1954.[117] In one October 17, 1957, newspaper photo, Queen Elizabeth II listens to Robinson's "spiel" with a smile on her face, but the photographer cut him out of the shot.[118] Other photographs show Robinson and the queen shaking hands; Robinson wears a suit and smiles at her. In newspaper accounts, Robinson is directly identified by his full name. In programmatic planning, he is referred to as "a Canada-born Negro guide" and "the old custodian."[119] Though no film exists of the queen and Robinson's interaction, it may have been the only time she directly heard from a Black interpreter while in Virginia.[120]

A question still remains: Why did Robinson tell this story for the royal couple? Was it on the recommendation of the Queen Mother? Did Bagby advocate for Robinson's inclusion? The festival planning documents do not reveal clear answers, but it is evident that Robinson was well known. However, his sycamore story adheres to white expectations of Black storytellers. It is a tale rooted in nature, superstition, and the otherworldly. It did not break down other social barriers at the Jamestown Festival. Robinson was not invited to dine with the festival's dignitaries. He did not speak stories of Jamestown's white male colonial leaders, like John Smith and John Rolfe. Though his voice was heard, Robinson's story was confined to expected storytelling content. His linkage to the sycamore is terribly problematic, and it is difficult to imagine the festival and Jamestown administrators were unaware of trees as spaces for violence. It just did not matter in their planning or their consideration of Robinson.

The Spectral Sycamore

Just as it was removed time and time again within Robinson's narrative, the sycamore tree was finally uprooted for the last time in 2007. It no longer grows in the historic churchyard, but other large trees still populate the island.[121] Despite the physical tree no longer attracting visitors, the spectral sycamore "remains" on the site through ghost tours and their associated publications. It "lives on" in Flickr galleries and outdated websites.[122] Robinson's voice is preserved on YouTube over fifty years after he died.[123] News outlets still trot out the Mother-in-Law Tree story around Halloween to elicit goose bumps and drum up tourism to the region. When the sycamore is conjured into narrative existence now, Sarah Harrison Blair quickly disappears from the discussion. Much as the sycamore fragmented and absorbed her tomb in the early twentieth century, Blair remains one-dimensional and undeveloped in modern retelling. Her biography is even less known than Robinson's. There is yet an opportunity to recover Blair, much as her tomb was recovered from the sycamore's roots.

At Jamestown, the sycamore tree as a memory-making device might fade from the physical and symbolic landscape, but recent scholarship about the island promises to commemorate a "sense of history" that includes polyvocal storytelling. Historian Manning Marable writes that the American master narrative is "an inevitable series of conquests" over people, places, and things. To counter this narrative of American exceptionalism, Marable argues for Black "living history projects" to reconstruct American collective memory through oral history, multimedia archiving, and civic activism.[124] This reconstruction centers Black storytelling about American history in order to reorient the focus from whiteness. Though Robinson's sycamore story did not subvert racial stratification, it is important to preserve and share his interpretative intervention at Jamestown. Robinson remains in Jamestown's collective memory because of the sycamore tree—and vice versa.

New interpretative interventions bubbled up as Jamestown prepared for the 1619 commemorations. Archaeologists excavated and interpreted the Angela site, where a captive African woman lived in bondage during the first decades of the colony.[125] There were "First Africans" walking tours and an opportunity to "meet" Angela in the form of an actor-interpreter. Guests were encouraged to "listen as [Angela recalled] her former home in Angola, her capture and her new life in Virginia." Programming included discussions about Jamestown's commemorative power into the twentieth century. First offered in February 2019, the "American Heartbreak: Historical Memory and Racial Amnesia" program told audiences about "the civil rights struggle to acknowledge black history" at historic sites and African Americans' significant presence within American history.[126] This latter program mentioned Robinson's legacy, and a recent Historic Jamestowne website photograph shows an actor-interpreter portraying Robinson for twenty-first-century audiences.[127] The image shows him standing where the sycamore once stood.

At Jamestown, there is a long history of public history. Robinson's role as arbiter of white knowledge and speaker of the sycamore's story is just one of the island's complicated narratives. Histories of race and violence were overshadowed by the white nationalism fueled by preservationist groups like the APVA. In more recent museum work, interpretation by curators, guides, archaeologists, and scientists slowly and deliberately unearthed narratives underneath the nostalgic and whitewashed "sense of history" long associated with Jamestown. The now imagined sycamore roots Robinson to the landscape through newspaper articles, regional histories, institutional archives, and perhaps most powerfully, personal reminiscences. *This* famous tree outlives "the allotted lifespan of [humans]" and carries its "associations through generations."[128] It symbolizes how other narratives grow at a historic site—narratives often unrelated to the prominent, well-circulated interpretation.

As historic sites across the country approach the 250th commemoration of the Declaration of Independence in 2026, public historians and museum professionals aim to "reassemble the southern plantation museum" and consider "how the word is passed" at these problematic places.[129] Much of this work must occur by historicizing both landscape *and* museum. They are intimately tied to the public history they share while composed of their own historical processes. Too often, visitors tour a site and see its parklike qualities: the lush green grass, the bright flower beds, and the spectacular tree cover. Not only does this belie the historical realities of agricultural chaos; it also creates a facade whereby the general visitor experiences the physical museum as an ahistorical institution. Twenty-five years ago, public historian Patricia West wrote that "the history of American historic house museums . . . [was] manufactured out of human needs bound by time and place."[130] Often, cultural institutions fed this need by storytelling. In order to examine how visitors remember historic sites—an important project in the twenty-first century, where much of public memory comes from a purposefully imagined past—we should spend time with the storytellers and their content. Robinson's sycamore is a microhistory of how historic sites commemorated themselves. Though the 1957 Jamestown Festival's intent was to entertain a queen, current interpretation provides a more nuanced look at who tells a story with deep roots.

FIGURE 14. The Fox Oak in Flushing, New York—the tree under which George Fox, the Quaker, preached in 1672. Photograph by George Stacy, ca. 1860. https://www.loc.gov/item/2016653334/.

Chapter Nine

The Fox Oaks of Flushing, New York

QUAKER PULPIT AND BOWNE FAMILY SHRINE

Evan Haefeli, Texas A&M University

Few trees have earned the privilege of a historical marker, but Flushing, in the New York City borough of Queens, has created two for a pair of white oak trees that once stood across the street from the historic Bowne House, erected in 1661 on what is now Bowne Street. The oaks had been around for centuries before the Bownes arrived, but the Bownes outlasted them. The first oak died in 1841; the second in 1862 (or maybe 1863). Bowne descendants held on to the house until 1945, after which it became a historic home preserved and operated by the Bowne House Historical Society. It was probably in no small measure due to their influence that, in 1907, Flushing's Historical Society placed a large triangular chunk of granite on the site where the oak trees had stood. Engraved upon the George Fox Stone, as the nearby metal historical marker calls it, is the message "Here stood the FOX OAKS beneath whose branches GEORGE FOX founder of the Society of Friends preached June 7th 1672." The more recently erected metal marker adds additional context, explaining that this was "one of the most important events in the history of the Quaker community in Flushing." Fox, it explains, passed through town during his tour of America's first Quaker congregations. Originally intending to preach in the Bowne House, he had to move to the shade of the two oak trees after hundreds of people showed up. The marker concludes with the less than fully accurate claim that the two trees "were destroyed by storms" in 1863.[1]

The oaks are even more interesting than these markers let on. While they were alive, they served as a public pulpit several times for three notable Quaker preachers, one a woman. Since their demise, their remnants have helped commemorate the region's Quaker history—and the Bowne family's leading role in it. The case of the Fox Oaks demonstrates how memory, religion, environment, and preservation can effectively reinforce one another for centuries—even through the challenging circumstances of an urbanizing community flooded with immigrants from around the world. What in the mid-nineteenth century was described as a "village" of "about 2000 inhabitants in a square mile," most of whom were Protestants of English origin, is now the most ethnically and religiously diverse city in America, full of an extraordinary range of immigrants and religions, primarily from Asia.[2] The Bownes are gone, as is the rural, Anglo-American version of Flushing they once presided over, replaced by modern apartment buildings full of people of very different historical and religious origins. Nevertheless, the stone marker and metal plaque remain, visible to everyone walking down the street. They are just the most publicly visible efforts to preserve the memory of the Fox Oaks. Private initiatives by the Bowne family in both word and deed did the crucial work of keeping this past alive for generations before those public markers were created. The history of the Fox Oaks is as meaningful to them as the community of Flushing or Quakerism more broadly.[3]

The Bownes were originally English Puritans who had migrated to New England. They then moved down to Flushing in what was then the Dutch colony of New Netherland, where they converted to Quakerism. They quickly displayed a special capacity for preserving local history by associating it with physical objects that could be seen and touched by later generations, long after any living connection to those events had disappeared. The memorialization of the Fox Oaks is just one of their more notable accomplishments. Apart from recording an interesting episode of early Flushing history, the Fox Oaks have served as a testament to the Bownes' faith while also highlighting their family's role in the history of Flushing. The Bowne descendants' knack for blending genealogy with local history along with their continuing adherence to the Quakerism of their ancestors kept this memory alive for both personal and spiritual reasons, but their success as "pastkeepers" benefited enormously from their ability to retain the ancestral property for almost three centuries.

That accomplishment enabled them to preserve relevant items and documents long enough to hand them over to the care of professional archivists and museum staff in the mid-twentieth century. These included various items carved out of the wood of the trees as well as literary works composed by Bowne descendants (a poem and a novel) and illustrations drafted with their encouragement. Once published, the illustrations helped spread the story of the trees farther around the country and even overseas to Quakers in England. Indeed, by the 1850s, the one surviving oak had become so famous that, as a newspaper article described it, the tree, as "high as can well be reached," had "been despoiled of its venerable bark to be preserved as relics."[4]

What began as a family project in the eighteenth century thus spread to a wider community of people eager for a tangible connection to history. The mix of personal and public ambitions in this process is exemplary of early modern forms of memory making, which often involved recurring practices connected to physical objects. This approach is noticeably different from modern (post-1800) ways of memory making where, as scholars have emphasized, the role of elites or the state was decisive in shaping public memory, even when they contrasted with the increasingly sophisticated versions of personal memories made accessible through either studies of the more abundant documentation or interviews with living individuals. In earlier periods, memory work was more personal. Rooted in families, it lacked formal archives or professional oral historians. The story of the Fox Oaks offers an excellent case study of how this amateur style of memory making worked while also demonstrating its ability to persist into the modern era. The Bownes successfully attached a particular version of the past to specific objects so firmly that long after the trees have gone, their memory lives on in artifacts made of their wood, in memorials of stone and metal placed where they once stood, and now in digital articles posted on the internet.[5]

Trees have long served humans as symbols for all sorts of purposes. As with the Fox Oaks, they often figured as important parts of a community's emotional and even religious life. Before and after the Christianization of Europe, for example, trees, together with springs and other notable natural features, were objects of worship and devotion. Unfortunately, trees' propensity to die and eventually disappear places a limit on their ability to fulfill these roles without assistance from humans. Sometimes their importance drew hostile human attention. Since the days of the early Christian missionaries, religious reformers deliberately attacked trees to transform local religious beliefs and practices. Others assaulted them to clear land for roads or other improvements. In early modern England, trees' importance in marking local boundaries and preserving historical memories could stir people to actively resist their removal. Trees were not only beautiful: they helped recall vital information. Losing them damaged people's sense of place and belonging. Even in the modern era the loss of certain trees could be a newsworthy event. In Deerfield, Massachusetts, the "death of each old tree" felt like the loss of an "organic connection with the past," as historian Michael Batinski notes. The collapse of an old elm in 1885 seemed like the end of a historic era. The local paper reported how Deerfielders took pictures of themselves standing among its tangled remains, trying to preserve what they could of its memory. Sadly, the specific significance of that tree has since been forgotten. In Flushing, however, the meaning of the Fox Oaks remains clear because their memory was carefully cultivated by multiple generations of the Bowne family. Well before the trees began to decay, the Bownes had transformed them into compelling historical curiosities of special religious significance.[6]

Associating the oaks with the preaching of George Fox tied Flushing to the founding father of a major religious movement with important influence in early America. In commemorating George Fox through this local piece of nature, the Quakers of Flushing were merely imitating their fellows back in England. Since the earliest days of their movement, Quakers had commemorated key moments in George Fox's career by associating them with outstanding elements in the local landscape. For example, a yew tree and a rock in Westmoreland, England, where Fox preached some of the first Quaker sermons, were treasured for their connection to this foundational moment in Quaker history. When the aging yew eventually blew down in January 1877, a piece of it was preserved in a nearby Quaker meetinghouse. The large rock, known as Fox's Pulpit, is still there. Around the turn of the twentieth century, a commemorative plaque was affixed to its base. It can still be read by passersby.[7]

Fox's visit to Flushing took place barely fifteen years after Quakerism took hold in the town. Named after the Dutch city of Vlissingen, Flushing was chartered in 1645 and settled by a mixture of Dutch and English colonists. Dutch officials had purchased the land it was built on in 1639 to shore up the eastern frontier of New Netherland. Bowne family tradition claims that John Bowne, who built the family's house, bought his land directly from its Indigenous owners. With remarkable precision, it claims that he paid six silver guilders and four fathoms of wampum for it. No documentation of the transaction survives. If John Bowne did purchase his land from the Indigenous Matinecocks, he likely would have done so in the early 1650s, when he arrived in town—and before he had become a Quaker. He nevertheless would have had to secure a title from the Dutch as well.[8]

In addition to the tradition about the land purchase, the Bowne family recalls their ancestors' arrival in Flushing with a wooden object: a crutch. Cherished for generations, it has been displayed in the Bowne House since at least the late nineteenth century. Family tradition claims the crutch belonged to John Bowne's father, Thomas, who moved to Flushing with his son. Soon after arriving, Thomas was confronted by a bear in the nearby woods. To save his life, he allegedly shoved the crutch down the bear's throat and killed it. This story has been carefully handed down in the family along with the cane.[9]

Today, Flushing is famous for religious tolerance and diversity, but its early history involved a series of religious conflicts. Dutch law allowed individuals liberty of conscience but forbade those who were not Reformed Protestants (Presbyterians, in other words) from gathering for worship. They did not have to belong to the official Dutch Reformed Church, but they could not set up alternative congregations. Like many of the initial inhabitants of Flushing, John Bowne was English. Most of the English people in Flushing had fled New England because they disagreed with the religious orthodoxy that took hold in Massachusetts and Connecticut. A number had connections to Rhode Island, the most religiously radical part of New England. Unlike Massachusetts and Connecticut, Rhode Island had no orthodox religious establishment. Instead, it tolerated a wide range of Protestant dissidents, including Baptists and Quakers. A Baptist from Rhode Island visited Flushing soon after it was established. He made several converts. In 1657 came Quaker missionaries. They too made converts, including the Bownes. However, both the Baptists and Quakers were harassed by their Reformed Protestant English and Dutch neighbors who upheld the Dutch law forbidding members of other religions from worshipping together.[10]

Today, Flushing proudly remembers its struggle for religious liberty. It treasures a petition many of its inhabitants signed in December 1657 to protest a Dutch law passed to deny Quaker missionaries the right to proselytize within New Netherland. This so-called Flushing Remonstrance (which John Bowne did not sign—probably because he was out of town) is one of the first and most passionate defenses of religious freedom to appear in America. The document, accorded special care by the New York Archives, is regularly pointed to as a precedent for American religious liberty. It also has been a touchstone for efforts by the Bowne House Historical Society to draw attention to their site and hopefully raise it to the status of a national park honoring Flushing's role in the history of American religious freedom.[11]

Although he did not sign the Flushing Remonstrance, John Bowne is intimately associated with Flushing's struggle for religious liberty. As one of the first people in town to convert to Quakerism, he hosted Quaker worship services in his home. For his efforts, Bowne suffered harassment, imprisonment, and exile at the hands of the Dutch authorities. The period of Dutch rule lasted until August 1664, when an English invasion captured the colony and abolished the hegemony of the Dutch Reformed Church that gave Bowne and other religious dissidents so much trouble. Eventually, in the 1690s, Bowne and others were able to construct a (still-standing) Quaker meetinghouse to worship in.[12]

In English New York, Quaker worship was tolerated but not freed from religious conflict. One of the likely purposes of Fox's 1672 visit was to reinforce Quaker morale after they had suffered for upholding the Peace Testimony that forswore armed violence and military conflict. Fox had articulated this doctrine at the time of the restoration of England's monarchy in 1660, but it was a few years before it was fully adopted by Quakers across Britain. It had reached Flushing by 1667, when, in the midst of the Second Anglo-Dutch War, a number of men in Flushing's militia company refused to fulfill their compulsory military service. New York's governor was furious. Chastising the men of Flushing in a letter, he fulminated, "You have given me just reason to suspect your fidelities & your courage." To punish the militia company, its flags and "twelve Match Locks" were returned to the store at Fort James in Manhattan. The individual offenders were prohibited from entering New York City for three months. This was just the first of several incidents where Quakers in colonial New York and other English colonies were punished for their adherence to the Peace Testimony and refusal to undertake military service.[13]

The offenders of 1667 were not named, so we do not know if John Bowne was among them, but he probably was. Certainly, by the time Fox visited Flushing a few years later, Bowne was the town's most prominent Quaker. George Fox passed through in the spring of 1672, on his way to Rhode Island as part of his mission to organize all the colonial Quaker congregations. The Society of Friends (as Quakers call themselves) inspired by George Fox's preaching was new. It had only begun in the late 1640s. Colonial Quakerism had emerged in the 1650s with no direct involvement from Fox. He had had little control over what was happening in America and was concerned that some colonial Quakers were being drawn to the radical preaching of John Perrot. Moreover, outside of Rhode Island, colonial Quakers lived in provinces ruled by non-Quakers, some of whom, like the governors of Virginia and New York, persecuted them. Fox had recently recovered from a severe illness and was determined to reform colonial Quakerism into an orthodox faith loyal to him. In addition to preaching, he set up the system of regular monthly and quarterly meetings he had recently developed in Britain to shore up order and control over the faithful. Adopting this uniform system of worship, Quakers began communicating with other congregations and keeping regular records. These procedures strengthened the ties between American and English Quakers, which had weakened in recent years. After the initial burst of missionary visits between 1656 and 1664 had died down, few Quakers crossed the Atlantic to America. After Fox's tour, transatlantic visits by Friends became the norm—in both directions. American Quakers, including John Bowne and his wife Hannah, visited Europe. European Quakers visited America.[14]

The Fox Oaks became both a participant and symbol of transatlantic Quakerism, beginning with Fox's trip to Flushing. Our main source of information on the visit is the journal George Fox kept of his travels. Unfortunately for local historians, he said nothing about the oaks or the Bownes. He only noted the size of his audience and the effect of his preaching. Fox was a transatlantic celebrity in 1672, the first famous person to visit New York. Accordingly, his arrival sparked the curiosity of all sorts of New Yorkers, not just Quakers. What began as a Quaker meeting quickly turned into a major public event. Fox recorded that "many hundreds of the world," meaning non-Quakers, came to hear him speak. No wonder he had to preach outdoors. The audience included the new "governor" Francis Lovelace, who had recently replaced the governor that had punished Flushing's Quakers for resisting militia duty. Fox noted, "[Lovelace had] heard of me and was loving and said that he had been in my company." Perhaps he had seen Fox back in England. Altogether, it was a harmonious, successful meeting.[15]

There is no reason to doubt the Bowne family tradition that John Bowne hosted Fox, even if there is no other evidence for it. He had a thriving family living in a solid house that was the center of local Quaker worship. In yet another demonstration of their skill at keeping historical memory alive, the Bownes preserved the daybed they claim George Fox slept in. It is still on display in the Bowne House. Admittedly, the style of the bed suggests it could not have been built before the 1690s. Since Fox died in 1691 and never returned to America after his 1672 tour, it is unlikely that he slept in this exact bed. Nevertheless, the bed, currently displayed in the oldest room of the house under a portrait of Fox, provides useful testimony of John Bowne's close connection to George Fox.[16]

Under Dutch rule, John Bowne had been persecuted for holding Quaker meetings in his home. The fact that he could now, under English rule, host an enormous outdoor meeting with the approval of the governor would certainly have been worth remembering. It is likely that the Bownes began the process of memory making soon after Fox left Flushing. It would have been easy enough to tie the oaks to the memory of Fox's visit. One can imagine John Bowne and his family standing outside their house and pointing to the two oaks across the street as they recalled Fox's preaching. Since John Bowne lived for twenty-three years after Fox's visit, he had numerous occasions to hone the story for friends and visitors. His children and grandchildren absorbed and retold the story, honoring their ancestor's devotion to Quakerism by recalling his special relationship to George Fox.

Curiously, the Bownes never mentioned that Fox actually returned to Flushing at the end of the summer. Fox held another meeting in Flushing on his journey back from Rhode Island. This gathering too probably took place under the Fox Oaks. Again, Fox recorded nothing about the oaks or the Bownes in his journal, but there is no reason to doubt that he was there, for he again preached to a large crowd of Quakers and non-Quakers. In the words of Fox (our sole source for the incident), there were once again "many hundreds of the people of the world" in attendance. Some had come "about thirty miles," including a justice of the peace "and his family, and many considerable persons." Strikingly, Fox had more to say about this meeting than the first one, probably because this time around it was more controversial. Some non-Quakers confronted him on questions of religious doctrine. A "priest's son" (that is, the son of a minister) "stood up" at the end of the meeting and "laid down three things that he would dispute." These were three of the basic problems that Reformed Protestants had with Quakers—namely, "the ordination of ministers," allowing women to speak in meetings, and the idea that Quakers "held a new way of worship." If Fox is to be believed, he emerged from the debate triumphant.[17]

The Bowne family probably overlooked this second visit by George Fox because it involved confrontation and dispute, not religious community, leadership, or harmony, the key themes of the Fox Oaks story. Consequently, the second visit was less important to the Bownes and Flushing than it was to Fox himself. Fox's first visit had earned the Bownes attention and respect, even from the governor of New York. It proved that they were now a respectable and recognized community. The second visit was a reminder that their religion was still not welcome among a significant portion of their neighbors. Fox, accustomed to controversy, rose to the challenge, but the local community had other interests. And so the tradition took hold that there was just one visit from Fox—the harmonious first one in June—not two.

We do not know exactly how the story was passed down over the generations, but it happened. The first documented evidence of the existence of the Fox Oaks is also the first instance of the Bowne family taking an active role in preserving their history. In a note scribbled around 1800, the Reverend Samuel Miller, a Presbyterian minister interested in writing a history of New York, recorded, "[There] are now standing, in the town of Flushing, two large oak trees, under which George Fox preached when he was in this country. Mr. Aspinwall of Flushing proposed, not many years since, to cut these trees down." John Bowne's great-grandson John Bowne III (1742–1804), "for the sake of sparing them, agreed to pay Mr. Aspinwall a sum of money, which was esteemed the market price of them."[18] Bowne had effectively ransomed the oaks. He did not buy the land they stood on. There is no record of him owning any of the property on the other side of the street in either his will or any other Bowne family documents.[19]

The Mr. Aspinwall who threatened to cut down the Fox Oaks was most likely Gilbert Aspinwall (1768–1819), whose family also originated in New England. However, their history was quite different from the Bownes. They were seafarers, merchants, and Anglicans who made their fortune in New York City. Gilbert was the eldest surviving son of Captain John Aspinwall (1706–74). Around 1760, Captain Aspinwall had earned enough money to purchase the country seat in Flushing for his retirement. Thereafter, the Aspinwalls became an increasingly prominent part of New York City's wealthy merchant class while still holding on to the house in Flushing. In the 1850s, Gilbert's grandson William Henry Aspinwall earned fame as the sponsor of a railway across the Panama peninsula. The Aspinwalls also intermarried with regional elites. Gilbert's granddaughter, Mary Rebecca, became the grandmother of Franklin Delano Roosevelt.[20]

The contrast between the Aspinwalls and the Bownes illuminates the precarious nature of early modern memory making. Not being Quakers and having only recently arrived in Flushing, the Aspinwalls had no special attachment to the Fox Oaks. Their focus was on their business in Manhattan, which had an ever-expanding need for capital. Bowne's ransom would have been a welcome addition to this ambitious family's assets. Two moments from the 1790s stand out as likely times for the transaction. In 1791, Gilbert moved to New York City to launch his trading firm. He surely could have used some extra money. In 1794, his younger brother John Aspinwall (1774–1847) joined the firm, then headed off to Britain with a respectable amount of cash to improve their overseas business contacts (along the way he was introduced to John Jay). Whenever the deal with John Bowne was made, the Aspinwalls remained true to it. They left the oaks alone and allowed them to die a natural death.[21]

John Bowne's ransom of the Fox Oaks seems to have been the spark that brought them public recognition. Before he paid for them, Flushing had had some famous visitors, but none of them mention the oaks: a notable contrast to later visitors. George Washington made the trip from Manhattan to Flushing in 1789, just after becoming president of the United States. Accompanied by a delegation that included Vice President John Adams, the governor of New York, and several other important men, Washington stopped by the nursery run by William Prince, who supplied some of the fruit that ended up on Washington's dinner table. Perhaps significantly, Washington does not seem to have interacted much with the Quaker part of the community. Apart from expressing his disappointment with "Prince's fruit Gardens and shrubberies," Washington only noted, "Inhabitants of this place shewed us what respect they could, by making the best use of one Cannon to Salute." Such a military ceremony is not one that Quakers would have eagerly participated in. Neither Washington nor Adams said anything about the Fox Oaks. Nor did Thomas Jefferson, who also visited Prince's nursery in June 1791.[22]

Rescuing the Fox Oaks from the Aspinwalls' axe seems to have galvanized the Bowne family into more actively promoting their memory and significance. After the death of John Bowne III, Bowne women led the way. The house's owners lost the Bowne surname after 1806, when John Bowne III's daughter Mary (1784–1839), who had inherited it, wed the Quaker minister Samuel Parsons (1774–1841). A farmer as well as a minister, Parson acquired a chunk of nearby land along with the house. His son Samuel Bowne Parsons (1819–1906) transformed the land into a successful nursery that specialized in growing and selling trees and shrubs. The Parsons Nursery earned its place in American tree history in 1847, when Samuel Bowne Parsons brought back a weeping beech from Belgium. It was the first of its kind in America. The notable tree flourished for over a century before it died in 1997. By then it had become one of only two trees to become a New York City landmark. Some of the former nursery land next to the Bowne House is now a public park named Weeping Beech Park in its honor. To celebrate the family's long-standing arboricultural interests, the historic Bowne House hosts an annual tree giveaway.[23]

The survival of the Bowne House made the task of commemoration much easier. By 1815, the family had expanded the house out from the initial room of 1661 to its current size. By (more or less) holding on to the property until 1945, the family had space to preserve a variety of objects and the traditions associated with them. The Bowne House Historical Society, formed to purchase and preserve the Bowne House, has used those objects and traditions to organize the exhibits it launched after opening the house for tours in 1947. Since then, the society has promoted the significance of the house and its connections to American history in various ways. In addition to the Flushing Remonstrance, it highlights the abolitionist sentiments of the house's antebellum owners and their participation in the Underground Railroad (the house is a member of the National Park Service's National Underground Railroad Network to Freedom).[24]

In the meantime, the network of Bowne women carried relics and recollections of the Fox Oaks out of state. Jane Bowne, a cousin of Mary Bowne Parsons, married the Philadelphia Quaker Rueben Haines III in 1812. Moving to the Haines family house in Germantown (now the Wyck Historic House), Jane took with her a wooden tea caddy that, as a small plaque on its lid claims, was "made from one of the old Oak trees at Flushing L.I. under which George Fox Preached the Gospel A.D. 1672." A note preserved with the tea caddy explains that Jane Bowne bequeathed the caddy to her daughter, Jane Reuben Haines. In July 1886, she in turn passed it on to her niece, Jane Bowne Haines, on her seventeenth birthday.[25]

This extended family, connected through Bowne women, did much to spread the fame of the Fox Oaks to the broader community. In 1822, a drawing was done "of the two venerable Oak Trees in the town of Flushing, under which Geo Fox preached in the year 1672 with the assemblage of people at that day." Perhaps this is the illustration depicting Fox preaching under the oaks with the Bowne House across the street printed on a postcard currently in the Bowne House Archives. Henry Post Jr. wrote to Reuben Haines III in Philadelphia to solicit the support of him and his wife, Jane Bowne Haines, for the artist so that a "copperplate engraving" could be made of the picture. Post noted that it included pictures of Quakers dressed in their "usual" garb, as well as "a View of the house such as it stands." The picture was attracting "a considerable attention" in New York, "especially by those who are attached to friends—as well as the friends of the fine arts & efforts are making to give the author a generous support." The picture, "associated with the communion of the society of friends in that place," was generating excitement as "one of the first efforts of the kind." Post expected support for its reproduction would come from Quaker communities across America as well as England.[26]

The plea to publish the image of the Fox Oaks evidently worked. At some point, the Haines family acquired an engraving of the picture. It was set in a frame allegedly made "of wood from the same oak tree" under which Fox is portrayed as preaching. They also acquired a print of the Bowne House and framed it with Fox Oak wood. Finally, they obtained a picture of George Fox's English residence, Swarthmore Hall (it does not seem to have been framed with Fox Oak wood). There could be no clearer statement about the direct links being drawn between George Fox, the headquarters of Quakerism in England, the Bowne House, and the Fox Oaks. These associations raised the Bowne House to a special level as an important seat of American Quakerism. Materially and conceptually, it was an integral part of a united front of transatlantic Quakerism.[27]

These images likely played a role in carrying the oaks' reputation across the Atlantic. When the noted English Quaker preacher Joseph John Gurney came to Flushing in 1839, he made a point of preaching underneath the Fox Oaks. He even spent several months resting in Flushing during an extended tour of American Quaker communities. It seems that he was a guest of the Parsons in the Bowne House, for Gurney noted that the "two venerable oaks"—"under which George Fox, nearly two hundred years before," had "held a large and impressive meeting"—stood just opposite his host's home. Gurney also remarked that he "had long believed that it would be [his] duty to hold a meeting" beneath "these oaks." Like Fox, Gurney was on a special mission to help American Quakers adapt to the changing world around them. He represented an evangelical turn in Quakerism that sought to reconcile it with prevailing Protestant norms. Like other evangelical Protestants, Gurney's preaching emphasized the importance of the Bible as a source of religious authority. He also encouraged his listeners to devote themselves to Jesus Christ, hoping they would have a conversion experience like that of other evangelical Protestants. Gurney was also an abolitionist. After spending a year in America, he decided that Flushing was the place to speak out on the theme.[28]

Like Fox before him, Gurney preached under the oaks because there was "no suitable place of worship in the village, large enough to accommodate the people." His account of the event implies it was endorsed and protected by a higher power. The day started off gloomy. Gurney worried that his voice was not up to the task, but by "five o'clock, the sky cleared, the wind abated, and a multitude of peoples were seen flocking to the spot." Like Fox before him, Gurney was a transatlantic celebrity. His preaching attracted "large numbers of the upper class, and many of the labouring inhabitants of the district, including the coloured people, and Irish Roman Catholics." His voice proved strong enough "to speak to them for upwards of an hour." As soon as he stopped, "a slight shower fell, which, had it occurred a few minutes sooner, would have robbed the meeting of its best and most solemn moments." He believed it "was, indeed, a good meeting." He mused that "George Fox might, perhaps, have applied to it his epithet 'glorious.'"[29]

Soon after Gurney's visit, images and other records of "The Flushing Oaks" began to proliferate. One was published around 1840.[30] In 1841, surveyor Elijah A. Smith drew up a map of Flushing that included "The Oaks" across the street from the Bowne homestead.[31] That same year, the oaks gained national renown with the publication of an account of Flushing in the *Historical Collections of the State of New York*. This popular series of state histories by John W. Barber and other authors recorded the "Most interesting Facts, Biographical Sketches, Varied Descriptions, etc. Relating to the Past and Present" of the different states, along with "Geographical Descriptions" of their "Counties, Cities, and Principal Villages." Often, an account of a town was accompanied by an engraved illustration. In the case of Flushing, the engraving is of the "Bowne Mansion-house." The view looks north up what is now Bowne Street. The Bowne House is on the right. In the middle of the street stands a young family admiring the Fox Oaks. The text notes that the house "is believed to be the oldest house now standing on Long Island, having been erected in 1661, by John Bowne, of the society of Friends." Along with its "antiquity," the house's "historic interest" made it worthy of note. "The celebrated George Fox, the founder of the society of Friends, has lodged within the walls of this house," it affirms. Indeed, the house "was the place for the yearly meeting for the whole body of Friends in the province of New York" until 1690, when a proper meetinghouse was finally erected a block and a half away on today's Northern Boulevard. It then notes the "two ancient oaks" on "the left of the engraving, on the opposite side of the street from the house . . . under which Fox preached when in this country in 1672." It concludes by praising Fox's "martyr spirit" even though he differed "in some of his tenets from the majority of those professing the Christian name." The text also notes that Flushing was the home of former colonial governor Cadwallader Colden and his descendants. Still, the most obviously significant aspect of Flushing was the Bowne House, the oaks, and the connection to George Fox.[32]

Unfortunately, just as they reached the peak of their fame, one of the oaks was "blown down by a violent storm" in September 1841.[33] Samuel Bowne Parsons, the nursery owner and heir to the Bowne House, composed the following poem as an elegy:

The ancient oak lies prostrate now.
Its limbs embrace the sod.
Where in the Spirit's strength and might,
Our pious fathers trod;
Where, underneath its spreading arms,
And by its shadows broad,
Clad in simplicity and truth,
They met to worship God.

No stately pillars round them rose.
No dome was reared on high;
The oaks their only columns were.
Their roof the arching sky;
No organ's deep-toned notes arose,
Or vocal songs were heard;
Their music was the passing wind,
Or song of forest bird.
And as His Spirit reached their hearts,
By man's lips speaking now,
A holy fire was in their eye,
Pure thought upon their brow;
And, while in silence deep and still,
Their souls all glowing were
With heartfelt peace and joy and love,
They felt that God was there.

Those pure and simple-minded men
Have now all passed away,
And of the scenes in which they moved
These only relics lay;
And soon the last surviving oak,

In its majestic pride,
Will gather up its failing limbs
And wither at its side.

Then guard with care its last remains,
Now that its race is run;
No sacrilegious hand should touch
The forest's noblest one.
And when the question may be asked,
Why that old trunk is there?
'Tis but the place in olden time
God's holiest altars were.[34]

Samuel Bowne Parsons commemorated the oak in more than just words. He is credited with carving out a cane from its wood that he gave to his dying father, then in the care of a New York doctor named Thomas Cook. Thomas Cook later became one of the founders of Haverford College. His granddaughter-in-law, Sarah E. Bowne, eventually inherited the cane and, in 1893, donated it to Haverford's Founders Hall "as a memento of her grandfather, Dr. Cook, and ancestor, John Bowne." It remains there to this day. No longer on display, it is a treasured piece of the college's special collections. The collection note describing it records that it came "from the 'Fox Oaks' . . . under which George Fox is supposed to have preached."[35]

In word and deed, then, Samuel Bowne Parsons—horticulturist, lover of trees, pious Quaker, and owner of the Bowne House—played a crucial role in perpetuating the memory of the Fox Oaks and other Bowne family lore. However, since the second of the two oaks remained standing for about twenty years after the first fell, some confusion arose over whether there were one or two Fox Oaks. Sources from the 1840s onward are as likely to speak of the "Fox Oak" as the "Fox Oaks." The surviving tree's significance is highlighted in a newspaper article published sometime between 1852 and 1862. It draws the most explicit connection possible between the tree, the Bowne family, their house, and George Fox: "Six John Bownes have come and gone in the old house, where the daughter of the last still lives." That daughter was Ann Bowne (1785–1863), a spinster and the last surviving sister of Mary Bowne Parsons (her spinster sister Eliza, who had also lived in the house, died in 1852). "An aged oak opposite stretches out its gaunt arms and seems like a giant spectre," the article says, making no mention of the tree's lost companion. Instead, it emphasizes, "Four hundred years it has stood in its majesty." If only it were a "talking oak," muses the author. Speculating about the notable historical incidents the tree could recount, the writer imagines the "crowds assembled in its shade" to hear how "the venerated George Fox spoke in long remembered tones." Then, "it could speak of the British soldiers encamped within the ken of its vision, it could tell of the shouts that rent the air when Washington was an honored guest at Flushing." Alas, as the writer, who was neither a Bowne nor a Quaker, notes, "The oak, like the Friends of whose founder it stands a memorial, is silent [a reference to the Quaker practice of silent worship], though suggestive—a golden silence rich with precious thoughts." Sadly, "decay is silently eating away the strength of this oak that has so well fulfilled its mission. . . . It is said that there is a curious sympathy between the tree and the family, who have for centuries dwelt beneath its shadow, that a branch died as each proprietor passed away, till now on the old trunk, as in the old house, but one living branch remains."[36]

Meanwhile, the oak continued its service to Quakerism by sheltering yet another Quaker preacher. This time it was a woman (female preachers being another distinctive aspect of Quakerism). In 1848, the abolitionist Abigail Kelley Foster came down from Massachusetts. Her mission was more political than religious, for she wanted to discourage people from supporting the anti-slavery Free Soil Party. The sort of political engagement it represented seemed to her to be a distraction from the greater cause of abolition. Perhaps because of its political purpose, her meeting was less peaceful than those of her predecessors. Hecklers showed up and pelted her with rotten eggs. Unscathed and undeterred, she successfully finished the meeting.[37]

Soon thereafter, the national fame of the Fox Oak(s) was secured. In 1851, the account of Flushing and the Fox Oaks, along with the illustration, was reprinted in a new edition of the *Historical Collections of the State of New York*. By the spring of 1862, the surviving oak was famous enough to be profiled in *Harper's New Monthly Magazine*. The article, the last in a series of articles about "American Historical Trees," was accompanied by a lovely sketch of the tree made in August 1861. Invoking their connection to George Fox's 1672 visit, it notes that both oaks had been rotting for some time before the first one fell in 1841. Those who examined its rings claimed it was about four hundred years old at the time. The one still standing was not even alive anymore. Down in Philadelphia, someone, probably Jane Reuben Haines, placed a copy of this article in the tea caddy made of Fox Oak wood she had inherited from her mother.[38]

Within a year, the remaining oak also fell.[39] Soon afterward, a marble slab was laid on the spot. An 1878 newspaper article describing the slab said it marked "where George Fox stood in 1672, beneath two old oaks, and addressed a congregation, the most notable of its time, which had gathered from far and near to the number of hundreds." The slab did not last very long. Its current whereabouts are unknown.[40]

In the meantime, the Bowne family briefly lost control of the house. Then, in 1886, a local newspaper happily reported that "Mrs. Robert Parsons" was able to purchase the home for "$10,100," returning it and its wealth of memories to the Bowne family. The article recalls Fox's 1672 sermon under the oaks. It is also the only piece of evidence to specify their species: "two great white oaks." It notes that one "was blown down on Sept. 25, 1841"; the other, called the "Fox Oak," stood "until 1862." Attached to the article is an illustration depicting a figure preaching to a crowd under the "Fox Oaks." That May, Mr. and Mrs. Robert B. Parsons sent out invitations for a "celebration" of the "225th Anniversary" of the Bowne House, to be held on the afternoon of June 8. One of those invitations made it to the Bowne relatives living in the Wyck House in Germantown, who then attached it to the back of their engraving of the Bowne House "framed in oak from the 'George Fox' tree."[41]

Thanks to the continuing efforts of the Bowne family, local reverence for the oaks remained strong into the twentieth century. In May 1893, Dr. J. W. Barston delivered an address on "The Trees of Flushing" to the Good Citizenship League. In it, Barston speculated on the demise of the "'Fox oaks' in Bowne Avenue." He thought they "were probably sacrificed to the spirit of progress which laid out that beautiful street. The grading of the surface doubtless disturbed the roots and led to their premature decay." At the time of his speech (it was not published until twenty-one years later), only three "of Flushing's primeval trees" remained. Barston wondered, "Shall their ancient dignity and their majestic endurance appeal to us in vain?"[42]

That same year, the memory of the Fox Oaks was again promoted out of state, this time in New Jersey. On December 25, 1893, an article in the *New York Sun* reported that "a relic" was "on exhibition in the show window of a store" in Rahway, New Jersey. Mrs. Isaac F. Wood, "of Rahway," was putting the "Cane Carried by John Bowne, the Quaker, Persecuted by Stuyvesant" (as the headline described it) on display before donating it to Haverford. Around the same time, the "Elizabeth Journal" (probably the *Elizabeth Daily Journal*, the paper of Elizabeth, New Jersey) ran essentially the same announcement of this "interesting relic of olden times" being exhibited "at Moore's stationery store." A "silver plate" above the "glass case" holding the cane noted that it came "from the Fox oak at Flushing, under which preached George Fox, the founder of Quakerism." Noting that Fox had been "entertained by John Bowne at his residence at Flushing," it emphasized that Bowne was one of Fox's enthusiastic followers. It then retold the story of Bowne's persecution at the hands of Peter Stuyvesant, before concluding with the dramatic (but false) claim that the "'Fox Oaks' were destroyed by lightning in 1849."[43]

The Bowne family also made a point of cultivating the memory of the oaks with powerful people. In 1897, Jane C. Moon, a probable Bowne descendant, visited the Bowne House along with her husband, Jonathan Chace. Chace was a prominent Quaker from Rhode Island. He had represented that state in both the House of Representatives and the Senate. At one point during their visit, they walked to the "opposite side of [the] road from" the house to "the spot where the George Fox oak stood." Perhaps because Chace was so important, someone took a picture of him and his wife standing on the spot. The photograph was then passed down through the family until it made its way into the Bowne House Historical Society Archives.[44]

In the twentieth century, the Bownes got even more creative in their memory work. In 1911, another Bowne descendant, Cornelia Mitchell Parsons, included the Fox Oaks in her novelization of seventeenth-century Quaker history. The main character of *The Quaker Cross* is George Fox. Robert Barclay and William Penn only get a chapter each. In an entire chapter devoted to Fox's visit to America, Cornelia Parsons describes how, when he got to Flushing, hundreds of people "from far and near had gathered under the oak trees in the lane, where they could all be sheltered from the scorching rays of the June sun. . . . The great trees swayed their branches and whispered, 'Come, come, come.'" After providing a fictionalized version of Fox's sermon (the actual one was never recorded), she has the crowd sit "as if spellbound. As they looked around them at the trees, the green grass under their feet . . . all nature appeared the same." Unsurprisingly, the Bowne family plays an important role in this part of the story. The family's preparations for Fox's arrival are detailed. Then, "after the meeting was over, all were invited to partake of John and Hannah Bowne's hospitality." Later, John turns to his wife to make a prophetic observation that says much about his house's importance to his descendants and the local Quaker community: "Hannah, dear heart, I feel as if this holy man hath left a benediction behind him. Our home will be more hallowed than ever before, and bearing our daily cross cheerfully, we must be drawn heavenward."[45]

The blending of history, religion, and nature with the Bowne House did not stop at the Fox Oaks. The title of Cornelia Parsons's novel, *The Quaker Cross*, refers to another piece of family lore that linked Quakerism with a material object and, eventually, some plants still preserved on the house site. As an undated typescript from the mid-twentieth century explains, this legendary jeweled cross had been a treasured heirloom of the Percy family in England. It eventually was inherited by Mary Becket, a Quaker who moved to America and married John Bowne's son Samuel in 1691. According to the tradition, just after she arrived in Flushing, she noticed a secret spring in the cross. When pressed, the cross opened to reveal a paper saying, "God forbid that I should glory save in the cross of our Lord Jesus Christ, whereby the world is crucified unto me, and I unto the world." Accordingly, she then gladly sold the jeweled cross "to help defray expenses of bringing William Penn back from England to his people in Pennsylvania." In the 1950s, Mary Dixon, with the help of "Mrs. Samuel D. Jones . . . and Mr. Laurence B. Halleran," planted a "Quaker Cross Garden" at the Bowne House. This floral memorial consisted of a stately boxwood in the shape of a cross interspersed with "lovely flowers that change as the seasons change." The attractive arrangement quickly became a favorite with visitors. The home's "hostess" gladly explained to them "the story of how the garden got its name."[46]

In comparison, the memory of the Fox Oaks threatened to fade away. When August Kapka wrote his short pamphlet *The Trees of Flushing* in the 1940s, he mentioned the Parsons Nursery and its weeping beech but said nothing about the Fox Oaks. Admittedly, Kapka's interest was in living trees, not legendary ones. He closed his account with Joyce Kilmer's famous 1913 poem "Trees," inspired by the living trees of New Jersey. No legendary trees feature in these texts.[47]

Nevertheless, the Fox Oaks have yet to be forgotten. The granite memorial sitting across the street from the Bowne House has told their story since 1907. More recently, a historic marker was added to explain more about the oaks' significance. In the fall of 1991, *Newwyck*, the newsletter of the Wyck House, published an article mentioning the "tea caddy made with wood from the oak under which Quaker, George Fox preached in Flushing, Long Island in 1672." It remembered that Jane Bowne Haines, "who grew up in Flushing," had received the "chest" as a gift, which "then passed to her daughter and eventually to her granddaughter." The chest was just one of several family relics the family still owned in the twentieth century. More recently, in June 2016, a French blogger with a passion for history included the illustration of Fox preaching under the Fox Oaks in his account of Fox's visits to Flushing for his online timeline of US history. The memory of the Fox Oaks has now gone from the material to the digital world. Who knows where it will go next.[48]

In his recent sweeping study of trees and historical memory in the United States, Jared Farmer emphasizes their association with acts of violence and dispossession. Looking primarily at notable trees from the eighteenth century forward (Farmer's earliest tree is the Penn Treaty Tree of the 1680s), he found most of them were associated with violence: colonialism, hanging, lynching, slavery, or war. Given these grim associations, he suggests one might be forgiven for preferring to see them chopped down and the history associated with them forgotten. He does not include the Fox Oaks in his analysis. Their peaceful Quaker legacy—dating back a decade before William Penn arrived in America—evokes a very different set of relationships between history, memory, and trees. Here, religious and dynastic associations prevail. The astounding history of the oaks' survival—decades beyond what their eighteenth-century owner would have allowed—and their extensive commemoration in word, picture, artifact, and deed, demonstrate the lengths people can go to commemorate trees if they attach enough personal as well as public meaning to them.[49]

While still standing, the Fox Oaks provided a communal worship space for the people of Flushing, one where Quakers could share their preaching with their non-Quaker neighbors. The persistence of their memory is a rare success story of early modern memory culture in the United States. Their enduring legacy reveals the power of generations of work to sustain an account of an otherwise poorly documented history. For over two and a half centuries, members of the Bowne family, both those who lived across the street from the oaks and those who moved out of state, passed on the story of George Fox's visit using a variety of media: oral tradition, literature, and material culture. The Bownes' creative use of a wide range of techniques—items carved out of their wood, a poem, a novel, engravings, photographs, letters, speeches, and social gatherings—helped fix this memory in the minds of their descendants, neighbors, and, now, tourists. Their willingness to put their money where their mouth was is also significant. They purchased the oaks. They held on to their house, even buying it back when it fell out of family control. They offered hospitality to visitors sustaining the tradition of preaching beneath them inaugurated by George Fox. Finally, they turned their home over to an organization capable of maintaining it as a museum and historic site. Now that the Bowne family has left town, archivists and museum staff at several Quaker-linked institutions in the mid-Atlantic continue the task of preserving this memory. Meanwhile, across the street in Flushing, the large hunk of granite and metal street sign still maintain their vigil on the sidewalk.

The variety of methods and media used to preserve the memory of the Fox Oaks—and their often intimate material connection to the trees themselves—provides a remarkably detailed case study of how early modern forms of memory making worked and continue to work. The role of a prosperous family personally invested in the history and its religious significance cannot be underestimated. The Bownes had the social and economic stability to remain neighbors of the oaks for two centuries while they existed, then almost another full century after they had vanished from the landscape. The successful preservation of their memory and significance was a genuinely intergenerational affair. It also depended on the work of both the men and women of the Bowne family. Family history has been recognized as a matter of particular concern for women since the early modern period.[50] Here, the women of the Bowne family proved especially crucial in enrolling their non-Bowne husbands and relatives into the cause. The Fox Oaks show how family history, religious interests, and local pride can survive by wrapping themselves around a specific object—in this case, a pair of trees.

While this mix of family tradition and documented history has proven powerful, it has also produced a less than perfectly historically accurate account of George Fox's time in Flushing, the early religious history of the town, and even the fate of the oaks. The Bownes commemorated Fox's first visit, not his second, contentious one. Accurate details of what happened with the oaks are hard to come by. Inaccurate statements have proliferated over the years, adding to the legend by obscuring the history. In short, the Fox Oaks phenomenon also demonstrates the limits of early modern memory making. The granite monument on Bowne Street was completed just two years before the Queensboro Bridge provided a direct link to Manhattan and unleashed the rapid urbanization of what had remained a largely agricultural town. With urbanization came immigration and demographic changes that, especially since the mid-twentieth century, transformed Flushing into one of the most religiously and ethnically diverse—and least Christian—communities in all of America. Few, if any, Quakers are left in town. Instead, the streets are full of representatives of various forms of Hinduism, Buddhism, Islam, Korean Protestantism, Confucianism, various Japanese sects, and more. The granite memorial is now easily obscured by parked cars. Whether the memory of the Fox Oaks will persist as a relevant story for the current residents of Flushing remains to be seen. However, as long as the Bowne House and its historical society continue to exist, the town's Quaker origins will remain a source of local pride and wonder. Not bad for a family legacy.

FIGURE 15. Two white pine coniferous trees planted by the Children of Shingwauk Alumni Association on the front lawn of Shingwauk Hall. Photograph by the Shingwauk Residential Schools Centre, 2024.

Chapter Ten

Pine Trees and the Legacy of the Shingwauk Site

Krista McCracken, Algoma University

The Shingwauk Residential School

The Anishinaabemowin (Ojibway) word for pine tree is *Shingwauk.* This chapter connects the history of the Shingwauk Residential School and the use of pine trees as commemorative markers on the Shingwauk site. The site that is now home to the Sault Ste. Marie campus of Algoma University was home to the Shingwauk Indian Residential School from 1874 to 1970. The Shingwauk Residential School—like residential schools across Canada and Indian boarding schools in the United States—aimed to assimilate Indigenous children and erase the culture, language, and identity of Indigenous peoples.[1] Residential schools were designed to remove the connection of children to the family, community, and identity. They were places of genocide and harmed many generations of Indigenous people. Today, many residential schools in Canada and the United States are conducting site searches for unmarked burials.[2] Unmarked burials are but one example of the horrible trauma and violence that took place at these institutions.

In Canada, residential schools were operated through a partnership between religious organizations and the Canadian government. There were over 135 residential schools, which operated from the 1830s until 1996, located across Canada as part of the residential school system. The Shingwauk School was run by the Government of Canada in partnership with the Anglican Church of Canada. It was one of the eighteen residential schools located in Ontario and one of the approximately three dozen schools across Canada that were run by the Anglican Church. Students from all across Canada and the upper United States attended Shingwauk, and it was one of the largest and longest-running Anglican residential schools in Ontario.[3]

Residential schools and boarding schools were part of a larger agenda of colonization in Canada and the United States. The first prime minister of Canada, Sir John A. MacDonald, asserted that one of the main goals of the Canadian government was to assimilate Indigenous people into Canadian society.[4] Residential schools were part of the colonial agenda, alongside various other pieces of government policy, including the reserve system, the pass system, day schools, and many other forms of colonial control. In 1847, Egerton Ryerson, the chief superintendent of education for Upper Canada, argued in favor of establishing industrial residential schools.[5] Ryerson's work was followed by the work of Nicolas Davin, who issued the 1879 *Davin Report*, which recommended funding residential schools through a partnership with church organizations. Davin's report was based on observing Indian education in the United States, particularly the Carlisle Boarding School, and was the foundation for the large-scale residential school system that would expand across Canada.[6] This residential school system, which existed in Canada until 1996, was designed to forcibly assimilate Indigenous children into Canadian society. The impact of the Shingwauk School and other residential schools is still being felt by many who attended, their families, and their communities today.[7]

Most residential schools were named after their physical location or a religious figure. For example, there were multiple schools named St. Mary and St. Peter. The Shingwauk School in Sault Ste. Marie is an unusual case, as it was named after Anishinaabe Chief Shingwaukonse, from Garden River First Nation. Shingwaukonse died in 1854, prior to the Shingwauk Residential School opening. However, the first principal of the Shingwauk School, Reverend E. F. Wilson, worked closely with Shingwaukonse and his descendants to advocate for a school in the Garden River First Nation region. It is this relationship that resulted in the naming of the school after Chief Shingwaukonse. He was an Anishinaabe political, thought, and educational leader.[8] According to Janet E. Chute, Shingwaukonse had three major goals for the Anishinaabe people: "To establish linkages with the government agencies that were just beginning to exercise jurisdiction in the Upper Great Lakes region; second to preserve an environment in which Native cultural values and organizational structures could survive; and finally, to devise new strategies that would promote the formation of band governments capable of assuming a degree of proprietorship over resources on First Nations lands."[9] Shingwaukonse's leadership was tied to Anishinaabe sovereignty, cultural stewardship, and connection to the land. The name "Shingwaukonse" is translated to English as "Little Pine." In addition to his political and legal position, Chief Shingwaukonse had a vision of "teaching wigwams," places where Anishinaabe could learn from white settlers and white settlers could learn about Anishinaabe worldviews and teachings.[10] It is this vision that inspired him and his descendants to work with E. F. Wilson to advocate for education. However, Chief Shingwaukonse's vision was lost through the residential school era, with the Shingwauk Residential School operating like every other residential school in Canada with the goal of assimilating Indigenous peoples. Shingwaukonse's name may have been tied to the residential school building, but his vision was not present throughout the duration of the residential school's operation.

The original vision of cross-cultural education held by Chief Shingwaukonse continues today through the Children of Shingwauk Alumni Association (CSAA), Shingwauk Kinoomaage Gamig, and Algoma University. The CSAA is a group of survivors and intergenerational survivors from the Shingwauk and Wawanosh Residential Schools, Shingwauk Kinoomaage Gamig is an Indigenous-run educational institute, and Algoma University is a mainstream postsecondary institution.[11] As partners on the Shingwauk site, these three groups, along with other stakeholders, continue to talk about Chief Shingwaukonse, his vision, and the importance of learning across cultures. In 2008, when Algoma University became an independent university, it was given a special mission by the province of Ontario as part of its charter. This legal mandate notes, "It is the Special Mission of the University . . . to cultivate cross-cultural learning between Aboriginal communities and other communities, in keeping with the history of Algoma University College and its geographic site."[12] The legacy of Chief Shingwaukonse's vision for cross-cultural education was written into the legal framework that governs Algoma University. Practically, this means that Algoma University places an emphasis on incorporating Anishinaabe culture into curricula, support systems, and administrative structures. Algoma University uses its "history and stories to teach the truth about the residential schools history in Canada while at the same time, moving forward with Chief Shingwauk's original vision for education on this site to be one of cross-cultural learning and teaching."[13] Algoma University has publicly committed to supporting cross-cultural education and teaching about the legacy of residential schools. Additionally, the special mission supports Algoma University's relationship with Indigenous partners such as Shingwauk Kinoomaage Gamig to help facilitate cross-cultural learning through the delivery of an Anishinaabe studies degree and a degree in the Anishinaabemowin language. Algoma University also works closely with the CSAA—survivors of the Shingwauk School and their descendants—to honor the residential school legacy that is tied to the Algoma campus. The CSAA has been working on the Shingwauk site since the late 1970s to ensure that the vision of Chief Shingwaukonse and the legacy of residential schools are not forgotten. In 1979, Dan Pine, a descendant of Chief Shingwaukonse and a survivor of the Shingwauk School, spoke publicly about the legacy of the Shingwauk site. He said, "The Shingwauk School never closed. It just entered a new phase of development. It has to be given a chance to finish what it started. It has to put back what it took away. It is the people who went there that will care. Bring the people together. Let them gather and they will know what to do."[14] Dan Pine's words were a call to remember Chief Shingwaukonse's vision of teaching wigwams and the importance of returning to traditional ways of knowing and honoring the past. These words were also a call to bring together survivors of the Shingwauk Residential School and begin ongoing dialogues about the future of the Shingwauk site. The legacy of Shingwauk, residential schools, and Chief Shingwaukonse is still deeply connected to the work of Algoma University as a place of postsecondary education and as a place for the community to honor the past. This history is directly tied to two pine trees that stand on the front lawn of the Shingwauk site.

Pine Trees as Monuments

In 1981, the CSAA held the first Shingwauk reunion. This reunion was eleven years after the Shingwauk School had closed and welcomed former students and their families to return to the Shingwauk site to begin to talk about their experiences at the residential school. The date of this reunion is significant, as in the 1980s, residential schools were still open elsewhere in Canada, and nationally, there was not a conversation occurring about the harms of the school system.[15] During the organizing of the reunion, the CSAA wasn't sure how many people would attend. They thought if they got fifty people, the event would be considered a success. Over the course of the weekend, over three hundred people participated in the reunion. There was a strong community desire to begin talking about the impact of residential schools and to connect with others who lived through the same experience. The 1981 reunion was the catalyst for the CSAA to begin nationally organizing and connecting survivors across the country.[16] The CSAA has since expanded to be a survivor organization open to others from different residential schools and a national organization that has worked to support survivors throughout the healing process. As part of this work, the CSAA has held many other reunions, gatherings, and sharing circles and established a community archives—now known as the Shingwauk Residential Schools Centre (SRSC).[17]

The 1981 Shingwauk reunion also saw the planting of a white pine tree on the front lawn of the Shingwauk site as a way to commemorate the history of the Shingwauk Residential School and the Shingwauk/Algoma site. The tree, as a commemorative marker, was chosen by the survivors. It was planted by a combination of survivors and members of the local diocese of the Anglican Church, which had run the Shingwauk School. Unfortunately, this first pine tree did not survive due to a landscaping mishap when the young tree was clipped by a lawn mower. Not to be discouraged, survivors planted two more white pine trees during the next Shingwauk reunion, which was held in 1991. The pine trees were planted next to a monument marking the location of the original Shingwauk School building, which existed on the site from 1874 to 1935. The stone monument has an inscription that is dedicated to Reverend E. F. Wilson, the first principal of the Shingwauk School. By placing the pine trees next to the stone monument, the Shingwauk survivors were actively countering government and church historical narratives about residential schools and creating space to honor the students who attended the Shingwauk School. Survivor and founding CSAA member Shirley Horn was present at the planting and considers the trees as a reflection of the growth of the reconciliation movement. The first pine tree didn't make it, but the two that were planted afterward were protected and have grown in strength. According to Shirley, this mirrors the resilience of survivors.[18] Likewise, when the trees were originally planted as small saplings, no one was really talking about residential schools in public forums. In the 1980s and 1990s, many survivors were only beginning to deal with their traumas, and many were just starting their healing journeys. Now, decades later, the trees are tall and easily visible, reflecting the spread of information about residential schools, the continuing growth of reconciliation in Canada, and the progress many survivors have made on their healing journeys.

As a public historian, archivist, and white settler who has worked at Algoma University in the SRSC since 2010, I am incredibly grateful for the knowledge that has been shared about these trees and the community care that has gone into honoring the past with the planting and maintenance of them. I also acknowledge as a white settler that sacred Indigenous knowledge is not mine to share. The information shared in this chapter is publicly available, or I have been granted explicit permission to share it in this forum. Any information about traditional ecological Indigenous knowledge relating to trees in this chapter is information that has been widely published and discussed in academic forms. It in no way represents sacred or traditional Indigenous knowledge. Rather, this chapter is a discussion of community commemoration and local history in connection to two pine trees. To contextualize the Shingwauk pine trees, this chapter will discuss the trees in relation to Indigenous understandings of pine trees, explore the lives of the white pine trees themselves, and situate the trees in relation to the legacy of residential schools. Now situated on the front lawn of Algoma University, these trees represent the journey of residential school survivors and are markers of trauma, resilience, and strength within the survivor community.

Trees and Knowledge Holders

The idea of trees as markers and keepers of history is not something new. Since time immemorial, Indigenous peoples have had relationships with trees. These relationships have been cultural, spiritual, and resource based. Trail marker trees are an example of Indigenous communities using trees as markers, signage, and directional aids.[19] Indigenous peoples from numerous communities "turned trees themselves into signs—'trail trees,' 'message trees,' 'signal trees,' 'bent trees'—by training the trunk or one large branch to grow in an irregular direction."[20] This training of a trunk or branch can be seen as a metaphor for education, as a parallel to the challenges associated with growing into and learning new knowledge. Trail marker trees are keepers of ecological knowledge and information about trade routes and have cultural importance. For over several hundred years, Indigenous people in North America have intentionally changed or modified trees to record memories, to share information, and for cultural practices.[21] These trees sometimes mark trails or locations. Trees have also been modified to mark memories, events, or cultural activities.

Trees have also been used by Indigenous peoples to represent relationships and tell the history of communities. For example, the Great Tree of Peace, an eastern white pine tree, is recognized as representing the unity and strength of the Haudenosaunee Confederacy.[22] The eastern white pine has clusters of five needles, representing the five nations that came together to make up the Haudenosaunee Confederacy. The white pine is also noted for its strength and physical characteristics: "As the tallest tree, the white pine also has strong roots, deep and widespread, rather than a single taproot. The deep, wide roots indicate stability, but they also become the carriers of the metaphor for the spreading of the peace. White pines are also relatively fire-resistant: they survive most surface fires due to their thick bark, branch-free trunks, and moderately deep roots. Metaphorically, they survive the fires of war."[23] The Great Tree of Peace—the white pine—is deeply connected to Haudenosaunee concepts of peace, unity, strength, and community. This is one example of trees holding knowledge of Indigenous communities and representing relationships. The Great Tree of Peace being a pine tree is significant. It was chosen in part for its physical strength and deep roots. The symbolic importance of the deep roots and strength of the pine tree can be tied back to the two pine trees on the Shingwauk site. In the case of Shingwauk, the strength of the pine trees reflects the strength of healing and the survivor community. The white pine is also culturally significant to the Kitcisakik Algonquins, who view the white pine "as the 'king' or 'chief' (*Okima*) of the forest because of the great trunk size and height."[24] The Kitcisakik community also speaks about the importance of the white pine in providing a sense of peace in forests, the role of the white pine in providing shade, and the use of the trees to provide directional guidance.[25] Similarly, the white pine is known for its medicinal value and the use of all parts of the tree to treat illness. The pine tree has many meanings and cultural teachings both for the students who attended the Shingwauk Residential School and for many other Indigenous communities across the land.

In contrast to Indigenous culture, Eurocentric culture has commodified white pines in a number of ways. Historically, this is seen in the use of white pines by the British shipping industry, where the pines were used to create ship masts, tying the trees directly to colonization and the expansion of the British Empire. This exploitation and use of white pines by Britain is further seen by the British enacting policy in the 1700s to claim all white pines over twenty-four inches for their navy.[26] By the 1800s, the white pine was heavily logged in Canada and the United States, resulting in the destruction of many of the older, taller white pine stands in both countries. White pine is commonly used for furniture and interior finishings. Today, white pines are further colonized through their use as Christmas trees and as landscaping plants. The white pine is easy to shape, making it ideal for Christmas trees, which all conform to the same aesthetic. The treatment of pines by colonial industry is a stark contrast to the use of white pines as knowledge keepers in Indigenous culture.

Pinus strobus and the Physicality of White Pines

The two pine trees planted on the Shingwauk site are eastern white pines (*Pinus strobus*). The white pine is a long-lived, needled evergreen native to the northeastern United States and Canada. It is a conifer species that provides habitats and food for wildlife, and it is commonly found in both forested and urban landscapes.[27] The eastern white pine is the provincial tree of Ontario, Canada, and is the state tree of both Maine and Michigan. Additionally, Maine's state flower is the pine cone and needles of the white pine tree.[28] The bark of the mature white pine is gray brown with furrowed ridges. The bark furrows with age, growing in thickness and strength over time. White pine growth is slow and steady. A three-year-old tree is only around five inches tall, a five-year-old tree is twelve inches, and an eight-to-ten-year-old tree is fifty-four inches. Growth then speeds up as the tree ages, with trees growing an average of forty-one inches a year.[29] Trees reach fifty to eighty feet in cultivation and will grow over one hundred feet tall in the wild.[30] Precolonial stands of pine trees were known as being the tallest in eastern North America, with some trees being over 230 feet in height.[31] The slow initial growth of white pines parallels the residential school survivor movement, with it starting off slowly on a local level at Shingwauk, gaining strength in increments, and then eventually growing in strength and expanding to the national level. White pines are also long-lived, often reaching 200 years, with some trees being over 450 years.[32] Residential school survivors have been working for decades to have their experiences heard, persevering through time and space like a strong white pine tree.

The needles of the eastern white pine are light green and grow in bundles. Each bundle has five needles.[33] Indigenous peoples have used the needles of the pine for tea and for making pine needle baskets. When selecting pine needles for use, only the longest needles are collected, leaving the shorter ones to continue to grow and be used in the future. Harvesting needles is seen as a form of care, with harvesting supporting the new growth of needles, when done correctly.[34] In some cases, the needles of pine trees have uses beyond their practical application. They are tied to Indigenous knowledge and used as part of Indigenous learning and understanding. For example, the five needles of the white pine tree are tied to Kanyen'kehá-ka understanding of history, with the white pine telling about the Haudenosaunee Confederacy, the Great Law of Peace, and the traditional geography of the five Haudenosaunee Nations.[35] The needles of the pine tree have many uses—both practical applications and as mnemonic devices and storytellers. Similar to the needles, the resin, pitch, or sap from pine trees also have many uses. Pine tree resin can be used as an adhesive, for making candles, for waterproofing, and for starting fires. The resin from pine trees can be used to hold things together. The Shingwauk pine trees hold together community history, survivor voices, and survivor resilience.

The seeds of the pine tree come in the form of pine cones. Pine trees don't begin to produce pine cones until they are twenty to thirty years old, and then seed growth comes in waves—with every three to five years being good seed years.[36] Cones start off green and take time to mature, turn brown, and fall to the ground. Henry David Thoreau, an American naturalist and author, recorded his observations of the white pine. He noted, "As for the white pine, you have all observed its clusters of sickle-shaped green cones at the top chiefly of the tallest trees, well nigh inaccessible to man. About the middle of September these turn brown and open in the sun and wind. . . . How little observed are the fruits which we do not use! How few attend the ripening and dispersion of the white-pine seed!"[37] Pine cones are commonplace on yards, forest floors, and wherever there are stands of pine trees. These small cones have the potential to grow into white pine trees, which carry knowledge and strength. The Shingwauk trees have grown with the narrative of residential school survivors, strengthening with age and mirroring the growth of survivors, healing, and truth telling.

Community Commemoration

I pass by these trees every day when I go to work, and I've had the privilege of sitting with survivors—like Shirley—who were at the Shingwauk reunion and hearing them speak about the planting of the pine trees. The location, story, and preservation of these trees matter. The SRSC staff routinely provide historical site truth walks to over twenty thousand visitors per year. These historical truth walks focus on the history of the Shingwauk Indian Residential School and commemoration efforts of the CSAA and place the history of the Shingwauk School in the larger context of Canada, the residential school system, and colonization. These walks include information on the historic buildings on the site, ongoing commemoration efforts, and general site history. There are a number of formal monuments and markers on the site, including a memorial cairn located in the cemetery dedicated to all students who passed away at Shingwauk, a stone cairn dedicated to the first principal of Shingwauk, a government heritage plaque, and a monument put up in 2012 by survivors that is dedicated to all those who attended residential schools across the land. The two pine trees sit close to the stone cairn and the 2012 monument, which back onto each other. It's tempting to skip over the pine trees and be drawn into the more formal monuments. However, while engaged in delivering historical walks of the Shingwauk site, staff often make sure to reference the two pine trees. This walk stop is used to explain the significance of the trees and is an opportunity to talk about language, honoring the past, and preserving the history of Shingwauk. It's also an opportunity to talk about community and the ways in which the survivor community has chosen to remember and represent the past. The pine trees were intentionally placed and prioritized over another stone marker. They are commemorative markers, even if they do not appear so at first glance. They represent the legacy of Shingwaukonse, the resilience of the survivor community, and the legacy of residential schools. The trees are markers to the community and tell a story of a movement, a community, and the growth of knowledge. The pine trees are a fundamental part of the legacy of the Shingwauk site, and they act as constant reminders of the legacy of Shingwaukonse and his vision for cross-cultural education. The trees also serve as a reminder of the pain of the residential school era and the ongoing healing work related to residential schools. The pine trees have grown up alongside the healing journey of many survivors and serve as markers of hope and resilience.

The word *Shingwaukonse*—Little Pine—is deeply connected to the history of residential schools in Sault Ste. Marie. From the initial vision of Chief Shingwaukonse to the naming of a residential school after him, the word *Shingwauk* is embedded in narratives around Indigenous education and residential schools. It is fitting, then, that pine trees have been chosen as a form of commemoration and honoring, as a way to draw on the connection to the Shingwauk family and the legacy of residential schools. The two pine trees stand silently but speak volumes about community, healing, and commemoration.

FIGURE 16. The "whipping tree" in Laurel Grove South bears a scar belt more than five feet up its trunk. Local tour guides believe the marks were created by an overseer's lash, but dendrologists know them to be the signs of a naturally forming tree canker. Photograph courtesy of Alena Pirok, 2024.

Chapter Eleven

Oaks of Ill Repute

DARK TOURISM, DISSONANT HERITAGE, AND SAVANNAH'S HANGING TREES

Alena Pirok, Georgia Southern University

As any promotional photo can attest, Savannah, Georgia, is filled with large mature trees. The city's nineteenth- and early twentieth-century buildings are framed by magnolias, pride of India, and sweet gums. The twenty-two eighteenth-century squares and numerous parks are littered with twisty Spanish moss–covered oaks. In the cemeteries, pine, live oak, and palms intermingle with the graves and headstones of the city's former residents. Of the city's 28,764 acres, 44 percent is covered in trees and has been for as long as any resident today can remember.[1] Many think fondly of the trees, some seeing them as deeply "intertwined" with the relationship the city has with its past and present.[2] But, unlike the buildings or colonial-era layout, few people know why the trees are in the city. They are not part of the official narrative of the city's past, and they don't have an officially written story of their own.

Savannah's official history is told between the trees, on over one hundred signs and plaques that public and private ventures have planted generously throughout downtown and are interpreted by an ever-fluctuating number of historical tour guides. Be it on foot or in buses, they share a well-trodden route, matching narratives to signs. They talk about General Oglethorpe founding Georgia and befriending Tomochichi in the shadow of his monument,

Juliette Gordon Lowe and the Girl Scouts out front of her house museum, immigrant hard work at Leopold's Ice Cream outside the Broughton Street parlor, the epics of the Historic Savannah Foundation's restoration efforts at the Davenport House, and the birth of the winter classic "Jingle Bells" under its official marker outside of the Unitarian Church.

The clear stops and stories speak in a cohesive and overwhelming positive voice. The officially marked history compliments the lovely yesterday-aesthetic created by the architecture, tight roads, and large trees and seeks only to challenge guests to imagine the little city as a major player in the national narrative. Stories that ask more of guests or reveal the city as a site of pain as well as beauty are not represented in official markers and are easily forgotten or dismissed on most tours. The guides who share the unmarked stories of whippings, lynchings, and hangings look to the trees to orient their disturbing tales.

The old oaks function remarkably well for this work. They, like the historical markers, are everywhere tourists want to visit and are largely unremarkable and freely inscribable. Without a voice of their own or an accessible history, the guides present the trees as timeless objects. It is common in Savannah to understand the trees as witnesses of the city's entire history and thus living remnants of the past situated in the present-day. They are also, to the untrained eye, unremarkable. The most used trees—the Candler Oak, the hanging tree in Colonial Park Cemetery, the hanging tree in Wright Square, and the whipping tree in Laurel Grove South Cemetery—are largely indistinguishable from the thousands of other trees in Savannah. The tour guides make them remarkable through the stories they tell under their branches and by teaching guests a kind of pseudo-dendrology that enables them to read trunk scars and moss as indisputable evidence of dissonant heritage. In doing so, they not only inject the painful realities of the region's past within the historical marker landscape; they also transform the city's trees into powerfully defiant objects, whose presence alludes to the nation's ever-present yet silenced history of violence.

Ascribing meaning to trees is not exclusive to Savannah, of course. Historian Eric Rutkow argues that much of US history "has been defined by trees."[3] From the early colonial Europeans who set eyes on North America's massive forests to the endless uses humans have made for trees, people have filled volumes about all that trees are, can be, and have been to them.

Despite humans' love of trees through time, historians have not granted trees a formal recognition in the same way that nonhistorians have.[4] Scholars' treatment of trees tends to focus on humans' relationship to them—how humans plant them, organize them, and wield them in their urban environments. In most cases, trees are treated not as individual resources but rather as examples of a larger practice. Part of the reason for this limitation comes from what Dipesh Chakrabarty calls "the age-old humanist distinction between natural history and human history,"[5] or the idea that the natural world, trees included, is present but separate from human history. Trees, while a common part of all human life, do not have agency. Trees across the nation, as in Savannah, have long been background characters in a human-focused story. They have been used to create food, tools, and shelter and have been approached largely from a colonial lens, one in which humans are responsible for action, and trees are passive.

This way of thinking makes oaks, maples, and sweet gums of all kinds ideal candidates for human meaning making. As such, people have been identifying trees as markers, symbols, and witnesses of historical events in the United States for hundreds of years.[6] From founder trees, inaugural trees, lone trees, and mother trees, as Jared Farmer explains, trees make for good historical symbols because they can be recontextualized easier than human-made monuments. Furthermore, he explains that as living things, their life and death are easily compared to that of humans and romanticized.[7]

Sentimentality and romance dominate the meaning that people ascribe to trees. So much so, as Farmer points out, the seemingly unproblematic tree narratives often harbor more nuanced pasts as liberty/vigilance trees and treaty/massacre trees.[8] These new critical categories challenge the older interpretations of tree-marked stories by recognizing how Americans have used trees to celebrate and reinforce a sense of colonial power. For this reason, he explains, historical trees further racialize American nature and naturalize racial hierarchies.[9] The trees that I discuss in this chapter are what Farmer would call vigilance trees. All of them are remembered for the unwilling role they played in murder or the beatings of those deemed criminal. But they do not fit neatly into Farmer's categories due to the unofficial nature of peoples' interpretation of these trees.

The ease by which people inscribe meaning onto trees increases when there is no bureaucratic entity through which one needs to officiate their interpretation. Such is the case in Savannah; the trees themselves are not officially recognized as historical, and guides' interpretations are not subject to any kind of peer review. With this freedom, history and ghost tour guides have transformed the city's trees from aesthetic background objects into passive participants in the city's undesirable history.

Of course, the "dark" nature of the stories attached to the trees is hard to ignore and lends itself to interpreting Savannah's oaks of ill repute as examples of what scholars have termed *dark tourism*. According to Philip Stone, dark tourism "alludes to a sense of apparent disturbing practice and morbid products (and experiences) within the tourism domain."[10] He gives examples like Ground Zero in New York, Auschwitz-Birkenau, the killing fields of Cambodia, execution sites, prisons, graveyards, slavery-heritage sites, celebrity death sites, and battlefield sites and argues that people visit these sites to embrace their dark qualities. As sites of human violence, it is not hard to see the guides' interpretation of the trees in this category.

Other scholars have asserted that dark tourism is more of a label that researchers have assigned to places than something that tourists feel or seek out. Stephan Miles's 2014 piece reveals that when asked, visitors showed "no evidence of a considered appreciation" of the studied "sites' 'darker' aspects."[11] He argues that visitors expressed a "lighter set of values" and asserts that the commercial aspect of the sites—in this case, English battle sites—kept the darkness at bay. In a similar way, Michael S. Bowman and Phaedra Pezzullo argue that, among other things, calling tourist practices "dark" contributes to "the already-formidable body of criticism and popular opinion that attributes only vulgar, base, and superficial motives to tourism." They go on to ask, "If we jettison historical tragedies as not part of the broader desire for heritage tours, don't we continue to marginalize stories of subaltern, emergent, and counter public voice by marking 'their' sites as 'dark' and privilege the sites of those in power and 'heritage'?"[12]

Historian Tiya Miles offers an alternative vision of dark tourism by exploring how ghost tours' embrace of dark tourism harms their ability to tell historical truths.[13] Her work reveals that while tours in Savannah and other southern cities explain their embrace of dark tourism as a way to present the history of slavery that other tours ignore, their commercial treatment of the horrors of slavery does more harm than good.

This is not the case for all ghost stories or tales of woe; not all that is undesirable is fully insensitive. Other scholars have carved out a part of what has been called dark tourism and relabeled it as dissonant heritage to highlight how difficult histories need not be the insensitive romps that Miles found on ghost tours and Stone theorized about sites of violence. As Sharon Macdonald describes, dissonant heritage is different from dark tourism in that the "majority of the population would prefer not to have" the stories dissonant heritage includes.[14] People seek it out not for enjoyment but rather in recognition of past wrongs. Her work focuses on historical Nazi sites in Europe, but the term and application fit when applied to the Jim Crow South as well.[15]

I tend to favor Macdonald's "dissonant heritage" over "dark tourism" when describing painful sites with lore or stories of hauntings. The admittedly less sexy label, dissonant heritage, is a more fitting ground floor for analysis than dark tourism, which comes prepackaged with negative assumptions of intention and insensitivity.[16] As such, I approached guides' interpretation of hanging and whipping trees from the point of view that, like sociologist Avery Gordon says of ghost stories, they have the potential to be "one way that abusive systems make themselves known and their impacts felt" in people's "everyday lives."[17] This vision allows for the Candler Oak, the hanging tree in Colonial Park Cemetery, the hanging tree in Wright Square, and the whipping tree in Laurel Grove South Cemetery, as Eric Rutkow wrote of trees in 2012, to be "the loudest silent figures" in the city's history.[18] However, as this chapter shows, while the potential for dissonant heritage is present in each of Savannah's historical trees, only half avoid the dark tourism mark.

The Candler Oak is one of them. In fact, few trees are better suited for making the "abusive systems" known in Savannah than this prominently placed old oak. As the only tree with a name and the sole resident of a parking lot, it stands out physically and symbolically among the other trees and has thus become the owner of a recorded—though widely unknown—history.

Residents know the oak to be the oldest tree in the city. Dendrochronologists believe the acorn that would become the mighty live oak found its way to comfortable soil three hundred years ago, around 1730, when English colonists began to transform the area into the European-style colonial settlement of Savannah. It is likely that the tree, if planted at that time, was part of a larger colonial project of de- and reforestation. When English Parliamentarian James Oglethorpe laid out a plan for Savannah in 1733, the first step the colonists undertook was to "cut down Trees, build houses, fortify towns," and "sow the land."[19] The original trees would factor in as fuel and building materials. Colonists added new trees in great numbers outside of the city, which at the time stuck close to the river. Each settler was required to plant five hundred mulberry trees in their out-of-town five-hundred-acre lots for the cultivation of silkworms.[20] Surely, an oak tree seed managed to find its way into the mix, and the early city ordinance against cutting trees without expressed permission ensured that it continued to grow unmolested long after its neighboring mulberry trees failed to produce the much-hoped-for silkworms.

In 1819, the Savannah Poor House and Hospital was built on the land near the tree. The then wooded area made the hospital an ideal respite from the busier city that lay just shy of a mile to the north. Later, during the Civil War, it served as both a Confederate and Union hospital, and the nondescript area around the tree served as a stockade. The building became a medical school after the war and continued taking patients under various names.[21] In 1931, the Methodist Church purchased the property and dubbed it the Warren A. Candler Hospital and lent the old tree the name Candler as well.

The Candler Hospital and the Candler Oak lived a long life together. As the city expanded and automobiles became the main form of transportation, the hospital created a parking lot and over the years extended it closer and closer around the old oak tree. By midcentury, patients and visitors could park under the tree's long branches, and if they were not careful, they could crash their bumpers right into its trunk.

The encroaching parking lot, though arguably disrespectful to the tree, illustrated an unverbalized idea that the tree belonged there and ought to stay. It had been on that spot as long as anyone could remember, and it seems no one seriously considered removing it from the parking lot. Situated on the hospital's private property, it was not subject to any of the city codes that applied to the trees along the streets, in the squares, and in the parks. It would have been a simple task to remove the tree and pave over its spot, and yet it stayed. Perhaps without expressing it, the residents felt the tree connected the hospital to the adjacent park and helped maintain its pleasant and serene surroundings. It was equally as likely that because the tree had not made itself a problem, no one gave it a thought.

It seems that no one gave much consideration to the tree until 1984, when Huntington II Ltd. and an absentee landlord named William E. Hamby of Atlanta purchased the property that the tree sat on. At this point, the Savannah Tree Foundation (STF), a local activist group, began to raise a concern. The foundation's lead members—Page Hungerpiller, Suzanne Williams, and Lynda Beam—noted that the large, nearly three-hundred-year-old oak tree in front of former Candler Hospital was looking worse for wear and sought to offer the new owner "expert advice" on how to relieve the tree's root system from the "paved parking area."[22] Subsequent conversations between President

Hungerpiller and the landowner's son very quickly evolved from a discussion about tree care into a plan to give the STF protective ownership over the oak.[23]

What the handover lacked in drama, the easement made up for in pure oddity.[24] The Candler Oak's easement was the first of its kind given to a singular tree. Easements are usually to protect tree lines, forests, waterways, and the like from development. This easement was granted to a singular tree without any formal historical claim or cultural value. At the time of its protection, the Candler Oak was not spoken about as if it had a great meaning in the city. There was no romance in the tree and no attempt to connect it to the city's history of planting trees, nor was there an attempt to tie it to the city's founding or before. It was enough that the STF wanted to protect it.

After the success of the easement agreement, newspapers made modest attempts to sensationalize the story. A 1987 article in *Dixie Living* told the Candler Oak's easement story as a battle between a greedy big-city developer and a character-rich small town. In this telling, Hamby had hatched a plan to cut Candler Oak down and pave it over to increase the property's parking allotment by a measly fourteen parking spots.[25] Hungerpiller explained to the paper that when she heard about this plan, she told Hamby, "We don't do those things in Savannah."[26] "Unlike in Atlanta," she added, "beauty" was more "important than business or entertainment" for Savannahians' "quality of life."[27] But the story did not stick.

Since then, the Candler Oak has prospered. The STF takes great care of the tree. In their pride for the tree, the people of Savannah have tried to incorporate the old oak into the city's celebrated historical identity. According to the sun-faded sign that sits inside the oak's protective fencing, the tree has been recognized for its history twice: first by the Georgia Landmark and Historic Tree Register in 2001 and then in 2004 by the now defunct National Register of Historic Trees. According to the Georgia Register, the Candler Oak is considered historical because the "land around the tree has housed hospitals," and during the Civil War, General Sherman "erected a barricade around the Candler Oak with which he kept wounded Confederate Soldiers."[28] This little-known history was enough to include the tree on the list, but its inclusion is largely unknown in the city. It is perhaps for lack of a clear connection to Savannah's past that one local tour guide has transformed the Candler Oak into a hanging tree.

While Savannah's house museums and tours have slowly begun to recognize slavery, the violence of Jim Crow is largely skipped over by all but one tour: Black History Tour Company.[29] Led by a local man, Johnny Brown, these Black history tours aim to correct the kind of selective memory that has become iconic for historical sites and cities in the United States.[30] Like all the others, Brown's tour uses the city's many historical markers and signs as stops on the tour. Guides lead guests to the Revolutionary War Haitian soldier's statue in Franklin Square, the emancipation statue on River Street, and the Candler Oak on the property of the old Candler Hospital. While the statues are self-explanatory, the Candler Oak begs for interpretation. According to Brown, it was Savannah's hanging tree—the tree from which white southerners hanged their Black neighbors.

While the reality of lynching in the United States is undeniable and white Americans did hang Black Americans from trees in the name of white supremacy, the Candler Oak bore no strange fruit. It was not a hanging tree. But without an official story, it is easy to interpret the special tree's silence as an attempt to obscure the city's history of racial violence.

Other than Brown's tour, there is no documented evidence of a hanging being performed on the Candler Oak. The public nature of lynching in the South and the very prominent place that the tree occupies in the city suggest that there would have been some photos or reports of such an event happening in Savannah. A lynching was not a secretive event but rather a public performance of political power.[31] A white mob did not lynch someone to simply end their life; to do so would just be murder. Lynchings were done to show victims' friends and family that the mob had the power to kill without reprisal. If someone was hanged from the Candler Oak, records would have been created in the form of photographs or news reports to ensure that the Black community understood the power of the white community.

However, for this chapter's purposes, the lack of historical data to support the claim matters less than the claim itself. For the Black History Tour Company, the Candler Oak offers a physical marker to situate the history of lynching in Savannah in a way that will linger with guests long after the tour ends. In this way, the interpretation alters how guests view the city and its trees, shrinks the distance between the past and present, and pulls back the curtain on Savannah's rosy history.

One guest, Dana Carmel Bell, formerly from Los Angeles, writes that before she took the tour, she was apprehensive about visiting Savannah in general. Slavery, Jim Crow, "the injustices that spurred the Civil Rights Movement," and scores of stories from her family made it "hard" for her to "be a fan" of the "cute city near the Georgia coast."[32] But, she explains, the city's charm "enraptured" her, especially the Candler Oak. Before she had heard it was a hanging tree on Brown's tour, she writes that she felt it was a "beautiful tree" that stood out and seemed special in the forest city. When Carmel Bell learned that the beautiful tree was "used as a hanging tree," she could not put words together to express her feelings. As if betrayed by the Candler Oak's beauty, the only response that felt appropriate was to recall the heartbreaking lyrics of Billie Holiday's "Strange Fruit."

Like Carmel Bell, the history of lynching is not news for most adults in the United States, but when placed inside Savannah's pleasant surroundings, the reality of the Jim Crow South becomes an abrupt intrusion. The city's beauty disarms people, and its official histories encourage them to understand it in terms of past heroics and aesthetics. The choice to place the history of lynching on the Candler Oak, and by association the other trees, acknowledges the hidden-in-plain-sight nature of Jim Crow's history. Just as the trees are both vital to the overall look of Savannah and not often thought about, the history of Jim Crow violence shaped the South and the economic inequality that made the polarized built landscape of grand mansions and shabby workers' homes that Savannah presents.

Carmel Bell was not the only observer disturbed by the interpretation of the Candler Oak as a hanging tree. A photograph of the tree posted on Flickr with the caption "This tree was used to hang black people in the Civil Rights period" has gained mixed attention over the years.[33] One commenter says that an oak outside of a hospital was an unlikely hanging tree.[34] Another points out that there is no "history to support the claim" that it was a hanging tree but that there are records of people being hanged in Colonial Park Cemetery.[35] The most recent commenter argues that a lack of data on lynchings is not convincing enough evidence to claim that none took place on the oak—and adds that when they visited the spot, the tree gave off "lynch vibes all day."[36] Though it is unclear what "lynch vibes" are, it may be safe to assume they are the same discomfort Dana Carmel Bell felt after the tour.[37]

For those who meet the Candler Oak as a lynching tree by way of Brown's history tour, the knowledge that such a prominent tree was used for murder hits hard. For those who learn the Candler Oak was a hanging tree from the city's many ghost tours, the story comes across as less symbolic and thus less disturbing. According to the haunting-focused tours, like Savannah Terrors, the tree's use as a hanging tree is nothing more than an example among a list of disquieting things that happened in the hospital's early years.[38] This treatment of the tree's past disassociates it with lynching or anything real and obscures the Jim Crow–era lesson embedded in Brown's interpretation. Plus, the Candler Oak is usually left off of walking tours because it is just outside of the major tourist area and thus holds very little significance to the city's ghost tours. Instead, most ghost tours go to the two other hanging trees that sit within a mile of the Candler Oak.

The closest hanging tree may or may not be in Colonial Park Cemetery. The city of Savannah opened what would later become Colonial Park Cemetery in 1750 as the public burial ground.[39] Unlike the iconic graveyards of the Victorian era, most eighteenth-century graveyards were sparse landscapes purposely placed outside of town to make them avoidable.[40] There is reason to believe that Savannah's burial ground was nothing out of the ordinary. It served the city well and was closed in the early 1800s. After Reconstruction in 1897, it was given to the Park and Tree Commission to improve and run as a park.[41] The commission sent crews to pave a strolling path, turn headstones right side up, plant trees, and install "shrubbery" throughout.[42] These efforts gave the cemetery a friendlier look and inspired stories around its trees.

Unlike the Candler Oak, whose history as a hanging tree lacks a narrative, the hanging tree in the cemetery is associated with the well-known ghost story of Rene Rondolier. Like any piece of lore, the details of the story change, but the general narrative holds that Rondolier was born in 1770, grew to be larger than average, and was kept prisoner by his parents.[43] He escaped from his home jail in 1820 and committed a string of murders. Some say he was a gentle man, like Lenny in *Of Mice and Men*, who "didn't understand his own strength," but other stories characterize him as mad.[44] No matter the details, the gruesome tale turns into a ghost story when the people of Savannah, seeking vigilante justice, hanged Rondolier from the tree for the murders they believed he committed.

The story is well known, but the location of the tree that was used to hang Rondolier is contested. First, depending on the story, Rondolier was hanged from a tree in the cemetery, one in a nearby swamp, or a tree in one of the city's squares.[45] Second, there are many trees in the cemetery, some of which could date to his story but were most likely planted after. Residents and guides often assume that the city's trees were planted during the colonial period and have witnessed all the city's history, when in fact the city only began planting in the city parks and squares in 1810. The first recorded order to plant trees in Colonial Park Cemetery came in 1846.[46] By the 1880s, many of them had been ruined by a "terrific tempest," or killed off by illness.[47] In 1886, one resident proclaimed that the time "when the beauty of the trees in Savannah" made the "city famous" was over.[48] It is safe to say that the vast majority of trees in Savannah today, save for the Candler Oak, did not exist before 1900.[49]

Shannon Scott, a local ghost tour guide, is one of the few people to claim to know the tree where Rondolier was hanged from and to have sat under it. He explains that the three-hundred-year-old "capitol live oak" sat in the center of the cemetery until the city removed it.[50] According to his knowledge, the reputed tree from the Rondolier story was removed because of its status as a real, not legendary, hanging tree. He explains that in 1911, the city of Savannah imprisoned an unnamed Black man who was "falsely accused of raping a white woman."[51] While he awaited trial, the white men of Savannah took him from his jail cell and lynched him in Colonial Park Cemetery.

Scott offers no evidence of the events other than word of a photograph that he once saw on display at the Martin Luther King Center in Atlanta of a man lynched. In his writing, Scott describes the photo as simply "something else" and lets his mind wander back to his pleasant memories sitting under the tree. Unburdened by the lynching history, Scott wonders how long the tree bore marks from the tragic event. For him, the tree's potential scarring and later removal were the great injustices. As he explains, when people "threw a rope over one of its grand branches," the old oak tree had "no say in the matter."[52]

Perhaps Scott's inability to feel what Carmel Bell felt when learning about a lovely tree being used as a hanging tree was due to his confused information. Like the Candler Oak, there is no record of a man, Rondolier or the unnamed Black man, being lynched in Colonial Park Cemetery and little evidence of the tree being removed. It is possible that the image Scott saw did transform his beloved tree into something more heinous because the image was of a different man and a different tree.

There is only one recorded lynching in the city of Savannah, and according to the records of the National Association for the Advancement of Colored People (NAACP), it took place out of town. This event occurred nine years before the story Scott shares but has some similarities. In 1902, a white mob captured a Black man they claimed was Richard Young. Mr. Young had been accused of murdering another man named Dower Fountain and was assumed to be missing. The mob went looking for Young and found another man, captured him, and lynched him. Afterward, they brought his body to Young's mother for disposal.[53] It was there at Young's mother's door, the *Chicago Record-Herald* reports, that the mob learned they had burned the unnamed man "in error." But the NAACP's records still reflect Richard Young as the man whom the mob lynched near Savannah.[54] There is a possibility that two men were lynched that year, but there is no record of this happening in Colonial Park Cemetery or in 1911.[55]

Despite the confusion of data and the possibility that the tree in question may have never existed, the stories around the trees in the cemetery offer guides a place to talk about vigilante mob violence in Savannah. Unfortunately, due to the unofficial nature of this interpretation, few, if any, tour guides choose to interpret the trees in that way. The tours that talk about Rondolier or Young's hanging in the cemetery do so to contrast the city's daytime loveliness with stories of a seedy yesterday. In all cases, the tours promote the idea that the effects of mob or judicial hangings are limited to ghost sightings and have no real-world effects or reflections today.

The same can be said of the story around the hanging tree in Wright Square. Most ghost tours and historical records place the story of Georgia's first executed criminals, Alice Riley and Richard White, in Wright Square. Local legend identifies the tree on the north end of the square that, unlike its neighbors, does not feature Spanish moss as the one used for the hanging. Tour guides use the oak's lack of moss to situate the hanging and the murders inside of the present-day city and likewise use the hangings to explain why that particular oak lacks the Spanish moss that so many of the city's other trees have.

The basics of the story are true and were recorded in a series of letters written to James Oglethorpe in the eighteenth century updating him on the goings-on of the colony.[56] In 1734, Irish indentured servants Alice Riley and Richard White murdered their master, William Wise. They attempted to run out of town but were caught, tried, and sentenced to death. White was executed first, but Riley's execution was delayed so she could give birth to her son. Shortly after she gave birth and was executed, the baby died, and the two were buried next to Wright Square. *Savannah Morning News* claims the burial site is now located at 9 West York Street, today home to handsome and expensive apartments that don't appear to be haunted.[57]

Despite there being a documented record of the events, there is no evidence to suggest that Riley and White were hanged from any of the trees in Wright Square. As previously established, the squares were not treed until much later, and most of the precolonial trees were removed during Oglethorpe's first mission. Like the other hanging trees, the significance of the tree lies not in its facts but in how tour guides talk about it and transform it into an unofficial historical marker.

Many ghost tours in Savannah begin the tale of this hanging tree with a dramatic recounting of Riley and White's dream of freedom in Ireland and their perilous journey across the Atlantic Ocean.[58] From there, the stories explain the life of indentured servants. Tours often mention that while some people were contracted out to "benevolent Masters," Riley and White were not so lucky and were made to work "extremely hard."[59] Others call Wise a "tyrant," recalling Revolutionary-era language of the oppressed, or point out his "lecherous" actions toward Riley.[60] Some stories also mention the colony's head magistrate, Thomas Causton, and his rumored anti-Irish prejudice and history of "manipulating trial juries."[61] No matter the angle, most narratives make it clear that Riley and White's actions were justified, if not a favor to all the women of Savannah, and end with Riley's pregnancy and her son's tragic incarcerated birth and death.[62]

At this point, the historical tale transforms into a ghost story. While on her way to the gallows, tour guides explain that Riley cried out for her baby or placed a curse on the city.[63] The wail produced Riley's ghost, who continues to cry out for her child and is rumored to have been recorded in local police department records due to the volume of people calling officers to the square to help a woman look for her lost child.[64] The curse manifested itself in the tree's lack of Spanish moss. Ghost City Tours offers the explanation that "Spanish Moss will never grow where innocent blood has been spilled."[65]

The clever moss explanation stands out. First, the lack of Spanish moss is not as uncommon as the lore would lead one to believe. Gordon Denny of the city's Park and Tree Commission told WSAV in 2015 that none of the squares north of Broughton Street have Spanish moss, and only one south of the street has it.[66] Rather than weakening the story, the presence of mossless trees in the city transforms the ghost story into a powerful, unnerving punch. Like the Candler Oak story, which reminds viewers that the history of lynching just barely hides in plain sight, the story of Ann Riley trains guests to interpret the lack of Spanish moss as evidence of unjust murder. The prevalence of moss-less trees in the city leaves open the possibility that the morning after their ghost tours, guests will gaze into the city's treetops and find a history of injustice on each limb—hidden in plain sight. But like the stories told in the Colonial Park Cemetery, there is little evidence to support that the guides intend to present this more dissonant heritage-type interpretation.

The guests who comment on the tree's status as a hanging tree do so without any obvious understanding of the tree or the story's historical significance. They may comment on it being the site of Georgia's first hanging for murder, but the tree is not made to represent any larger historical narrative.[67] This is likely because the story is introduced to people on ghost tours, which generally lack historical follow-through or a clear argument of significance. Unlike the Candler Oak story, which uses the tree to tell a larger story about lynching in the South, the tree in Wright Square is used as evidence to authenticate Riley's ghost rather than talk about the city's history of judicial hangings or murders. For a tree with a deeper historical meaning, visitors must leave the historical downtown and venture into a place more comfortable with death and dying, like the Laurel Grove Cemetery.

The last of Savannah's oaks of ill repute is not a hanging tree but a whipping tree found in Laurel Grove South Cemetery. When Colonial Park Cemetery was deemed full in 1850, the city allocated a new plot of land for burials on the former grounds of the Springfield Plantation. The new cemetery was strictly segregated. Portions were set aside for white Christians, another for Jewish people, and a third portion, later called Laurel Grove South, for enslaved and Black Savannahians.[68] Over the years, the southern portion grew into the largest Black burial ground in the state of Georgia.

During the 1800s, both sides of the cemetery were designed in what is called a "Victorian style"[69]—meaning the cemetery is parklike and filled with trees, walking paths, and dramatic grave markers.[70] Laurel Grove North is home to an impressive marble sculpture of angels, a classic Confederate monument called Silence, and a town of bungalow-like tombs that range from Roman to Egyptian in style.[71] Unlike other well-visited cemeteries, Laurel Grove is not the final resting place of many nationally famous people. The founder of the Girl Scouts of America, Juliette Gordon Lowe, is buried there, but the Scouts more often pay their respects at her house than her grave.[72] The main draw for visitors is the cemetery's beauty. True to its Victorian style, it is a pleasant place to walk around. Visitors have called it "truly breath taking," historical, and "gorgeous," saying it exudes "old-fashioned Southern charm."[73]

The comments on Laurel Grove South differ. In 1968, the nation's continued effort to make car travel the most efficient mode of transportation came to Savannah and ran the new I-16 through the center of the cemetery. For many cities across the United States, new highways were synonymous with the destruction of economically marginalized, typically African American neighborhoods.[74] Many white leaders of the Jim Crow era saw this as a net positive. It cleared out shabby-looking neighborhoods, led to further segregation of white and Black residents, and helped obscure the unequally divided public resources. At Laurel Grove, this meant that the white cemetery was given more attention and more care than the Black cemetery.

As such, those who visit Laurel Grove South today comment more on the people buried than on the area's beauty. One visitor writes that it is the final resting place of "resourceful, intelligent and groundbreaking African Americans" but that the infrastructure of the cemetery is "badly in need of work."[75] Another agrees, saying the land is "badly" in "need of help and upkeep."[76] Due in great part to the economic limitations put on Black Americans throughout the Jim Crow era, Laurel Grove South does not have the same amount of remarkable or celebrated grave markers and generally sees fewer tourists.

Unsurprisingly, most of the tours that offer guests an interpretation of the cemetery and its architecture stick to Laurel Grove North. Johnny Brown's Black History Tour Company makes a point to take guests to Laurel Grove South. While in the cemetery, guests are treated to the wide range of Savannah's Black history. Unlike the downtown, the monuments in Laurel Grove South all recognize and celebrate Black residents. From the enslaved people's plots to the resting place of Savannah's civil rights leader W. W. Law, the graveyard is the place where guests are given the most detailed place-based Black history tour.

Among the graves, there are several trees that were planted in the unified cemetery's Victorian heyday and a few that Brown explains predated the cemetery. Brown argues that one tree originated from the plantation that once occupied the land and was used as a whipping tree.[77] On the tour and in photos, he points upward seven to eight feet to a band of diagonal cuts high up on a tree's trunk. These, he argues, are marks left by the overseers' lashes.

The damaged tree gives guests a vision of how hard enslavers and drivers beat enslaved people and offers evidence for the brutality of slavery.[78]

The existence of the whipping tree, like the Candler Oak and the hanging tree in Colonial Park Cemetery, is not supported by historical records, and according to plant biologists, a wounded tree would grow over scars, not push them upward. No matter, the tree's history, like that of many other historical trees, is less important than the story people tell.

Brown's telling of the whipping tree in Laurel Grove South reminds guests that the history of plantation slavery is present in Savannah. Americans often associate slavery with large rural rice and cotton farms rather than cities. Savannah benefits from this forgetting, and in general, the tours that interpret the city's past easily gloss over the presence of enslaved workers. There is change on the horizon. Select house museums have begun to interpret urban slavery. Most notably, the Owens-Thomas House, now Owens-Thomas House and Slaves Quarters, undertook a massive renovation that restored the slave quarters that had been used as office space and a gift shop.[79] Likewise, the Davenport House is currently reinterpreting and reconstructing the slave quarters in the home's basement and attic area, and Telfair Museums hosted a symposium on the legacy of slavery in Savannah.[80] Despite these institutional efforts, the tours have been slow to pick up the city's history of slavery; it is simply too easy to overlook slavery in the modern historical city. Laurel Grove South's whipping tree offers a different vision of Savannah and its past that is unmistakably linked to slavery.

Furthermore, the presence of the whipping tree reinforces not only that the cemetery includes the graves of enslaved people but also that they and hundreds of other Black Savannahians are interred on the grounds of a former plantation. This brings the plantation vision of slavery that most Americans can easily recall closer to the city's downtown. And like the Wright Square hanging tree, the marks in the whipping tree can teach visitors to understand tree scaring as evidence of an unofficial, hidden, or shameful history.

Interpreting Savannah's trees is still a relatively new practice among the city's commercial guides. The exploration of these interpretations has illustrated that there is a lot of potential for the city's oaks as dissonant heritage, but they face the common problem of popular ghost tours obscuring difficult realities with a thick layer of dark tourism. Efforts to counter the dark tourism might include the creation of an official history for the trees. A placard complete with the city's civic beautification projects and odd legal agreements may help to wrestle control of the trees' narratives from dark tourism, but lore does not follow rules and is hard to eliminate through official routes. Even if the ghost tours tend to obscure the full reality of hangings, the trees remain powerfully defiant symbols for those who are taught to read them. Plus, there are plenty of trees to use in town, and the oaks of ill repute remain convenient shady places to tell less-than-accurate stories of a very real and violent past.

FIGURE 17. Cornelius Johnson's Olympic Oak from the 1936 Berlin Olympic Games. The tree is located at 1156 S. Hobart Blvd., Los Angeles. Photograph by Christian Kosmas Mayer, 2014.

Chapter Twelve

Living Memory in Los Angeles

CORNELIUS JOHNSON'S 1936 OLYMPIC OAK IN ART, HISTORY, AND PRESERVATION; CHRISTIAN KOSMAS MAYER IN CONVERSATION WITH ALAINA SCAPICCHIO

Christian Kosmas Mayer, Vienna

Alaina Scapicchio, University of South Florida

The 1936 Olympic Games held in Berlin, Germany, are widely remembered as the tournaments hosted by the Nazi German Reich, as Adolf Hitler accumulated the power that ultimately resulted in World War II and the Holocaust. As the world prepared for the games, talk of boycotting the event swirled around the Olympic committees of several countries, including the United States. With many world leaders aware of the anti-Semitic Nuremberg Laws passed the year before, they debated the morality of their nations' participation. In an effort to appease their critics, Reich leaders pledged not to exclude Jewish Germans from their teams.[1] However, these were hollow promises, since Jews were classified as non-Aryans and denied citizenship in Germany, and noncitizens could not represent their country at the Olympics.

Ultimately, the United States decided to participate in the 1936 Games. After much deliberation, African American athletes from the United States chose to compete, aiming to debunk Hitler's racial ideologies through their prowess and victories. This decision was a deliberate act to confront and disprove the Nazi propaganda of racial inferiority. One prominent example is African American track-and-field star Jesse Owens shattering records as the first American to win four gold medals in an Olympiad. Cornelius Johnson was another African American track-and-field athlete who set the Olympic high jump record at the 1936 Games. Johnson, Owens, and many other gold-medal-winning athletes that summer were presented small potted oak trees in addition to their official medals by Nazi Germany.

These trees were a powerful symbol for the Germans, but for the winners themselves, they were viewed as trophies, curiosities, and living objects of memory. Cornelius Johnson brought his oak tree back to his hometown of Los Angeles, California, and planted it in the backyard of his family's home at the western edge of the city. Over the decades, it grew to full size. However, as it grew, so too did the neighborhood around the tree. The Johnson home changed as well. By the time German artist Christian Kosmas Mayer became aware of the tree in 2014, a new family resided in the former Johnson home and had forged new connections to the historic tree.

Mayer is a visual artist currently living and working in Vienna, Austria. He studied at the Academy of Fine Arts Vienna and developed a body of work that challenges the imagined divisions between nature and culture. In describing his work, he says, "I often deal with historical issues. I have a deep fascination with concepts of time and temporality, particularly in how we memorialize events and interact with the natural world. My interest lies in examining how cultural significances are projected onto nature and in exploring the ways we assign meaning to phenomena beyond our direct experience. By doing so, I often use or work with living organisms like plants or trees and try to involve them in my art as some sort of co-authors who become active participants in the creation of my work."[2]

In 2014, Mayer was awarded a fellowship from the Museum of Applied Arts (MAK) in Vienna, which enabled him to spend six months in Los Angeles, California. During his stay, he stumbled upon the Olympic Oak, which had by then been all but forgotten. As a German artist with a well-developed interest in and experience with the boundaries between nature and culture, Mayer found the Olympic Oak a fascinating subject. Aiming to simultaneously preserve the tree while telling its story in art, he eventually created an extensive project that involved propagating acorns from the tree. That project began in 2017 and was titled *The Life Story of Cornelius Johnson's Olympic Oak and Other Matters of Survival.* Mayer's work and his incubating propagated oak seedlings were exhibited internationally in various museums in the subsequent years. Mayer's work caught the attention of people in Los Angeles who reached out to him when development threatened the tree. Mayer has joined forces with a group of concerned residents and institutions to lobby the Los Angeles Cultural Heritage Commission to secure historical status for the Olympic Oak and the Johnson family home itself. In August 2022, only weeks after this interview, the commission designated both the tree and the home historic cultural monuments. The main challenge the tree faces today is its deteriorating health—a fact that highlights the challenges in caring for living monuments.

Mayer is in conversation with Alaina Scapicchio, who is a public history doctoral candidate at the University of South Florida, where she is working on a dissertation examining the public commemoration and memory of witch trials in the Atlantic world. What follows is a discussion that highlights several of the themes that the various authors of this anthology have touched on, specifically those of race, heritage, and preservation.[3]

ALAINA SCAPICCHIO: Can you tell us a bit about the tree and its neighborhood?

CHRISTIAN KOSMAS MAYER: On my initial exploration, armed only with an address and a sense of curiosity, I made my way there, as one often does in Los Angeles, by car, unsure if the tree was even still alive. I was greeted by a quaint neighborhood dotted with small, single-family homes, many of which bore the charming patina of age. The streets were lined with the quintessential palm trees that define the city's landscape, along with a variety of other trees. Amid this leafy setting, an imposing oak tree suddenly commanded my attention, standing as the undisputed giant of the neighborhood. It majestically towered over a modest house and leaped over the fence to stake its claim on the streetside. I instantly realized that this magnificent tree had to be the Olympic Oak I had been seeking.

AS: Can you recount for us the story of Cornelius Johnson and his winning gold in the high jump at the 1936 Berlin Olympics? What was he doing before this event, and how did he become an Olympic-quality athlete?

CKM: Cornelius Johnson began his athletic journey in school, quickly distinguishing himself as a promising high jumper during his high school years. His talents were recognized early on, leading to significant achievements. After attending Berendo Junior High, which was near his home, he moved on to LA High School. There, he broadened his athletic repertoire, excelling not only in the high jump but also in sprinting and relay races. His prowess in these events won him numerous competitions. Remarkably, while still in high school and only eighteen years old, he qualified for the 1932 Los Angeles Olympic Games that took place not far from his neighborhood. In a memorable high jump competition, he found himself in a four-way tie, all athletes having cleared the same height. This led to a jump-off to decide the victor, where Johnson secured fourth place. Though he narrowly missed out on a medal then, under current regulations, his performance would have earned him a silver medal.

So he was already one of the best high jumpers in the world when he made it to the Berlin Olympic Games in 1936. He went there with a large US team, including nineteen African American athletes. He was competing in the high jump on the first day of the Olympic Games, August 2, 1936.

The first day of the Olympic Games included two or three other disciplines, and then came the high jump. He won this competition, setting a new Olympic record, which was an amazing achievement because the Berlin Olympia stadium was filled with a cheering audience. It was a great atmosphere, and he won. Two of his teammates won silver and bronze, so all three medals went to the US team.

There's a famous scene in the Leni Riefenstahl movie about the Olympic Games where you can see him making his final jump, and it's quite impressive. It was an amazing victory. Then there was this highly discussed incident where he was snubbed by Adolf Hitler, who had been in the stadium watching all the competitions. The athletes who won gold medals before Cornelius Johnson were German and Finnish, fitting the Nazi idea of an Aryan athlete, and Hitler welcomed them in his private balcony after the medal ceremony. When Cornelius Johnson won, Hitler left the stadium, pretending he had an important meeting, probably because he didn't want to shake Johnson's hand.[4]

Interestingly, it was the International Olympic Committee, not the US Olympic Committee, that protested with Hitler, telling him he had to invite all Olympic champions to his balcony or none. Hitler decided not to invite any champions after that. This incident is often referred to in relation to Jesse Owens, but it's clear it happened with Cornelius Johnson.

During the medal ceremony, there was a sort of silent protest by Johnson and the other two American athletes. When the national anthem was played and people were supposed to salute the flags, all Germans in the stadium gave the Nazi salute. Johnson and his teammates made a salute that looked similar to the Nazi salute but was different, as the palms of their hands were raised upward. It's known as the Bellamy salute, a distinctly American patriotic gesture created by James B. Upham in the late nineteenth century. So by choosing this salute, they used this very public event to show a gesture against the nationalism the Nazis presented, replacing it with a self-confident American posture, which had a very different meaning if an African American athlete did it at that time.

Cornelius Johnson and his teammates actually had a good time in Berlin. There was a lot of discussion before they left about whether it was a good decision to go to Nazi Germany for the Berlin Olympic Games, knowing the racist agenda and theory of superiority. They decided to go because they understood they could use the Olympic Games as a public event to show the world that the Nazi ideas were wrong, that African Americans could represent self-confident, victorious subjects. The Nazis tried to use the Olympic Games as a big propaganda event, but African American athletes were welcomed by the audience, and Jesse Owens became a big star of the Olympic Games. So the Nazis didn't like that much but accepted it, as they were interested in making the Olympic Games an event that would assure the world Germany was a good and civilized country.

During the medal ceremony, Cornelius Johnson received a little potted oak tree, which he brought back not so much because it represented Nazi Germany or Adolf Hitler but because it represented his victory in Berlin. He was proud and happy about his success, and the tree was a very personal memory he brought back and decided to take care of.

Of course, there was racism in Germany at the time, which they must have felt, but when they came back to the US, they were returning to a country full of racism as well. It was clear there were two different sorts of Olympic champions coming back: the African American ones and the white ones. This was obvious when President Roosevelt invited some representatives to the White House, and not a single African American was among them. Barack Obama tried to make good on this in 2016 by inviting representatives of the families of the African American athletes of the 1936 Olympics to the White House.

Upon their return, many of these African American athletes did not receive the hero's welcome or reap the benefits of their success that one might have expected. Most of them had to return to rather simple and not very well-paid jobs. Cornelius Johnson moved back in with his parents in the house where he was born. He first worked as a letter carrier for the post office, then joined the Merchant Marine and worked on a ship as a cook. Then, in 1946, he got really sick on the ship and died on the way to the hospital, only ten years after his Olympic victory and at only thirty-four years old.

AS: Does anyone know the exact circumstances around his planting of the tree?

CKM: Well, there's no real documentation or anything about this one moment because I think it was a rather unspectacular, very private moment for him when he came back carrying this oak tree with him and moving back in with his parents. They just decided where to plant it, made a little hole, and put it there. I am not aware of any documents from this event, but we know from oral history within the family that they did it and took great care of this tree. For them, it was more than just a tree, especially after Cornelius Johnson had died, as it became a living memorial for someone who had passed.

AS: Do we know what genus of oaks the Germans gave the winning athletes?

CKM: It's a pedunculate oak, or *Quercus robur*, which is its official Latin name. It's a very common tree all over Europe. Which is interesting because the Germans always used the term *German oak*. For them, it represented something very specific: German strength, rootedness, like the typical German man they envisioned, a soldier maybe, who is rooted in the German soil, very strong and tall. That's why the Nazis were so obsessed with the symbol of the oak. It was all over the place: the acorn, oak leaves, oak laurels. This builds on a long history. These sorts of trees were considered to be special already back in Celtic and Germanic tribes' times. They were considered to be sacred trees or spiritual trees. Then, only later on in the German context, it became kind of burdened, I would say, by these nationalists' ideas. Especially in the nineteenth century, when Germany was all these small states that were still representing only parts of Germany, and there was no German nation yet, and all these nationalist, also anti-Napoleon movements had been very strong, and they were kind of figuring out what this Germanness is. That's a time when the oak tree as a symbol became more and more used to represent this specific Germanness. The Nazis based their ideology on such symbolism. They amplified this nineteenth-century notion of the oak tree as a symbol of Germany or Germanness, ultimately perverting it, to use a more precise term. So, of course, when they handed out these little oak trees to the Olympic champions, for them, it was also a gesture to hand out a symbol of Germanness or of these ideas of racial superiority through a living object. And through that, spread it all over the world. Almost like a representation of something that is to come. Because they dreamed of Nazism conquering the whole world at some point. This is why it's fascinating to see how this tree we're discussing has undergone a profound transformation in ideological and representational terms. The Nazis had their intentions for these oaks, aiming to embody their twisted values. Yet today, when we view this tree through the lens of its various social and geographical layers that have since enveloped its original symbolism, it's clear the narrative has shifted dramatically, even reversed. The tree's current significance, especially when connected to the story of an African American athlete, stands in stark opposition to what the Nazis aimed to symbolize during the Olympic Games.

AS: Was the gift a unique Nazi innovation? Or was there a tradition of giving oaks as an award?

CKM: The concept originated from a Berlin-based German gardener who proposed, "Why don't we give every Olympic champion a small potted German oak?" He brought this idea before the German Olympic Committee, which was predominantly comprised of Nazi officials. They were quite taken with the idea. While it's not definitively known if the proposal was directly approved by Adolf Hitler, it's highly probable given that nearly all decisions of this nature required his consent. Consequently, the idea received approval, and the tradition was born. This gesture of gifting trees to Olympic champions was unprecedented and has not been replicated in any subsequent Olympic Games.

AS: Who actually handed the trees to the athletes?

CKM: The individuals responsible for distributing the trees were officials from the Olympic committees. Adolf Hitler himself did not personally distribute any items during the Olympic Games. Instead, he observed the events from his private booth, situated high on a balcony.

AS: So Cornelius Johnson brought this symbol-rich tree back to Los Angeles. What was the story of his own family and the tree's new home?

CKM: When we presented the issue to the Los Angeles Cultural Heritage Commission, we chose to highlight not just the oak tree but also the house for permanent protection. The rationale was clear: the Johnson family, who had made their home there, embodied a unique and significant part of history that merited preservation alongside the tree. The family's roots trace back to the 1890s, with Johnson's maternal ancestors hailing from Texas and his paternal lineage originating in North Carolina. They migrated to Los Angeles in search of better opportunities, a move made during a time when the South offered limited prospects for African Americans. Los Angeles presented a relatively more welcoming environment, albeit still fraught with challenges. The Johnsons were pioneers, settling in what was then known as Pico Heights well before the Great Migration. This area, at the time, was on the outskirts of Los Angeles, marked by its pastoral scenery with sheep grazing to the north and barley fields to the east. The Johnsons were among the first to build a life in this nascent community, contributing to the westward expansion of the city. Their story and the home they established offer a window into a pivotal era in Los Angeles history, deserving of recognition and protection.

Johnson's father, Shadrak Johnson, originally a plasterer from North Carolina, built their Los Angeles home in 1905. This dwelling likely stands as one of the earliest, if not the very first, self-constructed homes by an African American family in the area, and remarkably, it remains intact today. The maternal side of Johnson's family, the Coopers, also migrated from Texas to Los Angeles with hopes of a better life. They became pillars of the local community, actively contributing to its cultural and spiritual life, particularly through church activities. Their efforts were instrumental in fostering a sense of community in an area where none had existed before. This rich history imbues the Johnson home with significant cultural and historical value, underscoring its importance not just as a physical structure but as a testament to the pioneering spirit of the family and their enduring legacy in shaping the community.

AS: Has the local community seen the home and tree as historically significant?

CKM: When I began researching this tree and visited it for the first time, engaging with the family residing in the house, I discovered its story was not widely known in the neighborhood. The house, having been in the possession of the Johnson family until 1994, housed nearly ninety years of memories. Throughout their tenure, they cherished and preserved the legacy of the tree, even placing a sign to commemorate Cornelius Johnson's Olympic victory. Yet the narrative shifted when the property was sold to the Tomas family, who had migrated from Oaxaca, Mexico, in the 1970s, seeking better prospects similar to the Johnsons. Unconnected to the tree's historical significance or to African American history, this family valued the tree more for its presence and the shade it provided than for its storied past. To them, it became a cherished family tree, a play area for the children, and a source of comfort during warm afternoons.

Over time, as the original narrative of the tree dimmed within the community, my involvement from 2014 to 2017 helped rekindle interest in its rich history. This resurgence of attention, fueled by my efforts, reached a point where a neighbor, aware of the tree's significance due to my work, alerted me to its potential peril a year ago.

AS: Can you explain the nature of the danger?

CKM: The Tomas family sold the property to a developer in 2019. This man intended to replace the existing structures with new construction to profit from the sale, necessitating the removal of both the historic house and the oak tree, as the tree occupied a significant portion of the property. However, the onset of the COVID pandemic inadvertently delayed these plans, offering a temporary reprieve. It was during this slowed period that I was contacted, giving me the opportunity to devise a strategy for preserving the tree and house before any irreversible actions could be taken.

AS: Can you share the story of the preservation effort?

CKM: In June 2021, a neighbor from the vicinity sent me an email, a message that would set a new course for the oak tree's future. He wrote, "Hey, I remember your work with this oak tree. I've just passed the house and noticed a 'demolition notice' sign on the fence. I'm worried it might affect the tree as well." I was grateful for his alert; being far away, I would have otherwise remained unaware until it was perhaps too late.

Motivated by a sense of urgency to protect the tree, I reached out for support within Los Angeles. I first reached out to the MAK Center, my previous hosts and collaborators in research, where I spoke with director Jia Yi Gu. She was immediately supportive, suggesting we rally more allies to our cause. Concurrently, I reengaged with the Huntington Botanical Gardens, my partners in creating saplings from the oak, and reconnected with Tim Thibault, curator of the Woody Plant Materials collection. With Jia's assistance, I also engaged with officials from Los Angeles City Planning, drawn by a new Los Angeles policy prioritizing the preservation of living objects, particularly trees, as historic cultural monuments. This initiative, along with a growing recognition of the underrepresentation of African American history, meant we found a supportive audience for our cause. Jia then introduced me to Susan Anderson, history curator at the California African American Museum, whose expertise was invaluable in navigating the historical complexities involved.

Initially, relocation seemed the only option for the tree's preservation, prompting discussions with the Huntington team on logistics and survival probabilities. However, the conversation shifted when the possibility of nominating the site as a historic cultural monument emerged, offering a more sustainable solution that avoided the risks associated with moving the tree.

Susan and I undertook the substantial task of preparing the nomination paperwork for the Historic Heritage Commission of the City of Los Angeles—a meticulous process due to the private ownership of the property and potential legal challenges. After months of diligent effort, we submitted our proposal in spring 2022. The committee's initial acceptance of our nomination for further review was a promising first step, granting temporary protection to the tree and house. Finally, on August 8, 2022, the commission voted in favor of our application, and both the tree and house have since been protected as Historic-Cultural Monuments.

AS: What is the natural lifespan of this tree?

CKM: Determining the lifespan of oaks like this one is challenging, as they can live for five to six hundred years under favorable conditions. At nearly ninety years old, this tree is relatively youthful by oak standards. Historically robust and visually striking, its health has declined significantly over the past three years following the property's sale and the cessation of regular watering. The Tomas family had diligently watered it, a necessity due to much of its root zone being encased in concrete, leaving limited areas for water absorption. This care became even more critical with the recurring droughts in California, exacerbated by climate change. Building activities on neighboring properties, which have damaged its roots, have been another problem. As a result, the tree's condition has worsened, now vulnerable to thirst, disease, and pests.

Addressing the tree's immediate needs has become my priority, with the goal of preserving it until we can gain regular access to it. There's a hopeful pathway forward: acquiring the property through fundraising and ideally transitioning it into an educational space for younger generations, incorporating artistic activities as well.

This oak's narrative is more than local history; it's a living testament to broader historical events, embodying a connection to the past that static monuments cannot replicate. Its existence as a living being adds layers of experience and connection—historical, intellectual, and visceral. This dynamic between being a living organism and a symbol of history is what draws me to this project, highlighting the unique and profound relationship between humans and the natural world around us.

AS: Can you talk more—well, maybe this is a good place to move to your personal connection. What do you see artistically in the tree, and where does your own investment in the project come from?

CKM: As a German artist, my connection to Germany's history, including its darkest chapters, naturally influences my work. I am drawn to exploring the concept of memory—how we remember and vow never to forget the lessons of the past, yet face the challenge of preserving these memories as the last eyewitnesses depart from this world. In this era, our reliance shifts entirely to historical records like documents, books, films, and photographs, without the firsthand narratives to accompany them. This transition prompts the question, How do we keep memory alive in a meaningful way that informs our future?

It was this contemplation that led me to see the oak tree not just as a living entity but as a vehicle for exploring memory. This tree offers a unique opportunity to engage with history, to memorialize a period that reshaped world history through some of humanity's most profound misdeeds. Yet unlike static monuments, the tree remains alive, bridging past and present, making history tangible in our everyday lives.

In my exhibition, I aimed to create a space where visitors could immerse themselves in this concept, experiencing history through a direct connection with life. While the oak itself could not be present, its saplings could. These young trees serve as a living link to the story of the oak, allowing visitors to experience history not just as a narrative but as a living dialogue.

This approach to the exhibition led to an unexpected realization: history is not merely a series of events to be recounted but a living, breathing presence that interacts with the present and future. The saplings, with their potential to grow and create their own stories, underscore this notion. They challenge the conventional linear narrative of history, suggesting instead a more complex interweaving of time and memory. This perspective, where history is alive and evolving, forms the core of my artistic exploration, emphasizing that our understanding and memory of the past are not static but continuously in flux.

AS: Can you expand a bit more on your exhibit with the saplings?

CKM: In my exhibition, I suspended metal boxes from the ceiling, each open on one side and outfitted with a lab-like interior, including a reflective silver lining and grow lamps emitting a mix of red and blue light—creating a distinctly artificial ambiance. Within these containers, I placed in vitro saplings from the Olympic Oak of Los Angeles, each encased in a small lab glass, thriving in their own miniature environments. These saplings, delicate and diminutive, were not just exhibits but narrators of living history.

Surrounding each box, narratives were silk-screened onto the metal and gold leaf, each telling a different story connected to the tree. One narrated the life of Cornelius Johnson, another delved into the saga of the Olympic Oaks, a third explored the oak's symbolic significance in German culture, a fourth discussed the story of a Mexican descendant family's connection to the tree and its legacy, while the fifth summoned my efforts to bring these saplings to life. This diversity of narratives offered visitors a multifaceted perspective on the tree's history and its impact on various lives and cultures.

The exhibition was designed to be interactive, allowing visitors to weave through these stories at their own pace, drawing connections between the oak's past and their own experiences. To complement the physical displays, a video filmed with a drone provided a dynamic visual context. It began at the tree's base, showing the family that then lived beside it, before ascending through its branches to offer an aerial view of its surroundings. This transition from the intimate space around the tree to the broader landscape of the neighborhood aimed

FIGURE 18. In vitro saplings of Cornelius Johnson's Olympic Oak featured in Christian Kosmas Mayer's art installation at the Museum of Modern Art (Mumok), Vienna. Photograph by Klaus Pichler, 2017.

to illustrate the interconnectedness of personal stories and community history, underscoring the oak's significance not just as a botanical specimen but as a living monument within the fabric of the city.

AS: What became of your saplings?

CKM: The saplings currently reside in a lab of the Huntington Botanical Gardens, still in their in vitro phase and quite delicate. Fascinatingly, I faced challenges in transporting them into the European Union (EU) due to stringent regulations against importing certain plants from the US to prevent the spread of harmful bacteria. Ironically, the European oak, the species of our saplings, falls under the category of trees banned for importation into the EU from the US, leading me to covertly bring them in for the exhibition.

This situation sparked an intriguing consideration regarding the identity of the saplings: How closely do they reflect the essence of the original Olympic Oak? The Huntington and I debated whether to pursue cloning, which would result in a genetically identical copy, or to grow a hybrid from an acorn, likely cross-pollinated with a native Californian oak. The cloning route presented a metaphorical overlap with discussions on purity and mixed heritage, prompting me to opt for the hybrid, embracing the complexity and richness it represents. This decision opened up broader reflections on identity and legacy, underscoring the depth and breadth of the project's implications.

AS: What do we know about the other Olympic Oaks given away in 1936?

CKM: During the Olympic Games, 129 gold medals were awarded, and with each medal, an Olympic Oak was gifted, totaling 129 oaks. Presently, we have knowledge of only twenty-nine of these oaks, their whereabouts, and their survival status, while the fate of the others remains unknown, with many presumed dead or simply forgotten.

In an effort reminiscent of a bygone era, the historian J. R. Constandt embarked in the 1990s on a quest to uncover the stories of these oaks, utilizing a method that predated the digital age: he sent letters to various regional Olympic committees inquiring, "Do you know what happened to the Olympic Oak?" This pursuit shed light on the stories of some oaks, though, notably, Cornelius Johnson's oak eluded discovery at the time.

Most of the surviving oaks are found in Germany, which is perhaps unsurprising. In the US, it is believed that three remain, including those associated with Cornelius Johnson and Jesse Owens—the latter having received four oaks, in line with his four gold medals. One of Owens's oaks thrives in Cleveland, Ohio, near his former high school.

The destinies of these trees are as varied as they are fascinating. In New Zealand, an oak associated with Jack Lovelock, the country's first Olympic gold medalist in athletics, has become a symbol of national pride and a popular attraction. Conversely, in some nations, the trees were viewed through a lens of their association with Nazi Germany, leading to their destruction during periods of conflict, such as in England during World War II.

This narrative underscores the diverse legacies of the Olympic Oaks—ranging from cherished living monuments to victims of historical associations. These twenty-nine oaks that we know of continue to tell a story that intertwines sports, history, and the complex shadows of the past.

AS: This is just a great story. It's a great project. It's exciting to see the ripple effect in the preservation effort moving from individual to community to institution. It demonstrates that these "living monuments," as you have phrased it, can inspire people of all backgrounds to engage with the past and the biosphere.

CKM: I share that sentiment and am pleased that it's beginning to receive the attention it merits—though certainly, it deserves even more. Remarkably, to my knowledge, there exists no monument dedicated to Cornelius Johnson or to celebrate the remarkable achievements of African American athletes of that era. Their success stands as a significant symbol against the backdrop of a very different America for African Americans. The story embodied by this tree and this place has the potential to serve as a powerful representation of their history. I harbor the hope that our efforts will ultimately culminate in the recognition and commemoration it rightly deserves.

Afterword

BRANCHING OUT FURTHER

David Glassberg, Department of History,
University of Massachusetts Amherst

Where do we go from here? This first anthology to explore the public history of trees marks a productive convergence between the fields of environmental history and public history. Environmental historians have written about trees for decades; the Forest History Society, founded in 1946, predates the American Society for Environmental History by thirty-one years. With the important exception of studies analyzing the meanings of trees in Indigenous societies, nearly all environmental histories discuss trees as natural resources rather than cultural ones. Public historians also analyze trees primarily as natural rather than cultural resources. When public historians mention trees at all, it is usually in the context of ways to document and care for trees on the site of a historic building or battlefield to enhance its historical character. Except for cultural landscape studies, most public histories consider trees as the natural setting in the background and buildings as the historical artifacts in the foreground.

By contrast, the preceding essays analyze trees as historic artifacts in and of themselves. They shift our perspective and challenge prevailing Western beliefs that trees are only "natural," existing apart from human history, and only change over time in response to natural cycles and disturbance events such as diseases, extreme weather, and wildfires independent of human action and control. In the face of mounting scientific evidence of the inseparability of humans and nonhuman nature, especially in relation to humans' impact on a changing climate, the belief that somewhere a natural world exists untouched by human intervention persists in popular culture and many aspects of movements for wilderness preservation.[1]

One common theme in the preceding essays is the unique character of trees as historic artifacts. For example, living trees are vulnerable to disease and a changing climate in ways that nonliving historic structures are not. At the same time, the aliveness of trees allows them to adapt to changing environmental conditions in ways that nonliving historical structures cannot.

As Christian Kosmas Mayer observes in his conversation with Alaina Scapicchio about Cornelius Johnson's oak, because trees are living and growing, the public relates to them differently than nonliving historical artifacts. Their aliveness allows us to form a deep emotional attachment to them as biological entities, since we are biological entities ourselves.

Several authors note that living trees can endanger the preservation of nearby historical structures by fueling wildfires, hosting invasive insects, or simply falling on them in a storm. Leah Glaser's essay on managing Connecticut's historic landscape cautions that characteristic of trees makes them targets for removal for public safety reasons without consideration of their ecological or historical significance. In fact, when trees are removed, for whatever reason, they cease to hold soil, leaving the area even more vulnerable to flooding and mudslides during extreme weather events.

A characteristic of trees as historical artifacts left unexplored in the preceding essays is how trees, living or dead, provide historical evidence of past natural phenomena. A stand of ghost trees testifies to the salinification of freshwater areas. The Petrified Forest National Park in Arizona demonstrates the process of petrification to the public. Trees also provide historical evidence of the passage of time through tree rings and dendrochronology, which archaeologists and historians employ to date and interpret the history of standing structures, as well as trace the history of rainfall in a region.

Living trees can not only provide historical evidence but also hide it. Trees often overgrow the site of a former farm or battlefield, concealing traces of past human occupation or conflict. As a tree grows taller, it can obscure the view; as it grows thicker, it can bury within it items associated with torture, such as a hasp used for whipping enslaved African Americans, evident in a photograph of a tree taken in St. Helena, South Carolina, in the 1890s but invisible today.[2]

FIGURE 19. A handwritten caption identifies this late nineteenth-century photograph from St. Helena Island, South Carolina, as follows: "Tree on Frogmore Plant[ation] with the iron bolt in it at which the people were tied for punishment." Photograph by Helen C. Jenk in the Penn School Papers #3615, Southern Historical Collection, Wilson Library, University of North Carolina at Chapel Hill.

A second common theme in the preceding essays is the historical services that trees provide as sites of memory. Historians are accustomed to discussing the economic value of trees, whether harvested as lumber, cultivated as an orchard for growing fruit, or preserved as parkland for recreation. More recently, scientists and planners have discussed the ecological services that trees provide—among them shade, carbon sequestration, holding soil, filtering toxins, and habitat for wildlife.

In that context, the preceding essays analyze trees as both "historical and ecological assets."[3] George Washington's cherry tree, Sam Robinson's sycamore, Cornelius Johnson's oak, and the Fox Oaks in Flushing all functioned as monuments, sites where stories and memories could be attached to locales, then communicated across generations. Like monuments, trees and their stories do not necessarily express a community's collective memory but rather serve as places of collected memory, where diverse memories converge and are made tangible.[4] Various stories converged around "George Washington's" cherry tree, which, as Philip Levy notes, was a local black cherry that stood in for the original. Ironically, the tree that in Mason Weems's fable imparts the lesson that Washington "could not tell a lie" was implicated in a continuous series of lies about its origin.

Sometimes, as these essays show, the memorial function of trees is intentional—such as the trees planted in St. Louis in 2013 to memorialize victims of street violence or, as Krista McCracken notes, the pine trees planted at the Shingwauk Indian Residential School in Ontario in the 1980s and 1990s. Sasha Coles describes how in the early twentieth century, when mulberry trees in Utah no longer had economic value for silk production, they were celebrated for their memorial value as symbols of pioneer women's economic production. Another example of this transformation, as Carolyn Barske Crawford notes in her essay on the American chestnut and Evan Haefeli notes in his essay on the Fox Oaks of Flushing, New York, is that following death, trees can be made into furniture or other artifacts with historical associations.

The historical services trees provide often have considerable economic value, as Alena Pirok demonstrates in her essay about visitors touring the "hanging trees" in Savannah. Another example, unexplored in the preceding essays, is the effort by Florida nurseryman Jeff Meyer in the 1990s to gather seeds from trees throughout the country associated with famous people and sell the saplings for consumers to plant in their yards. Partnering with American Forests (formerly American Forest Society) to market "Famous and Historic Trees" to the public, a flyer from 1998 offers seedlings and cuttings from the "Lafayette Sycamore" in Chadds Ford, Pennsylvania, which the "dashing Frenchman" leaned against "to have a leg wound treated during the Battle of Brandywine"; the "Gettysburg Address Honeylocust," "the last living tree that was present during the Gettysburg Address"; and the "Sam Houston Kissing Bur Oak," beneath which Houston "kissed young ladies who presented him with a flag" in San Marcos, Texas, in 1857. Each tree came with a "personalized Certificate of Authenticity" recounting its history.[5]

The preceding essays also offer examples of how the memorial function of trees is often unintentional. The overwhelming majority of trees identified as "historical" were not planted by humans, at least not in living memory. Their historical meaning evolved over time either as "witness trees" associated with a nearby historical event or, as Brian Dempsey's essay about the Old

FIGURE 20. Brochure advertising saplings from American Forests, Famous and Historic Trees, 1998. The featured tree is located on Johns Island, South Carolina, seventy-five miles from the tree on Frogmore Plantation pictured in figure 19.

Hickory grove near Cleveland, Mississippi, demonstrates, through everyday local memories and attachments that accrete over time.[6]

A third common theme in the preceding essays is the call for public historians to build on the popular appeal of historical trees to develop projects that advance racial justice and public action on the climate emergency. Andrew Hurley's essay on the Missouri Place Stories project in St. Louis is especially promising in this regard, offering a model for conducting community-engaged research on the interaction of historical trees and contemporary urban residents that other public historians might follow. Several other essays employ oral history methods to bring neglected stories from marginalized communities into public view.

In addition to fostering new community-engaged research projects, the essays identify several other historical topics worth investigating further. Several essays mention in passing the collaboration of nature conservation and historic preservation organizations at the turn of the twentieth century. Liz Sargent's essay on Michaux State Forest notes that in Pennsylvania, the Association for the Promotion of Scientific Forestry "routinely joined forces with . . . the Historical Society of Pennsylvania," an effort that paralleled that of the American Scenic and Historic Preservation Society in New York, founded in 1895, which merged the conservation of "natural scenery" and historic landmarks.[7]

Lastly, worth further investigation is the history of efforts to identify and catalog famous historical trees. Evan Haefeli's essay on the Fox Oaks refers to a series of articles on "American Historical Trees" that *Harper's New Monthly Magazine* published in 1862; Mariaelena DiBenigno's essay on Sam Robinson's sycamore refers to the US Department of Agriculture's book of *Famous Trees*, published in 1938; and Alena Pirok's essay on Savannah's "hanging trees" refers to the creation of a National Register of Historic Trees sometime in the early 2000s. One might add to that the story of how the US National Park Service established the rather unfortunately named National Witness Tree Protection Program in 2006.[8]

The public history of trees can help raise awareness and understanding of the interdependence of humans and nonhuman nature in a changing climate. As global temperatures rise, the human impact on many aspects of the natural world previously thought to be independent of human action—extreme weather events, wildfire, diseases—becomes evident even in places like Antarctica, where few humans have been. Like other living creatures, trees respond to the environmental conditions created for them, conditions that in recent years have changed faster than many species can adapt. Humans also become acclimated to particular places and environmental conditions and often experience distress when their familiar surroundings—including trees—change faster than they can comprehend. The preceding essays on the public history of trees therefore demonstrate how historical trees serve as uncertain sites of memory in a changing climate. They also demonstrate how the practice of public history, which is rooted in concepts of place and memory, can assist communities in making sense of what is happening to the environment around them and become empowered to take the collective social and political actions necessary to improve it.[9]

Notes

Foreword

1 Jörg Matthies, "Symbol der Unabhängigkeit: Zur Motiv- und Denkmalikonographie der Schleswig-Holsteinischen Doppeleiche," in *Gartenkultur und nationale Identität: Strategien nationaler und regionaler Identitätsstiftung in der deutschen Gartenkultur*, ed. Gert Gröning and Uwe Schneider (Worms: Wernersche Verlagsgesellschaft, 2001), 52–74.

2 Jared Farmer, "Taking Liberties with Historic Trees," *Journal of American History* 105, no. 4 (March 2019): 816.

3 Eduard Mielck, *Die Riesen der Pflanzenwelt* (Leipzig: Winter'sche Verlagsbuchhandlung, 1863), figure XVI, 121–24. For an early assessment of the age of baobabs, see Carl Ludwig Willdenow, *Grundriss der Kräuterkunde* (Berlin: Haude and Spener, 1792), 292.

Introduction

1 Frank Carini, "Historic Preservation Can Pit Old Buildings vs. [*sic*] Mature Trees," ecoRI News, September 23, 2018, https://ecori.org/2018-9-21-historic-preservation-can-pit-old-buildings-vs-mature-trees-1/.

2 Jim Kimball, "Brown Wins Historic Preservation Award for Relocation, Renovation of Sharpe House," News from Brown, October 31, 2022, https://www.brown.edu/news/2022-10-31/preservation.

3 Carini, "Historic Preservation."

4 Carini.

5 Providence city code defines a tree of significance as being one that is larger than thirty-two inches in diameter. See "City of Providence Zoning Ordinance," City of Providence, November 24, 2014, 15-3, https://www.providenceri.gov/wp-content/uploads/2021/02/Zoning-Ordinance-Article15-Trees-Landscaping.pdf; and Carini, "Historic Preservation."

6 Dipesh Chakrabarty, "The Climate of History: Four Theses," *Critical Inquiry* 35, no. 2 (Winter 2009): 201.

7 Ed Lewis, "Gettysburg Monument with Local Interest Spared from Tree Damage," *Times Leader*, January 13, 2020, https://www.timesleader.com/news/769127/gettysburg-monument-with-local-interest-spared-from-tree-damage.

8 One commercially available photograph of a turn-of-the-twentieth-century veteran visit to the site showed that there were no trees on site. A similar site photograph from roughly the same time shows the monument unshaded. "Photograph of 143rd Pennsylvania Volunteer Infantry Monument at Gettysburg," Wikimedia, accessed September 4, 2024, https://upload.wikimedia.org/wikipedia/commons/e/e1/143rd_PA_Infantry_p683.jpg.

9 Jared Farmer, "Taking Liberties with Historic Trees," *Journal of American History* 105, no. 4 (March 2019): 815–42. There is an emerging trend of people opting for interment in a tree-growing pod. See Georgette Kilgore, "Tree Pod Burial: How It Works in 2023," 8 Billion Trees, January 20, 2023, https://8billiontrees.com/eco-friendly-natural-products/tree-pod-burial/.

10 "Rooted in History: Gettysburg's Witness Trees," CBS News, Sunday Morning, July 8, 2018, https://www.cbsnews.com/news/rooted-in-history-witness-trees-gettysburg-national-military-park/. Also see Joan E. Cashin, *War Stuff: The Struggle for Human and Environmental Resources in the American Civil War* (New York: Cambridge University Press, 2018), 82–107; and Kelby Ouchley, *Flora and Fauna of the Civil War: An Environmental Reference Guide* (Baton Rouge: LSU Press, 2010), 5–110.

11 Nicholas C. Kawa, Bradley Painter, and Cailín E. Murray, "Trail Trees: Living Artifacts (*Vivifacts*) of Eastern North America," *Ethnobiology Letters* 6, no. 1 (2015): 183–88; Chakrabarty, "Climate of History," 201.

12 "Select Tree Cutting on Little Round Top," National Park Service, Gettysburg, February 1, 2022, https://www.nps.gov/gett/learn/news/little-round-top-select-tree-cutting.htm.

13 Karen Chavez, "Hiker Killed on Appalachian Trail," *Citizen Times*, March 24, 2015, https://www.citizen-times.com/story/girls-gone-outdoors/2015/03/16/hiker-killed-on-appalachian-trail/24863089/.

14 Jonathan Griffin, "New Timeline to California's Deadliest Wildfire Could Guide Lifesaving Research and Action," NIST, February 8, 2021, https://www.nist.gov/news-events/news/2021/02/new-timeline-deadliest-california-wildfire-could-guide-lifesaving-research.

15 Talia Lakritz, "10 Famous Monuments That Were Destroyed by Fire," Insider, April 16, 2019, https://www.insider.com/famous-monuments-destroyed-in-fire-2019-4#royal-clarence-hotel-devon-england-7.

16 Dana Varinsky, "California's Historic 'Drive-Through' Tree Has Fallen Down," Yahoo Finance, January 9, 2017, https://finance.yahoo.com/news/california-historic-drive-tree-fallen-164500460.html.

17 Jared Farmer focuses on the age of trees and maintains a global frame. Age—or the appearance of age—plays a role in American historical trees. See Jared Farmer, *Elderflora: A Modern History of Ancient Trees* (New York: Basic Books, 2022).

18 George Perkins Marsh, *Man and Nature; or, Physical Geography as Modified by Human Action* (1864; repr., New York: Charles Scribner, 1871).

19 A curious exception is the racist practice of interpreting Native American culture as part of the natural world. Derek Bousé, "Culture as Nature: How Native American Cultural Antiquities Became Part of the Natural World," *Public Historian* 18, no. 4 (Autumn 1996): 75–98.

20 Aldo Leopold as quoted in Donald Worster, "Transformations of the Earth: Toward an Agroecological Perspective in History," *Journal of American History* 76, no. 4 (1990): 1087. This essay was part of a pivotal forum that helped crystallize the field. Those essays included 76 (March 1990), 1087–1106, esp. 1089. Other articles in the *Journal of American History* roundtable discussion are Alfred W. Crosby, "An Enthusiastic Second," 1107–10; Richard White, "Environmental History, Ecology, and Meaning," 1111–16; Carolyn Merchant, "Gender and Environmental History," 1117–21; William Cronon, "Modes of Prophecy and Production: Placing Nature in History," 1122–31; Stephen J. Pyne, "Firestick History," 1132–41; and Donald Worster, "Seeing beyond Culture," 1142–47.

21 John Herron, "Because Antelope Can't Talk: Natural Agency and Social Politics in American Environmental History," *Historical Reflections / Réflexions Historiques* 36, no. 1 (2010): 34.

22 Worster, "Transformations of the Earth," 1088.

23 Alfred W. Crosby Jr., *The Columbian Exchange: Biological and Cultural Consequences of 1492* (London: Praeger, 2003), xxv.

24 Paul S. Sutter, "The World with Us: The State of American Environmental History," *Journal of American History* 100, no. 1 (2013): 94–119.

25 Paul J. Crutzen and Eugene F. Stoermer, "The Anthropocene," *International Geosphere-Biosphere Programme Newsletter* 41 (2000): 17.

26 Chakrabarty, "Climate of History," 206.

27 Eric Rutkow, *American Canopy: Trees, Forests, and the Making of a Nation* (New York: Scribner, 2013); Thomas J. Campanella, *Republic of Shade: New England and the American Elm* (New Haven, CT: Yale University Press, 2003); Sonja Dümpelmann, *Seeing Trees: A History of Street Trees in New York City and Berlin* (New Haven, CT: Yale University Press, 2019); Jill Jonnes, *Urban Forests: A Natural History of Trees and People in the American Cityscape* (New York: Penguin, 2016); Jared Farmer, *Trees in Paradise: A California History* (New York: W. W. Norton, 2013); Farmer, *Elderflora*; Ellen Stroud, *Nature Next Door: Cities and Trees in the American Northeast* (Seattle: University of Washington Press, 2012); Steven J. Pyne, *Between Two Fires: A Fire History of Contemporary America* (Tucson: University of Arizona Press, 2015).

28 "Cultural Landscapes: Cultural Landscape Recognition, 1981–2000," National Park Service, accessed January 29, 2023, https://www.nps.gov/subjects/culturallandscapes/cltimeline5.htm; Melody Webb, "Cultural Landscapes in the National Park Service," *Public Historian* 9, no. 2 (Spring 1997): 77–89; Gerald D. Patten, "Cultural Landscapes: The Intent and the Tenor of the Times," *CRM* 14, no. 6 (1991): 1, 3; Robert R. Page, Cathy A. Gilbert, and Susan A. Dolan, *A Guide to Cultural Landscape Reports: Contents, Process, and Techniques* (Washington, DC: US Department of the Interior, National Park Service, Park Historic Structures and Cultural Landscapes Program, 1998).

29 Thomas J. Schlereth, "Plants Past: An Historian's Use of Vegetation as Material Culture Evidence," *Environmental Review* 4, no. 1 (1980): 20–28.

Chapter One: Arboreal Memories

The author would like to thank Laura Schatzman for help in identifying tree species.

1 Dave, "Mary's Tree," Missouri Place Stories, November 2015, https://placestories.missouriepscor.org/archive9.

2 Max Page, *Why Preservation Matters* (New Haven, CT: Yale University Press, 2016).

3 Robin Mearns and Andrew Norton, eds., *Social Dimensions of Climate Change: Equity and Vulnerability in a Warming World* (Washington, DC: World Bank, 2010).

4 David-Paul B. Hedberg, "Seeing Portland's Urban Forest for Its History," *Western Historical Quarterly* 47 (Winter 2016): 463–70; Jennifer Britton, Elisa K. Boyd, and William A. Hoch, "The State of Heritage Tree Programs in the Rocky Mountain / Interior Plain Province," *Land Research Record*, no. 4 (2015): 138–49; "Heritage Tree Program," Minneapolis Parks and Recreation Board, 2021, https://www.minneapolisparks.org/park_care__improvements/trees/heritage_tree_program/; Myles Ritchie, "Establishing Consensus or the Protection of Heritage Trees" (MA thesis, Department of Geography, University Hawaii at Manoa, 2019); "Heritage Tree Program," Seattle Department of Transportation, 2021, http://www.seattle.gov/transportation/projects-and-programs/programs/trees-and-landscaping-program/heritage-tree-program.

5 "Legacy Initiative: Canopy Story," Portland State University, 2021, https://www.pdx.edu/sustainability/canopy-story. Another exemplary storytelling project, coordinated by Leah Glaser at Central Connecticut State University, generated fifteen student-researched and student-narrated audio recordings about trees that witnessed meaningful pasts and merited recognition as living memorials to historic events and actors. "Rooted in History: Connecticut's Trees," June 29, 2021, in *Grating the Nutmeg*, produced by Leah Glaser and Mary Donohue, podcast, audio, 1:05:17, https://gratingthenutmeg.libsyn.com/121-rooted-in-history-connecticuts-trees.

6 Award number 11A-1355406. Any opinions, findings, conclusions, or recommendations expressed in this essay are those of the author and do not necessarily reflect those of the National Science Foundation.

7 The following students made substantial contributions to the project: Paige Fensterman Ballard, Lauren Cooley, Shuron Jones, Mark Loehrer, Eliza Murray, Rebecca Rea, and Brenda Thacker. Faculty contributors included the author and Maris Gillette, currently professor of social anthropology, School of Global Studies, University of Gothenburg.

8 *Report of the Kingshighway Commission* (St. Louis: City of St. Louis, 1903).

9 "City Will Supply Shade Trees Guaranteed to Grow, for $4 Each," *St. Louis Star and Times*, January 10, 1919, 3.

10 "WPA Buys 4,300 Trees for Planting in City," *St. Louis Star and Times*, May 11, 1937, 3; "WPA Grants $144,901 for Trees in City," *St. Louis Star and Times*, March 28, 1939, 3.

11 Raymond W. Vodicka, "Beauty: $4 Million for a 'City of Trees,'" *St. Louis Post Dispatch*, December 12, 1988, 1N, 2N.

12 The list was refined several times as the project evolved. The last revision included the following categories: a vulnerable place that needs to be protected; a place that shows how the neighborhood has changed, for better or worse; a place that provides environmental benefits; a place that reflects local heritage; a place to go during very hot weather; a place to go on a rainy day; a place that promotes community or contributes to neighborhood identity; a place that needs to be eliminated; a beautiful place; a scary or unpleasant place; and a place that inspires hope for the future.

13 Peter H. Raven, foreword to *St. Louis in the Century of Henry Shaw: A View beyond the Garden Wall*, ed. Eric Sandweiss (St. Louis: Missouri Historical Society Press, 2003), xi–xiv; Carol Grove, *Henry Shaw's Victorian Landscape: The Missouri Botanical Garden and Tower Grove Park* (Amherst: University of Massachusetts Press, 2005.) The arboretum, established in 1860, remained in its planning stages on the date of the garden's grand opening.

14 Mary M. Stiritz, "Shaw Avenue Place," National Register of Historic Places Inventory-Nomination Form, September 3, 1980, https://mostateparks.com/page/84916/st-louis-city-national-register-listings; "Another Mystery," *St. Louis Post Dispatch*, September 25, 1878, 1.

15 "A Big Real Estate Deal," *St. Louis Globe-Democrat*, June 7, 1887, 5; advertisement for lots on Tyler Place, *St. Louis Post Dispatch*, November 18, 1888, 9.

16 On the vast social and political forces that reshaped St. Louis in the decades after World War II, including white flight, urban renewal, and inner-city disinvestment, see Colin Gordon, *Mapping Decline: St. Louis and the Fate of an American City* (Philadelphia: University of Pennsylvania Press, 2009); Richard Rothstein, *The Color of Law: A Forgotten History of How Our Government Segregated America* (New York: W. W. Norton, 2017); and Walter Johnson, *The Broken Heart of America: St. Louis and the Violent History of the United States* (New York: Basic Books, 2020).

17 Hank Webber and Todd Swanstrom, "Rebound Neighborhoods in Older Industrial Cities: The Story of St. Louis" (working paper, Center for Social Development, Washington University, 2014), 30–40; Shelley Smithson, "The Greening of McRee Town," *Riverfront Times*, October 8, 2003.

18 Robert, "Flora Place Park," Missouri Place Stories, October 2015, https://placestories.missouriepscor.org/.

19 Jametta, "Playground," Missouri Place Stories, July 2015, https://placestories.missouriepscor.org/.

20 Patrick, "Community Garden," Missouri Place Stories, July 2015, https://placestories.missouriepscor.org/.

21 Brittany, "Old Tree," Missouri Place Stories, July 2015, https://placestories.missouriepscor.org/.

22 James Sheire, "Missouri Botanical Garden," National Register of Historic Places Inventory-Nomination Form, June 1976, https://mostateparks.com/page/84916/st-louis-city-national-register-listings.

23 Tami, "Missouri Botanical Garden," Missouri Place Stories, February 2016, https://placestories.missouriepscor.org/.

24 Rob, "Tower Grove Park," Missouri Place Stories, March 2016, https://placestories.missouriepscor.org/.
25 Sean, "Flora Place," Missouri Place Stories, October 2015, https://placestories.missouriepscor.org/.
26 Sean, "Magnolia," Missouri Place Stories, October 2015, https://placestories.missouriepscor.org/.
27 Jacque, "Church Lot," Missouri Place Stories, October 2015, https://placestories.missouriepscor.org/.
28 Scholars across multiple disciplines have employed the concept of hybridity to describe settings that blend natural and human-constructed features. For a small sampling of the relevant literature, see Moura Quayle and Tilo C. Driessen van der Lieck, "Growing Community: A Case for Hybrid Landscapes," *Landscape and Urban Planning* 39 (November 1997): 99–107; Richard White, "From Wilderness to Hybrid Landscapes: The Cultural Turn in Environmental History," *Historian* 66, no. 3 (2004): 557–64; John Wylie, *Landscape* (Oxford: Routledge, 2007); and Marina Alberti, *Cities That Think like Planets: Complexity, Resilience, and Innovations in Hybrid Ecosystems* (Seattle: University of Washington Press, 2016).
29 Paul Hampel, "Prayer then Violence Erupts and Shaw Shooting Scene in St. Louis," *St. Louis Post Dispatch*, October 10, 2014, A4.
30 Monte, "Shaw Memorial Grove," Missouri Place Stories, October 2015, https://placestories.missouriepscor.org/.
31 Shaw Forum meeting notes, May 11, 2016, in author's possession.
32 Personal notes, Walnut Park Workshop no. 2, October 30, 2017, in author's possession.
33 "MSD Project Clear, City of St. Louis Begin $13.5 Million Program to Demolish Buildings," City of St. Louis, March 23, 2017, https://www.stlouis-mo.gov/government/departments/street/news/msd-project-clear-and-city-begin-program-to-demolish-buildings.cfm.
34 Rolla Wells, *Episodes of My Life* (St. Louis: W. J. McCarthy, 1933), 17.
35 Elizabeth Rosin, "Walnut Park School," National Register of Historic Places Inventory-Nomination Form, October 23, 2012, https://mostateparks.com/page/84916/st-louis-city-national-register-listings; Norbury Wayman, *History of St. Louis Neighborhoods: Walnut Park* (St. Louis: City Plan Commission, 1978).
36 "For Sale—1480 Goodfellow," *St. Louis Globe-Democrat*, May 19, 1912, 8A.
37 "For Sale by John F. McMahon," *St. Louis Globe-Democrat*, April 28, 1895, 19.
38 "Annual Report of the City Forester," in *The Mayor's Message with Accompanying Documents to the Municipal Assembly of the City of St. Louis for the Fiscal Year Ending April 13, 1908* (St. Louis: Municipal Assembly of the City of St. Louis, 1909), 861.
39 John Curley, "Elms Are in Again," *St. Louis Post Dispatch*, July 1, 2002, A1.
40 "Horticulture," Bellefontaine Cemetery and Arboretum, 2021, https://bellefontainecemetery.org/destination/horticulture/.
41 St. Louis City Plan Commission, *Comprehensive City Plan, St. Louis, Missouri* (St. Louis: City Plan Commission, 1947), plate 23.

42 John, "Trees on Plover Ave.," Missouri Place Stories, July 2017, https://placestories.missouriepscor.org/.
43 Reggie, "Lot with Tree," Missouri Place Stories, October 2017, https://placestories.missouriepscor.org/.
44 Sylvester, "The Neighborhood," Missouri Place Stories, July 2016, https://placestories.missouriepscor.org/.
45 Ernest, "Harney and Thrush Apple Tree" and "Harney and Genevieve Fruit Trees," Missouri Place Stories, October 2017, https://placestories.missouriepscor.org/.
46 Reggie, "Trees of Walnut Park East Past," Missouri Place Stories, October 2017, https://placestories.missouriepscor.org/.
47 Joyce, "Climate Change," Missouri Place Stories, July 2016, https://placestories.missouriepscor.org/.
48 Tyanna, "Calvary Cemetery," Missouri Place Stories, January 2018, https://placestories.missouriepscor.org/.
49 William, "History on Arlington Avenue," Missouri Place Stories, November 2017, https://placestories.missouriepscor.org/.
50 Valerie, "Terry Avenue Tree," Missouri Place Stories, June 2016, https://placestories.missouriepscor.org/.
51 Eltereon, "Volunteer Trees," Missouri Place Stories, November 2017, https://placestories.missouriepscor.org/.
52 Harlem Creek Community Advisory Council meeting notes taken by author, October 9, 2017; Walnut Park East Vacancy to Vibrancy Workshop no. 1 notes taken by author, October 5, 2017. All notes in author's possession.
53 Carolyn Finney, *Black Faces, White Spaces: Reimagining the Relationship of African Americans to the Great Outdoors* (Chapel Hill: University of North Carolina Press, 2014), 62–66.
54 Renate Chancellor and Shari Lee, "Storytelling, Oral History, and Building the Library Community," *Storytelling, Self, Society* 12, no. 1 (2016): 39–54.

Chapter Two: "The Most Useful Tree"

The author wishes to thank Dr. Carmen Burkhalter for introducing her to the story of the American chestnut and the American Chestnut Foundation for all their assistance with this project. Dr. John Scrivani, "Forest Inventory and Analysis," *Journal of the American Chestnut Foundation* 25, no. 3 (May/June 2011): 18, https://acf.org/wp-content/uploads/2016/09/Volume-XXV-No.-3-May-Jun-2011.pdf.

1 Edward K. Faison and David R. Forster, "Did American Chestnut Really Dominate the Eastern Forest?," *Arnoldia* 72, no. 2 (2014): 21, https://www.jstor.org/stable/24706421.
2 "Why American Chestnut," American Chestnut Foundation, accessed May 13, 2021, https://tacf.org/history-american-chestnut/why-american-chestnuts/.
3 "Welcome to the Carolinas Chapter," American Chestnut Foundation, accessed January 15, 2021, https://acf.org/nc-sc/.

4 Ralph Lutts, "Like Manna from God: The American Chestnut Trade in Southwestern Virginia," *Environmental History* 9, no. 3 (July 2004): 497, https://www.jstor.org/stable/3985770.
5 "FAQs," American Chestnut Foundation, accessed May 13, 2021, https://acf.org/resources/faqs/.
6 See Frances Jenkins Olcott, "The Chestnut Kettle," in *The Red Indian Fairy Book* (Chapel Hill: Yesterday's Classics, 2006), 139; and Paul Hamel and Mary Chiltoskey, *Cherokee Plants: Their Uses—a 400-Year History* (Cherokee, NC: Cherokee Publications, 2014).
7 For an example of a poem by a TACF enthusiast, see Krista Jackson Butterfield, "The Sentinel," *Journal of the American Chestnut Foundation* 10, no. 1 (Summer/Fall 1996): 14–15, https://acf.org/wp-content/uploads/2016/09/journ_vol10-1_96.pdf.
8 Donald Davis, *Where There Are Mountains: An Environmental History of the Southern Appalachians* (Athens: University of Georgia Press, 2000); Lutts, "Like Manna from God," 497–525.
9 George Hepting, "Death of the American Chestnut," *Journal of Forest History* 18, no. 3 (July 1974): 59, https://www.jstor.org/stable/3983346.
10 Hepting, 61; Chris Bolgiano, ed., *Mighty Giants: An American Chestnut Anthology* (Bennington, VT: Images from the Past, 2007), 172.
11 William A. Powell, Andrew E. Newhouse, and Vernon Coffey, "Developing Blight-Tolerant American Chestnut Trees," in *Perspectives on Engineering Plants for Agriculture*, ed. P. Arnold (Cold Spring Harbor, NY: Cold Spring Harbor Perspectives in Biology, 2019), 3, doi:10.1101/cshperspect.a034587.
12 Hepting, "Death of the American Chestnut," 61.
13 Jane Hodgins, "What It Takes to Bring Back the Near Mythical American Chestnut Trees," US Department of Agriculture, accessed June 4, 2021, https://www.usda.gov/media/blog/2019/04/29/what-it-takes-bring-back-near-mythical-american-chestnut-trees.
14 Myra McAllister, "Of the Rural Appalachians," *Journal of the American Chestnut Foundation* 10, no. 1 (Summer/Fall 1996): 20, https://acf.org/wp-content/uploads/2016/09/journ_vol10-1_96.pdf.
15 Lutts, "Like Manna from God," 497.
16 Tom Horton, "Revival of the American Chestnut," *American Forests*, Winter 2010, https://www.americanforests.org/magazine/article/revival-of-the-american-chestnut/ (page no longer extant).
17 Hepting, "Death of the American Chestnut," 62.
18 Mary Hosier, Charles R. Burnham, and Paul E. Read, "Breeding Strategy for a Blight-Resistant American Chestnut," *Journal of the American Chestnut Foundation* 1, no. 1 (July 1985): 2–3, https://acf.org/wp-content/uploads/2016/09/journ_vol1-1_85.pdf; "Letters to the Journal," *Journal of the American Chestnut Foundation* 7, no. 1 (Fall/Winter 1992): 3, https://acf.org/wp-content/uploads/2016/09/journ_vol7-1.pdf.
19 Hepting, "Death of the American Chestnut," 64.
20 Hepting, 66.

21 Sandra L. Anagnostakis, "The American Chestnut: New Hope for a Fallen Giant," Connecticut Agricultural Experiment Station, bulletin 777, December 1978, 2, https://portal.ct.gov/-/media/CAES/DOCUMENTS/Publications/Bulletins/B777pdf.pdf.
22 Hosier, Burnham, and Read, "Breeding Strategy," 3.
23 Hosier, Burnham, and Read, 4.
24 Hosier, Burnham, and Read, 4.
25 Hosier, Burnham, and Read, 4.
26 Frederick V. Hebard, "Meadowview Notes," *Journal of the American Chestnut Foundation* 7, no. 1 (Fall/Winter 1992): 5, https://acf.org/wp-content/uploads/2016/09/journ_vol7-1.pdf.
27 Dennis Fulbright, "The Survival of American Chestnut Trees in Michigan," *Journal of the American Chestnut Foundation* 1, no. 2 (August 1986): 3–5, https://acf.org/wp-content/uploads/2016/09/journ_vol1-2_86.pdf.
28 "About," American Chestnut Research and Restoration Project, accessed May 5, 2021, https://www.esf.edu/chestnut/about.asp.
29 "Homepage," American Chestnut Cooperators' Foundation, accessed May 5, 2021, http://accf-online.org/.
30 Donald Willeke, "Introduction to the Journal of the American Chestnut Foundation," *Journal of the American Chestnut Foundation* 1, no. 1 (July 1985): 2, https://acf.org/wp-content/uploads/2016/09/journ_vol1-1_85.pdf.
31 Elizabeth Daniels, "Voices of the Past," *Journal of the American Chestnut Foundation* 17, no. 1 (Fall 2003): 28–29, https://acf.org/wp-content/uploads/2016/09/journ_vol17-1_03.pdf.
32 Jeanne Coleman, "From the Editor," *Journal of the American Chestnut Foundation* 20, no. 2 (Fall 2006): 5, https://acf.org/wp-content/uploads/2016/09/JrnlFall2006.pdf.
33 Jules Smith, phone conversation with the author, June 3, 2021.
34 David Cameron, "Charlotte Ross and the Chestnut Connection," *Journal of the American Chestnut Foundation* 15, no. 2 (Spring 2002): 7–8, https://acf.org/wp-content/uploads/2016/09/Journal_vol15_02_spring2002.pdf.
35 Davis, *Where There Are Mountains*, 192.
36 Lutts, "Like Manna from God," 498.
37 Davis, *Where There Are Mountains*, 198.
38 Samantha Bowers, "Black History Month: The Community of Coe Ridge, KY," American Chestnut Foundation, accessed August 26, 2021, https://tacf.org/black-history-month-the-community-of-coe-ridge-ky/.
39 Davis, *Where There Are Mountains*, 196.
40 Gary Carver, "Creating Artwork from American Chestnut Is Both a Joy and a Challenge," *Journal of the American Chestnut Foundation* 18, no. 2 (Fall 2004): 27, https://acf.org/wp-content/uploads/2016/09/journal_fall04.pdf.
41 Both Edward G. Lowell and Richmond Curtis describe working with the wood as children in shop class. See Edward G. Lowell, "Of Suburban Long Island, New York," *Journal of the American Chestnut Foundation* 10, no. 1 (Summer/Fall 1996): 21, https://acf.org/wp-content/uploads/2016/09/journ_vol10-1_96.pdf;

and Richmond Curtis and Sally Curtis, "Of Urban New Haven, Connecticut," *Journal of the American Chestnut Foundation* 10, no. 1 (Summer/Fall 1996): 22, https://acf.org/wp-content/uploads/2016/09/journ_vol10-1_96.pdf.

42 Georganna Rice et al., "Memories of the American Chestnut," *Journal of the American Chestnut Foundation* 15, no. 1 (Fall 2001): 27, https://acf.org/wp-content/uploads/2016/09/Journ_vol15-1_01.pdf. This is an excerpt from *Foxfire 6: Shoemaking, One Hundred Toys and Games, Gourd Banjos and Songbows, Wooden Locks, a Water-Powered Sawmill, and Other Affairs of Just Plain Living* (Garden City, NY: Anchor/Doubleday, 1980), 397–421, http://archive.org/details/foxfire6shoemaki0000unse.

43 William A. Banks, "My Life with the Chestnut," *Journal of the American Chestnut Foundation* 19, no. 1 (Spring 2005): 20, https://acf.org/wp-content/uploads/2016/09/journ_vol19-1.pdf.

44 Coleman, "From the Editor," 5.

45 David Lowenthal, *The Past Is a Foreign Country* (Cambridge: Cambridge University Press, 1985), 7.

46 Lowenthal, *Past Is a Foreign Country*, 7.

47 Lowenthal, 8.

48 Philip Rutter, "The President's Message," *Journal of the American Chestnut Foundation* 1, no. 2 (August 1986): 13, https://acf.org/wp-content/uploads/2016/09/journ_vol1-2_86.pdf.

49 Jack Stillman, "A Chestnut Treasure," *Journal of the American Chestnut Foundation* 8, no. 2 (Fall/Winter 1994): 6, https://acf.org/wp-content/uploads/2016/09/journ_vol8-2.pdf; Ellsworth Barnard, "Excerpt from *In a Wild Place: A Natural History of High Ledges*," *Journal of the American Chestnut Foundation* 14, no. 1 (Summer 2000): 34, https://acf.org/wp-content/uploads/2017/11/journ_vol14-1_00.pdf.

50 Lowenthal, *Past Is a Foreign Country*, 11.

51 Jeremy Davies, "Sustainable Nostalgia," *Memory Studies* 3, no. 3 (July 2010): 262, https://journals.sagepub.com/doi/pdf/10.1177/1750698010364819.

52 "Portrait of a Pioneer: Angus W. McDonald, Jr.," *Journal of the American Chestnut Foundation* 8, no. 1 (Winter/Spring 1994): 7, https://acf.org/wp-content/uploads/2016/09/journ_vol8-1.pdf; Nadia Atia and Jeremy Davies, "Nostalgia and the Shapes of History," *Memory Studies* 3, no. 3 (July 2010): 181, https://journals.sagepub.com/doi/pdf/10.1177/1750698010364806.

53 Rutter, "President's Message," 13.

54 William A. Good, interview by Charles Miller, in Bolgiano, *Mighty Giants*, 61.

55 Rice et al., "Memories," 29.

56 Katie L. Burke, "Chestnuts and Wildlife," *Journal of the American Chestnut Foundation* 27, no. 2 (March/April 2013): 8, https://acf.org/wp-content/uploads/2016/09/Volume-XXVII-No.-2-Mar-April-2013.pdf.

57 McAllister, "Of the Rural Appalachians," 20.

58 "Of North Bridgewater, Susquehanna County, Pennsylvania, circa 1920," *Journal of the American Chestnut Foundation* 11, no. 1 (Summer 1997): 28, https://acf.org/wp-content/uploads/2016/09/journ_vol11-1_97.pdf.

59 Rice et al., "Memories," 28.

60 Rice et al., 28.
61 "Medicinal Monday—American Chestnut Tree, the Redwoods of the East," Stories from the Wigwam, accessed August 26, 2021, https://nativeamericanmuseum.blogspot.com/2019/11/medincinal-monday-american-chestnut.html.
62 Donald Davis, "Excerpts from *Where There Are Mountains: An Environmental History of the Southern Appalachians*," *Journal of the American Chestnut Foundation* 13, no. 1 (Spring 1999): 35, https://acf.org/wp-content/uploads/2016/09/journ_vol13-1_99.pdf.
63 Rice et al., "Memories," 27.
64 Rice et al., 29.
65 Dr. William Lord, "The Blue Ridge Parkway Agronomist," *Journal of the American Chestnut Foundation* 15, no. 1 (Fall 2001): 32, https://acf.org/wp-content/uploads/2016/09/Journ_vol15-1_01.pdf.
66 Donald McCall, "Sweet Chestnuts," *Journal of the American Chestnut Foundation* 15, no. 2 (Spring 2002): 14, https://acf.org/wp-content/uploads/2016/09/Journal_vol15_02_spring2002.pdf.
67 William B. Wood, "The Last Great Chestnut: A Story Based upon My Childhood Experiences in Western North Carolina," *Journal of the American Chestnut Foundation* 24, no. 1 (Winter 2010): 11, https://acf.org/wp-content/uploads/2016/09/Journal_vol_24_winter2010.pdf.
68 P. L. Buttrick, "Excerpts from Commercial Uses of Chestnut," *Journal of the American Chestnut Foundation* 13, no. 1 (Spring 1999): 21, https://acf.org/wp-content/uploads/2016/09/journ_vol13-1_99.pdf.
69 Georgia Miller, "Chestnuts before the Blight," *Journal of the American Chestnut Foundation* 15, no. 2 (Spring 2002): 16, https://acf.org/wp-content/uploads/2016/09/Journal_vol15_02_spring2002.pdf; John Alger, "The Chestnut Loggers," *Journal of the American Chestnut Foundation* 16, no. 2 (Spring 2003): 26, https://acf.org/wp-content/uploads/2016/09/journ_vol16-2_03.pdf.
70 "Survivors: An Interview with Daniel Hallett," *Journal of the American Chestnut Foundation* 24, no. 1 (Winter 2010): 13, https://acf.org/wp-content/uploads/2016/09/Journal_vol_24_winter2010.pdf.
71 Dr. William Lord, "How Things Happen: The Story of the Chestnut Tree and a Chemist," *Journal of the American Chestnut Foundation* 28, no. 3 (May/June 2014): 23–27, https://acf.org/wp-content/uploads/2016/09/Volume-XXVIII-No.3-May-June_2014.pdf.
72 Patrick Chamberlin, "A Practical Way for the Layman to Participate in Breeding Resistance into the American Chestnut," *Journal of the American Chestnut Foundation* 2, no. 2 (Fall/Winter 1991): 8–11, https://acf.org/wp-content/uploads/2016/09/journ_vol6-2.pdf.
73 "One Goal," *Chestnut: The New Journal of the American Chestnut Foundation* 29, no. 3 (Fall 2015): 40, https://acf.org/wp-content/uploads/2017/03/Chestnut_Fall2015FINAL_lr.pdf.
74 Ernest Souther, "His DNA Had a Cambium Layer," *Journal of the American Chestnut Foundation* 27, no. 6 (November/December 2013): 26, https://acf.org/wp-content/uploads/2016/09/Volume-XXVII-No.6-Nov-Dec-2013.pdf.

75 Jill Willson, "One Man's Dream—the Return of the American Chestnut," *Journal of the American Chestnut Foundation* 8, no. 2 (Fall/Winter 1994): 8–9, https://acf.org/wp-content/uploads/2016/09/journ_vol8-2.pdf.

76 Tom Horton, "Will We Ever Be Able to Pull the American Chestnuts Out of the Fire?," *Bay Journal*, April 8, 2021, https://www.bayjournal.com/columns/chesapeake_born/will-we-be-able-to-pull-the-american-chestnuts-out-of-the-fire/article_0b80d740-93c7-11eb-b49c-634b2209e56b.html.

77 Willson, "One Man's Dream," 8–9.

78 Jim Casada "Youth and the American Chestnut: Instilling a Love of Nature in the Next Generation," *Journal of the American Chestnut Foundation* 24, no. 3 (November 2010): 20–22, https://tacf.org/wp-content/uploads/2016/09/Volume-XXIV-No.-4-November-2010.pdf.

79 "TACF Success Rooted in the Work of Talented Volunteers," *Journal of the American Chestnut Foundation* 25, no. 4 (July/August 2011): 16, https://acf.org/wp-content/uploads/2016/09/Volume-XXV-No.-4-Jul-Aug-2011.pdf.

80 Dan Hale, "Curt Laffin: Tireless Advocate for the American Chestnut," *Journal of the American Chestnut Foundation* 25, no. 6 (November/December 2011): 7, https://acf.org/wp-content/uploads/2016/09/Volume-XXV-No.-6-Nov-Dec-2011.pdf; Paul Franklin "James Curtis: Environmental Volunteer and Renaissance Man," *Journal of the American Chestnut Foundation* 25, no. 6 (November/December 2011): 7, https://acf.org/wp-content/uploads/2016/09/Volume-XXV-No.-6-Nov-Dec-2011.pdf; Dave Armstrong and Sara Fitzsimmons, "Tracy Coulter," *Journal of the American Chestnut Foundation* 26, no. 2 (May/June 2012): 7, https://acf.org/wp-content/uploads/2016/09/Volume-XXVI-No.-3-May-June-2012.pdf; "Ellery 'Woods' Sinclair," *Journal of the American Chestnut Foundation* 27, no. 4 (July/August 2013): 12, https://acf.org/wp-content/uploads/2016/09/Volume-XXVII-No.4-July-Aug-2013.pdf.

81 Glen Rea, "One Million and Seven," *Journal of the American Chestnut Foundation* 25, no. 2 (March/April 2011): 5, https://acf.org/wp-content/uploads/2016/09/Volume-XXV-No.-2-Mar-Apr-2011.pdf.

82 Casada, "Youth and the American Chestnut," 22; fifth-grade class of Elwood Kindle Elementary School, "Our Chestnut Challenge," *Journal of the American Chestnut Foundation* 26, no. 1 (January/February 2012): 23, https://acf.org/wp-content/uploads/2016/09/Volume-XXVI-No.-1-Jan-Feb-2012.pdf; Tyler Kulfan, "On the Necessity of a Cross-Generational Approach to Restoring the American Chestnut," *Journal of the American Chestnut Foundation* 27, no. 5 (September/October 2013): 26–27, https://acf.org/wp-content/uploads/2016/09/Volume-XXVII-No.5-Sept-Oct-2013.pdf.

83 Charles C. Mann and Mark L. Plummer, "Forest Biotech Edges Out of the Lab," *Science* 295, no. 5560 (March 1, 2002): 1628, https://www.jstor.org/stable/3075945.

84 Brian C. McCarthy, Jenise M. Bauman, and Carolyn H. Keiffer, "Mine Land Reclamation Strategies for the Restoration of the American Chestnut," *Ecological Restoration* 26, no. 4 (December 2008): 292–94, https://www.jstor.org/stable/43443158.

85 Julie Grant, "Restoring the American Chestnut with Genetic Engineering Splits the Conservation Community," *Allegheny Front*, October 16, 2020, https://www.alleghenyfront.org/restoring-the-american-chestnut-with-genetic-engineering-splits-conservationists/.

86 Douglass F. Jacobs, Harmony J. Dalgleish, and C. Dana Nelson, "A Conceptual Framework for Restoration of Threatened Plants: The Effective Model of American Chestnut (*Castanea dentata*) Reintroduction," *New Phytologist* 197, no. 2 (2013): 378–93, http://www.jstor.org/stable/newphytologist.197.2.378.

87 Lutts, "Like Manna from God," 497.

88 "History," Forest Restoration Alliance, accessed 5.13.2021, https://threatenedforests.com/about-us/history/.

89 Suki Casanave, "The Quest to Restore American Elms: Nearing the Finish Line," Cool Green Science: Stories of the Nature Conservancy, accessed August 15, 2023, https://blog.nature.org/2017/08/09/quest-restore-american-elms-nearing-finish-line/.

90 Kathleen S. Knight et al., "American Elm (*Ulmus americana*) in Restoration Plantings: A Review," *Proceedings of the American Elm Restoration Workshop*, 2016, 133, https://www.fs.usda.gov/nrs/pubs/gtr/gtr-nrs-p-174papers/15knight-et-al-gtr-p-174.pdf.

91 Kim Steiner and Bryan Burhans, "Why Bring Back the American Chestnut?," *Journal of the American Chestnut Foundation* 27, no. 1 (January/February 2013): 3, https://acf.org/wp-content/uploads/2016/09/Volume-XXVII-No.-1-Jan-Feb-2013.pdf.

92 "Fond Memories of the Tree," Ozark Chinquapin Foundation, accessed May 13, 2021, https://ozarkchinquapinmembership.org/interviews/.

93 Donald C. Willeke, "From Thirty Years Ago to Thirty Years from Now," *Journal of the American Chestnut Foundation* 27, no. 6 (November/December 2013): 20, https://acf.org/wp-content/uploads/2016/09/Volume-XXVII-No.6-Nov-Dec-2013.pdf.

94 Bryan Burhans, "Individual Creativity—TACF's Largest Asset," *Journal of the American Chestnut Foundation* 25, no. 6 (November/December 2011): 6, https://acf.org/wp-content/uploads/2016/09/Volume-XXV-No.-6-Nov-Dec-2011.pdf.

Chapter Three: An Island of Trees Called *Old Hickory*

1 Satellite view of Cleveland, Mississippi, Google Earth, June 18, 2021, https://earth.google.com/web/search/cleveland+missisippi/@33.743922,-90.73036205,41.84546505a,9665.27763783d,35y,0h,0t,0r/data=CigiJgokCYkmlglY3UBAEYKbqweH3EBAGWrtcUHrrlbAIWWabMGDr1bA.

2 "Overcup Oak," US Department of Agriculture, accessed January 31, 2022, https://www.srs.fs.usda.gov/pubs/misc/ag_654/volume_2/quercus/lyrata.htm; John D. Hodges, David L. Evans, and Linda W. Garnett, *Mississippi Trees*, 2nd ed. (Jackson: Mississippi Forestry Commission, 2016), 144–45.

3 Dan Flores, "Place: An Argument for Bioregional History," *Environmental History Review* 18, no. 4 (Winter 1994): 5. The following definition for *bioregion*

is useful: "Bioregion is short for 'bio-cultural region' and are geographically based areas defined by physical traits; land or soil composition, watershed, climate, flora, and fauna; as well as the cultural traits of the inhabitants that live within them, and act upon them. Ultimately, they are defined by the people living within them." "Defining a Bioregion," Cascadia Department of Bioregion, accessed September 9, 2023, https://cascadiabioregion.org/what-is-a-bioregion.

4 Dana Prince, "What about Place? Considering the Role of Physical Environment on Youth Imagining of Future Possible Selves," *Journal of Youth Studies* 17, no. 6 (July 2014): 2.

5 James C. Cobb, *The Most Southern Place on Earth: The Mississippi Delta and the Roots of Regional Identity* (New York: Oxford University Press, 1992).

6 Richard Grant, *Dispatches from Pluto: Lost and Found in the Mississippi Delta* (New York: Simon & Schuster, 2015).

7 W. Ralph Eubanks, *A Place like Mississippi: A Journey through a Real and Imagined Literary Landscape* (Portland, OR: Timber Press, 2021).

8 "Mississippi River Alluvial Plain Ecoregion," Landscope America, accessed April 13, 2021, https://libguides.heidelberg.edu/chicago/web.

9 As quoted in Eubanks, *Place like Mississippi*, 185. While the Delta is inherently flat, farmers and developers often engage in precision leveling of the ground, rendering an agricultural field almost perfectly flat.

10 Mikko Saikku, "An Environmental Historian's Perspective on the Mississippi Delta," in *Defining the Delta: Multidisciplinary Perspectives on the Lower Mississippi River Delta*, ed. Janelle Collins (Fayetteville: University of Arkansas Press, 2015), 57; William H. Conner et al., "Silviculture and Management Strategies Applicable to Southern Hardwoods," in *Southern Forest Science: Past, Present Future Productivity*, ed. H. Michael Rauscher and Kurt Johnsen (Asheville, NC: US Department of Agriculture, Forest Service, Southern Research Station, 2004), 52, 53.

11 Cobb, *Most Southern Place*, 8; Robert K. Nelson at el., "The Forced Migration of Enslaved People," American Panorama, accessed April 7, 2021, https://dsl.richmond.edu/panorama/forcedmigration; Charles Reagan Wilson, "Mississippi Delta," Southern Spaces, accessed April 8, 2021, https://southernspaces.org/2004/mississippi-delta/. Old Hickory is located in Cleveland, Mississippi—Bolivar County.

12 As quoted in John Solomon Otto, *The Final Frontiers: Settling the Southern Bottomlands* (Westport, CT: Greenwood Press, 1999), 23.

13 Some postbellum African American farmers secured "rent-free" acres from planters or absentee landowners with the understanding that in exchange they would clear the thick swamplands for cultivation. Otto, *Final Frontiers*, 40; John C. Willis, *Forgotten Time: The Yazoo-Mississippi Delta after the Civil War* (Charlottesville: University Press of Virginia, 2000), 4, 107, 113.

14 Cobb, *Most Southern Place*, 98, 99, 100.

15 Charles Reagan Wilson, "Mississippi Delta," *Mississippi Encyclopedia*, accessed April 8, 2021, https://mississippiencyclopedia.org/entries/delta/; Mikko Saikku,

This Delta, This Land: An Environmental History of the Yazoo-Mississippi Floodplain (Athens: University of Georgia Press, 2005), 220; Albert E. Cowdrey, *This Land, This South: A Environmental History*, rev. ed. (Lexington: University Press of Kentucky, 1996), 83.

16 US Department of Agriculture, Weather Bureau, *Index: Monthly Weather Review*, vol. 39 (Washington, DC: US Department of Agriculture, 1911), 402; Florence Warfield Sillers, members of the Mississippi Delta chapter of the Daughters of the American Revolution, and the County History Committee, comps., *History of Bolivar County, Mississippi* (n.p.: MSGenWeb Project, n.d.), 226, 227, accessed May 18, 2021, https://www.msgw.org/index2.html, http://msgw.org/bolivar/HBCLater.pdf.

17 Michael Tarrant and Bruce Hull, "Forest Values and Attitudes in the South: Past and Future Research," in Rauscher and Johnsen, *Southern Forest Science*, 233; Saikku, *This Delta, This Land*, 222; Cowdrey, *This Land, This South*, 130.

18 Sonja N. Oswalt, "Mississippi's Forests, 2013," USDA Forest Service, Southern Research Station, bulletin SRS-204, 2015, 2; Wilson, "Mississippi Delta," Southern Spaces; Saikku, *This Delta, This Land*, 226; Charles E. Snipes et al., "Current Agricultural Practices of the Mississippi Delta," Mississippi Agricultural & Forestry Experiment Station, bulletin 1143, December 2005.

19 Eubanks, *Place like Mississippi*, 191.

20 Saikku, *This Delta, This Land*, 226.

21 Phillip Gordon, "The Delta and Yoknapatawpha: The Layering of Geography and Myth in the Works of William Faulkner," *Study the South*, November 28, 2016, https://southernstudies.olemiss.edu/study-the-south/delta-yoknapatawpha/.

22 Cobb, *Most Southern Place*, 326.

23 See Prince, "What about Place?," 697–716. Prince writes, "Individuals utilize aspects of their daily physical environments to maintain a coherent sense of self. For example, everyday places may offer respite, privacy, and retreat to re-center self." Prince, 4. See also M. Drenthen, "Rewilding in Culturally Layered Landscapes," *Environmental Values* 27 (2018): 325–30. In his criticism of some tenets of modern rewilding efforts, Drenthen counters the idea that landscapes are immutable or possessive of an ideal continuity. He writes, "A more nuanced approach to the role of history in the landscape is needed, in which more attention is paid to the layered nature of historic landscapes." Drenthen, 328. See also Rachel D. Kroencke et al., "Knowledge of Neighborhood Nature Is Associated with Strong Sense of Place among Milwaukee Youth," *Children, Youth and Environments* 25, no. 3 (2015): 129–44.

24 Frances Ryfield et al., "Conceptualizing 'Sense of Place' in Cultural Ecosystem Services: A Framework for Interdisciplinary Research," *Ecosystem Services* 36 (2019): 3.

25 Rebecca Wheeler, "Mining Memories in a Rural Community: Landscape, Temporality and Place Identity," *Journal of Rural Studies* 36 (October 2014): 22–32.

26 Yi-Fu Tuan, *Topophilia: A Study of Environmental Perception, Attitudes, and Values* (New York: Columbia University Press, 1974), 27–28.

27 Jennifer Ladino, *Memorials Matter: Emotion, Environment, and Public Memory at American Historical Sites* (Reno: University of Nevada Press, 2019), 9, 11.
28 "Cleveland Design Guidelines," City of Cleveland, Cleveland Heritage Commission, Mississippi Department of Archives and History, 2008, 15, 20.
29 *Cleveland Quadrangle, Mississippi*, 1934, 7.5-minute series, 1:62500, US Department of the Interior, US Geological Survey.
30 "Edgar," interview by author, Cleveland, Mississippi, May 20, 2019.
31 "You from the Delta Ain'tchu," private Facebook group, July 2019.
32 Research query posted to "You from the Delta Ain'tchu," July 2, 2019:

> Hello Delta Folks! My name is Brian Dempsey, and I am originally from Cleveland, Mississippi. I am now a history professor at the University of North Alabama, and working on a research project about a specific site in Cleveland. I am collaborating with Will Jacks—Cleveland photographer, storyteller, and educator—and we both remember a small stand of woods in a field just off Yale St. called "Old Hickory." As kids we would sneak over to ride bikes on the trails in that small clump of woods. Some brief informal conversations reveal that the site has been known locally as "Old Hickory" for many generations. We are writing a history of the site, capturing it via photography and documentary film, and plan to submit the project for publication this year. An important part of the project will be to gain local perspective, and we now seek your help! If you know about Old Hickory, would you kindly offer any memories, stories, historical knowledge, ideas of where the name originates, or photographs in reply to this post? We are also planning to conduct formal interviews in Cleveland in the coming months, so we'd love to hear from you if you are interested. We welcome and would greatly appreciate any feedback, and we look forward to learning more about Old Hickory.

33 Daschel Franz et al., "Using Facebook for Qualitative Research: A Brief Primer," *Journal of Medical Internet Research* 21, no. 8 (August 12, 2019): e13544, https://doi.org/10.2196/13544; "10 Facts about Americans and Facebook," Pew Research Center, accessed January 31, 2022, https://www.pewresearch.org/fact-tank/2021/06/01/facts-about-americans-and-facebook/.
34 Replies included stand-alone responses, follow-up posts, and dialogue between group members.
35 Responder 1, "Boy [those] were the good ole days . . . ," Facebook, July 2019.
36 Responder 2, "Oh wow! Old Hickory . . . ," Facebook, July 2019.
37 Responder 3, "Man we had bicycles . . . ," Facebook, July 2019.
38 Responder 4, "The inside of these woods . . . ," Facebook, July 2019.
39 Responder 5, "We built bridges across the ditch . . . ," Facebook, July 2019.
40 John, "During the mid-fifties . . . ," Facebook, July 2019.
41 Responder 6, "Mound with collapsed caves/tunnels . . . ," Facebook, July 2019.
42 John, "Wow . . . I wonder if the mounds . . . ," Facebook, July 2019.
43 John, interview by author, January 29, 2020.
44 John, interview.

45 John, interview.
46 Responder 7, "Heard my older brothers talking . . . ," Facebook, July 2019.
47 Lance, "As a kid I had a dirt bike . . . ," Facebook, July 2019.
48 Kathy Rhodes, "The Big Woods," Kathy Rhodes, July 3, 2019, https://kathyrhodes.wordpress.com/2019/07/03/the-big-woods/.
49 Kathy Rhodes, email interview with author, December 9, 2020.
50 Tuan, *Topophilia*, 118, 119.
51 Mayor Billy Nowell, personal interview, June 8, 2021.
52 Dr. Brady Self, personal interview and site fieldwork, June 8, 2021.
53 Saikku, *This Delta, This Land*, 225.
54 *Cleveland Quadrangle, Mississippi*; US Department of Agriculture, Agricultural Adjustment Administration, aerial surveys, Bolivar County, Mississippi, January 20, 1943; Dr. Brady Self, email communication with author, April 25, 2022; satellite view of Cleveland, Mississippi, Google Earth, June 18, 2021.
55 US Department of Agriculture, in cooperation with Mississippi Agricultural Experiment Station, *Soil Survey, Bolivar County Mississippi*, series 1951, no. 5 (Washington, DC: US Department of Agriculture, 1958), 3.
56 Alan Feduccia, email communication, December 27, 2020.
57 Alan Feduccia, email communication, January 5, 2021.
58 Jean-Marc Serme, "Stormy Weather at Andrew Jackson's Halcyon Plantation, in Coahoma County, Mississippi, 1838–1845," *Revue Française d'Études Américaines* 98 (2003): 32–47; John D. W. Guice, "Andrew Jackson," *Mississippi Encyclopedia*, accessed January 29, 2004, http://mississippiencyclopedia.org/entries/andrew-jackson/.
59 Alan Feduccia, email communication, December 27, 2020.
60 Alan Feduccia, email communication, January 5, 2021.
61 The Salvatore A. Feduccia and Maria Grace Serio Feduccia Trust has contributed to more than twenty charitable organizations in the area, including the Feduccia Endowed Scholarship Fund at Delta State University.
62 Alan Feduccia, email communication, September 7, 2021. Ultimately, the city purchased the parcels owned by the family and the charitable trust for about one-fourth of its value.
63 Alan Feduccia, email communication, December 27, 2020.
64 Alan Feduccia, email communication, January 5, 2021. Dr. Feduccia also mentioned that the woods stand in a low, damp area of the field, reinforcing the idea that this is why the trees were never cut over during the earlier clearing process.
65 Alan Feduccia, email communication, December 30, 2020.
66 As a follow-up to the initial social media query, fifteen members of the private Facebook group responded to a brief survey I posted designed to assess a sense of place value. This very small sampling is not definitive, nor does it significantly alter impressions garnered via the social media responses. But the majority of those taking the survey rated the following words as "excellent" descriptions of Old Hickory: *unique*, *important to preserve*, *authentic*, *fun*, and *adventurous*. A majority also "agreed" that the site makes them "think about living in the Delta" and "think about their childhood" and that it is a "place to meet with friends."

67 Tarrant and Hull, "Forest Values and Attitudes," 236.

68 Suzanne Simard, "Conversations in the Forest: The Roots of Nature's Equanimity," Nature Conservancy Canada, accessed September 26, 2023, https://www.natureconservancy.ca/en/blog/archive/conversations-in-the-forest.html.

69 The Natural Capital Project at Stanford University "operates as a partnership between the Chinese Academy of Sciences, the University of Minnesota, the Stockholm Resilience Centre, The Nature Conservancy, and the World Wildlife Fund. [They] are an interdisciplinary team of academics, software engineers, and real-world professionals all working to make valuing natural capital easier and more accessible to everyone." "Natural Capital Project," Stanford University, accessed February 2, 2022, https://naturalcapitalproject.stanford.edu/.

70 "What Is Natural Capital," World Forum on National Capital, accessed January 22, 2022, https://naturalcapitalforum.com/about.

Chapter Four: When a Tree Falls

I dedicate this essay to the memory of my mother, Rochelle Sosne Glaser, who fully enjoyed her shaded garden and instilled in me an appreciation for street trees.

1 Daryl C. Borst and Barbara L. Borst, *Self-Guiding Nature Trail in Sleeping Giant State Park*, 7th ed. (Hamden, CT: Sleeping Giant Park Association, 2019), https://sgpa.org/wp-content/uploads/2022/09/Nature-Trail-Guide-7th-Edition-2019.pdf.

2 Helen McDonald, "On Nature: Dead Forests and Living Memories," *New York Times Magazine*, September 20, 2015, 24, 26.

3 Latif Nasser, Ekedi Fausther-Keeys, and Maria Paz Gutierrez, "The Fellowship of the Tree Rings," July 14, 2023, in *Radiolab*, produced by Maria Paz Gutierrez and Pat Walters, podcast, audio, 31:39, https://radiolab.org/podcast/fellowship-tree-rings.

4 "New England States Are Losing Their Forest Cover," *New Hampshire Public Radio*, May 12, 2016, https://www.nhpr.org/nh-news/2016-05-12/new-england-states-are-losing-their-forest-cover; Khalilah Brown-Dean et al., "Branching Out: How Trees Are Key to New England's Environmental Future," *Disrupted*, WNPR, August 11, 2021; Barbara Moran, "New England Forests Can Help Slow Climate Change, a New Report Shows Exactly How Much," WBUR, accessed September 14, 2021, https://www.wbur.org/news/2021/09/14/deforestation-new-england-carbon-sequestration-climate-change.

5 Gregg Mangan, "The Great September Gale," in *On This Day in Connecticut History* (Charleston, SC: History Press, Arcadia Publishing, 2015), 221; Sidney Perley, *Historic Storms of New England* (Carlisle, MA: Commonwealth Editions, 2001), 2; Katherine S. Grandjean, "New World Tempests: Environment, Scarcity, and the Coming of the Pequot War," *William and Mary Quarterly* 68, no. 1 (January 2011): 77, 80–81, 83; "Great New England Hurricane of 1635 Even Worse Than Thought," Associated Press, November 21, 2006; William Hubbard, *A General History of New England: From the Discovery to MDCLXXX* (Boston: Little and Brown, 1848), 199–200.

6 The annual powwow is still held near this site, but the sacred space of the red tree grove is closed to those outside the tribe. Lisa Brooks, *The Common Pot: The Recovery of Native Space in the Northeast* (Minneapolis: University of Minnesota Press, 2008), 105; Mohegan Tribe, "The Sacred Tree, or Tree of Life, is the spiritual entity that connects one generation to the next. With roots deeply embedded in the earth and the bodies of the ancestors, its branches reach," Facebook, May 1, 2020; Melissa Tantaquidgeon Zobel, "Fort Shantok, CT," in *American Indian Places: A Historical Guidebook*, by Frances H. Kennedy (Boston: Houghton Mifflin, 2008), 38–39.

7 Thomas J. Campanella, *Republic of Shade: New England and the American Elm* (New Haven, CT: Yale University Press, 2003), 11–12, 21–22; William Cronon, *Changes in the Land: Indians, Colonists, and the Ecology of New England* (New York: Hill and Wang, 1983), 38–53, 108–26.

8 Jamie M. Bolker, "The Trees That Marked America," *Beehive* (blog), Massachusetts Historical Society, January 2022, https://www.masshist.org/beehiveblog/2021/12/the-trees-that-marked-america/.

9 "The Legend of the Charter Oak," Connecticut Humanities, ConnecticutHistory.org, accessed February 17, 2020, https://connecticuthistory.org/the-legend-of-the-charter-oak/; Perley, *Historic Storms*, 134, 130.

10 An 1878 tornado struck Wallingford, Connecticut, located between New Haven and Hartford. Perley, *Historic Storms*, 281.

11 Richard Judd, *Second Nature: An Environmental History of New England* (Amherst: University of Massachusetts Press, 2014), ix–xi, 12–13.

12 Campanella, *Republic of Shade*, 78–79, 80–81.

13 Working and Natural Land Working Group, "Forests Sub-Group Draft Report," Department of Energy and Environmental Protection, State of Connecticut, September 10, 2020, https://portal.ct.gov/-/media/DEEP/climatechange/GC3/GC3-working-group-reports/GC3_WNL_Forests_DRAFT_report_public_comment_091120.pdf.

14 R. Douglas McDonald, "Multiple Use Forestry in Megalopolis: A Case Study of the Evolution of Forest Policies in Connecticut" (PhD diss., Yale University, 1969), 30.

15 Austin F. Hawes, "History of Forestry in Connecticut, 1849–1943," box 1, folder 28, Austin Foster Hawes Papers, Manuscripts and Archives, Yale University, New Haven, CT (hereafter cited as Hawes Papers).

16 Ellen Stroud, *Nature Next Door: Cities and Trees in the American Northeast* (Seattle: University of Washington Press, 2013), 97, 148, 159.

17 Campanella, *Republic of Shade*, 3–5.

18 Mark Stoll, "'Sagacious' Bernard Palissy: Pinchot, Marsh, and the Connecticut Origins of American Conservation," *Environmental History* 16, no. 1 (2011): 4–37; Mark Stoll, *Protestantism, Capitalism, and Nature in America* (Albuquerque: University of New Mexico, 1997), 154–55, 412.

19 See Char Miller, *Gifford Pinchot and the Making of Modern Environmentalism* (Washington, DC: Island Press, 2001). Also, professors Samuel W. Johnson and William H. Brewer from the Sheffield Scientific School at Yale helped begin the Connecticut Agricultural Experiment Station (CAES). The state forestry

program and the CAES and Brewer helped organize the Yale School of Forestry. McDonald, "Multiple Use Forestry," 28.

20 See more at Leah S. Glaser, "Dynamic Tensions: Conservation and Development up to the 1920s," Connecticut Humanities, ConnecticutHistory.org, accessed March 6, 2020, https://connecticuthistory.org/.

21 Walter Mulford was a researcher at the Connecticut Agricultural Experiment Station in New Haven. McDonald, "Multiple Use Forestry," 49–51.

22 Austin Hawes, "Connecticut: Scattering the Seeds" and "Connecticut: No Loss without Some Small Gain," in *Forests and Forestry in the American States: A Reference Anthology*, ed. Ralph Widner (Washington, DC: National Association of State Foresters, 1968), 100–106, 230.

23 Harold K. Steen, *The U.S. Forest Service: A History* (Seattle: University of Washington Press, 2004), 122; Austin F. Hawes, "History of Forestry"; Austin F. Hawes, "Forestry Progress in Connecticut," *Woodland and Roadside* 5, no. 1 (1906): 8–9.

24 Richard William Judd, *Common Lands, Common People: The Origins of Conservation in Northern New England* (Cambridge, MA: Harvard University Press, 2000), 91; Ney C. Landrum, *The State Park Movement in America: A Critical Review* (Columbia: University of Missouri Press, 2004), 15–20.

25 Gifford Pinchot was reportedly named for Hudson River Valley School painter Sanford Gifford.

26 The father and brother of future NPS director Conrad Wirth, respectively, served as superintendent of parks in the city of Hartford, Connecticut, from 1896 to 1905 and New Haven from 1929 to 1946. Conrad Wirth, *Parks, Politics, and the People* (Norman: University of Oklahoma Press, 1980), 3–5.

27 For a broader national context on the state park movement, see Landrum, *State Park Movement*.

28 Turner to Chapman, February 10, 1917, Turner to Harold Caparn, December 31, 1921, series 2, box 1, folder 1B, RG 079:017, State Park and Forest Commission, Connecticut State Archives, Hartford, CT (hereafter cited as Connecticut State Archives).

29 "How Soon Will Our Connecticut Hills Be Bare of Trees?," *Hartford Courant*, August 17, 1919, https://ccsu.idm.oclc.org/login?url=https://www.proquest.com/historical-newspapers/how-soon-will-our-connecticut-hills-be-bare-trees/docview/556720502/se-2.

30 Personal letters (transcribed), June 1900–1901, compiled 1949, box 1, folder 7, Hawes Papers; "Report of the Sub-Committee of State Forests 1943–45," box 1, folder 26, MS 637, Hawes Papers; George McLean Milne, *Connecticut Woodlands: A Century's Story of the Connecticut Forest and Park Association* (Connecticut Forest and Park Association, 1995), 15, 23; Austin Hawes, "Memo to the Joint Congressional Committee on Forestry: Forestry Problems, Objectives, and Solution in CT," box 1, folder 8, Hawes Papers.

31 Austin Hawes, "Recreation Facilities of the State Forests," 2, Hawes Papers, folder 19, box 9, Subject Files, RG 169-007, State Forest and Park Association, Connecticut State Archives, Hartford, Connecticut.

32 Hawes, "Memo."
33 Stroud, *Nature Next Door*, 97; Austin Hawes, "The Preservation of the Forests by Wise Use," March 12, 1906, to Wesleyan College Scientific Association, 14, box 1, folder 14, Hawes Papers.
34 See Dona Brown, *Inventing New England: Regional Tourism in the Nineteenth Century* (Charlottesville: University of Virginia Press, 1995), 4–5, 8–9.
35 Austin Hawes, "Touring Connecticut," Division of Forestry Records, n.d., old letters, folder 1, box 6, RG 079:017, Connecticut State Archives.
36 Roos, CF&PA secretary to officers and directors, August 30, 1930 (IMG_0750), and Robert M. Ross to officers of the CF&PA, CF&PA publication no. 41, January 1940, 3–4.
37 Joseph Woodruff, Natural Resource Committee, New England Regional Planning Commission, *The Development of State Provision for Recreation in Connecticut* (Hartford: Connecticut State Planning Board, 1935), 22, https://collections.ctdigitalarchive.org/node/42639.
38 Campanella, *Republic of Shade*, 112–13.
39 Campanella, 3.
40 George A. Cromie and Walter A. Filley, *The Planting and Care of State and Highway Trees* (New Haven, CT: Documents of Civic Federation of New Haven No. 8, 1912).
41 P. L. Buttrick, "Highway Trees and Roadside Improvement for Connecticut," CFA publication no. 16, June 1926; "Roadside Shade Trees: A Manual of Roadside Improvement for Tree Wardens and Others Interested," CFA publication no. 18, January 1928, 7, 29, 37.
42 "Report of the Committee on Street Trees to the West Hartford Chamber of Commerce," 8, CT forester boxes, Connecticut State Archives.
43 "Tree in New Haven, 227 Years Old Cut Down," *New York Times*, May 3, 1927, 1.
44 Campanella, *Republic of Shade*, 147–48, 165; "Dutch Elm Disease in Connecticut," Connecticut Agricultural Experiment Station, circular 106, January 1935.
45 Stephen Long, *Thirty-Eight: The Hurricane That Transformed New England* (New Haven, CT: Yale University Press, 2016), 118–19.
46 "Dollars from Your Woodlot," CF&PA publication no. 39, 1938.
47 Woodruff, *Development of State Provision*, 7–8.
48 Herman Chapman, "CT State Forest Purchase Program," CF&PA publication no. 27, March 13, 1935.
49 Woodruff, *Development of State Provision*, 7–8.
50 "An account of my last visit with Gifford Pinchot written immediately afterwards," folder 24, box 1, Hawes Papers.
51 Woodruff, *Development of State Provision*, 7–8.
52 Katherine Matthies, *Trees of Note in Connecticut* (New Haven, CT: Yale University Press, 1934).
53 Patrick Mahoney, "The Great Atlantic Hurricane Hits Connecticut," Connecticut Humanities, ConnecticutHistory.org, September 14, 2020, https://connecticuthistory.org/the-great-atlantic-hurricane-hits-connecticut/; H. C.

Sumner, "The North Atlantic Hurricane of September 8–16, 1944," *Monthly Weather Review* 72, no. 1419 (December 5, 1944): 187–89.

54 David Taylor, "When Planting Trees Expresses Love of Country," arbordayblog.org, April 3, 2020; Shaul E. Cohen, *Planting Nature: Trees and the Manipulation of Environmental Stewardship* (Berkeley: University of California Press, 2004); "After World War II 1945–1967," foresthistory.org, accessed October 3, 2021.

55 Eric Rutkow, *American Canopy: Trees, Forests, and the Making of a Nation* (New York: Simon and Schuster, 2012), 277–78.

56 Community Builders' Council, *Community Builders Handbook* (Washington, DC: Urban Land Institute, 1947), 73–75.

57 "Tree-Planting Gains Support of Homeowners," *Hartford Courant*, March 20, 1958; Country Women's Council, *You Need Trees: 6 Lessons in Tree Planting* (Washington, DC: United States Forest Service, Department of Agriculture, US Government Printing Office, 1952), 10.

58 Campanella, *Republic of Shade*, 39–42, 164–65; Jared B. Standish, "Story of the Great Elm, 1750–1950," Wethersfield Historical Archives, Wethersfield, CT, accessed October 20, 2021, https://www.wethersfieldhistory.org/articles/story-of-the-great-elm-1750-1950/; Frank H. Lamb, *Book of the Broadleaf Trees: The Story of the Economic, Social, and Cultural Contribution of the Broadleaved Trees* (New York: W. W. Norton, 1939), 236.

59 Chapman, "An Administrative Director for the Park and Forest Commission: An Analysis," June 15, 1944, 19, folder 56, box 2, Hawes Papers; "Report of the Sub-Committee"; McDonald, "Multiple Use Forestry," 192. McDonald implies that the conflicts were more about personality conflict than theories about forestry, but my interpretation is the conflict was over qualifications and scientific training and who had the expertise to make such decisions about forest use.

60 Chapman continued to fight for forestry and the original independence of the forester's position through the private State Forest and Park Association, which had considerable lobbying influence. In a tribute article for the *Hartford Courant*, Hawes described Chapman as "a fighter for causes, which he believes are right, and a staunch opponent of inefficiency, waste of public money, and charlatanism." Chapman made sure his records and accounts of the situation were ever-present in his legacy through his papers and deposits to the State Library. Austin Hawes, "America's Forests Owe Him a Great Debt," *Hartford Courant*, January 30, 1949, sm3; S. Herbert Evison, interview with Donald B. Alexander, National Park Service Oral History Collection, HFCS 1817, Harpers Ferry History Center, Harpers Ferry, WV, April 13, 1971.

61 McDonald, "Multiple Use Forestry," 206.

62 R. M. Ricard, "Tree Wardens and the Evolution of Urban Forestry in New England," in *Proceedings of the 1996 Society of American Foresters Convention* (Bethesda, MD: Society of American Foresters, 1997), 80–85.

63 See Lawrence Vale, *From the Puritans to the Projects: Public Housing and Public Neighbors* (Germany: Harvard University Press, 2009).

64 Dave Drury, "Officials Say Tree-Trimming Program Helped Cut Power Losses," *Hartford Courant*, August 25, 1989, C3D; "Some See NU's Tree-Trimming as

Search and Destroy Mission," *Hartford Courant*, June 3, 1989, A1G; Anthony Giorgianni and Daniel P. Jones, "Trimming Trees Cuts Utilities' Failures," *Hartford Courant*, November 14, 1995.

65 Janice Posada, "Connecticut's Love of Trees Threatens Electrical Service," *Hartford Courant*, September 13, 2011; Robert Miller, "Power Struggle," Newstimes.com, April 12, 2012; "Tree Trimming Will Affect Historic Landscapes," *Connecticut Preservation News* 34, no. 6 (November/December 2011): 4; Katharine Q. Seelye, "Spate of Harsh Weather in New England Shifts Sentiment on Trees," *New York Times*, December 2, 2012; "Preserving Street Trees," *Connecticut Preservation News* 37, no. 2 (March/April 2014): 1, 14.

66 "Utility Poles: The Timber Product That Helps Power America," American Tree Farm System, Tree Farmer Bulletin, Winter 2013, https://www.treefarmsystem.org/bulletin-the-product-that-helps-power-america; Leah S. Glaser, "The EMA Transmission Line," no. AZ-6-B, Historic American Engineering Record (HAER), National Park Service, Western Region, 1996. In addition to HAER reports that document transmission and distribution line technology, Daniel Wuebben and Eugene Levy have studies about the aesthetics of power lines and their historic place on the American landscape. Daniel L. Wuebben, *Power-Lined: Electricity, Landscape, and the American Mind* (Lincoln: University of Nebraska Press, 2019); Eugene Levy, "The Aesthetics of Power: High Voltage Transmission Systems and the American Landscape," *Technology and Culture* 38, no. 3 (July 1997): 575–607.

67 April Mulqueen, "The Natural History of the Wooden Utility Pole," San Francisco Policy and Planning Division: California Public Utilities Commission, July 2017.

68 Tatiana Pina, "Hurricane Gloria Takes a Toll on City's Tree Population," *Hartford Courant*, December 12, 1985; Drury, "Tree-Trimming Program."

69 "Cutting of Trees Opposed," *Hartford Courant*, November 26, 2002.

70 Loretta Waldman, "Giving Trees a New Life: Historic District's Giants Showing Their Age," *Hartford Courant*, February 20, 2010, B3.

71 Daniela Altimair, "Panel Looks at CL&P Tree-Trimming Policies: Company Cut Fewer Miles of Trees in 2010 than in 2001, Documents Show; Storm Response," *Hartford Courant*, November 10, 2011; Steve Grant, "One Rough Year for Old Trees: Two Storms Put Many in Jeopardy; Living History," *Hartford Courant*, April 9, 2012, A1.

72 Campanella, *Republic of Shade*, 167.

73 Greg Gordon, *When Money Grew on Trees: A.B. Hammond and the Age of the Timber Baron* (Norman: University of Oklahoma Press, 2014); Stroud, *Nature Next Door*; Jill Jonnes, *Urban Forests: A Natural History of Trees and People in the American Cityscape* (New York: Penguin Books, 2016); Sonja Dümpelmann, *Seeing Trees: A History of Street Trees in New York City and Berlin* (New Haven, CT: Yale University Press, 2019).

74 Connecticut's Notable Trees (website), Connecticut Botanical Society, the Connecticut College Arboretum, and the Connecticut Urban Forest Council, accessed March 10, 2020, http://oak.conncoll.edu:8080/notabletrees/; Jeffrey G. Meyer and Sharon Linnea, *America's Famous and Historic Trees: From George*

Washington's Tulip Poplar to Elvis Presley's Pin Oak, 1st ed. (Boston, MA: Houghton Mifflin Harcourt, 2001); Lindsey K. Kerr, "Tree Preservation Ordinances: Protections for Our Communities' Heritage Trees" (MA thesis, University of Georgia, 2009), https://getd.libs.uga.edu/pdfs/kerr_lindsey_k_200908_mhp.pdf.

75 Susan A Dolan, *Fruitful Legacy: A Historic Context of Orchards in the United States, with Technical Information for Registering Orchards in the National Register of Historic Places* (Washington, DC: National Park Service, US Department of the Interior, 2009); Jennifer Pfaff, Burlingame Historical Society, Howard-Ralston Eucalyptus Tree (El Camino Real Trees), Burlingame, California, July 31, 2011, National Register of Historic Places Registration Form, approved March 15, 2012, https://burlingamehistoricalsociety.org/wp-content/uploads/2012/04/final-ralston-howard-ohp-spring-2012.pdf; Bruce B. Bingham, Robert E. Bennetts, and Andy Hubbard, "Integrating Science and Management: The Road to Rico-Chico," *George Wright Forum* 24, no. 2 (2007): 21–25; R. Diamant, C. Marts, and N. Mitchell, "Rethinking Traditional Preservation Approaches for Managing a Forested Cultural Landscape: The Case of Marsh-Billings-Rockefeller National Historical Park's Mount Tom Forest," in *The Conservation of Cultural Landscapes*, ed. Mauro Agnoletti (Wallingford, UK: CABI Digital Library, 2006), 155; Jesus M. Garcia, "The Legacy of the Trees: Edible Landscapes in Arizona," Smithsonian Center for Folklife and Cultural Heritage, November 19, 2019, https://folklife.si.edu/magazine/preserving-historical-edible-landscapes-arizona; Leimomi Hooper and Carrie Mardorf, "Preserving Heritage Trees: History Thrives at Kalaupapa," NPS Park Cultural Landscapes Program, January 22, 2016, https://npsparkclp.tumblr.com/post/137825899722/preserving-heritage-trees-history-thrives-at.

76 Thomas J. Schlereth, "Plants Past: An Historian's Use of Vegetation as Material Culture Evidence," *Environmental Review* 4, no. 1 (1980): 20–28.

77 "Replacing Trees in Cultural Landscapes," *Clippings: Concepts and Techniques for Maintaining Cultural Landscapes*, accessed April 27, 2020, http://npshistory.com/publications/landscapes/clippings-replacing-trees.pdf; Historic Tree Care (website), accessed April 27, 2020, http://www.historictreecare.com; C. Y. Jim, "Urban Heritage Trees: Natural-Cultural Significance Informing Management and Conservation," in *Greening Cities*, ed. Tan Puay Tok and C.Y. Jim, Advances in 21st Century Urban Settlements (Singapore: Springer, 2017), 279–305; C. Y. Jim, "Evaluation of Heritage Trees for Conservation and Management in Guangzhou City (China)," *Environmental Management* 33 (January 2004): 74–86; Wan Noor Anira et al., "The Morphology of Heritage Trees in Colonial Town: Taiping Lake Garden, Perak, Malaysia," *Procedia—Social and Behavioral Sciences* 222 (May 2016): 621–30.

78 S. F. Fitzsimmons et al., "Germplasm Conservation for Species Restoration: Examples from Efforts to Restore the American Chestnut," in *Gene Conservation of Tree Species—Banking on the Future*, ed. Richard A. Sniezko et al. (Portland, OR: US Department of Agriculture, Forest Service, Pacific Northwest Research Station, 2017), 157; "Replacing Trees in Cultural Landscapes."

79 Jill Nathanson, "Hamden Tree Commission Names 'Notable Tree,'" Hamden Tree Commission, press release, September 2018.

80 Altimair, "Panel Looks at CL&P," B8; Leah S. Glaser, "Guidelines for Historic Tree Preservation," *History@Work* (blog), October 5, 2021, http://www.ncph.org. Also see Paul Bogard, ed., *Solastalgia: An Anthology of Emotion in a Disappearing World* (Charlottesville: University of Virginia Press, 2023).

Chapter Five: The Trees of the South Mountain Cultural Landscape

The author wishes to thank her husband, Ted Corcoran, for always graciously helping to answer my writing questions. Thanks also to Peter Benton and Jocelyn Kelley for collaborating on the cultural landscape project at South Mountain.

1 Rothrock's advocacy likely resonated with his audience all the more because of the importance of forests to the state's identity based on its name, assigned by King Charles of England in 1681, which means Penn's Woods.

2 For more information on cultural landscapes, see Charles A. Birnbaum, *Protecting Cultural Landscapes: Planning, Treatment and Management of Historic Landscapes*, Preservation Briefs 36 (Washington, DC: National Park Service, 1994), https://www.nps.gov/tps/how-to-preserve/briefs/36-cultural-landscapes.htm.

3 Stone quarries where metarhyolite was mined are found in several locations at South Mountain. In fact, one of the largest and most accessible outcroppings of the metarhyolite within the eastern United States can be found within Michaux State Forest. The outcropping is listed in the National Register of Historic Places for the information it has provided about pre-European contact use of the stone, natural resource exploitation, cultural mobility, and trade. "Antiquity of the South Mountain Landscape," Indiana University of Pennsylvania, accessed August 18, 2024, https://www.iup.edu/anthropology/research/antiquity-of-the-south-mountain-landscape.html; "Penn's Woods Strategic Plan," Pennsylvania Department of Conservation & Natural Resources, accessed August 18, 2024, https://www.dcnr.pa.gov/Conservation/ForestsAndTrees/StateForestManagement/PennsWoodsStrategicPlan/Pages/default.aspx.

4 "Michaux State Forest Management," Pennsylvania Department of Conservation & Natural Resources, accessed August 18, 2024, https://www.dcnr.pa.gov/StateForests/FindAForest/Michaux/pages/default.aspx.

5 For more information, see James H. Merrell, *Into the American Woods: Negotiators on the Pennsylvania Frontier* (New York: W. W. Norton, 2000), which considers the different meanings of wilderness to the Indigenous people and the colonists.

6 For more information, see the Conestoga-Susquehannock Tribe (website), accessed August 18, 2024, https://www.conestogasusquehannocktribe.com/home.

7 A cultural hearth is a hub from which cultural traditions originate and are disseminated.

8 For more information about the history of slavery in the region, see Cooper H. Wingert, *Slavery and the Underground Railroad in South Central Pennsylvania*

(London: History Press, 2016). In fact, one of the iron companies located within present-day Michaux State Forest at South Mountain—the Caledonia Iron Works—was owned by Congressman Thaddeus Stevens from 1837 until the 1860s. Stevens fought for abolition in Washington, DC, while the Caledonia Iron Works furnace foreman William Hammet was a conductor for the Underground Railroad prior to the Civil War.

9 *LiDAR* is an acronym that stands for "light and detection ranging" or "laser imaging, detection, and ranging." It is an aerial survey technique that measures the time for reflected light targeted using a laser to return to a receiver. LiDAR is used to develop 3D models of terrain and picks up topographic anomalies such as the leveled area of charcoal hearths with good resolution.

10 Claire J. Woods, "A History as Strong as the Trees It Protects," Pennsylvania Center for the Book, Spring 2010, https://pabook.libraries.psu.edu/literary-cultural-heritage-map-pa/feature-articles/history-strong-trees-it-protects.

11 Woods, "History."

12 Henry D. Gerhold, *A Century of Forest Resources Education at Penn State, Serving Our Forests, Waters, Wildlife, and Wood Industries* (University Park, PA: Penn State Press, 2007).

13 Henry E. Clepper, *Forestry Education in Pennsylvania* (University Park, PA: Penn State–Mont Alto Alumni Association, 1957).

14 Gifford Pinchot, born in Pennsylvania, was appointed the head of the nascent US Division of Forestry by President William McKinley in 1898 and the first chief of the US Forest Service in 1905. Pinchot was an advocate of conservation, an interest he shared with his friend President Theodore Roosevelt. Pinchot was named the head of the Pennsylvania Forestry Division in 1920 and governor of the state in 1922. He was an ardent supporter of President Franklin Delano Roosevelt's New Deal programs during the Great Depression.

15 Mont Alto was the second forestry school established in the United States. The first was the Biltmore Forest School, overseen by German forester Dr. Carl A. Schenck. George Vanderbilt, who was working with Frederick Law Olmsted and Gifford Pinchot to establish Biltmore Estate, funded the school. For more information on the Biltmore Forest School, see Dave Tabler, "First Forestry School in the USA," AppalachianHistory.net, May 7, 2019, https://www.appalachianhistory.net/2019/05/first-forestry-school-in-usa.html. For more information on Mont Alto, see Penn State Mont Alto (website), accessed August 18, 2024, https://montalto.psu.edu/.

16 Elise Vider, "Celebrating 125 Years of PA's State Parks and Forests," Keystone Edge, May 31, 2018, https://www.keystoneedge.com/2018/05/31/celebrating-125-years-of-pas-state-parks-and-forests/.

17 Elizabeth H. Thomas, "Forest Protection and the Founding of Pennsylvania's First Forestry School, 1901–1903," *Pennsylvania History: A Journal of Mid-Atlantic Studies* 44, no. 4 (1977): 293.

18 For more information, see Lester A. Decoster, *The Legacy of Penn's Woods: A History of the Pennsylvania Bureau of Forestry* (Harrisburg: Pennsylvania Historical and Museum Commission, 1995).

19 The Appalachian Trail Conservancy describes the trail as the longest hiking-only trail in the world.

20 For more information on National Scenic Trails, see "National Scenic Trails," National Trails System, National Park Service, December 6, 2021, https://www.nps.gov/subjects/nationaltrailssystem/national-scenic-trails.htm.

21 For more information, see the Appalachian Trail Museum (website), accessed August 18, 2024, https://www.atmuseum.org/.

22 For more information, see Patrick L. Metcalf, "The Pine Grove Prisoner of War Camp," Gardner Digital Library, accessed August 18, 2024, https://gardnerlibrary.org/journal/pine-grove-prisoner-war-camp.

23 For more information, see "Penn's Woods Sustaining Our Forests," Pennsylvania Department of Conservation and Natural Resources, accessed August 18, 2024, https://elibrary.dcnr.pa.gov/PDFProvider.ashx?action=PDFStream&docID=1741347&chksum=&revision=0&docName=sf-Penns_Woods_Strategic_Plan&nativeExt=pdf&PromptToSave=False&Size=409196&ViewerMode=2&overlay=0.

24 Lewis F. Southard, "The History of Cooperative Forest Fire Control and the Weeks Act," *Forest History Today* 17, nos. 1 & 2 (Spring/Fall 2011): 17.

Chapter Six: Mormon Women, Mulberry Trees, and Environmental Transformation in the American West

I would like to thank the editors of this volume for the invitation to contribute and their feedback on the essay. I am grateful for the anonymous reviewers who provided careful and useful recommendations for revision. I would also like to thank Jan Hemming for her introduction to the Daughters of Utah Pioneers Yale Crest camp. The Church History Library in Salt Lake City, the Tanner Humanities Center at the University of Utah, and Penn State's History Department provided critical support for the research behind this publication.

1 "Plaque Honors Silk Industry in Pioneer Utah," *Deseret News* 364, no. 40 (November 15, 1941): 6.

2 "Plaque Honors Silk Industry in Pioneer Utah," *Improvement Era* 45, no. 3 (March 1942): 184.

3 Clark S. Monson, "Mulberry Trees: The Basis and Remnant of the Utah Silk Industry," *Economic Botany* 50, no. 1 (1996): 130–38.

4 Ned Blackhawk, *Violence over the Land: Indians and Empires in the Early American West* (Cambridge, MA: Harvard University Press, 2006), chap. 7.

5 The foremost study of Mormon economic self-sufficiency is Leonard J. Arrington, *Great Basin Kingdom: An Economic History of the Latter-day Saints, 1830–1900* (Urbana: University of Illinois Press, 1958).

6 Sasha Coles, "Homespun Respectability: Silk Worlds, Women's Work, and the Making of Mormon Identity" (PhD diss., UC Santa Barbara, 2021).

7 Chris Rigby Arrington, "The Finest of Fabrics: Mormon Women and the Silk Industry in Early Utah," *Utah Historical Quarterly* 46, no. 4 (Fall 1978): 376–96. For a more recent investigation of the local silk production, see Coles, "Homespun Respectability."

8 Jared Farmer, *On Zion's Mount: Mormons, Indians, and the American Landscape* (Cambridge, MA: Harvard University Press, 2008), 371.

9 For a helpful, succinct synopsis of this literature, see David Glassberg, "Public History and the Study of Memory," *Public Historian* 18, no. 2 (Spring 1996): 7–23.

10 Davis Bitton, "The Ritualization of Mormon History," *Utah Historical Quarterly* 43, no. 1 (Winter 1975): 67–85.

11 Eric A. Eliason, "The Cultural Dynamics of Historical Self-Fashioning: Mormon Pioneer Nostalgia, American Culture, and the International Church," *Journal of Mormon History* 28, no. 2 (Fall 2002): 139–73.

12 Sara M. Patterson, *Pioneers in the Attic: Place and Memory along the Mormon Trail* (Oxford: Oxford University Press, 2020), chaps. 6, 7.

13 Bitton, "Ritualization of Mormon History," 83–84; Melodie Moench, "Nineteenth-Century Mormons: The New Israel," *Dialogue: A Journal of Mormon Thought* 12, no. 1 (1979): 42–56; Jan Shipps, *Mormonism: The Story of a New Religious Tradition* (Urbana: University of Illinois Press, 1985), 52–53; Michael H. Madsen, "The Sanctification of Mormonism's Historical Geography," *Journal of Mormon History* 34, no. 2 (Spring 2008): 230, 239; Barry Laga, "In Lieu of History: Mormon Monuments and the Shaping of Memory," *Dialogue: A Journal of Mormon Thought* 43, no. 4 (Winter 2010): 146.

14 Sarah K. Nytroe, "Taming the Past to Conquer the Future: The Pioneer Jubilee of 1897," *Journal of Mormon History* 42, no. 4 (October 2016): 125–46; Clyde A. Milner II, "Why Don't Mormons Have a Lost Cause?," *Journal of Mormon History* 44, no. 2 (April 2018): 37–54; Konden Smith Hansen, *Frontier Religion: Mormons and America, 1857–1907* (Salt Lake City: University of Utah Press, 2019), chaps. 5, 6; Cynthia Culver Prescott, *Pioneer Mother Monuments: Constructing Cultural Memory* (Norman: University of Oklahoma Press, 2019), chap. 4.

15 For accounts of the racial components and colonial legacies of Mormon pioneer nostalgia, see Elise Boxer, "'This Is the Place!' Disrupting Mormon Settler Colonialism," in *Decolonizing Mormonism: Approaching a Postcolonial Zion*, ed. Gina Colvin and Joanna Brooks (Salt Lake City: University of Utah Press, 2018), 77–79; and Angela Pulley Hudson, "There Is No Mormon Trail of Tears: Roots, Removals, and Reconstructions," in *Reconstruction and Mormon America*, ed. Clyde A. Milner II and Brian Q. Cannon (Norman: University of Oklahoma Press, 2019), 35.

16 Peter Coles, *Mulberry* (London: Reaktion Books, 2019), 20, 28, 74, 88.

17 Ben Marsh, *Unravelled Dreams: Silk and the Atlantic World, 1500–1840* (Cambridge: Cambridge University Press, 2020), 26.

18 For historical and more recent descriptions of the mulberry tree in North America, see Nathaniel Lord Britton, *North American Trees* (New York: H. Holt, 1908),

361–66; Charles Sprague Sargent, *Manual of the Trees of North America*, vol. 1 (New York: Dover, 1965), 328–32; Michael Albert Dirr, *Photographic Manual of Woody Landscape Plants: Form and Function in the Landscape* (Champaign, IL: Stipes, 1978), 203–4; John Laird Farrar, *Trees of the Northern United States and Canada* (Ames: Iowa State University Press, 1995), 238–40; and Gil Nelson et al., *Trees of Eastern North America* (Princeton, NJ: Princeton University Press, 2014), 406–8.

19 Coles, *Mulberry*, chaps. 1 and 2, quote from p. 117.

20 Coles, 43–48, 180, 199, 206.

21 For a detailed study of colonial and antebellum American silk activities, see Marsh, *Unravelled Dreams.*

22 Ben Marsh, "The Republic's New Clothes: Making Silk in the Antebellum United States," *Agricultural History* 86, no. 4 (Fall 2012): 206–34.

23 Coles, *Mulberry*, 135–40.

24 Dan L. Flores, *The Natural West: Environmental History in the Great Plains and Rocky Mountains* (Norman: University of Oklahoma Press, 2001), 124–44; Jeff Nichols, "Before the Boom: Mormons, Livestock, and Stewardship, 1847–1870," in *The Earth Will Appear as the Garden of Eden: Essays on Mormon Environmental History*, ed. Jedediah S. Rogers and Matthew C. Godfrey (Salt Lake City: University of Utah Press, 2019), 155–72; Thomas G. Alexander, "Lost Memory and Environmentalism: Mormons on the Wasatch Front, 1847–1930," in Rogers and Godfrey, *Earth Will Appear*, 57–63.

25 For studies of Mormon economic life in the nineteenth century, see Arrington, *Great Basin Kingdom*; Leonard J. Arrington, Feramorz Y. Fox, and Dean L. May, *Building the City of God: Community and Cooperation among the Mormons* (Salt Lake City: Deseret Book, 1976); and Dean L. May, *Three Frontiers: Family, Land, and Society in the American West, 1850–1900* (Cambridge: Cambridge University Press, 1994).

26 "Silk," Council of Fashion Designers of America, accessed August 16, 2024, https://cfda.com/resources/materials/detail/silk.

27 Louis A. Bertrand, "Sericulture—Feeding the Worms," *Deseret News* 18, no. 4 (March 3, 1869): 45.

28 Louis A. Bertrand, "Silk Culture—the Mulberry," *Deseret News* 17, no. 46 (December 23, 1868): 363.

29 Louis A. Bertrand, "Silk Culture—the Soil," *Deseret News* 17, no. 47 (December 30, 1868): 375.

30 "Summary of Instructions," *Deseret News* 14, no. 45 (August 9, 1865): 354.

31 "Correspondence," *Deseret News* 17, no. 5 (March 11, 1868): 33.

32 For analyses of how religious and economic spheres overlapped in nineteenth-century Mormon communities, see Arrington, *Great Basin Kingdom*, 5; Richard V. Francaviglia, *The Mormon Landscape: Existence, Creation, and Perception of a Unique Image in the American West* (New York: AMS, 1978); Mark P. Leone, *Roots of Modern Mormonism* (Cambridge, MA: Harvard University Press, 1979), 103; Shipps, *Mormonism*, 125; and May, *Three Frontiers*, 219, 270–71.

33 Alexander, "Lost Memory and Environmentalism," 52.

34 Sarah Dant, "The 'Lion of the Lord' and the Land: Brigham Young's Environmental Ethic," in Rogers and Godfrey, *Earth Will Appear*, 30, 33.
35 Flores, *Natural West*, 135.
36 Nichols, "Before the Boom," 157.
37 Coles, "Homespun Respectability," chaps. 2, 3.
38 *Treatise on Silk Raising*, Deseret Silk Association, 1877, 6, 638.2 D451t, Church History Library, Church of Jesus Christ of Latter-day Saints, Salt Lake City (hereafter cited as Church History Library).
39 Clarissa Young Spencer and Mabel Harmer, *Brigham Young at Home* (Salt Lake City: Deseret Book, 1961), 249–51; Elinor G. Hyde, "The Brigham Young Farm House," in *Brigham Young's Homes*, ed. Colleen Whitley and Sandra Dawn Brimhall (Logan: Utah State University Press, 2002), 147–72.
40 "Home Items," *Deseret News* 14, no. 40 (July 5, 1865): 313.
41 "Correspondence," 4. For several years, Forest Farm functioned as a source of information and raw materials for silk producers in Salt Lake City and beyond. See Margaret Schow Potter, "The History of Sericulture in Utah" (MS thesis, Oregon State College, 1949), 18.
42 "Utah Silk," *Salt Lake Herald-Republican* 12, no. 50 (August 4, 1881): 8.
43 For more on Schettler, see Jacob W. Olmstead and Fred E. Woods, "'Give Me Any Situation Suitable': The Consecrated Life of the Multitalented Paul A. Schettler," *BYU Studies* 41, no. 1 (2002): 109–26.
44 Paul A. Schettler to editors, *Salt Lake Herald*, December 20, 1872, in George A. Smith et al., *Correspondence of Palestine Tourists; Comprising a Series of Letters by George A. Smith, Lorenzo Snow, Paul A. Schettler, and Eliza R. Snow, of Utah* (Salt Lake City: Deseret News Steam Printing Establishment, 1875), 88.
45 R. Simpson, "Sericulture," *Deseret News* 26, no. 6 (March 14, 1877): 81.
46 Marsh, *Unravelled Dreams*, 106, 145–46, 445–46.
47 Alice Kessler-Harris, *Out to Work: A History of Wage-Earning Women in the United States* (New York: Oxford University Press, 1982), chap. 2; Christopher Clark, *The Roots of Rural Capitalism: Western Massachusetts, 1780–1860* (Ithaca: Cornell University Press, 1992), chap. 4; Jeanne Boydston, *Home and Work: Housework, Wages, and the Ideology of Labor in the Early Republic* (New York: Oxford University Press, 1994).
48 David John Rossell, "The Culture of Silk: Markets, Households, and the Meaning of an Antebellum Agricultural Movement" (PhD diss., State University of New York at Buffalo, 2001), 85–102; Coles, "Homespun Respectability," chap. 1.
49 Potter, "History of Sericulture in Utah"; Arrington, "Finest of Fabrics," 382–83; Jude Daurelle, "Produce What You Consume: The Silk Industry in Utah," *Piecework* 2, no. 4 (August 1994): 45–47; Kathleen Haggard, "'In Union Is Strength': Mormon Women and Cooperation, 1867–1900" (MS thesis, Utah State University, 1998), 27–50; Coles, "Homespun Respectability."
50 Margaret C. Eccles autobiographical sketch, April 1945, MS 10270, Church History Library.
51 Minutes of the Senior and Junior Retrenchment Association, March 6, 1875, CR 100 904, Church History Library. As one of the earliest converts to the church

and a plural wife of the first two church presidents, Young enjoyed a relatively comfortable economic position and political and ecclesiastical influence. In the words of historian Maureen Ursenbach Beecher, she and a small cohort of "leading sisters" held the "reins of leadership" among nineteenth-century Mormon women. Maureen Ursenbach Beecher, "The 'Leading Sisters': A Female Hierarchy in Nineteenth Century Mormon Society," *Journal of Mormon History* 9 (1982): 25–39.

52 Arrington, "Finest of Fabrics," 383; Coles, "Homespun Respectability," chap. 3.

53 Marsh, *Unravelled Dreams*, 27.

54 Saint George Utah Stake Relief Society minutes and records, February 7, 1878, LR 7836 14, Church History Library.

55 Coles, *Mulberry*, 59.

56 Louis A. Bertrand letter to Brigham Young, August 27, 1869, Brigham Young Office Files, CR 1234 1, box 33, folder 1, Church History Library.

57 "Sericulture," *Deseret News* 21, no. 40 (November 6, 1872): 599; Daurelle, "Produce What You Consume," 46.

58 Deseret Silk Association minutes, March 6, 1876, MS 14029, Church History Library.

59 See, for example, "Culture of Silk," *Deseret News* 17, no. 7 (March 25, 1868): 52; and Emmeline B. Wells, "Officers Meeting," *Woman's Exponent* 27, no. 5 (August 1, 1898): 21.

60 Haggard, "In Union Is Strength," 43–44, 48, 54; Maureen Ursenbach Beecher, "Women's Work on the Mormon Frontier," *Utah Historical Quarterly* 49, no. 3 (Summer 1981): 287.

61 "The Silk Industry," *Woman's Exponent* 21, no. 19 (April 1, 1893): 148.

62 S. A. S., "On Raising Mulberry Brush," *Woman's Exponent* 22, no. 5 (September 15, 1893): 34.

63 Utah Stake Silk Association minutes, July 15, 1892, LR 9629 36, folder 1, Church History Library.

64 Utah Silk Commission, *Sericulture: Instruction in the Art of Producing Silk* (Salt Lake City: Geo. Q. Cannon & Sons, 1897), 8 (italics in original).

65 "Utah Abandons Silk Culture," *Deseret Evening News*, March 1, 1905, 5; "Senate Kills Batch of Bills," *Salt Lake Herald-Republican*, March 1, 1905, 3. For more on why investment in local silk production declined, see Coles, "Homespun Respectability," chap. 5.

66 Utah Stake Silk Association minutes, 1906, LR 9629 36, folder 1, Church History Library.

67 Joe Fehr, "Utah's First Arbor Day Present," *Salt Lake Herald-Republican* 186, no. 71 (April 15, 1919): 12.

68 Edward Leo Lyman, *Political Deliverance: The Mormon Quest for Utah Statehood* (Urbana: University of Illinois Press, 1986), chaps. 3, 4, 5; Thomas K. Hafen, "City of Saints, City of Sinners: The Development of Salt Lake City as a Tourist Attraction 1869–1900," *Western Historical Quarterly* 28, no. 3 (Autumn 1997): 342–78; David Walker, *Railroading Religion: Mormons, Tourists, and the Corporate Spirit of the West* (Chapel Hill: University of North Carolina Press, 2019), chap. 6.

69 The foremost study of the "Americanization" process is Thomas G. Alexander, *Mormonism in Transition: A History of the Latter-day Saints, 1890–1930* (Urbana: University of Illinois Press, 1986). For other discussions about how Mormonism "modernized" at the turn of the century, see Leone, *Roots of Modern Mormonism*; Lyman, *Political Deliverance*; Kathleen Flake, *The Politics of American Religious Identity: The Seating of Senator Reed Smoot, Mormon Apostle* (Chapel Hill: University of North Carolina Press, 2004); Gordon Shepherd and Gary Shepherd, *A Kingdom Transformed: Early Mormonism and the Modern LDS Church*, reprint ed. (Salt Lake City: University of Utah Press, 2015); and Thomas W. Simpson, *American Universities and the Birth of Modern Mormonism, 1867–1940* (Chapel Hill: University of North Carolina Press, 2016).

70 For discussions of this evolution, see Jill Mulvay Derr and C. Brooklyn Derr, "Outside the Mormon Hierarchy: Alternative Aspects of Institutional Power," *Dialogue: A Journal of Mormon Thought* 15, no. 4 (Winter 1982): 32; Joan Iversen, "Feminist Implications of Mormon Polygyny," *Feminist Studies* 10, no. 3 (Autumn 1984): 519; Alexander, *Mormonism in Transition*, 125–27, 292–94; Jill Mulvay Derr, "'Strength in Our Union': The Making of Mormon Sisterhood," in *Sisters in Spirit: Mormon Women in Historical and Cultural Perspective*, ed. Maureen Ursenbach Beecher and Lavina Fielding Anderson (Urbana: University of Illinois Press, 1987), 191; Kathryn M. Daynes, *More Wives than One: Transformation of the Mormon Marriage System, 1840–1910* (Urbana: University of Illinois Press, 2001), 208; and Jill Mulvay Derr, Janath Russell Cannon, and Maureen Ursenbach Beecher, *Women of Covenant: The Story of Relief Society* (Salt Lake City: Deseret Book, 1992), 150–61.

71 For more recent studies on Mormon women and the church's "Americanization," see Lisa Olsen Tait, "Between Two Economies: The Business Development of the Young Woman's Journal, 1889–1900," *Journal of Mormon History* 38, no. 4 (Fall 2012): 1–54; and Josh E. Probert, "Leah Dunford Witdsoe, Alice Merrill Horne, and the Sacralization of Artistic Taste in Mormon Homes, circa 1900," in *Mormon Women's History: Beyond Biography*, ed. Rachel Cope et al. (Madison, NJ: Fairleigh Dickinson University Press, 2017), 167–84.

72 Carol Cornwall Madsen, ed., *Battle for the Ballot: Essays on Woman Suffrage in Utah, 1870–1896* (Logan: Utah State University Press, 1997).

73 Colleen McDannell, *Sister Saints: Mormon Women since the End of Polygamy* (New York: Oxford University Press, 2018), chap. 3.

74 Jennifer Reeder, "'To Do Something Extraordinary': Mormon Women and the Creation of a Usable Past" (PhD diss., George Mason University, 2013).

75 This event constituted "the most dramatic contact of Utah silk with the outside world," writes historian Chris Rigby Arrington. See Arrington, "Finest of Fabrics," 392.

76 Visitors encountered exhibits of enormous manufacturing capacity, rapid technological and scientific advancement, "backward" non-Western societies, and "uncivilized" people. See Robert W. Rydell, *All the World's a Fair: Visions of Empire at American International Expositions, 1876–1916* (Chicago: University of Chicago Press, 1987), chap. 2; and John P. Burris, *Exhibiting*

Religion: Colonialism and Spectacle at International Expositions, 1851–1893 (Charlottesville: University of Virginia Press, 2002), chaps. 4, 5.

77 Hansen, *Frontier Religion*, 173.

78 In their speeches and pamphlets, they cast themselves as "moral, progressive, patriotic" American citizens standing "on the cutting edge of suffrage activism." See Andrea Radke-Moss, "Mormon Women, Suffrage, and Citizenship at the 1893 Chicago World's Fair," in *Gendering the Fair: Histories of Women and Gender at World's Fairs*, ed. TJ Boisseau and Abigail M. Markwyn (Urbana: University of Illinois Press, 2010), 98.

79 The silk displays also earned several medals for Utah Territory. See Coles, "Homespun Respectability," chap. 6.

80 Nytroe, "Taming the Past."

81 "Plant Better Trees," *Washington County News* 7, no. 16 (May 14, 1914): 1.

82 "Mulberry Tree Here and in Germany," *Ogden Daily Standard* 45, no. 306 (November 27, 1915): 4.

83 See, for example, City Tree Commission, "Plans Made for City Beautiful," *Washington County News* 24, no. 11 (March 19, 1931): 5; "Tree Planting Regulations Announced," *Washington County News* 24, no. 12 (March 26, 1931): 1; "Mayor Sets Special Tree Planting Days," *Washington County News* 25, no. 2 (January 14, 1932): 1, 2; "Tree Committee Makes Report to Council," *Parowan Times* 17, no. 21 (March 18, 1932): 1; and "Council Grants DUP Use of Old Schoolhouse as Meeting Place, Museum," *Pleasant Grove Review* 29, no. 7 (April 26, 1940): 5.

84 Monson, "Mulberry Trees," 134, 136.

85 See, for example, "Suggestive List of Trees for Arbor Day Planting," *Gunnison Gazette* 15, no. 24 (April 10, 1914): 4; "Little Things Picked Up in Orchard," *Wasatch Wave* 26, no. 45 (January 8, 1915): 2; N. Byhower, "Ornamental Gardens Add to Home Beauty," *Salt Lake Telegram* 14, no. 39 (March 14, 1915): 6; "Old 'Dixie' Land Is Admired by Visitors," *Richfield Reaper* 28, no. 45 (September 16, 1916): 1; "To Beautify Logan and Cache County," *Logan Republican* 18 (February 24, 1920): 1; and "Trees and Shrubs Arrive to Be Planted in County," *Garfield County News* 22, no. 12 (March 4, 1943): 1.

86 See, for example, "How to Fight the High Cost of Living," *Logan Republican* 11 (July 19, 1913): 6; "Let Woods Help Sweet Store," *Salt Lake Telegram* 17, no. 172 (July 30, 1918): 13; "Soups of Summer Fruits," *Roosevelt Standard*, no. 52 (August 20, 1919): 6; D. Laney, "Provide Birds with Fruits," *News Advocate* 9, no. 26 (October 29, 1915): 5; "Many Nutritious Foods Found in the American Forests," *Ogden Daily Standard* 48, no. 17 (January 19, 1918): 28; and George C. Fraser, *Journeys in the Canyon Lands of Utah and Arizona, 1914–1916*, ed. Frederick H. Swanson (Tucson: University of Arizona Press, 2005), 11.

87 Coles, *Mulberry*, chap. 6.

88 "Indorses Move to Preserve Our Trees," *Salt Lake Telegram* 29, no. 207 (August 24, 1930): 4.

89 George M. Cannon, "Trees of Modern Zion," *Improvement Era* 37, no. 4 (April 1934): 198–99, 223.

90 Alice Merrill Horne, "Mormon Pioneer Culture," *Relief Society Magazine* 31, no. 8 (August 1944): 419–22. For more biographical information about Horne, see Harriet Horne Arrington, "Alice Merrill Horne, Art Promoter and Early Utah Legislator," *Utah Historical Quarterly* 58, no. 3 (Summer 1990): 261–76.
91 Farmer, *On Zion's Mount*, chap. 3.
92 Orson Ferguson Whitney, *Popular History of Utah* (Salt Lake City: Deseret News, 1916), 18–19.
93 Thomas G. Alexander, "Irrigating the Mormon Heartland: The Operation of the Irrigation Companies in Wasatch Oasis Communities, 1847–1880," *Agricultural History* 76, no. 2 (Spring 2002): 172–87.
94 They ultimately surpassed this goal by fifteen thousand members. Cannon, Derr, and Beecher, *Women of Covenant*, 247, 287.
95 Cannon, Derr, and Beecher, 286.
96 Quoted in Vera White Pohlman, "Relief Society Celebrates Its Centennial," *Relief Society Magazine* 29, no. 4 (April 1942): 225–26.
97 Cannon, Derr, and Beecher, *Women of Covenant*, 284. This was not the first time that Relief Society women used trees to mark an occasion. In the 1930s, for example, they, along with many other Americans, planted elm, redwood, ash, and pine trees to signify the two-hundred-year anniversary of George Washington's birth. See Cannon, Derr, and Beecher, 262.
98 Pohlman, "Relief Society Celebrates," 227.
99 Cannon, Derr, and Beecher, *Women of Covenant*, 284.
100 Amy Brown Lyman, "Address," *Relief Society Magazine* 29, no. 4 (April 1942): 249.
101 Lyman, "Address," 248.
102 "Tree Planting Ceremony Well Attended Here on Wednesday Afternoon," *Washington County News* 37, no. 9 (March 19, 1942): 1.
103 "Plant Better Trees," 1.
104 "Tree Planting Ceremony Well Attended," 1. This commentary reflected the growing international presence of the Relief Society, which by the 1940s counted members in Europe, South America, Asia, and Africa. Cannon, Derr, and Beecher, *Women of Covenant*, 344. The increasingly international character of the membership ultimately catalyzed a change in the organization's name. In June 1945, the leadership transitioned from the "National Woman's Relief Society" to "Relief Society of the Church of Jesus Christ of Latter-day Saints." Cannon, Derr, and Beecher, *Women of Covenant*, 307.
105 Arrington, Fox, and May, *Building the City of God*, chap. 15. As described by historians Brian Q. Cannon and Charles S. Peterson, "The focus [during the Depression] upon individual industry and initiative, retrenchment in expenditures, and local production and exchange closely resembled the self-sufficient economic outlook Brigham Young had advocated in the pioneer era." Charles S. Peterson and Brian Q. Cannon, *The Awkward State of Utah: Coming of Age in the Nation, 1896–1945* (Salt Lake City: University of Utah Press, 2015), 277.
106 Cannon, Derr, and Beecher, *Women of Covenant*, 291–92; Peterson and Cannon, *Awkward State of Utah*, 329–30.

107 Cannon, Derr, and Beecher, *Women of Covenant*, 269.
108 Jessie L. Embry, "Grain Storage: The Balance of Power between Priesthood Authority and Relief Society Autonomy," *Dialogue: A Journal of Mormon Thought* 15, no. 4 (Winter 1982): 59–66.
109 Connie Lamb, "Symbols of the LDS Relief Society," *Mormon Historical Studies* 14, no. 1 (Spring 2013): 115–16, 118–20.
110 Cannon, Derr, and Beecher, *Women of Covenant*, 255–61, 277–78, 290–92; McDannell, *Sister Saints*, chap. 4.
111 "Daughters of Utah Pioneers," *Salt Lake Tribune* 42, no. 1 (April 14, 1901): 3; Derr, "Strength in Our Union," 183.
112 "Home," Daughters of Utah Pioneers, accessed August 19, 2024, http://www.dupinternational.org/index.php; "Organization of Daughters of Utah Pioneers," Daughters of Utah Pioneers, accessed August 19, 2024, http://www.dupinternational.org/dyn_page.php?pageID=43.
113 Jan Hemming, "President Eyring Points to Then-Unseen Successes of Utah's Silkworm Industry at Monument Commemoration," *Church News* (blog), October 18, 2021, https://www.thechurchnews.com/leaders-and-ministry/2021-10-18/president-henry-b-eyring-silkworm-industry-daughters-of-utah-pioneers-monument-commemoration-229291.
114 In 2007, this neighborhood made it on to the National Register of Historic Places. For the application, see Yalecrest Historic District, National Register of Historic Places Registration Form, October 1990, http://www.slcdocs.com/Planning/Historic%20Districts/YNR.pdf.
115 Gertrude S. Romney letter to Ida M. Kirkham, September 6, 1935, Pioneer Memorial Museum, Salt Lake City, UT (hereafter cited as Pioneer Memorial Museum).
116 Gertrude S. Romney letter to Leona Holbrook, September 23, 1938, Pioneer Memorial Museum.
117 Quoted in Eugene F. Fairbanks, *A Sculptor's Testimony in Bronze and Stone: The Sacred Sculpture of Avard T. Fairbanks*, rev. ed. (Salt Lake City: Publishers Press, 1994), 9.
118 Athelia T. Woolley, "Art to Edify: The Work of Avard T. Fairbanks," *Ensign* 17, no. 9 (September 1987): 34–38.
119 Cynthia Culver Prescott, "Representing the Ideal American Family: Avard Fairbanks and the Transformation of the Western Pioneer Monument," *Pacific Historical Review* 85, no. 1 (February 2016): 127.
120 Lamb, "Symbols," 126–27.
121 Avard T. Fairbanks, *Pioneering (Bell Tower Plaques)*, bronze, Salt Lake City, Utah, 1942.
122 Cannon, Derr, and Beecher, *Women of Covenant*, 283–84; Lamb, "Symbols," 126.
123 Prescott, *Pioneer Mother Monuments*, 130–31, 153, 159–63.
124 Prescott, "Representing," 113, 114.
125 Avard T. Fairbanks, *Daughters of Utah Pioneers Silk Industry Monument*, concrete, Salt Lake City, Utah, 1940.

126 "Monument Commemorates Pioneer Silk Industry," *Improvement Era* 44, no. 9 (September 1941): 542. See also "Monument Marks Utah Silk Industry," *Deseret News* 363, no. 17 (July 19, 1941): 5.

127 Coles, "Homespun Respectability," chap. 5. Historian Sarah Barringer Gordon refers to this period as a "second reconstruction." See Sarah Barringer Gordon, *The Mormon Question: Polygamy and Constitutional Conflict in Nineteenth-Century America* (Chapel Hill: University of North Carolina Press, 2002), 14.

128 Margaret and her and William's children lived in Salt Lake City only very briefly. They had to move on to smaller towns in and beyond Utah Territory. By staying away from her husband, she could help protect him from imprisonment. Margaret C. Eccles autobiographical sketch.

129 For more on the Eccles case, see Cleo G. Geddes, "A Study in Propaganda and the Eccles Case" (MS thesis, Utah State University, 1969); and B. Carmon Hardy, *Solemn Covenant: The Mormon Polygamous Passage* (Urbana: University of Illinois Press, 1992), 184–85.

130 "Plaque Honors Silk Industry," *Deseret News*, 6.

131 The journalistic coverage of the monument's unveiling in 1941 does not mention Eccles attending. "Monument Commemorates," 542.

132 This finding bears out historian David Glassberg's comment that memories of the past can be a product of power dynamics. Glassberg, "Public History," 20.

133 Prescott, *Pioneer Mother Monuments*, chap. 4; Hansen, *Frontier Religion*, chaps. 4–6; Patterson, *Pioneers in the Attic*.

Chapter Seven: George Washington's Cherry Tree

This photograph is in a scrapbook of collected images of Stafford County, Virginia. That album is in the collections of the George Washington Foundation in Fredericksburg, Virginia. The author would like to thank David Muraca, William E. Garner, and the George Washington Foundation. Thanks also to Sarah Carleton and the members of the University of South Florida Department of History and its graduate cohort who offered comments on an early draft of this essay.

1 Dipesh Chakrabarty, "The Climate of History: Four Theses," *Critical Inquiry* 35, no. 2 (Winter 2009): 201; Peter Coates, "Emerging from the Wilderness (or, from Redwoods to Bananas): Recent Environmental History in the United States and the Rest of the Americas," *Environment and History* 10, no. 4 (November 2004): 407–38; R. G. Collingwood, *The Idea of History* (New York: Oxford University Press, 1956), 212.

2 Eric Rutkow, *American Canopy: Trees, Forests, and the Making of a Nation* (New York: Scribner, 2013); Stephen J. Pyne, *Between Two Fires: A Fire History of Contemporary America* (Tucson: University of Arizona Press, 2015); Jared Farmer, *Trees in Paradise: The Botanical Conquest of California* (Berkeley: Heyday, 2017); Thomas J. Campanella, *Republic of Shade: New England and the American Elm* (New Haven, CT: Yale University Press, 2003); Sonja Dümpelmann, *Seeing Trees: A History of Street Trees in New York City and Berlin* (New Haven, CT: Yale

University Press, 2019); Jill Jonnes, *Urban Forests: A Natural History of Trees and People in the American Cityscape* (New York: Penguin, 2016); Jared Farmer, *Trees in Paradise: A California History* (New York: W. W. Norton, 2013); Ellen Stroud, *Nature Next Door: Cities and Trees in the American Northeast* (Seattle: University of Washington Press, 2012). Jared Farmer's recent *Elderflora: A Modern History of Ancient Trees* (New York: Basic Books, 2022) offers the first-of-its-kind study of trees as unique historical agents.

3 Richard Powers, *Overstory: A Novel* (New York: W. W. Norton, 2019); Peter Wohlleben, *The Hidden Life of Trees: What They Feel, How They Communicate—Discoveries from a Secret World* (New York: Greystone, 2013).

4 I discuss this in Philip Levy, *George Washington Written upon the Land: Nature, Memory, Myth, and Landscape* (Morgantown: West Virginia University Press, 2015); and Philip Levy, *Where the Cherry Tree Grew: The Story of Ferry Farm, George Washington's Boyhood Home* (New York: St. Martin's Press, 2013). See also Philip Levy, "'Crystallized into Solid Reality': How Mason Locke 'Parson' Weems Shaped George Washington's Boyhood Home," *Virginia Magazine of History and Biography* 120, no. 1 (April 2013): 107–45.

5 Nicholas C. Kawa, Bradley Painter, and Cailín E. Murray, "Trail Trees: Living Artifacts (*Vivifacts*) of Eastern North America," *Ethnobiology Letters* 6, no. 1 (2015): 183–88.

6 The idea of trees playing a central role in place-based nostalgia is explored somewhat in Jason E. Pierce, "Marvelous, Maligned, and Misunderstood: The Strange History of the Mesquite Tree in Texas," *Southwestern Historical Quarterly* 117, no. 4 (2014): 347–70. See also R. Bruce Allison, "Every Root an Anchor: Wisconsin's Famous and Historic Trees," *Wisconsin Magazine of History* 89, no. 1 (2005): 42–45. For more examples of the way scholars have discussed historical trees, see Janet Harvill Standard, "Trees of Legend and Lore in Historic Washington-Wilkes," *Georgia Review* 21, no. 3 (1967): 345–53.

7 Jared Farmer makes this point in "Taking Liberties with Historic Trees," *Journal of American History* 105, no. 4 (March 2019): 816. See also Farmer, *Trees in Paradise*; and Daegan Miller, "Reading Tree in Nature's Nation: Toward a Field Guide to Sylvan Literacy in the Nineteenth-Century United States," *American Historical Review* 121 (October 2016): 1114–40.

8 Farmer, "Taking Liberties," 816.

9 Jared Farmer offers a historian's overview of the natural cycles of trees' lives. See Farmer, *Elderflora*, 18–29; and Chakrabarty, "Climate of History."

10 James Cook questions what he calls "ocularcentrism" in "Seeing the Visual in U.S. History," *Journal of American History* 95, no. 2 (2008): 432–41. See (as it were) also Mark M. Smith, "Getting in Touch with Slavery and Freedom," *Journal of American History* 95, no. 2 (2008): 381–91.

11 "Washington Farm to Go to Auction," *New York Times*, October 22, 1939, 8; "Washington's Home as Boy Will Be Put Up at Auction," *New York Times*, February 3, 1940, 12.

12 "Farm Will Become Washington Shrine," *New York Times*, February 23, 1930, 38.

13 Levy, *George Washington Written*, 148–55; Francois Furstenberg, "Mason Locke Weems: Spreading the American Gospel," in *In the Name of the Father: Washington's Legacy, Slavery, and the Making of a Nation* (New York: Penguin, 2006), 105–45.

14 The reigning text on this story remains Peter Novick's *That Noble Dream: The "Objectivity Question" and the American Historical Profession* (New York: Cambridge University Press, 1988).

15 Henry Cabot Lodge, *George Washington, in Two Volumes* (Boston: Houghton Mifflin, 1889), 1:10–11.

16 Rupert Hughes, *George Washington: The Human Being and the Hero, 1732–1762* (New York: William Morrow, 1936), 16, 23; Joseph Dillaway Sawyer, *Washington* (New York: Macmillan, 1927), 79; William Woodward, *George Washington: The Image and the Man* (New York: Boni and Liveright, 1926), 16. See also Levy, *George Washington Written*, 25–58; and Lengel, *Inventing George Washington*, chap. 6, 140–58.

17 R. Tripp Evans, *Grant Wood: A Life* (New York: Alfred A. Knopf, 2010), 265–74.

18 Woodward, *George Washington*, 16.

19 Dixon Wecter, *The Hero in America: A Chronicle of Hero Worship* (New York: Charles Scribner and Sons, 1941), 133; Peter Onuf's introductory essay in Mason Locke Weems, *The Life of Washington*, ed. Peter Onuf (Armonk, NY: M. E. Sharp Press, 1996); Garry Wills, *Cincinnatus: George Washington and the Enlightenment* (Garden City, NJ: Doubleday, 1984), 27–53; Karal Ann Marling, *George Washington Slept Here: Colonial Revivals and American Culture, 1876–1986* (Cambridge, MA: Harvard University Press, 1988); Cathy Davidson, *Revolution and the Word: The Rise of the Novel in America* (New York: Oxford University Press, 2004), 83; Scott Casper, *Constructing American Lives: Biography and Culture in Nineteenth-Century America* (Chapel Hill: University of North Carolina Press, 1999), 72; Furstenberg, *In the Name of the Father*; Edward Lengel, *Inventing George Washington: America's Founder, in Myth and Memory* (New York: HarperCollins, 2011), 18–26. The most thorough biography of Weems remains Lewis Leary, *The Book-Peddling Parson* (Chapel Hill: Algonquin, 1984), although Emily Ellsworth Ford Skeel's *Mason Locke Weems: His Works and Ways in Three Volumes* (New York: privately published, 1929) also contains a wealth of information about Weems and his publication history.

20 John Bodnar, *Remaking America: Public Memory, Commemoration, and Patriotism in the Twentieth Century* (Princeton, NJ: Princeton University Press, 1992). See also Michael Kammen, *Mystic Chords of Memory: The Transformation of Tradition in American Culture* (New York: Alfred A. Knopf, 1991); Kirk Savage, *Standing Soldiers, Kneeling Slaves: Race, War, and Monument in Nineteenth-Century America* (Princeton, NJ: Princeton University Press, 1997); and David Glassberg, *Sense of History: The Place of the past in the American Life* (Amherst: University of Massachusetts Press, 2001).

21 "Folk Feel 'Slight' to Fredericksburg," *Washington Post*, January 16, 1931, 18.

22 Emily Fleming, "America's Historic Horse-Chestnut Tree," *Daughters of the American Revolution Magazine* 60, no. 4 (April 1926): 226–27.

23 "Charles Arthur Hoppin to Mrs. H. L. Rust," April 5, 1928, correspondence, Hoppin, box 1, folder 3, GWA Papers, George Washington Birthplace National Monument, Westmoreland, VA.

24 Wecter, *Hero in America*, 135.

25 George Allan England, "Washington's Old Home Farm," *Daughters of the American Revolution Magazine* 59, no. 12 (December 1925): 738.

26 England, 738.

27 William Miller, "Washington Lore," *Washington Post*, February 24, 1936, 6.

28 "Defends Story of Cherry Tree," *New York Times*, February 13, 1927, E5.

29 "Defends Story of Cherry Tree."

30 "Defends Story of Cherry Tree."

31 Anders Greenspan, *Creating Colonial Williamsburg: The Restoration of Virginia's Eighteenth-Century Capital*, 2nd ed. (Chapel Hill: University of North Carolina Press, 2020); Alena Pirok, "Goodwin's Ghosts: Williamsburg's Uncanny Legacy," *Public Historian* 41, no. 3 (August 2019): 9–30; Jesse Swigger, *"History Is Bunk": Assembling the past at Henry Ford's Greenfield Village* (Amherst: University of Massachusetts Press, 2014); William D. Moore, *Shaker Fever: America's Twentieth-Century Fascination with a Communitarian Sect* (Amherst: University of Massachusetts Press, 2020).

32 Jared Farmer touches on this idea in "Taking Liberties," 817.

33 "Farm Will Become Washington Shrine," *New York Times*, February 23, 1930, 38.

34 "Farm Will Become Washington Shrine."

35 Mason Locke Weems, *The Life of Washington* (Philadelphia: Mathew Carey, 1809), 14.

36 Identifying this specific tree from photographs is not easy. None of the posed photos show foliage, and those that do show foliage are at such a distance that identifying leaves is not possible. Nevertheless, the size and branch profile provide conclusive evidence. Rogers McVaugh, "A Revision of the North American Black Cherries (Prunus Serotina Ehrh., and Relatives)," *Brittonia* 7, no. 4 (1951): 279–315. Kanchi N. Gandhi, James L. Reveal, and Luc Brouillet, "(1886–1887) Proposals to Conserve the Names Prunus Serotina and P. Virginiana (Rosaceae) with Conserved Types," *Taxon* 58, no. 1 (2009): 312–14; James B. Beck et al., "Reduced Genetic Variation in Populations of Black Cherry (Prunus Serotina Subsp. Serotina, Rosaceae) at Its Western Range Limit in Kansas," *Northeastern Naturalist* 21, no. 3 (2014): 472–78.

37 David Marquis, "Black Cherry," Southern Research Station, accessed August 14, 2024, https://www.srs.fs.usda.gov/pubs/misc/ag_654/volume_2/prunus/serotina.htm.

38 "Prunus Serotina," Lady Bird Johnson Wildflower Center, University of Texas, accessed August 14, 2024, https://www.wildflower.org/plants/result.php?id_plant=prse2.

39 *Virginia Gazette* ad quoted in George H. S. King, "Washington's Boyhood Home," *William and Mary Quarterly*, 2nd ser., 17, no. 2 (April 1937): 275.

40 "How Old Can a Cherry Tree's Life Span Be?," Week&, October 11, 2020, https://homeguides.sfgate.com/old-can-cherry-trees-life-span-be-48143.html.

41 Marquis, "Black Cherry."
42 Sasha Degnan, "How Soon Does a Black Cherry Prunus Serotina Tree Make Cherries?," Week&, May 26, 2022, https://homeguides.sfgate.com/soon-black-cherry-prunus-serotina-tree-make-cherries-67821.html.
43 Photography is a uniquely valuable tool for scholars trying to chart the growth and decline of historical trees and forests. See James K. Agee and P. J. Ryan, "Historic Trees of John Muir National Historic Site," *Journal of Forest History* 24, no. 1 (1980): 40–46; and Daniel E. Ressler and John A. Kilmer, "Street Tree Inventory of Selinsgrove, Pennsylvania," *Journal of the Pennsylvania Academy of Science* 86, no. 1 (2012): 46–53.
44 S. Millett Thompson, *A Diary Covering Three Years and a Day* (Boston: Houghton Mifflin, 1888), 94.
45 Jane Hollenbeck Conner, *Lincoln in Stafford* (Stafford, VA: Parker, 2006), 13.
46 Correspondence of the Herald, May 13, 1862, Quiner Collection, State Historical Society of Wisconsin copies in Ferry Farm Collection, file 2, "Civil War Letters" (hereafter cited as FFCWL); Horace Currier, letter, May 18, 1862, file 2, FFCWL.
47 James F. Gibson, "Fredericksburg, Va. View of Town from Tyler's Battery," Prints & Photographs Online Catalogue, Library of Congress, accessed August 14, 2024, https://www.loc.gov/pictures/item/2018666271/.
48 Civil War–era photographers were attuned to the value of trees when they served as witnesses to conflict. Although Fredericksburg was the focus of the images, the trees were not irrelevant. For an example, see Maura Lyons, "An Embodied Landscape: Wounded Trees at Gettysburg," *American Art* 26, no. 3 (2012): 44–65.
49 Lyons, "Embodied Landscape," 44–65.
50 For context, see Megan Kate Nelson, *Ruin Nation: Destruction and the American Civil War* (Athens: University of Georgia Press, 2012).
51 "Fredericksburg, the Home of Washington's Boyhood, and the Burial Place of His Mother," *Frank Leslie's Popular Monthly* 19, no. 2 (February 1885): 2–3. I refer to the copy available through the American Periodicals Database, and thus my pagination reflects theirs.
52 "Fredericksburg," 2.
53 John Hennessy, "Fredericksburg's Lost Buildings" Fredericksburg Remembered, April 22, 2011, https://fredericksburghistory.wordpress.com/2011/04/22/an-umnatched-visual-record-the-1888-steeple-shots-reveal-some-of-fredericksburgs-lost-buildings/.
54 Levy, *George Washington Written*, 169–200.
55 HABS report, "George Washington's Surveying Office," architectural drawing and text report, LOC, HABS Files, HABS no. VA-90. The entire archive of HABS drawings and reports is available online through the Library of Congress website.
56 See Miller, "Reading Tree in Nature's Nation," 1114–40.
57 "Virginia Will Plant Cherry Trees Today," *New York Times*, February 22, 1936, 17.

58 Mai Hoang, "'Wipe Out:' Little Cherry Disease Poses a Big Problem for Washington Growers," *Yakima Herald-Republic*, July 28, 2019, https://www.yakimaherald.com/news/local/little-cherry-disease-poses-a-big-problem-for-washington-growers/article_37b19927-3324-5b30-840e-3e0a773d9cf6.html.
59 Matthew R. Costello, *The Property of the Nation: George Washington's Tomb, Mount Vernon, and the Memory of the First President* (Lawrence: University of Kansas Press, 2019), Word MS copy, pp. 106–7, 236.
60 Jared Farmer, "Witness to a Hanging: California's Haunted Trees," *Boom: A Journal of California* 3, no. 1 (2013): 70–79.
61 Charles H. Wade, "Legends in the Landscape: Myth as Material Culture at Dartmouth College," *Material Culture* 45, no. 2 (2013): 34–35.
62 This is a spin on Ferdinand de Saussure's idea of the signified and signifier.
63 Kirk Savage, *Monument Wars: Washington DC, the National Mall, and the Transformation of the Memorial Landscape* (Berkeley: University of California Press, 2005).
64 "Virginia Group to Perpetuate Cherry Tree Legend," *Washington Post*, February 21, 1935, 10.
65 "Virginia Will Plant," 17; Amanda Varnam, "History of the Cherry Blossom Trees in Washington DC," Arlington National Cemetery Tours, accessed August 14, 2024, https://www.arlingtontours.com/dc-cherry-blossom-history.
66 Melanie Marquis, "Interview with Barbara Segar," October 18, 2010, Ferry Farm Oral History Collections, Ferry Farm, Fredericksburg, Virginia.
67 "Washington's Boyhood Home Sold at Auction for $25,000," *Washington Post*, February 4, 1940, 1–2.
68 "Washington's Boyhood Home," 1–2.
69 Marquis, "Interview with Barbara Segar."
70 Melanie Marquis, "Interview with Charles B. Linton," March 5, 2007, Ferry Farm Oral History Collections, Ferry Farm, Fredericksburg, Virginia.
71 Marquis, "Interview with Barbara Segar."; Marquis, "Interview with Charles B. Linton."
72 Marquis, "Interview with Charles B. Linton."
73 Marquis, "Interview with Charles B. Linton." See also Melanie Marquis, "Souvenirs from Ferry Farm: Two Centuries of Myths at George Washington's Boyhood Home," paper on file at Ferry Farm, Fredericksburg, Virginia.
74 Wesley G. Pippert, "A Boyhood Recalled," *Washington Post*, February 24, 1974, G4.
75 "Ferry Farm, the Childhood Home of Washington, Gets Few Visitors," *Washington Post*, February 21, 1984, B6.
76 A later sign erected by the Department of Historical Resources in 1997 noted Weems's "popular fable" about the cherry tree.
77 Mason Locke Weems, *The Life of Washington* (Philadelphia: Mathew Carey, 1809), 6.
78 Levy, *George Washington Written*, 169–200.
79 HABS report, "George Washington's Surveying Office."

Chapter Eight: Sam Robinson's Sycamore

1 Avery Gordon, *Ghostly Matters: Haunting and the Sociological Imagination* (Minneapolis: University of Minneapolis Press, 1997), 8.

2 Robinson's middle name is recorded as "Andrews" in his Selective Service draft card. I have decided to use "Andrew" as used on Robinson's death certificate and grave marker.

3 Sam Robinson, *The Mother-in-Law Tree* (Richmond, VA: Whittet & Shepperson, 1957).

4 Sarah Harrison Blair's popular tale is shared in other folklore collections and local ghost tour publications, including L. B. Taylor, *The Ghosts of Williamsburg . . . and Nearby Environs* (Lynchburg, VA: Progress Printing, 1983), 12–16; Pamela Kinney, *Haunted Virginia: Legends, Myths, and True Tales* (Atglen, PA: Schiffer, 2009), 53–56; and Pamela Kinney, *Virginia's Haunted Historic Triangle* (Atglen, PA: Schiffer, 2011), 96–99. For this layer, I rely on the following account: Robinson, *Mother-in-Law Tree*.

5 All quoted material comes from Robinson, *Mother-in-Law Tree*.

6 David Silkenat, *Scars on the Land: An Environmental History of Slavery in the American South* (New York: Oxford University Press, 2022), 56.

7 Sandy Alexandre, *The Properties of Violence: Claims to Ownership in Representations of Lynching* (Oxford, MS: University Press of Mississippi, 2011); Orlando Patterson, *Rituals of Blood: The Consequences of Slavery in Two American Centuries* (New York: Basic Civitas, 1998).

8 Glayds-Marie Fry, *Night Riders in Black Folk History* (Chapel Hill: University of North Carolina Press, 1975), 66–69; Tiya Miles, *All That She Carried: The Journey of Ashley's Sack, a Black Family Keepsake* (New York: Random House, 2022), 198–204; Tiya Miles, "Every Pecan Tree: Trees, Meaning, and Memory in Enslaved People's Lives," Arnold Arboretum, YouTube video, 1:05:14, April 9, 2021, https://www.youtube.com/watch?v=rCyQYMPZ46Y.

9 Walter Johnson, "The Carceral Landscape," in *River of Dark Dreams: Slavery and Empire in the Cotton Kingdom* (Cambridge, MA: Harvard University Press, 2013), 209–43.

10 Shannon Lee Dawdy argues for archaeology to focus on present and future problems, like climate change, agricultural sustainability, urbanizations, and disaster and recovery, rather than "reconstructions of the past." See Shannon Lee Dawdy, "Millennial Archaeology. Locating the Discipline in the Age of Insecurity," *Archeological Dialogues* 16, no. 2 (2009): 131–42.

11 For recent scholarship on Jamestown, see Karen Ordahl Kupperman, *The Jamestown Project* (Cambridge, MA: Harvard University Press, 2008); Joseph Kelly, *Marooned: Jamestown, Shipwreck, and a New History of America's Origin* (New York: Bloomsburg, 2018); David A. Price, *Love & Hate in Jamestown: John Smith, Pocahontas, and the Start of a New Nation* (New York: Vintage Books, 2003); Jim Horn, *A Land as God Made It: Jamestown and the Birth of America* (New York: Basic Books, 2005); Jim Horn, *1619: Jamestown and the Forging of American Democracy* (New York: Basic Books, 2018); William M. Kelso,

Jamestown: The Buried Truth (Charlottesville: University of Virginia Press, 2008); and William M. Kelso, *Jamestown: The Truth Revealed* (Charlottesville: University of Virginia Press, 2017).

12 Philip L. Barbour, ed., *The Jamestown Voyages under the First Charter, 1606–1609*, vol. 1 (Cambridge: Cambridge University Press, 1969), 45–54.

13 Philip L. Barbour, *The Three Worlds of Captain John Smith* (Boston: Houghton Mifflin, 1964), 3–63.

14 Horn, *Land as God Made It*, 218.

15 Julia A. King, "Ruins of Jamestown," *Buildings and Landscapes* 26, no. 1 (Spring 2019): 11–31.

16 "New Towne," Jamestown Rediscovery, Preservation Virginia, accessed August 18, 2024, https://historicjamestowne.org/visit/plan-your-visit/new-towne/.

17 James Lindgren, *Preserving the Old Dominion: Historic Preservation and Virginia Traditionalism* (Charlottesville: University of Virginia Press, 1993), 21.

18 Lindgren, *Preserving the Old Dominion*, 94–95.

19 Lindgren, 55.

20 Lindgren, 98–99.

21 Lindgren, 114.

22 For more discussion of public history, tourism, and nation building, see the growing body of scholarship that includes Seth C. Bruggeman, *Here, George Washington Was Born: Memory, Material Culture, and the Public History of a National Monument* (Athens: University of Georgia Press, 2008); Anders Greenspan, *Creating Colonial Williamsburg: The Restoration of Virginia's Eighteenth-Century Capital* (Chapel Hill: University of North Carolina Press, 2009); Michael Kammen, *Mystic Chords of Memory: The Transformation of Tradition in American Culture* (New York: Vintage, 1991); Marguerite S. Shaffer, *See America First: Tourism and National Identity, 1880–1940* (Washington, DC: Smithsonian Books, 2001); Patricia West, *Domesticating History: The Political Origins of America's House Museums* (Washington, DC: Smithsonian Institution Press, 1999).

23 Charles E. Randall and D. Priscilla Edgerton, *Famous Trees* (Washington, DC: US Department of Agriculture), 110.

24 To be clear, I am referencing the actual site of James Fort where English colonists landed in 1607 that was "rediscovered" in the 1990s by archaeologists. Preservation Virginia and the National Park Service jointly run Historic Jamestowne. Confusingly, there is also the Jamestown Settlement, a living history museum operated by the Commonwealth of Virginia with a reconstructed fort, ships, and an Indian village. It is located about two miles from the island. Though the settlement was built for the 1957 commemoration, it does not factor in this discussion today, although it does operate as a simulacrum for the actual fort site—a kind of ghostly double that many schoolchildren (myself included) believed *was* Jamestown. In this essay, I refer to the actual site of the 1607 landing as Historic Jamestowne, Jamestown Island, and Jamestown.

25 Celia Naylor, *Unsilencing Slavery: Telling Truths about Rose Hall Plantation, Jamaica* (Athens: University of Georgia Press, 2022); Tiya Miles, *Tales from the*

Haunted South: Dark Tourism and Memories of Slavery from the Civil War Era (Chapel Hill: University of North Carolina Press, 2018).

26 Miles, *Tales from the Haunted South*, 125.

27 Miles, 132.

28 Miles, 113.

29 Miles, 125.

30 Miles, 113. See also E. Patrick Johnson, "'Quare' Studies, or (Almost) Everything I Know about Queer Studies I Learned from My Grandmother," in *Black Queer Studies: A Critical Anthology*, ed. E. Patrick Johnson and Mae G. Henderson (Durham, NC: Duke University Press, 2016), 141.

31 As of this writing, the recent reflection on Robinson came from Norfolk archivist/historian Robert Hitchings, "Jamestown Tour Guide Was a Gem," *Norfolk Virginian-Pilot*, February 24, 2019. Hitchings writes fondly of meeting Robinson during a 1960 field trip to Jamestown Island, noting that Robinson was "an outstanding storyteller."

32 Specifically, his draft card names Manning, South Carolina, a town located approximately sixty miles from Columbia, South Carolina. See Selective Service Records, "Samuel Andrews Robinson," WWII Draft Registration Cards for Virginia, October 16, 1940–March 31, 1947, box 624; and Virginia Department of Health, "Samuel Andrew Robinson," Virginia Deaths, 1912–2014.

33 Selective Service Records, "Samuel Andrews Robinson"; Myrtle S. Barnes, "Sam the Guide Allows as to How: Tree Growed Twixt Two Graves," *Times-Herald*, October 16, 1957, 17. To add further confusion, Sam's birth year is given as 1901 and 1906 in two separate newspaper articles, and his obituary mentions his "age is unknown": "Services Held for Sexton at Jamestown," *Daily Press*, November 11, 1965. Robinson's parents are dubiously named in "Samuel Andrew Robinson," Find a Grave, last updated April 6, 2019, https://www.findagrave.com/memorial/191417559/samuel-andrew-robinson.

34 Department of Commerce-Bureau of the Census, 1940 Census, Enumeration District 118–69, sheet 1.

35 Robinson was likely already working at Jamestown in the summer of 1937, as he was directly referenced in a letter from William Harrison Smith to Ellen Bagby, August 1, 1937, Bagby Family Papers, 1824–1960, Virginia Museum of History and Culture (hereafter cited as Bagby Family Papers).

36 Parke Rouse, "Miss Ellen Bagby: Power Puff Brunnhilde of Jamestown," *Daily Press*, August 15, 1982, C3. Hitchings retells the same story.

37 Shaffer, *See America First*, 6.

38 Shaffer, 4.

39 J. Douglas Smith, *Managing White Supremacy: Race, Politics and Citizenship in Jim Crow Virginia* (Chapel Hill: University of North Carolina Press, 2002), 4.

40 It appears that Robinson either did not drive or did not have access to a vehicle. Sam Robinson to William Harrison Smith, April 7, 1954, Records of the Virginia 350th Anniversary Commission, Library of Virginia (hereafter cited as Records of the Anniversary Commission).

41 William Harrison Smith to Ellen Bagby, June 30, 1943, Bagby Family Papers. This brief exchange also informs about Robinson's own urban travel experience.

42 Rouse, "Miss Ellen Bagby," 1982, C3.
43 Barnes, "Sam the Guide," 17. Barnes quotes Robinson directly: "I looks it up myself," he says. "I spends a lot of time in libraries, looking up family histories and things."
44 These letters are filed within the Rodney B. Taylor Papers at the Special Collections Research Center, William & Mary Libraries. Taylor was the son and stepson of Vivian and William Harrison Smith. He would have had firsthand knowledge of Robinson as a child.
45 As of 2019, satellite views of Robinson's Richmond address show a two-story brick duplex. See "Neighborhood Profile: Gilpin Court," *Richmond Architecture*, accessed October 31, 2019, https://architecturerichmond.com/neighborhood-profile-gilpin-court/.
46 Registration card, Samuel Andrews Robinson, order no. 1592-A, World War II.
47 According to Rodney Taylor, stepson of Jamestown Island's APVA superintendent William Harrison Smith, this recording was made by Jack L. Hiller, who worked for the Jamestown Foundation. See "1957 Audio Recording of Sam Robinson, Sexton of Jamestown Memorial Church, Jamestown, Virginia," Archive Williamsburg, YouTube video, 25:08, August 27, 2016, https://www.youtube.com/watch?v=vLzJQ70L7Lw. A 1964 reel copy of the recording is also in the Rodney B. Taylor Papers at the Special Collections Research Center, William & Mary Libraries. The original 1957 recording was returned to Robinson.
48 Virginia Department of Health, "Samuel Andrew Robinson."
49 "The Open Road," *Gettysburg Times*, October 22, 1938, 3; "Sycamore Tree Separates Graves," *Richmond Times-Dispatch*, May 8, 1938.
50 W. D. Brush, "The Utilization of the Sycamore," US Department of Agriculture, bulletin 884, October 12, 1920, 5, https://hdl.handle.net/2027/loc.ark:/13960/t3dz0wj1d?urlappend=%3Bseq=7; Ellen Powell, "Sycamore," Common Native Trees of Virginia, Virginia Department of Forestry, accessed August 18, 2024, https://dof.virginia.gov/wp-content/uploads/Common-Native-Trees-ID_pub.pdf; Gil Nelson, Christopher J. Earle, and Richard Spellenberg, *Trees of Eastern North America* (Princeton, NJ: Princeton University Press, 2014), 470–71.
51 Joan Maloof, *Teaching the Trees: Lessons from the Forest* (Athens: University of Georgia Press, 2005), 19.
52 Steve Nix, "Identifying the Common American Sycamore," Treehugger.com, August 11, 2019, https://www.treehugger.com/identify-common-american-sycamore-tree-1343174.
53 Maloof, *Teaching the Trees*, 19.
54 Christopher L.C.E. Witcombe, "Trees and the Sacred," personal website, accessed August 18, 2024, http://witcombe.sbc.edu/sacredplaces/trees.html.
55 H. S. Betts, "American Sycamore," US Department of Agriculture, September 1945, 1, accessed August 18, 2024, https://ia802205.us.archive.org/20/items/americansycamore1945bett/americansycamore1945bett.pdf.
56 Fiona Stafford, *The Long, Long Life of Trees* (New Haven, CT: Yale University Press, 2016), 157.
57 Stafford, *Long, Long Life of Trees*, 161–62.
58 "Curious Sycamore near Chester, South Carolina," *Frank Leslie's Illustrated Newspaper*, March 16, 1878, 27.

59 "An Account of a Remarkable Tree in the State of Ohio," *National Intelligencer*, August 4, 1821.
60 "A Wondrous Tree," *Raleigh Register*, August 20, 1824.
61 "A Large Tree," *Raleigh Register*, February 11, 1825.
62 "Open Road"; "Sycamore Tree Separates Graves."
63 William Meade, *Old Churches, Ministers, and Families of Virginia*, vol. 1 (Philadelphia: J. B. Lippincott, 1861), 114.
64 Lyon Tyler Gardiner, *The Cradle of the Republic: Jamestown and the James River* (Richmond, VA: Hermitage Press, 1906), 129, https://play.google.com/books/reader?id=4R4SAAAAYAAJ&pg=GBS.PP18&hl=en.
65 George Washington Coleman, "Along the Lower James," *Century Illustrated Magazine*, January 1891, 3.
66 Rouse, "Miss Ellen Bagby," C3.
67 "Tells of Eastern Trip," *Montrose Tidings*, August 10, 1939, 1.
68 "Audio Recording of Sam Robinson."
69 James Burke, "Tree Fire at Tomb Is a Mystery," *Richmond Times-Dispatch*, April 15, 1940, 4.
70 Rouse, "Miss Ellen Bagby," C3; "Guide and Historian: Sam's Fame," *Richmond News Leader*, January 18, 1951.
71 Fred Frechette, "Caretaker Spins Yarn about Jamestown Sycamore," *Richmond Times-Dispatch*, August 24, 1952, B5.
72 For recent discussions, see Katherine McKittrick, *Demonic Grounds: Black Women and the Cartographies of Struggle* (Minneapolis: University of Minnesota Press, 2006); Katherine McKittrick, "Plantation Futures," *Small Axe* 17, no. 3 (November 2013; no. 42): 1–15; Christy Hyman, "GIS and the Mapping of Enslaved Movement: The Matrix of Risk," Environmental History Now, August 19, 2021, https://envhistnow.com/2021/08/19/gis-and-the-mapping-of-enslaved-movement-the-matrix-of-risk/; and Christy Hyman, "The Disappearance of Eve and Sall: Escaping Slavery in North Carolina," *Black Perspectives* (blog), October 6, 2020, https://www.aaihs.org/the-disappearance-of-eve-and-sall-escaping-slavery-in-north-carolina/.
73 Silkenat, *Scars on the Land*, 4–5.
74 J. T. Roane, "Black Ecologies: Subaquatic Life, and the Jim Crow Enclosure of the Tidewater," *Journal of Rural Studies* 94 (2022): 229.
75 The National Council on Public History's president, Gregory E. Smoak, reflected on doing public environmental history in his 2022 presidential address. See Gregory E. Smoak, "Every History Has a Nature: Thoughts on Doing Public Environmental History," *Public Historian* 44, no. 3 (August 2022): 9–23.
76 Toni Morrison, *Beloved* (New York: Plume, 1987), 6; Alexandre, *Properties of Violence*, 122–45.
77 Paul Cloke and Eric Pawson, "Memorial Trees and Treescape Memories," *Environment and Planning D: Society and Space* 26 (2008): 109.
78 Jason Edward Black, "Here Is a Strange and Bitter Crop: Emmett Till and the Rhetorical Complications of Treescape Memory," *Argumentation and Advocacy* 55, no. 1 (July 2018): 38.

79 Amy Louise Wood, *Lynching and Spectacle: Witnessing Racial Violence in America, 1890–1940* (Chapel Hill: University of North Carolina Press, 2009), 1.

80 Brendan Wolfe, "Lynching in Virginia," *Encyclopedia Virginia*, Virginia Humanities, last modified February 9, 2023, https://encyclopediavirginia.org/entries/lynching-in-virginia/.

81 Wood, *Lynching and Spectacle*, 1. According to the Equal Justice Initiative, a white mob lynched Isaac Brandon in 1892 in Charles City County, Virginia—the only lynching documented close to Jamestown Island. "Lynching in America," Equal Justice Initiative, accessed August 18, 2024, https://lynchinginamerica.eji.org/explore/virginia. Brandon received a historical marker in 2019. See Jeremy M. Lazarus, "History Marker Dedicated to Charles City County Lynching Victim," *Richmond Free Press*, April 12, 2019, https://richmondfreepress.com/news/2019/apr/12/history-marker-dedicated-charles-city-county-lynch/.

82 Wood, *Lynching and Spectacle*, 75; Grace Elizabeth Hale, *Making Whiteness: The Culture of Segregation in the South, 1890–1940* (New York: Vintage Books, 1998), 199–239.

83 Smith, *Managing White Supremacy*, 16.

84 Smith, 15.

85 Smith, 223.

86 Smith, 89.

87 This group included the Anglo-Saxon Clubs, first started by John Powell in Richmond, Virginia. The group advocated for "the preservation and maintenance of Anglo-Saxon ideals and civilization" by increasing Jim Crow statutes and racial integrity across the Commonwealth. See Smith, 76–106.

88 Smith, 296.

89 "Barred from Jamestown," *Norfolk Journal and Guide*, October 4, 1930, 12.

90 "Barred from Jamestown."

91 "Barred from Jamestown."

92 "Burning Cross Warns NAACP Lawyer," *Miami Times*, August 13, 1955, 16; "Cross-Burning Probed at McKeldin's Mansion," *Washington Evening Star*, October 7, 1957, B3.

93 Alton Levy, "Mr. James Crow Invited to Attend," *Arkansas State Press*, May 17, 1957.

94 As of this writing, there are no known Black reporters covering Robinson's story and the sycamore. Further research may reveal such sources. Frechette, "Caretaker."

95 Fred E. Tarman, "'Mother-in-Law' Tree Story Spices Visit to Jamestown," *Norman Transcript* (Norman, Oklahoma), November 10, 1958, 6; Frechette, "Caretaker."

96 In his dissertation, Dr. Rex Ellis, the first African American vice president for the Colonial Williamsburg Foundation, mentions two Black interpreters by name: Alec Pleasant and Lydia Gardner. He erroneously notes that Robinson "interpreted at Jamestown during the turn of the century." See Rex Ellis, "Presenting the Past: Education, Interpretation and the Teaching of Black History at Colonial Williamsburg" (PhD diss., William & Mary, 1989), 4.

97 During World War II, Vivian Smith took over as superintendent and postmaster at Jamestown while her husband served in the US armed forces. In this capacity, she corresponded with Bagby about administrative, financial, and custodial matters. Vivian Smith to Ellen Bagby, undated, Bagby Family Papers.

98 "Services Held for Sexton."

99 Valarie Edinger, "Church Caretaker Is Star: Performance for a Queen," *Richmond Times-Dispatch*, October 10, 1957.

100 Sarah Gilbreath Ford, *Tracing Southern Storytelling in Black and White* (Tuscaloosa: University of Alabama Press, 2014).

101 Hale, *Making Whiteness*, 232–33.

102 Edinger, "Church Caretaker Is Star."

103 W. E. B. Du Bois to NAACP Board, November 5, 1956, in Herbert Aptheker, ed., *The Correspondence of W. E. B. Du Bois*, vol. 3 (Amherst: University of Massachusetts Press, 1978), 405–6.

104 The APVA "belatedly approved" a plan by Elder Lightfoot Solomon Michaux to commemorate the first Africans. See Kammen, *Mystic Chords of Memory*, 683.

105 Hale, *Making Whiteness*, 10.

106 *The Jamestown Festival: Plans for a National Celebration in 1957* (Richmond, VA: Whittet & Shepperson, 1957).

107 Walter J. Mueller, *History of the Colonial Capital Branch, Association for the Preservation of Virginia Antiquities, 1889–1988* (Williamsburg, VA: Association for the Preservation of Virginia Antiquities, 1988), 33.

108 *Report of the Virginia 350th Anniversary Commission, House Document No. 25* (Richmond, VA: Division of Purchase and Printing, 1956), 7. The economic boost is often discussed as a "permanent benefit of the Festival" in governmental planning documents. *Report of the Virginia 350th Anniversary Commission*, 20.

109 *Jamestown Festival*, 2. Stanley's term as governor oversaw the implementation of Massive Resistance and pushed for "separate but equal" schools. See Sara K. Eskridge, "Thomas B. Stanley (1890–1970)," *Encyclopedia Virginia*, Virginia Humanities, last modified December 22, 2021, https://encyclopediavirginia.org/entries/stanley-thomas-b-1890-1970/.

110 *Report of the Virginia 350th Anniversary Commission*, 7.

111 John L. Cotter and J. Paul Hudson, preface to *New Discoveries at Jamestown: Site of the First Successful English Settlement in America* (Washington, DC: National Park Service, 1957).

112 As executive director of the commission, Parke Rouse Jr. fielded multiple inquiries into dinner invitations for the queen's reception. Conrad L. Wirth, the then director of the Interior Department, chastised Rouse for neglecting to include certain persons. Rouse responded, "This whole operation is complicated and awkward, but I believe we will get through it alive." Wirth to Rouse, September 27, 1957, and Rouse to Wirth, October 4, 1957, Records of the Anniversary Commission.

113 L. D. Battle memo to committee members, October 1, 1957, Records of the Anniversary Commission, 1953–58.

114 Chief O. T. Custalow to Governor Thomas Stanley, September 12, 1957, Records of the Anniversary Commission, 1953–58.

115 Parke Rouse Jr. to Ellen Bagby, February 25, 1956, Records of the Anniversary Commission.

116 Herb Thompson and Harry Nash, "Queen Attends Service at Jamestown Church," *Daily Press*, October 16, 1957.

117 Thompson and Nash.

118 "Royal Pair Listen to Sam Robinson's Spiel at Jamestown," *Times-Herald Newport News*, October 17, 1957.

119 There are many draft schedules of the queen's time in Virginia. See Records of the Anniversary Commission.

120 This conjecture was shared by Preservation Virginia public historian Mark Summers during the Black History Month program "American Heartbreak: Historical Memory and Racial Amnesia" offered at Jamestown in February 2019.

121 "The Tombs of James and Sarah Blair," Historical Marker Database, accessed August 18, 2024, https://www.hmdb.org/m.asp?m=100108.

122 "The Legend of the Curse of the Mother-in-Law Tree," last updated November 16, 2010, https://www.flickr.com/photos/heyitsdebv/5181023042; "The Mother-in-Law Tree of Jamestown Island, VA," Colonial Ghosts, last updated August 6, 2024, https://colonialghosts.com/the-mother-in-law-tree-of-jamestown-island-va/.

123 "1957 Audio Recording of Sam Robinson."

124 Manning Marable, *Living Black History: How Reimagining the African-American Past Can Remake America's Racial Future* (New York: Perseus Books, 2006), 1.

125 I borrow "captive African" from a February 19, 2019, program, "The African and African-American Experience at Colonial National Historical Park," sponsored by All Together Williamsburg. First Africans Research Fellow Chardé Reid used the phrase to describe Africans who were either enslaved or indentured during the early period of English colonialism in Virginia.

126 This program was routinely offered at Historic Jamestowne and shared in outreach efforts with William & Mary's Lemon Project and the Williamsburg Regional Library. "'The American Heartbreak: Historic Memory and Racial Amnesia at Jamestown' Porch Talk," William & Mary, accessed August 18, 2024, https://events.wm.edu/event/view/wm/113534.

127 "Sam Robinson," Jamestown Rediscovery–Historic Jamestowne, accessed August 18, 2024, https://historicjamestowne.org/history/sam-robinson/.

128 US Department of Agriculture, *Famous Trees*, 1.

129 I take these quotes from two recent titles that call attention to the institutional histories at work within public history and how we must reorient discussions at historic sites. See Amy E. Potter et al., *Remembering Enslavement: Reassembling the Southern Plantation Museum* (Athens: University of Georgia Press, 2022); and Clint Smith, *How the Word Is Passed: A Reckoning with the History of Slavery across America* (New York: Little, Brown, 2021).

130 West, *Domesticating History*, 162.

Chapter Nine: The Fox Oaks of Flushing, New York

In addition to thanking the anonymous reviewers for their feedback and this volume's editors (especially Phil Levy, who recruited this piece) for helping see this essay into print, the author would like to thank the following individuals for their kind assistance with his research. At the Bowne House: Rosemary S. Vietor of the Board of Trustees, archivist Charlotte Jackson, Ellen Spindler, executive director Elise Helmers, and museum educator Emily Vieyra Haley. He also thanks Mary Crauderueff, curator of Quaker Collections at the Haverford College Libraries, and Cara Caputo, manager of Interpretation and Public Outreach, Wyck Historic House, Garden, and Farm.

1 George Fox Stone and "George Fox Stone" historical marker, Bowne Street, Flushing, Queens, visited August 17, 2022.

2 John W. Barber and Henry Howe, *Historical Collections of the State of New York* (New York: Clark, Austin, 1851), 291.

3 On modern Flushing and its efforts to promote itself as a community with an outstanding record for religious freedom dating back to the time of the first Bownes, see R. Scott Hanson, *City of Gods: Religious Freedom, Immigration, and Pluralism in Flushing, Queens* (New York: Fordham University Press, 2016).

4 Jacob Titus Bowne, *Bowne Family of Flushing, Long Island*, ed. Edith King Wilson (New York: Bowne, 1987); "The Old Bowne House . . . for the Commercial Advertiser" (1850s?, n.p.), box A7, "Newspaper Clippings," folder 4, Bowne House Historical Society Archive, Flushing, Queens (hereafter cited as BHHSA). On "pastkeepers," see Michael C. Batinski, *Pastkeepers in a Small Place: Five Centuries in Deerfield, Massachusetts* (Amherst: University of Massachusetts Press, 2004).

5 Judith Pollman, *Memory in Early Modern Europe, 1500–1800* (New York: Oxford University Press, 2017); Judith Pollman and Erika Kuijpers, "Introduction: On the Early Modernity of Modern Memory," in *Memory before Modernity: Practices of Memory in Early Modern Europe*, ed. Erika Kuijpers et al. (Brill: Leiden, 2013), 1–23.

6 Batinski, *Pastkeepers*, 168; Nicola Whyte, "An Archaeology of Natural Places: Trees in the Early Modern Landscape," *Huntington Library Quarterly* 76, no. 4 (Winter 2013): 499–517; Alexandra Walsham, *The Reformation of the Landscape: Religion, Identity, and Memory in Early Modern Britain and Ireland* (New York: Oxford University Press, 2011); Ann Hughes, "'When the Scotts Army Did March Thorow Our County': Space, Place and Remembering in the English Civil War," in *Remembering the English Civil Wars*, ed. Lloyd Bowen and Mark Stoyle (New York: Routledge, 2022), 43–59, esp. 50–51.

7 William C. Braithwaite, *The Beginnings of Quakerism*, 2nd ed., ed. Henry J. Cadbury (York: William Sessions Limited, 1981), 83, 84, 553; John Bainbridge, "The Sedbergh Quaker Trail," *Walking the Old Ways: Rambling in the British Countryside* (blog), accessed August 8, 2024, https://walkingtheoldways.wordpress.com/2019/03/20/the-sedbergh-quaker-trail/.

8 See "A Bowne House Indian Deed?," Bowne House Blogs: Profiles of the Flushing Charter Signers, Bowne House Historical Society (hereafter cited as BHHS),

accessed August 9, 2024, https://www.bownehouse.org/profiles-of-the-flushing-charter-signers. For the Dutch land purchase, see Charles T. Gehring, trans. and ed., *Land Papers* (Baltimore: Genealogical Publishing, 1980), 9.

9 Charlotte Jackson and Ellen Spindler, "Thomas Bowne's Crutch: Tale of an Unexpected Encounter," Bowne House Blogs: Bowne House Collection Spotlight, BHHS, July 2, 2020, https://www.bownehouse.org/collection-spotlight/.

10 On Flushing's early religious history and its Dutch colonial context, see Evan Haefeli, *New Netherland and the Dutch Origins of American Religious Liberty* (Philadelphia: University of Pennsylvania Press, 2014).

11 On the Flushing Remonstrance and its commemoration in New York history, see Harrop A. Freeman, "A Remonstrance for Conscience," *University of Pennsylvania Law Review* 106, no. 6 (1958): 806–30; Tabetha Garman, "Designed for the Good of All: The Flushing Remonstrance and Religious Freedom in America" (master's thesis, East Tennessee State University, 2006); David W. Voorhees, "The 1657 Flushing Remonstrance in Historical Perspective," *de Halve Maen* 81 (Spring 2008): 11–14; Dennis J. Maika, "Commemoration and Context: The Flushing Remonstrance Then and Now," *New York History* 89, no. 1 (2008): 28–42; Dennis J. Maika, "A Detestable Pamphlet," *New York Archives* 19, no. 3 (2020): 32–36; and Glenn Collins, "Precursor of the Constitution goes on Display in Queens," *New York Times*, December 5, 2008; "Document That Inspired Bill of Rights on Display at Federal Hall National Memorial," National Park Service, 2018, https://www.nps.gov/articles/flushing-remonstrance.htm. On the effort to raise the site to a national park, see "Flushing Remonstrance Special Resource Study," National Park Service, accessed August 9, 2024, http://npshistory.com/publications/srs/flre-srs-handout.pdf.

12 Haefeli, *New Netherland*, chaps. 6 and 10.

13 Edmund B. O'Callaghan and Berthold Fernow, eds., *Documents Relative to the Colonial History of the State of New York*, 15 vols. (Albany: Weed, Parson, 1853–87), 14:597–98; Rosemary Moore, *The Light in Their Consciences: The Early Quakers in Britain, 1646–1666* (University Park: Pennsylvania State University Press, 2000), 180–85.

14 Kenneth L. Carroll, "Some Thoughts on George Fox's Visit to America in 1672," *Quaker History* 61, no. 2 (Autumn 1972): 82–90.

15 John L. Nickalls, ed., *The Journal of George Fox* (Philadelphia: Religious Society of Friends, 1997), 619–20.

16 Elise Helmers, with Charlotte Jackson, "The George Fox Daybed: A Sacred Symbol," Bowne House Blogs: Bowne House Collection Spotlight, BHHS, August 21, 2020, https://www.bownehouse.org/collection-spotlight/.

17 Nickalls, *Journal*, 629.

18 "Notes on New York history," Miller Papers, vol. 2, BV Sec. M, New York Historical Society; Bowne, *Bowne Family*, 20.

19 Joseph Disponzio, Steven Whitesell, and Rachel Kramer, "Cultural Landscape Report for Weeping Beech Park, Queens, New York" (draft, 2008), 11.6.5, 11.7.12, BHHSA.

20 Algernon Aikin Aspinwall, *The Aspinwall Genealogy* (Rutland, VT: Tuttle, 1901), 47–49, 72–75. The Aspinwall house faced what is now Northern Boulevard, so the oaks were in the backyard. An early twentieth-century picture of the house is available at Eugene L. Armbruster, "Captain John Aspinwall House, 1922," Eugene Armbruster Drawings and Photographs, Queens Public Library Digital Archives, accessed August 8, 2024, http://digitalarchives.queenslibrary.org/browse/captain-john-aspinwall-house.

21 John Sloss Hobart to John Jay, November 20, 1794, Founders Online, https://founders.archives.gov/documents/Jay/01-06-02-0090; Aileen Sutherland Collines, ed., *Travels in Britain, 1794–1795: The Diary of John Aspinwall, Great-Grandfather of Franklin Delano Roosevelt, with a Brief History of His Aspinwall Forebears* (Virginia Beach: Parsons Press, 1994).

22 *The Diaries of George Washington*, vol. 5, *1 July 1786–31 December 1789*, ed. Donald Jackson and Dorothy Twohig (Charlottesville: University Press of Virginia, 1979), 458–59; Thomas Jefferson to William Prince, July 6, 1791, in Julian P. Boyd, ed., *The Papers of Thomas Jefferson* (Princeton, NJ: Princeton University Press, 1982), 20:603–4.

23 "History of the Bowne House," BHHS, accessed August 9, 2024, https://www.bownehouse.org/history-of-the-house; Disponzio, Whitesell, and Kramer, "Cultural Landscape Report"; M. P. and T. S. K. Johansson, "Samuel Bowne Parsons and the Golden Bees," *Journal of Long Island History* 9, no. 1 (Winter/Spring 1969): 21–31.

24 "History of the Bowne House."

25 Tea Caddy, 78.100, Wyck Association, Wyck Historic House, Philadelphia.

26 Henry Post Jr. to Reuben Haines III, December 17, 1822, Series II, box 18, folder 226, Wyck Association Collection, American Philosophical Society.

27 "Fox Oaks," print, 89.148, "Bowne House," print 89.147, and associated "Fox Oak Print Object Record," Wyck Association; "Swarthmore Hall," print 89.273, Wyck Association.

28 Joseph Bevan Braithwaite, ed., *Memoirs of Joseph John Gurney: With Selections from His Journal and Correspondence* (Philadelphia: Book Association of Friends, 1854), 353–54; Edward H. Milligan, "Joseph John Gurney (1788–1847)," in *Oxford Dictionary of National Biography*, online ed. (Oxford University Press, 2006–16).

29 Braithwaite, *Memoirs of Joseph John Gurney*, 354.

30 "The Flushing Oaks," image published by T. K. Wharton, c. 1835–41 (not sourced), BHHSA; "The Flushing Oaks, and the Old Bowne House," published by E. A. Smith, 1840, BHHSA.

31 Map of the village of Flushing, Queens County, L.I., 1841, Elijah A. Smith, surveyor, Queens Historical Society; details of the Bowne Homestead, 1841, Elijah A. Smith, surveyor, New York Public Library, both included in Disponzio, Whitesell, and Kramer, "Cultural Landscape Report."

32 John W. Barber and Henry Howe, *Historical Collections of the State of New York* (New York: S. Tuttle, 1841), 453–54.

33 Braithwaite, *Memoirs of Joseph John Gurney*, 354; "The Fox Oak at Flushing," *Harper's New Monthly Magazine* 24, no. 164 (May 1862): 740.

34 Samuel Bowne Parsons, "Fox Oak" (1841), poem 2 in "Poetry at the Bowne House," BHHS, accessed August 9, 2024, https://www.bownehouse.org/poetry.

35 Fox Oaks Cane, HC.MC.950.325.04.029, Quaker Objects Collection, HC.MC-950-325, Haverford College Quaker & Special Collections. My thanks to Mary Crauderueff, curator of Quaker Collections at the Haverford College Libraries, for sharing with me a picture of these items, as well as an update on their status. Mary Crauderueff email communications, August 29, August 30, and September 14, 2022.

36 "Old Bowne House," BHHSA.

37 Margaret Hope Bacon, *I Speak for My Slave Sister: The Life of Abby Kelley Foster* (New York: Thomas Y. Crowell, 1974), 149.

38 Barber and Howe, *Historical Collections* (1851); "Fox Oak at Flushing," 740; Tea Caddy, 78.100, Wyck Association.

39 A newspaper clipping, "Sale of an Old Landmark: The Old Bowne House in Flushing Sold at Auction—It's Interesting History," in BHHSA, box A7, "Newspaper Clippings," folder 7, says it was 1862. Dr. J. W. Barston claims it was 1863 in *The Trees of Flushing* (n.p., 1914), 14, in BHHSA, box A9, "Booklets," but he misdates the demise of its "twin" to 1851.

40 "Reunion of Quakers," n.p., 1878, in BHHSA, box A7, "Newspaper Clippings," folder 5.

41 "Sale of an Old Landmark," BHHSA; "Bowne House," print, 89.147, and associated "Fox Oak Print Object Record," Wyck Association.

42 Barston, *Trees of Flushing*, 15.

43 *New York Sun*, December 25, 1893, transcription, J. T. Bowne MSS, BHHSA; *Elizabeth Journal*, transcription, Fox Oaks Cane, HC.MC.950.325.04.029, Quaker Objects Collection, HC.MC-950-325, Haverford College Quaker & Special Collections.

44 Senator Jonathan Chace and Jane Moon Chace, photograph, Bowne House Archives; "Historical Note," Chace Family Papers, Rhode Island Historical Society.

45 Cornelia Mitchell Parsons, *The Quaker Cross: A Story of the Old Bowne House* (New York: National Americana Society, 1911), 191, 193, 194.

46 "The Quaker Cross Garden (typescript, n.d.)," box "Garden and Horticulture," folder 27; Disponzio, Whitesell, and Kramer, "Cultural Landscape Report."

47 August Kapka, *The Trees of Flushing*, pamphlet (1945?), box A9, "Booklets," BHHSA.

48 Tea Caddy, 78.100, Wyck Association; Gerard E. L. Tondu, "1672—Quaker Founder George Fox in America," U.S. Timeline, June 6, 2016, http://gerard-tondu.blogspot.com/2016/06/1672-quaker-founder-george-fox-in.html.

49 Jared Farmer, "Taking Liberties with Historic Trees," *Journal of American History* 105, no. 4 (March 2019): 815–42.

50 Katharine Hodgkin, "Women, Memory and Family History in Seventeenth-Century England," in Kuijpers et al., *Memory before Modernity*, 297–313.

Chapter Ten: Pine Trees and the Legacy of the Shingwauk Site

1 Countless works explain the Canadian government's colonization efforts that occurred through residential schools, but one might begin by looking at J. R. Miller's *Shingwauk's Vision: A History of Native Residential Schools* (Toronto: University of Toronto Press, 1996) or John S. Milloy's *A National Crime: The Canadian Government and the Residential School System, 1879 to 1986* (Winnipeg: University Manitoba Press, 1999).

2 Independent Special Interlocutor for Missing Children and Unmarked Graves and Burial Sites associated with Indian Residential Schools, *Sacred Responsibility: Searching for the Missing Children and Unmarked Burials Interim Report Findings* (Ohsweken, ON: Office of the Independent Special Interlocutor, 2023), https://osi-bis.ca/wp-content/uploads/2023/06/OSI_InterimReport_June-2023_WEB.pdf.

3 Krista McCracken, "Challenging Colonial Spaces: Reconciliation and Decolonizing Work in Canadian Archives," *Canadian Historical Review* 100, no. 2 (June 2019): 182–201.

4 Milloy, *National Crime*, 6.

5 Donald J. Auger, *Indian Residential Schools in Ontario* (Ottawa: Nishnawbe Aski Nation, 2005), 5.

6 Nicholas Flood Davin, "Report on Industrial Schools for Indians and Half-Breeds," Canadiana, March 14, 1879, https://www.canadiana.ca/view/oocihm.03651.

7 Truth and Reconciliation Commission of Canada, *Canada's Residential Schools: The Final Report of the Truth and Reconciliation Commission of Canada*, vol. 1 (Montreal: McGill-Queen's University Press, 2015).

8 For a detailed biography of Shingwaukonse and his family, see Janet Elizabeth Chute, *The Legacy of Shingwaukonse: A Century of Native Leadership* (Toronto: University of Toronto Press, 1998).

9 Chute, *Legacy of Shingwaukonse*, 3.

10 Shingwauk Residential Schools Centre, *Healing and Reconciliation through Education* (Montreal: eCampus Ontario, 2019), https://ecampusontario.pressbooks.pub/srsc/.

11 *Intergenerational survivors* refers to the children, grandchildren, or relatives of those who attended residential schools. It can also describe someone who attended a residential school as a second- or third-generation student.

12 Section 4(b), entitled "Special Mission," of the Algoma University Act, 2008, S.O. 2008, https://algomau.ca/special-mission/.

13 "Special Mission."

14 Dan Pine, public communication, 1979.

15 The last residential school did not close in Canada until 1996, and it was not until the mid-1990s that the harms of residential schools were covered by mainstream media in any large-scale conversation.

16 *Survivor* is the preferred term for those who attended residential schools.

17 Krista McCracken, "Community Archival Practice: Indigenous Grassroots Collaboration at the Shingwauk Residential Schools Centre," *American Archivist* 78, no. 1 (Spring/Summer 2015): 181–91.
18 Author conversation with Shirley Horn, 2020.
19 Nicholas C. Kawa, Bradley Painter, and Cailín E. Murray, "Trail Trees: Living Artifacts (*Vivifacts*) of Eastern North America," *Ethnobiology Letters* 6, no. 1 (2015): 183–88.
20 Jared Farmer, "Taking Liberties with Historic Trees," *Journal of American History* 105, no. 4 (March 2019): 820.
21 Carolyn Harwood and Alex K. Ruuska, "The Personhood of Trees: Living Artifacts in the Upper Peninsula of Michigan," *Time and Mind* 6, no. 2 (2013): 142.
22 H. W. Schroeder, "The Tree of Peace: Symbolic and Spiritual Values of the White Pine," in *Proceedings of the White Pine Symposium: History, Ecology, Policy and Management*, ed. R. A. Stine and M. J. Baughman (Minneapolis: Department of Forestry Resources, University of Minnesota, 1992), 73–83.
23 Kayanesenh Paul Williams, *Kayanerenkó: wa: The Great Law of Peace* (Winnipeg: University of Manitoba Press, 2018), 334.
24 Yadav Uprety, Hugo Asselin, and Yves Bergeron, "Cultural Importance of White Pine (*Pinus strobus* L.) to the Kitcisakik Algonquin Community of Western Quebec, Canada," *Canadian Journal of Forest Research* 43, no. 6 (2013): 546.
25 Uprety, Asselin, and Bergeron, 546–47.
26 Theodore E. Howard and James Hall, "The Lore and Lure of Eastern White Pine," in *Eastern White Pine: Today and Tomorrow. Compiled by TD Funk. USDA for. Serv. Gen. Tech. Rep. WD-51* (Durham: University of New Hampshire, 1986), 10–15.
27 Kara K. L. Costanza et al., "A Synthesis of Emerging Health Issues of Eastern White Pine (*Pinus strobus*) in Eastern North America," *Forest Ecology and Management* 423 (2018): 3–17.
28 "Pinus strobus / Eastern White Pine," American Conifer Society, accessed August 20, 2024, https://conifersociety.org/conifers/pinus-strobus/.
29 G. W. Wendel and H. Clay Smith, "*Pinus strobus* L. Eastern White Pine," *Silvics of North America* 1 (1990): 480–81.
30 "Pinus strobus," Missouri Botanical Garden, accessed August 20, 2024, https://www.missouribotanicalgarden.org/PlantFinder/PlantFinderDetails.aspx?taxonid=285004.
31 "Pinus strobus / Eastern White Pine."
32 Wendel and Smith, "Pinus strobus," 481.
33 Costanza et al., "Synthesis."
34 Enrique Salmón, "Kincentric Ecology: Indigenous Perceptions of the Human–Nature Relationship," *Ecological Applications* 10, no. 5 (2000): 1329.
35 James McCourt, "The Interconnectedness of Indigenous Pedagogy," in *Key Concepts in Curriculum Studies: Perspectives on the Fundamentals* (New York: Routledge, 2019), 129.
36 Wendel and Smith, "Pinus strobus," 479.

37 Henry D. Thoreau, *Faith in a Seed: The Dispersion of Seeds and Other Late Natural History Writings* (Washington, DC: Island Press, 1993), 34.

Chapter Eleven: Oaks of Ill Repute

1 "An Assessment of Urban Tree Canopy in Chatham County, Georgia," Savannah Tree Foundation, February 2015, https://savannahtree.org/wp-content/uploads/2023/11/Chatham-County-Urban-Tree-Canopy-Assessment.pdf.

2 Jim Morekis, "Editor's Note: Paving Paradise," *Connect Savannah*, February 20, 2019.

3 Eric Rutkow, *American Canopy: Trees, Forests, and the Making of a Nation* (New York: Scribner, 2013), 5.

4 Jared Farmer, *Trees in Paradise: The Botanical Conquest of California* (Berkeley: Heyday, 2017); Thomas J. Campanella, *Republic of Shade: New England and the American Elm* (New Haven, CT: Yale University Press, 2003); Sonja Dümpelmann, *Seeing Trees: A History of Street Trees in New York City and Berlin* (New Haven, CT: Yale University Press, 2019); Jill Jonnes, *Urban Forests: A Natural History of Trees and People in the American Cityscape* (New York: Penguin, 2016); Jared Farmer, *Trees in Paradise: A California History* (New York: W. W. Norton, 2013); Ellen Stroud, *Nature Next Door: Cities and Trees in the American Northeast* (Seattle: University of Washington Press, 2012).

5 Dipesh Chakrabarty, "The Climate of History: Four Theses," *Critical Inquiry* 35, no. 2 (Winter 2009): 201.

6 Rutkow, *American Canopy*.

7 Jared Farmer, "Taking Liberty with Trees," *Journal of American History* 105, no. 4 (March 2019): 815–42.

8 Farmer, "Taking Liberty with Trees," 816–17.

9 Farmer, 817.

10 Philip R. Stone, "A Dark Tourism Spectrum: Towards a Typology of Death and Macabre Related Tourists Sites, Attractions and Exhibitions," *Tourism* 54, no. 2 (2006): 146; Philip R. Stone, "Dark Tourism and Significant Other Death: Towards a Model of Mortality Mediation," *Annals of Tourism Research* 39, no. 3 (2012): 1565–87; Philip R. Stone, "Dark Tourism: Towards a New Post-disciplinary Research Agenda," *International Journal of Tourism Anthropology* 1, no. 3/4 (2011): 318–32.

11 Stephan Miles, "Battlefield Sites as Dark Tourism Attractions: An Analysis of Experiences," *Journal of Heritage Tourism* 9, no. 2 (2014): 134.

12 Michael S. Bowman and Phaedra C. Pezzullo, "What Is So 'Dark' about 'Dark Tourism'? Death, Tours, and Performance," *Tourist Studies* 9, no. 3 (2010): 190.

13 Tiya Miles, *Tales from the Haunted South: Dark Tourism and Memories of Slavery from the Civil War Era* (Chapel Hill: University of North Carolina Press, 2015); "Haunted Waters: Stories of Slavery, Coastal Ghosts, and Environmental Consciousness," in *Coastal Nature, Coastal Culture: Environmental Histories of the Georgia Coast*, ed. Paul S. Sutter and Paul M. Pressly (Athens: University Press of Georgia, 2018).

14 Sharon Macdonald, "Undesirable Heritage: Fascist Material Culture and Historical Consciousness in Nuremberg," *International Journal of Heritage Studies* 12, no. 1 (2006): 9–28.

15 Dorota Golanska, "Against the 'Moonlight and Magnolia' Myth of the American South, a New Materialist Approach to the Dissonant Heritage of Slavery in the US: The Case of the Whitney Plantation in Wallace, LA," *Museology and Cultural Heritage* 8, no.4 (2020): 137–60.

16 Alena Pirok, "Goodwin's Ghosts: Williamsburg's Uncanny Legacy," *Public Historian* 41, no. 3 (August 2019): 9–30.

17 Avery Gordon, *Ghostly Matters: Haunting and the Sociological Imagination* (Minneapolis: New University of Minnesota Press, 2008), xvi.

18 Rutkow, *American Canopy*, 9.

19 *A Brief Account of the Establishment of the Colony of Georgia, under Gen. James Oglethorpe, February 1, 1733* (Washington, DC: P. Force, 1835), 4.

20 Louis de Vorsey, "The Origins and Appreciation of Savannah, Georgia's Historic City Squares," *Southeastern Geographer* 52, no. 1 (Spring 2012): 93; *Colonial Records of the State of Georgia*, vol. 1 (Atlanta: Franklin Print and Publishing, 1904), 60.

21 "Warren A. Candler Hospital," Georgia Historical Commission / Department of Natural Resources, Historical Marker, Savannah, Georgia, 1964, https://georgiahistory.com/ghmi_marker_updated/warren-a-candler-hospital/.

22 Savannah Tree Foundation, "Minutes of 2nd Meeting of the Board of Directors," March 1, 1983, box 1, file "Board of Directors Meetings," Savannah Tree Foundation Records, Hargrett Rare Book and Manuscript Library, University of Georgia Libraries, Athens, Georgia (hereafter cited as STF Records). See also Letter from James E. Hamby to Page A. Hungerpiller, April 11, 1983, box 1, file "Board of Directors Meetings," STF Records.

23 Savannah Tree Foundation, "Minutes of the 3rd Meeting of the Board of Directors," April 5, 1983, box 1, file "Board of Directors Meetings," STF Records.

24 Candler Oak Conservative Easement, December 26, 1984, box 1, file "Board of Directors Meetings," STF Records. See also Letter from the Savannah Tree Foundation to Mr. W. E. Hamby, December 26, 1984, file "Board of Directors Meetings," MS4327, box 1, STF Records.

25 Alan Patureau, "Savannah: Going Out on a Limb to Preserve Its Trees," *Dixie Living*, November 8, 1987, 3H.

26 Patureau, "Savannah."

27 Patureau.

28 "Landmark & Historic Tree Register," Georgie Tree Council, 2021, https://gatreecouncil.org/what-wc-do/programs/landmark-historic-tree-register.html.

29 In this chapter, I call Brown's tour the Black History Tour Company. I have found the tour called many things, including Freedom Trail Tour, but the most common name seems to be Black History Tour Company.

The first major slavery interpretation project in Savannah was developed at the Owens-Thomas House in 2007 and was developed into a full exhibit in 2017. See Chuck Mobley, "Owens-Thomas House Adds New Interpretation to Its History," *Savannah Morning News*, February 21, 2007; and Ben Goggins, "Owens-Thomas House Tell Stories of Those Enslaved," *Savannah Morning News*, December 9, 2018.

30 James Oliver Horton and Lois E. Horton's now classic edited volume *Slavery and Public History: The Tough Stuff of American Memory* (Chapel Hill: University of North Carolina Press, 2006) features articles that look at the efforts to recognize African American history from slavery to the Civil War at the United States' high-profile sites. Mr. Brown's history tour is described as "an educational and interactive tour of Savannah's Black Heritage" in advertisements. See "Things to Do," Stay in Savannah, 2024, https://stayinsavannah.com/things-to-do-in-savannah/tours/historic-tours/black-history-tour-savannah/.

31 Amy Louis Wood, *Lynching and Spectacle: Witnessing Racial Violence in America, 1890–1940* (Durham: University of North Carolina Press, 2009). See also Cynthia Skove Nevel, *Lynching to Belong: Claiming Whiteness through Racial Violence* (College Station: Texas A&M University Press, 2007). Ana Lucia Araujo's recent *Slavery in the Age of Memory: Engaging the Past* (New York: Bloomsbury Academic, 2020) offers an expanded update on how slavery is being commemorated across the globe. Both illustrate projects that seek to fill gaps left by selective memory.

32 Dana Carmel Bell, "Southern Attitudes," thatgirlcarmel, July 18, 2013, http://www.thatgirlcarmel.com/racism-in-the-south/.

33 Comments on David Ferebee, "Candler Oak, 'The Hanging Tree,' Savannah GA," Flicker, April 5, 2011, https://www.flickr.com/photos/theeditroom/7055511543.

34 Comments on Ferebee.

35 Comments on Ferebee.

36 Comments on Ferebee.

37 Comments on Ferebee.

38 "Old Candler Hospital," Savannah Terrors, March 8, 2020, https://savannahterrors.com/old-candler-hospital/.

39 Brenna Elizabeth Weston, "Ghosts and Graveyards: Colonial Park Cemetery and Memory Construction on Ghost Tours in Savannah, Georgia" (MA thesis, North Dakota State University of Agriculture and Applied Science, July 2016), 7. Weston's work is a well-researched source on both the lore and documented history of the cemetery.

40 For more on graveyards in the South, see Ryan K. Smith, *Death and Rebirth in a Southern City: Richmond's Historic Cemeteries* (Baltimore: Johns Hopkins University Press, 2020).

41 Weston, "Ghosts and Graveyards," 15.

42 *Minutes of the Park and Tree Commission, 1896–1972*, vol. 1, City of Savannah Park and Tree Commission, 1896/1908, Record Series 5600PC-10, Research Library & Municipal Archives, https://dlg.usg.edu/record/gsg_5600pc-10_5600pc-010-vol1#item.

43 Ann Hoevel, "Walk Your Scaredy-Pants off in Savannah," *CNN*, October 31, 2003; T. A. Patterson, "Ghost Story of Rene Asche Rondolier," Gothic Bite Magazine, August 29, 2018. Hoevel, "Walk Your Scaredy-Pants," and Patterson,

"Ghost Story," report that Rondolier was an orphan who lived in the cemetery, the latter saying in underground tunnels below the cemetery.

44 Patterson, "Ghost Story."

45 Some stories have Rondolier hanged in a swamp. See Weston, "Ghosts and Graveyards." Hoevel, "Walk Your Scaredy-Pants," reports that the mob took Rondolier to a tree in the swamp to hang him and that his ghost continued to murder afterward. Savannah Terrors argues that his visitors may see his ghost hanging from a tree in the back of the cemetery but contends he was hanged in one of the squares. See "Rene Rondolier—Ghost of Colonial Park Cemetery," Savannah Terrors, accessed August 8, 2023, https://savannahterrors.com/colonial-park-cemetery/. Ghosts and Gravestones reports he was hanged from a specific hanging tree in the cemetery. "Rene Rondolier," Ghosts and Gravestones, accessed August 8, 2023, https://www.ghostsandgravestones.com/savannah/ghosts.

46 Michael Trinkley and Debi Hacker, *Identification and Mapping Historic Graves at Colonial Park Cemetery, Savannah, Georgia* (Columbia, SC: Chicora Foundation, 1999), 17.

47 "Terrific Tempest," *Savannah Morning News*, August 29, 1881.

48 J. J. W., "Savannah's Shade Trees," *Savannah Morning News*, June 16, 1886.

49 "Tree Mortality Is Small," *Savannah Morning News*, August 2, 1900.

50 Shannon Scott, "The Hanging Tree in Savannah," Shannon Scott Tours, February 5, 2015, https://www.shannonscott.com/the-hanging-tree-in-savannah/.

51 Scott, "Hanging Tree in Savannah."

52 Scott.

53 "Lynch Mob May Have Erred," *Chicago Record-Herald*, March 31, 1902.

54 "Lynch Mob."

55 *Thirty Years of Lynching in the United States, 1889–1918* (New York: National Association for the Advancement of Colored People, 1919), 59.

56 Michael Harris, "Murder & Lies: The Ghost of Savannah's Wright Square," *Savannah Morning News*, October 30, 2014, https://www.savannahnow.com/article/20141030/NEWS/310309723.

57 Harris, "Murder & Lies."

58 "The Haunted Wright Square in Savannah," Nightly Spirits, May 2, 2020, https://nightlyspirits.com/the-haunted-wright-square-in-savannah/.

59 "Haunted Wright Square."

60 Dale J. Young, "The Ghost of Alice Riley and the Legend of Spanish Moss," Dead Are Coming, 2017, https://dalejyoung.com/the-ghost-of-alice-riley-and-the-legend-of-spanish-moss/; Harris, "Murder & Lies."

61 Harris, "Murder & Lies."

62 Harris.

63 "Haunted Wright Square"; Lance, "Wright Square," Savannah Terrors, May 21, 2018, https://savannahterrors.com/wright-square/.

64 "The Ghosts of Wright Square: Many Haunted Houses Can Be Found on Madison Square," Ghost City Tours, accessed August 9, 2023, https://ghostcitytours.com/savannah/haunted-places/haunted-savannah-squares/wright-square/.

65 "Ghosts of Wright Square."

66 "WSAV Investigates Savannah's Squares Gathering No Spanish Moss," WSAV, November 8, 2015, https://www.wsav.com/news/wsav-investigates-savannahs-squares-gathering-no-spanish-moss/.

67 "Wright Square," Tripadvisor, September 15, 2019, https://www.tripadvisor.com/Attraction_Review-g60814-d107726-Reviews-Wright_Square-Savannah_Georgia.html.

68 "Laurel Grove South Cemetery," Savannah, accessed August 8, 2023, https://www.savannahga.gov/882/Laurel-Grove-South-Cemetery.

69 "Laurel Grove North Cemetery," Savannah, accessed August 8, 2023, https://www.savannahga.gov/880/Laurel-Grove-North-Cemetery.

70 "Laurel Grove North Cemetery."

71 Traci Rylands, "A Beautiful Decay: Visiting Laurel Grove North Cemetery," Adventures in Cemetery Hopping, November 7, 2014, https://adventuresincemeteryhopping.com/2014/11/07/a-beautiful-decay-visting-laurel-grove-north-cemetery/.

72 Scouts do visit her grave and leave her notes, but far more of them go to her house.

73 Alissa Lee Nicholsn, "Fascinating Tour with Shannon Scott Tours," Tripadvisor, July 2019, https://www.tripadvisor.com/ShowUserReviews-g60814-d2460590-r693283850-Laurel_Grove_North_Cemetery-Savannah_Georgia.html; Diane A., "Wonderfully Peaceful Cemetery for History Buffs," Tripadvisor, April 2015, https://www.tripadvisor.co.nz/ShowUserReviews-g60814-d2460590-r284284234-Laurel_Grove_North_Cemetery-Savannah_Georgia.html.

74 Deborah N. Archer, "'White Men's Roads through Black Men's Homes': Advancing Racial Equity through Highway Reconstruction," *Vanderbilt Law Review* 73, no. 5 (October 2020): 1259–1330.

75 Christinee2013, "Full of History but in Need of Help," Tripadvisor, August 2016, https://www.tripadvisor.com.sg/ShowUserReviews-g60814-d10920520-r418827625-Laurel_Grove_South_Cemetery-Savannah_Georgia.html.

76 Seamere, "African-Americans Savannah History," Tripadvisor, April 2018, https://www.tripadvisor.com.sg/ShowUserReviews-g60814-d10920520-r575472141-Laurel_Grove_South_Cemetery-Savannah_Georgia.html.

77 Dawn Baker, "Black History: Laurel Grove Cemetery South," WTOC, February 21, 2009, https://www.wtoc.com/story/9881231/black-history-laurel-grove-cemetery-south/.

78 Ron Stodghill, "Savannah, Both Sides," *New York Times*, October 5, 2014.

79 Alexander Marvar, "Uncovering History," *Savannah Magazine*, January 2, 2019.

80 Nick Robertson, "Davenport House Museum Develops New Exhibit to Recognize Enslaved Former Residents," *Connect Savannah*, January 17, 2021; Angie Miller, "Community-Driven Effort Out to Shatter Shackles of the Past," *Connect Savannah*, July 21, 2021.

Chapter Twelve: Living Memory in Los Angeles

The authors wish to thank Susan Anderson, MAK Center Los Angeles, Vienna's Museum of Applied Arts, the California African American Museum, the Huntington Botanical Gardens, Los Angeles City Planning, and the Los Angeles Cultural Heritage Commission. The initial interview was conducted in July of 2022; since that time, there have been some developments both in the story of the tree's preservation and in Mayer's art. The following edited version of the conversation reflects what was current in 2024. D. A. Kass, "The Issue of Racism at the 1936 Olympics," *Journal of Sport History* 3, no. 3 (1976): 223–35.

1 Kass, "Issue of Racism," 224.
2 Mayer has an extensive body of work that has been exhibited in Europe and the United States. *The Life Story of Cornelius Johnson's Olympic Oak and Other Matters of Survival* was most recently installed at New York's Austrian Cultural Forum in 2022 and 2023. See also Christian Kosmas Mayer, *Aeviternity* (Vienna: Verlag der Buchhandlung Walther Konig, 2019); and Christian Kosmas Mayer, *Christian Kosmas Mayer* (Berlin: Distanz, 2023). Readers can see more of his work at http://christiankosmasmayer.site.
3 Images of the Olympic Oak and Mayer's art can be found at Kim Cooper, "Save Cornelius Johnson's Olympic Oak," *Esotouric*, March 15, 2022, https://esotouric.com/2022/03/15/olympicoak.
4 See Michael Mackenzie, "From Athens to Berlin: The 1936 Olympics and Leni Riefenstahl's Olympia," *Critical Inquiry* 29, no, 2 (2003): 302–36; and Arnd Krüger, "Germany: The Propaganda Machine," in *The Nazi Olympics: Sport, Politics, and Appeasement in the 1930s*, ed. Arnd Kruger and William Murray (Urbana: University of Illinois Press, 2003), 17–43.

Afterword

1 See William Cronon, "The Trouble with Wilderness, or Getting Back to the Wrong Nature," *Environmental History* 1 (January 1996): 7–28.
2 Photograph reprinted with the caption "Former slaves recalled Blacks being bound to this tree for flogging on the Frogmore plantation, Saint Helena Island, South Carolina," in *Before Freedom Came: African-American Life in the Antebellum South*, ed. Edward D. C. Campbell Jr. and Kim S. Rice (Charlottesville: University Press of Virginia, 1997), 87. Original photo labeled "Whipping tree, Frogmore plantation, Saint Helena Island, South Carolina, ca. 1890," in Penn School Papers, Southern Historical Collection, University of North Carolina at Chapel Hill.
3 Andrew Hurley, "Memories: Recovering Historical Meaning in Neighborhood Trees," this volume, chapter 1.
4 On "collected" versus "collective" memory, see James E. Young, *The Stages of Memory: Reflections on Memorial Art, Loss, and the Spaces Between* (Amherst: University of Massachusetts Press, 2016), 15.

5 Meyer chronicled his efforts in *America's Famous and Historic Trees: From George Washington's Tulip Poplar to Elvis Presley's Pin Oak* (New York: Houghton Mifflin Harcourt, 2001). American Forests no longer lists this initiative or business relationship on its website. However, the identical ad copy appears on the website of an organization named American Heritage Trees (https://americanheritagetrees.org), now based at a nursery in Lebanon, Tennessee.

6 Brian Dempsey observes that no one seems to know how or when a stand of overcup oak acquired the name "Old Hickory" and whether this association, lost to memory, had any connection to Andrew Jackson's popularity in the area after the Battle of New Orleans.

7 Liz Sargent, "The Trees of the South Mountain Cultural Landscape," this volume, chapter 5. On the American Scenic and Historic Preservation Society, see Randall Mason, "Historic Preservation Public Memory, and the Making of Modern New York City," in *Giving Preservation a History: Histories of Historic Preservation in the United States*, ed. Randall Mason and Max Page, 2nd ed. (New York: Routledge, 2019), 67–99.

8 Despite the name, this project initiated by the National Capital Region did not transplant the trees and give them new identities. See Mike Townsend, "Silent Sentinels of Storied Landscapes," National Park Service, October 24, 2017, https://www.nps.gov/articles/silent-sentinels-of-storied-landscapes.htm.

9 For more on the responsibilities and opportunities of public historians in a changing climate, see the NCPH *History@Work* blog series "Public Historians in Our Climate Emergency" over 2021–22 (https://ncph.org/history-at-work/tag/climate-emergency-series/) and the special issue of *Public Historian* examining "Public History and Environmental Sustainability" in August 2014.

Index

Page numbers in *italics* refer to figures.